Curriculum Development
in East Asia

Curriculum Development in East Asia

Edited by

Colin Marsh and Paul Morris

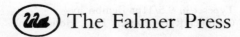 The Falmer Press

(A member of the Taylor & Francis Group)
London • New York • Philadephia

UK   The Falmer Press, 4 John St, London WC1N 2ET
USA   The Falmer Press, Taylor & Francis Inc., 1900 Frost Road, Suite
      101, Bristol, PA 19007

First published 1991

British Library Cataloguing in Publication Data
Curriculum development in East Asia.
   1. Asia. East Asia. Educational institutions. Curriculum.
   Development
   I. Marsh, Colin *1939–*   II. Morris, Paul *1946–*
375.001095

   ISBN 1–85000–685–7
   ISBN 1–85000–686–5 (pbk.)

Library of Congress Cataloging-in-Publication Data
Curriculum development in East Asia/edited by Colin Marsh
and Paul Morris.
   p.   cm.
   Includes bibliographical references (pp. 279–91) and index.
   ISBN 1–85000–685–7:—ISBN 1–85000–686–5 (pbk.):
   1. Education—East Asia—Curricula. 2. Education—East
Asia—Curricula—Case studies.   I. Marsh, Colin J.   II. Morris,
Paul.
LB 1564. E18C87   1991   90–48549
375'.001'095—dc20   CIP

Jacket design by Caroline Archer

Typeset in 9.5/11pt Bembo by
Graphicraft Typesetters Ltd., Hong Kong

*Printed in Great Britain by Burgess Science Press, Basingstoke on
paper which has a specified pH value on final paper manufacture of not
less than 7.5 and is therefore 'acid free'.*

Contents

Contents

List of Tables

List of Figures

Preface

Descriptions and analyses of the nature of, and problems affecting, curriculum development in Western industrial societies are numerous. Relatively few studies focus on countries in East Asia. Whilst educational developments in the USA, UK and other countries have had some impact on official educational policies in Asia the overall goals of curriculum policy, its form and the way it is disseminated and implemented have been substantially affected by the needs, priorities and context of the country in question.

The main purpose of this book is to provide an understanding of the purposes, nature and tensions which affect curriculum development in East Asian countries. This task is undertaken in three distinct stages which correspond to the three sections which make up this book.

Section I comprises three chapters which provide the reader with an introduction to the main concepts which can be used to describe and analyze the processes of and tensions within curriculum development. Chapter 1 focuses on analyzing the ways in which curriculum development can be described and distinguished. The second chapter looks at the problems and influences which affect curricula when they are used in classrooms. The third chapter focuses on the nature of, and impact on, the school curriculum of educational assessment.

Section II is made up of a set of country specific studies which describe the processes of curriculum development and the prevailing tensions and issues in seven East Asian countries. The chapters focus on: the People's Republic of China (two chapters), Hong Kong, Singapore, South Korea, Macau, Indonesia and Malaysia.

The countries included in section II contain a wide range of important and fascinating differences. For example, the vast size and scale of education in the PRC with over eight million teachers is in marked contrast to that of Macau with only 2500 teachers. The Islamic influence on the curriculum in Indonesia and Malaysia is in contrast to the influence of Confucian values in Singapore and South Korea. Whilst South Korea is a relatively homogeneous society in linguistic and cultural terms, Singapore and Indonesia are relatively heterogeneous societies. In political terms the countries studied range from that bastion of laissez-faire capitalism, Hong Kong, to the PRC, the world's largest Communist country. The colonial status of Hong Kong and Macau, up until 1997 and 1999 respectively, distinguishes them from the other sovereign states. In economic terms the relative affluence of Hong Kong, with a per capita GDP in 1989 of US$11,000 is in marked contrast to that of the PRC and of Indonesia with a per capita GDP of US$300 and US$500 respectively. The nature of the economies is also very different. Indonesia Malaysia, and the PRC are primarily agricultural economies with large rural populations, Singapore and Hong Kong are small, highly urbanized and technologically sophisticated economies which rely on their service and manufacturing industries. There are many other important contrasts between the countries which are described in this book.

Apart from their geographic location they also share a number of important features. First, with the exception of the PRC they are or have been colonies. Japan colonized South Korea up until 1945, the British colonized Malaysia and Singapore, and Hong Kong is still a British colony. Macau is a Portuguese colony and Indonesia was a Dutch colony. Second, economic modernization generally, and industrialization specifically, have occurred rapidly and recently in most Asian societies. The newly-industrialized countries (NICS) of Asia (South Korea, Hong Kong, Singapore and Taiwan) have, in the 1970s and 1980s, achieved the fastest rates of economic growth in the world and have now begun to compete with Japan as the world's main manufacturers and exporters. This economic development has been paralleled by a rapid shift toward urbanization in those countries which were dominated by an agricultural sector. Third, the populations of each of the countries described in this book, with the exception of Indonesia and Malaysia, share a common cultural heritage which has its roots in an essentially Confucian set of moral sentiments.

Finally, section III identifies and analyzes those concepts and issues which have arisen in the case studies. Chapter 12 focuses on the central role the curriculum plays in promoting social, moral and religious values in East Asian countries. It also compares and analyzes the other issues which emerged in section II, these include:

- the predominantly academic nature of the school curriculum;
- the central influence on the curriculum of ongoing nation building, the development of a national identity and of the inculcation of moral values;
- the close and comprehensive relationship between politics and the school curriculum;
- the centralized and bureaucratic nature of systems of curriculum development;
- the paramount influence of assessment practices on the styles of teaching and learning;
- the contradictions between official curriculum policy and the actual practices in schools.

These features existed within and were substantially affected by the prevailing social, political or cultural features and tensions which characterized the specific society in question.

The practical examples, ideas and concepts incorporated in this book have been obtained from various sources and countries but special mention needs to be made of colleagues at the University of Hong Kong and Murdoch University.

Finally, sincere thanks are due to Lynne Schickert, Roberta MacKay, Ivy Wong and Anita Tam for their skilful typing of the manuscript.

Colin Marsh and Paul Morris

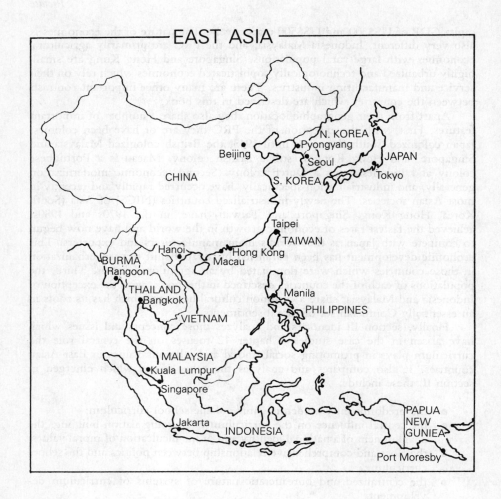

EAST ASIA

CHINA

Beijing

N. KOREA
Pyongyang
Seoul
S. KOREA

JAPAN
Tokyo

Taipei
TAIWAN

Hanoi
Hong Kong
Macau

BURMA
Rangoon

THAILAND
Bangkok

VIETNAM

Manila

PHILIPPINES

MALAYSIA
Kuala Lumpur

Singapore

PAPUA
NEW
GUNIEA

Jakarta
INDONESIA

Port Moresby

Section I
Curriculum Planning

Chapter 1

Curriculum Approaches

Colin Marsh

Introduction

The meaning of the term 'curriculum' in the field of education is very elusive. Other terms in education such as 'instruction' or 'administration' are far more specific and action-oriented. For example, 'instruction' is the 'act of instructing students' and is undertaken by an 'instructor'. Similarly, 'administration' is the 'act of administering' and is carried out by an 'administrator'. People have fairly definite ideas about what 'instructors' and 'administrators' do, how they behave, typical achievements and problems.

It is far more difficult to apply the same process to the term 'curriculum'. What term should be used to connote a person who spends most of his/her time on curriculum activities? The easy way out is to use more specialized functional terms such as a 'curriculum planner' or a 'curriculum developer'.

In this chapter the term 'curriculum' is studied initially by considering some important factors and by examining various definitions. Four conceptions or frames of reference about curriculum are then analyzed together with an examination of major influences which determine why some of the conceptions are more dominant in particular countries than others. Different levels of curriculum planning, content, methods and evaluation are each examined in turn and to conclude the chapter, one planning model is analyzed in some detail.

Some Factors Affecting Curriculum

The purposes which curricula are attempting to achieve and by which they are achieved are substantially affected by a range of social, economic and political factors. The main factors are:

(i) Political: Schools are frequently used to support and promote the political ideology of those persons in power. In the People's Republic of China (PRC) major political changes and sometimes minor changes of political leadership have resulted in rapid changes to the nature of the curriculum and of curriculum materials. In Hong Kong the return of sovereignty to the PRC has resulted in a number of changes to the school curriculum. Similarly, in South Korea major curriculum reforms have accompanied each change of government.

(ii) National Identity and Unity: The curriculum is frequently used to promote a sense of national pride and identity. In Korea, Japan and Taiwan the promotion of a sense of national identity and an essentially Confucian set of moral values are central goals of the school curriculum. Phrases such as hardworking, disciplined, collective will and character, perseverance have come to represent a set of uniquely Asian values which schools are expected to promote. In countries with a more heterogeneous ethnic mix, such as Singapore, the school curriculum is also expected to promote a sense of cohesion and unity amongst the various ethnic groups.

(iii) Economic: The attempt to achieve certain economic goals can also have an effect on the curriculum. The development of agriculture, industrialization or a service-oriented economy place different demands on school curricula. Attempts in various countries to develop a large industrial sector have for example usually been accompanied by an increased emphasis on scientific subjects. Thus, for example, the pursuit in the PRC of the four modernizations resulted in a reduced emphasis in the school curriculum on political education and an increased emphasis on mathematics, language and science.

(iv) Religious: In countries with a strong religious influence this can have a major effect on the curriculum. In Indonesia, for example, schools are expected to provide pupils with a knowledge of, and belief in, Islam. A substantial proportion of time is devoted in schools to learn the key religious texts such as the Koran. This has an effect on all aspects of the curriculum but especially on what is taught and the view of the nature and purposes of knowledge.

(v) The Development of Knowledge: Knowledge has been developed in different societies in different ways. Nakayama (1984) suggests that there are two major approaches to the development of knowledge, the documentary and the rhetorical. The rhetorical approach is the basis of western knowledge and is derived from a Judeo-Hebraic tradition. It does not depend on a written record but is dependent on verbal assertions and argumentation. Plato's 'Dialogues' are the classic example of this form of knowledge and these were written down by his students after they were originally presented. In contrast a documentary tradition developed in China where knowledge was recorded on paper. The core documents in the Confucian tradition were the Five Classics and the Four Books. Additions to knowledge were achieved through derivations from these sources which acted as a form of precedent. China developed a writing system and a body of written knowledge far earlier than western civilization and developed written examinations to test that knowledge much earlier than other societies.

The above-mentioned factors mean that different societies emphasize different educational goals and have different perceptions of what should be taught and how it should be presented. If education is viewed as a vehicle for promoting a political viewpoint or a religious creed then the content of the curriculum will be derived from the key publications of prominent political or religious leaders, and teachers will use a teaching style which is efficient for conveying content which is viewed as correct or true or not open to argument. Pupils will be assessed to determine the match between their knowledge and the material presented. A curriculum which is based on the premise that all knowledge is constructed through the use of logic and empirical investigation and is inherently open to question can be taught in quite different ways. The ideal outcome is for all to be able to exercise critical judgment. The tension between the desire to promote national and economic well-being through individual autonomy and scientific rationalism and the desire to promote a homogeneous society which shares a common political or religious creed lies at the heart of many curriculum issues. It is evident within Indonesia and Brunei Darussalam in the tension between the promoters of an Islamic revival and the secularists. In Singapore the tension is evident in the recent attempts to promote Confucian values in a highly technocratic society, and in the PRC it is evident in the oscillation between the promotion of economic modernization and the promotion of a socialist political ideology. In each of these countries the education system generally and the curriculum specifically becomes the vital arena which needs to be controlled if any group is to promote successfully its view of the nature of knowledge and of society. These factors are linked to the way knowledge has been developed in different societies.

Curriculum — Nature of the Term

Persons have interpreted the term 'curriculum' very differently over the years. Oliva (1988) provides us with an interesting range:

> Curriculum is that which is taught in school.
> Curriculum is a set of subjects.
> Curriculum is content.
> Curriculum is a set of materials.
> Curriculum is a set of performance objectives.
> Curriculum is that which is taught both inside and outside of school directed by the school.
> Curriculum is that which an individual learner experiences as a result of schooling.
> Curriculum is everything that is planned by school personnel. (pp. 5–6)

To define curriculum as 'what is taught in schools' is of course, very vague. Persons often talk about the 'school curriculum' in this general way and they tend to mean by this the range of subjects taught and the amount of instruction time given to each in terms of hours or minutes.

Curriculum defined as 'content' is an interesting emphasis and brings into question another term, namely the 'syllabus'. A 'syllabus' is usually a summary statement about the content to be taught in a course or unit, often linked to an external examination. This emphasis on WHAT content to be taught is a critical element of a 'syllabus' but a 'curriculum' includes more than this. For example HOW you teach content can drastically affect what is taught. Also, the extent to which students are sufficiently prepared and motivated to study particular content will affect very greatly what is learnt.

Curriculum is quite often defined as a product — a document which includes details about goals, objectives, content, teaching techniques, evaluation and assessment, resources. Sometimes these are official documents issued by the government or one of its agencies and which prescribe HOW and WHAT is to be taught (for example, in Singapore, Goh Report, 1980). Of course it is important to realize that a curriculum document represents the *ideal* rather than the *actual* curriculum. A teacher may not accept all aspects of a written curriculum and/or be unable to implement a curriculum exactly as prescribed due to lack of training and understanding. There can be gaps between the intended, ideal curriculum and the actual curriculum. It may be that the level and interests of the students, or local community preferences, may prevent a teacher from implementing a curriculum as prescribed.

Defining a curriculum as a 'set of performance objectives' or student learnings is a very practical orientation to curriculum. This approach focuses upon specific skills or knowledge that it is considered should be attained by students. Proponents of this approach argue that if a teacher knows the targets which students should achieve, it is so much easier to organize other elements to achieve this end, such as the appropriate content and teaching methods. Few would deny that another strength of this approach is the emphasis upon students. After all, they are the ultimate consumers and it is important to focus upon what it is anticipated that they will achieve and to organize all teaching activities to that end. Yet it must also be remembered that this approach can lead to an overemphasis upon behavioural outcomes and objectives which can be easily measured. Some skills and values are far more difficult to state in terms of performance objectives (see chapter 3). Also, a curriculum document which is simply a listing of performance objectives would have to be very large and tends to be unwieldy.

To define curriculum as 'that which is taught both inside and outside school, directed by the school' indicates that all kinds of activities that occur in the classroom, playground and community, comprise the curriculum. This emphasis has merit in that it demonstrates that school learning is not just confined to the classroom. However, it should be noted that the emphasis is upon 'direction' by the school which seems to indicate that the only important learning experiences are those which are directed by school personnel. Few would accept this statement and so it is necessary to look at other definitions.

To define curriculum in terms of 'what an individual learner experiences as a result of schooling' is an attempt to widen the focus. The emphasis here is upon the student as a self-motivated learner. Each student should be encouraged to select those learning experiences that will enable him/her to develop into a fully-functioning person. However, it should be noted that each student acquires knowledge, skills and values not only from the *official* or *formal* curriculum but also from the *unofficial* or *hidden* curriculum. As noted by Pollard and Tann (1987) the hidden curriculum is implicit within regular school procedures, in curriculum materials, and in communication approaches and mannerisms used by staff. It is important to remember that students do learn a lot from the hidden curriculum even though this is not intended by teachers.

The definition which refers to curriculum as 'everything that is planned by

Figure 1.1 *An illustrative definition of curriculum*

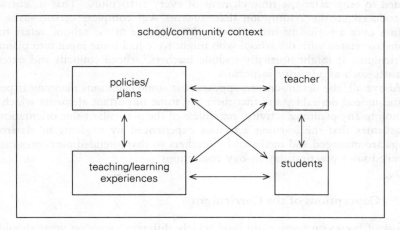

school personnel' is yet another orientation which emphasizes the planning aspect of curriculum. Few would deny that classroom learning experiences for students need to be planned although some unplanned activities will always occur (and these can have positive or negative effects). This definition also brings to bear the distinction that some writers make between curriculum and instruction. Some writers argue that curriculum is the WHAT and instruction is the HOW, or another way of expressing it — 'curriculum activity is the production of plans for further action and instruction is the putting of plans into action' (Macdonald and Leeper, 1965).

Although it can be important to separate out the two functions of WHAT and HOW, it tends to obscure the interdependence of *curriculum* and *instruction*. Classroom teachers do not separate out the two functions because they are constantly planning, implementing and monitoring in their respective classrooms. That is, it is not practical to separate out intentions from actions — there is really a fluid movement of interactions between plans, actions, change of plans, different actions.

To conclude this section it is important for the authors of this book to state their preferred definition of curriculum, based upon what one of them has stated elsewhere (Marsh and Stafford, 1988) 'an interrelated set of plans and experiences which a student completes under the guidance of the school' (p. 5). This definition needs amplification and illustration (see figure 1.1). The phrase 'interrelated set of plans and experiences' refers to the point that curricula which are implemented in schools are typically planned in advance but, that inevitably, unplanned activities also occur. Therefore the actual curricula which are implemented in classrooms consist of an amalgam of plans and experiences (unplanned happenings). The curriculum as experienced in the classroom is not a one-way transmission of ideas and information from the teacher to a group of passive recipients but a series of communications/reactions/exchanges between both groups.

The phrase 'which a student completes under the guidance of the school' is included to emphasize the time element of every curriculum. That is, curricula are produced on the assumption that students will complete certain tasks and activities over a period of time. 'Under the guidance of the school' refers to all persons associated with the school who might have had some input into planning a curriculum. It might normally include teachers, school councils and external specialists such as advisory inspectors.

Above all, the definition presupposes that some conscious planning is possible, and indeed desirable, and that there are some important elements which are common to any planning activity, regardless of the particular value orientation. It also assumes that the learning activities experienced by students in classroom settings are managed and mediated by teachers so that intended outcomes can be reconciled with practical day-to-day restrictions.

Conceptions of the Curriculum

Authors of books on curriculum hold widely different views on what should be taught in schools, and in many instances, why and how. It may seem strange that such conflicting viewpoints (which in some cases are diametrically opposed) are presented by curriculum experts, since most of them agree upon the process elements/components discussed earlier in this chapter.

The bases for these incompatibilities lie in different points of view about the *desired values and goals* in curriculum. These points of view cannot be dismissed as superficial whims and fancies since they are deep-seated differences which have been thought out and fully documented by authors. Over the last few decades many frames of reference have appeared, a number of which can be selected and amalgamated into four major categories.

The authors who have developed these frames of reference represent both practitioners and theorists. For example, Neill not only had a definite view or frame of reference about the curriculum he advocated, but in addition, had the opportunity to initiate and develop it at his Summerhill school in England. Other curriculum writers represent all shades of the theorist/practitioner spectrum including Piaget (1952), Torrance (1962), Bruner (1963), Kohlberg (1966), Taba *et al.* (1967) and Skinner (1968). As their approaches are not mutually exclusive, any attempt to develop four major frames of reference involves considerable overlap and perhaps gross oversimplification.

Just as research has not been able to decide on *the* single best way of teaching, it will become obvious that there is no *one* preferable frame of reference. What these four approaches can do is to indicate how different frames of reference may be suitable for certain education systems, schools, teachers and students.

Fortunately, a number of books detailing curriculum frames of reference have appeared in recent years. One of the most comprehensive was developed by Joyce and Weil in *Models of Teaching* (1980), although other notable curriculum writers have also focused upon this aspect, including Nuttall and Snook (1973), Eisner and Vallance (1974), and McNeil (1977, 1985). The following four approaches incorporate a substantial number of the categories listed by these authors:

Information Processing Orientation
Behaviour Modification Orientation
Social Interaction Orientation
Personal Development Orientation

Frame of Reference I: Information Processing Orientation

The explosion of knowledge during the twentieth century has caused many educators to doubt the amount of factual detail which can be or should be accumulated by students. More recently, a number of psychologists (Bruner, Goodnow and Austin, 1967; Ausubel, 1963) have stressed the need for students to develop cognitive skills for processing facts rather than concentrating upon the facts themselves. As Eisner (1974) termed it, this approach

> refers only rarely to curriculum content, focusing instead on the how rather than the what of education. Aiming to develop a sort of technology of the mind, it sees the central problem of curriculum as that of sharpening the intellectual processes and developing a set of cognitive skills that can be applied to learning virtually anything.

A number of curriculum writers have cited examples which include problem-solving and information-processing skills. One of the best known is the approach adopted by Taba, details of which were subsequently published in several textbooks and one curriculum project (Taba *et al.*, 1967).

Taba developed three postulates about thinking, which then formed the basis for her teaching strategies. These are:

   (i)   thinking can be taught;
  (ii)   thinking is an active transaction between the individual and the data;
 (iii)   the processes of thought evolve by a sequence which is governed by a law.

Schools exist because it is assumed that in a formal environment certain skills, including thinking skills, can be taught. Specific thinking skills cannot be taught in isolation, but if students examine factual data in a systematic way they can arrive at conclusions and make predictions. That is, the students themselves are actively involved in taking a series of mental steps with the factual data, resulting in some kind of explanations or conclusions. It is the task of the teacher to facilitate these thinking stages by initiating certain questions at appropriate stages. If this is carried out effectively, students will develop their own brand of thinking skills and be able to tackle progressively more difficult topics. It should be noted that a hierarchy of thinking skills is included in the Taba approach which therefore involves students mastering simple thinking skills before proceeding to more difficult ones. For Taba, this sequence of mental activities within a hierarchical framework follows a definite pattern and therefore has all the characteristics of a 'law'. If this assumption is considered a little unreal, it should be remembered that a number of educators, including Gagne (1962) and White (1973) have proposed similar sequences.

Colin Marsh

Figure 1.2   Simplification of the behaviour modification approach

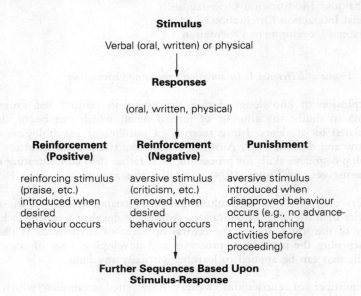

Stimulus

Verbal (oral, written) or physical

Responses

(oral, written, physical)

Reinforcement (Positive)	**Reinforcement (Negative)**	**Punishment**
reinforcing stimulus (praise, etc.) introduced when desired behaviour occurs	aversive stimulus (criticism, etc.) removed when desired behaviour occurs	aversive stimulus introduced when disapproved behaviour occurs (e.g., no advancement, branching activities before proceeding)

Further Sequences Based Upon Stimulus-Response

Frame of Reference II: Behaviour Modification Orientation

The Behaviour Modification orientation is an approach which emanated from the work of Stimulus-Response (S-R) psychologists, notably Skinner (1953), but its present-day exponents, especially the educational technologists, have evolved a number of variations. Their curriculum relies upon providing students with an efficient system of sequenced learning activities so that student behaviour can be changed. The behaviourist psychologists consider it possible to modify the behaviour of students by a sequence of stimulus-response-reinforcement procedures (figure 1.2). Their concern is only with observable behaviour. All kinds of hitherto labelled unobservable behaviour such as 'intuitive thoughts', 'critical thinking' and 'inquiry', can, according to the behaviourists, be categorized as observable processes of 'stimulus discrimination and generalization'.

The task of planning educational experiences is certainly simplified by this approach, so long as it is possible to isolate all the external variables which need to be taken into account. A number of learning programs have been produced by behaviourist-oriented writers in primary and secondary school subjects, the programs in mathematics having been specially successful. Material is presented in small, carefully designed sub-units each of which is designed to be relatively easy for a student to master; thereby obtaining reinforcement. Mastery of one sub-unit is prerequisite to studying the next in sequence. Ideally the student should master the entire programme without experiencing failure. Should a student fail to master a sub-unit it is usual to offer alternative parallel sub-units until mastery is achieved.

There is now a growing number of books about a further, technological,

10

Figure 1.3 Typical learning system design

1 Describe Current Status of System
↓
2 Derive and Write Learning Objectives
↓
3 Formulate Evaluation Plans
↓
4 Describe and Analyze Tasks
↓
5 Design and Implement Instructional Procedures
↓
6 Implement Evaluation Plan
↓
7 Redesign

(after Baker, 1973)

approach to curriculum. These writers believe that instructional procedures can be made more efficient by the use of modern techniques (computer programming) and media (audio, video) and by developing self-explanatory, individualized learning packages. Such educational technologists as Briggs (1970), Gagne (1968), and Baker (1973) have developed elaborate procedures based upon a systems approach to learning.

Inputs for the topic are carefully designated (needs of learners, society); throughputs (learning activities) and outputs (assessed outcomes) are included in elaborate models. Feedback loops are provided for students if they do not reach certain levels of performance (figure 1.3).

The language of the educational technologists is concise, terse and unambiguous. They prefer to identify specific behavioural objectives, because this enables the instructional activities to be more precisely designed. Although the technological approach is claimed to be successful with all kinds of curriculum frames of reference, observable, conventional classroom tasks have been those most frequently developed, indicating their learning toward the behaviourist point of view.

The benefit accruing from these behaviourist-oriented approaches is that learning can occur very efficiently if the tasks are well defined. On the debit side, this orientation requires a highly structured, sequenced approach to curriculum and minimizes the need for informal, interactive activities among children.

Frame of Reference III: Social Interaction Orientation

There are a number of curriculum writers who consider that the task of the school is to produce individuals capable of comprehending their own view of the world, their beliefs and values, and yet sensitive to the beliefs and values of others. The social interaction approach provides two gains, namely an understanding both of one's own 'world' and also of that of others. As Joyce and Weil (1980) put it, 'the resulting world is pluralistic and the essence of the democratic process is the creation of interaction among the unique, personal worlds of individuals so that a shared reality is created'.

An example of an approach which has been developed by Oliver and Shaver (1966) is illustrative of the social interaction frame of reference. These two curriculum writers consider that it is crucial for children to develop a respect for the point of view and dignity of other human beings. This can be achieved in the classroom by examining public issues and focusing upon the alternative views expressed. They maintain that the idea of a pluralist society needs to be developed by delaying early closure of a public issue with a 'correct' solution and instead taking time to show how different interpretations are due to differing value stances.

The predominant teaching technique involved is to require small groups of students to work cooperatively together exploring a public issue. They must have the opportunity to voice their interpretations, hear what others have to say and then be prepared to maintain or change their point of view. Once small groups start to examine the descriptive, analytic and normative elements of an issue, they are in a much stronger position to appreciate the many alternative solutions. Solutions to a public issue can be decided on either in small groups or by the total group.

Frame of Reference IV: Personal Development Orientation

In the Personal Development frame of reference, all the learning experiences are geared to the purposes of the individual. Writers who take this stance, such as Rogers (1969), Maslow (1962), Weinstein and Fantini (1970), and Brown (1971), emphasize that each individual should be allowed to construct and organize his/her own reality. For them, the development of self is a legitimate task of schools.

It is often difficult to extract from their books the specific classroom activities that these writers are proposing, and this can be expected in an orientation which stresses that outputs are emergent and not specified in advance. Nevertheless, it is possible to pinpoint some common approaches which might be used. The task of teachers, initially, is to seek out in a non-directive, non-threatening way, each student's needs with regard to schooling — their felt deficiencies, areas that they want to pursue further, and topics that they want to explore. Once teachers have an overall picture of the aims, aspirations and needs of each student, they are able to develop an appropriate classroom climate for each member but this will require the provision of a wealth of resource materials and specific instructions enabling individuals to gain access to them whenever required.

Making a Choice

Each of the four frames of reference described above contain very different value stances. For example, Behaviour Modification proponents maintain that detailed teaching materials need to be prepared in advance which are used to strictly control student behaviour.

In supporting any one frame of reference, decisions are automatically made about the relative weightings to be given to curriculum components. For example, the Information Processing adherents are likely to give higher priorities to 'students' abilities' than to 'needs of the disciplines'. Social Interaction followers are likely to consider 'needs of society' more important than 'students' interests'. It is not suggested that any one of the four orientations should, or could, be adopted entirely. Conditions peculiar to a given education system, schools, and teachers will limit the extent to which certain kinds of teaching can be used. It is likely, however, that Information Processing and Behaviour Modification frames of reference occur more commonly in East Asian countries than the other two.

Influences on Curriculum Conceptions

The fact that certain conceptions of curriculum occur widely in some countries and to a much lesser extent in others, can be traced to the influences that various individuals and groups (stakeholders) can exert on educational decision-making. The term 'stake-holder' is often used to indicate that individuals or groups consider that they have the expertise and/or are directly affected by certain decisions and must be part of the decision-making process. Many groups could be cited but major ones include:

* political leaders
* religious leaders
* head office officials
* teachers
* business groups/employers

Political leaders are very concerned about schools and the curriculum in that they expect children to understand their country's rules and institutions and to be committed participants when they attain adulthood. They exert control over the curriculum of schools using such measures as establishing academic standards and examinations, providing national curriculum guidelines, and requiring training programmes for teachers.

Religious leaders can have an enormous influence over the types and levels of schools that are provided for children and the nature of the curriculum practised in these schools. As noted by Thomas (1988b) the Islamic revival which occurred in a number of countries in the late 1970s has had an impact upon a number of East Asian countries, such as Indonesia. Curricula in Islamic schools have become more secular and give more attention now to communication skills, science, social science and vocational studies. But there has been a concomitant growth in non-formal Islamic programmes such as attendance at mosque prayers, daily prayers and pilgrimages to Mecca which clearly influence the goals and purposes of schooling (Holmes and McLean, 1989). Religious beliefs can influence in particular the amount of effort that students are prepared to devote to their studies and the extent to which families encourage and promote intensive study and commitment to learning in their children (Holloway, 1988).

Most education systems retain *head offices* or central administrative divisions to enable strategic policy decisions to be made about such matters as staffing, buildings, curriculum and standards. The degree of centralization/decentralization varies enormously from one system to another. In a highly centralized education system, curriculum documents and syllabus statements are specified in great detail and implementation procedures in schools are explicitly stated and systematically monitored. In such a situation a head office is obviously a very important stakeholder.

Teachers are also major stakeholders. The majority of teachers have chosen teaching as a career and take very seriously their responsibilities to provide for the intellectual, emotional, social and spiritual growth of their students. They receive some training in curriculum planning skills but they are constantly under pressures of time due to the daily demands of the classroom situation.

Where there is intense competition for goods and services, *employers* expect their employees to be not only literate and numerate, but also to have well developed problem-solving and social skills. The media often criticize the basic skills levels of newly employed youth. Employers tend to be extremely critical of schools and maintain that insufficient rigour and standards are required.

Different Levels of Curriculum Planning

Curriculum planning at the *system level* will always be significant even though the amount of centralization/decentralization varies considerably between countries and within each country over time. The size of an education system can vary from fewer than ten schools to hundreds of thousands of schools. In many systems subject guidelines or syllabuses are centrally developed for all schools.

Overlying the system level is *a national* level of curriculum planning. In some countries the system level may be a provincial level, but in others it may be synonymous with the national level (for example, Hong Kong and Singapore).

At the *school level* a certain amount of curriculum planning can occur. Some educationalists argue that the school is the natural organizing unit and that school-based curriculum development (SBCD) should be the dominant approach in all schools (Skilbeck, 1984; Caldwell and Spinks, 1988). SBCD activities can certainly provide intrinsic satisfactions for teachers because they plan and implement curricula which they 'own'. Other purported advantages include opportunities for teachers to undertake leadership, and opportunities for parents and students to work collaboratively with teachers. Yet, there are penalties. There is often insufficient time, expertise and money to enable classroom teachers to get involved in SBCD. Sometimes they get little recognition for their efforts. Teacher 'burn-out' is symptomatic of many SBCD endeavours.

At the *classroom level* a teacher still has the opportunity and responsibility to make important curriculum decisions even though a number of prescriptions may have already been made by others. For example, a primary teacher is usually assigned to teach a particular grade level and there is usually a designated syllabus for each subject that the teacher is required to follow. The school principal and other senior teachers may also supervise their teaching from time to time to ensure that certain standards are being attained. At the secondary school level, external examinations are often a major influence, and can provide very demanding restrictions on what content a teacher selects and how it is taught (for example, Singapore).

Even so, the classroom teacher is still able to make the ultimate decisions about day-to-day teaching practices. He/she can choose to use a certain teaching aid — a textbook reading — a guest speaker — or an excursion. As noted by various educators, what happens behind the classroom door can be quite different to what external forces may intend.

Content and the Curriculum

The content of the curriculum is critical to all teaching situations. It is important to stress the linkage between content and method. 'Content' only becomes important when it is transmitted to students by particular teaching methods. It is possible, of course, for important content not to be taught because inappropriate methods are used, or the reverse, where unimportant content is taught using appropriate methods.

Content is usually referred to as the subject-matter of teaching and includes knowledge, skills, values and attitudes. Knowledge is often described in terms of key concepts, generalizations and specific facts. Key concepts are especially important as they enable a teacher to organize large amounts of data within these terms. Generalizations link together several concepts to form main ideas or principles. Facts are specific happenings or events which can be used to illustrate and develop concepts. They have limited use by themselves but they are important in the development of concepts.

The knowledge that is actually taught in schools may have evolved from within the culture of a country or it could have been imported from advanced industrial societies. This can be the case especially with 'technical knowledge'. Holmes and McLean (1989) use the term 'dependence' to emphasize the extent to which a number of East Asian countries import technical knowledge via textbooks, educational experts, and training programmes (for example, the People's Republic of China and the Philippines).

Skills are also an important element of content. Some curriculum planners consider skills to be the highest form of content and that 'processes' rather than 'product' should be the major emphasis in all teaching. Skills cover a range of areas, and include thinking and inquiry skills, and communication skills.

Values and attitudes comprise the affective element of any content. Curriculum planners must take student motivations and attitudes into account in all their content selections (Egan, 1986). It is important that students develop positive attitudes about work habits and learning and this will only be achieved if content appropriate to student needs is selected. Then there is the issue of moral/ethical values implicit in many subject areas and which are strongly promoted by senior officials (for example, Indonesia, Singapore and the PRC).

Central agencies tend to prescribe content to teachers via syllabus documents or in teachers guides. They make their selections using such criteria as:

significance — Is the content selected fundamental to the subject in terms of specific facts, concepts, skills and values?

balance — Does the content permit development in both breadth and depth of understanding?

interest and needs — Is the content suited to the needs, interests and maturity level of students?

| utility | — Is the content consistent with the world around us — the social reality for students? |
| learnability | — Is the content arranged in such a way that it suits the ability of students and is learnable and understandable? |

At the classroom level, teachers are still faced with decisions even if general content areas have been prescribed in a syllabus. For example, should they use a textbook entirely or supplement it with a selection of references or discussion prints and charts?

Methods and the Curriculum

Decisions about content and method cannot be made independently. When students and teachers are involved in a learning situation it is obvious that content and methods are closely interlinked. Content will be used but how it is communicated and discussed will depend upon the methods selected.

Teachers tend to use methods with which they are familiar to impart content. It might be a very limited repertoire such as drill and recitation; question and answer; or laboratory presentation. However the list can be quite extensive as indicated below:

teacher talks
lectures
demonstrations
small group discussions
question and answers
recitation (students recite information back to the teacher)
practice drills
problem-solving
inquiry
role playing
simulation games
debates

It is desirable for teachers to use a wide range of methods to suit specific content and particular groups of students (see chapter 2). Research evidence indicates that in practice, teachers tend to use a small number of conventional methods (for example, a common one is 'recitation teaching' (Hargreaves, 1988). It is also apparent from recent research studies that no single method is better than another in all teaching situations. For example, drills may be most successful in imparting particular facts but not very efficient in fostering attitudes apart from obedience and uniformity.

Different methods can also be used to organize the content for teaching. Some typical methods include a *spiralling* process whereby a concept is re-introduced at regular intervals using content of increasing difficulty; an *activity* approach whereby student interests and activities provide the basis for what content is selected and taught; a *core curriculum* approach in which broad areas of social concern or academic disciplines are the focus and the content selected cuts across subject boundaries.

Evaluation and the Curriculum

This is an important aspect of curriculum planning and is described in detail in chapter 3.

For some teachers, 'grading', 'examinations' and 'assessment' are all the same and so the term 'evaluation' is only a new expression for the one thing. However, it is possible to make distinctions. Teachers assign marks or grades for work undertaken by students, such as a project, a maths test or a spelling test. Assessment of students' performance involves collecting a total picture of their performance as indicated by a range of grades and tests and students commonly receive assessment cards or report cards each term or semester. But the process of evaluation is, or should be, much wider than these terms and in fact includes them. Evaluation involves collecting and processing all kinds of data (grades, test results, observations, samples of work) and then making decisions or judgments about the students' performance. It should be emphasized that all kinds of data can be collected — formal and informal — objective and subjective — as the different categories complement each other and add to the total picture. Furthermore it is possible to evaluate the students' performance and the performance of the teacher, and indirectly, the relative effectiveness of the curriculum that was implemented.

The Context

Curriculum planners cannot ignore the importance of learning contexts. Even within the one country, schools can be very different. For example, they can vary one from another in such matters as:

school buildings and grounds
classroom spaces
availability of resources
staffing provisions
rules and regulations
discipline measures.

Some of these aspects can influence very greatly how curricula are taught. For example, cramped rooms and large classes may prevent certain activities and topics being selected and taught effectively by teachers. Further, the rules and regulations of a school might prevent teachers from using non-traditional methods of instruction. Many other aspects make each school unique. Some schools encourage a high degree of community participation in decision-making while others tend to minimize these activities. A school principal might encourage an open working environment, permitting staff to be heavily involved in decision-making. More frequently, some school principals insist upon a very authoritarian climate and do not encourage staff participation. SBCD activities are very difficult to initiate in school contexts which do not allow openness and freedom of discussion among staff (Pang *et al.*, 1985).

All schools are created to promote learning but the specific configuration of each school, in terms of its human and material resources, can produce very different results. Some of these variations become very apparent in the case study chapters in Section II of the book.

Planning Models

The planning of any curriculum requires mastery of a number of skills, some of which have been described above. For example, special skills are required in selecting:

content
teaching methods
objectives and goals
assessment and evaluation procedures.

In addition there are skills associated with:

using school resources efficiently
obtaining community support
communicating school achievements to external groups
obtaining support from other staff members.

Models can be helpful to curriculum planners in guiding him/her about activities to initiate and the criteria which might be used. As an illustration and to conclude this chapter, Tyler's model is presented in some detail as this has had a major influence on the way curricula have been developed, especially in countries with centralized systems of educational decision making.

Tyler's Model

Tyler's model first appeared in 1949 in his *Basic Principles of Curriculum and Instruction*. The book is such a fine example of clarity that, after half a century, it is still included in any list of highly rated works in the field of education.

Tyler warned in the introduction that his book 'is not a manual for curriculum construction since it does not describe and outline in detail the steps to be taken by a given school or college that seeks to build a curriculum'. It is merely 'one way of viewing an instructional programme' and 'the student is encouraged to examine other rationales and to develop his own conception of the elements and relationships involved in an effective curriculum'.

In the book, Tyler referred to a particular *rationale* which forms the basis for his viewpoint about curriculum-in-action. He argued that there are really four

Figure 1.4   Tyler's model: Rationale based on four questions

---

1   What educational purposes should the school seek to attain?
    Sources — studies of the learners themselves
            — studies of contemporary life outside the school
            — suggestions about objectives from subject specialists.
    The use of philosophy in selecting objectives.
    The use of a psychology of learning in selecting objectives.
    Stating objectives in a form to be helpful in selecting learning experiences and in guiding
    teaching.

2   How can learning experiences be selected which are likely to be useful in attaining these
    objectives?
    General principles in selecting learning experiences.

3   How can learning experiences be organized for effective instruction?
    Criteria for effective organization
    Elements to be organized
    Organizing principles
    The organizing structure.

4   How can the effectiveness of learning experiences be evaluated?
    Basic notions regarding evaluation
    Evaluation procedures

---

elements, or 'big questions' that curriculum makers have to ask (figure 1.4). In subsequent chapters of his book he devoted one to each of these four areas.

Educational purposes of school

In answering the first question on educational purposes of the school, Tyler accepted three sources: learners, contemporary society, and subject specialists. He was quite eclectic in this respect. Is it possible to combine all three sources even if they represent very different priorities? According to Tyler it can be done by putting together a number of potentially useable objectives from these three sources, and then using philosophy and psychology as screens to sieve off the important objectives.

Tyler did not address values issues directly, but his views become clear when reading his book. For example, he suggested that curriculum planners use scientific studies of students (such as norm-referenced tests on reading skills of 10-year-olds) to make decisions about whether these students at a specific school need to receive instruction in particular reading skills or not. That is, he perceived learner sources from a *scientific* testing point of view, and he obviously valued this data source more highly than data obtained informally from a class of students. Tyler accepted similar types of data as valid and reliable for deriving information about contemporary society and subject specialists.

It is not clear how the philosophy and psychology screens of question 1 in figure 1.4 are supposed to operate. In Tyler's view, each school will have its own values, stated or implied, about the nature of a good life and a good society.

Tyler is more specific about how psychology might be used as a screen, by his reference to certain psychology of learning principles, such as maturation levels and learning, and conditions amenable to effective learning. But he still throws the onus back upon the curriculum planner to make choices of objectives with very little guidance about how to undertake the task:

> However, each curriculum worker will need to formulate a theory of learning in which he has some confidence and use it as a basis for checking his educational objectives to see that they are consistent with his theory of learning. (p. 34)

Despite these weaknesses, the model does provide the curriculum planner with guidance by its emphasis on the need to have a purpose, or goals, or objectives. Furthermore, if planners can specify what they are trying to achieve with a particular curriculum, then the task of organizing the procedures becomes so much easier.

Selection of learning experiences
The emphasis upon goal-directed, means-end approach to planning is very evident in Tyler's second and subsequent components. For example, he asserted that learning experiences (see figure 1.4) must be selected so that the students have sufficient opportunity to experience and successfully complete the tasks required of them. He also suggested that the learning experiences must enable the students to gain satisfactions from carrying on particular kinds of behaviour. These principles about designing learning experiences were certainly very advanced for the 1940s when Tyler's book was published.

Organization for effective instruction
A range of helpful suggestions are also included by Tyler in his discussion of the third element, 'the organizing of learning experiences' (see figure 1.4). This section of the book makes it clear again that he placed considerable emphasis upon rational planning by the use of terms such as a 'coherent program', 'efficiency of instruction', and an 'effective organization'. Tyler thought that learning will be maximized if the learning experiences built upon earlier ones (vertical organization) and were reinforced by activities in other subjects (horizontal organization). He incorporated these concepts into three criteria for providing an effective organization, namely 'continuity', 'sequence' and 'integration'. In his view, it is essential for planners to identify the major concepts and skills which are then introduced and reintroduced in successive teaching units. Tyler stressed that continuity, sequence and integration have to be experienced by the learners, and not to be merely tools for the planner. Learners have to experience the continuity of particular concepts, they go into more detail each time a concept is resequenced, and then by their individual levels of understanding, achieve the necessary level of integration.

Evaluation
In the fourth and final element, Tyler emphasized the need for curriculum planners to see how far the learning experiences, as developed and organized by them, actually produced the desired results. He provided here again some innovative ideas about evaluation, including the need to evaluate students throughout a unit and not just at the end. He emphasized that evaluation involves getting evidence about behaviour changes in students and this is not necessarily confined

to merely given paper-and-pencil tests. For example, he advocated other techniques such as observations, interviews, questionnaires and work samples.

Despite certain ambiguities about objectives and sources of data, as outlined above, Tyler's model does highlight important elements for the curriculum planner. Many other models have been based upon Tyler's model. A lot of the excesses of these recent models have been criticized but there has also been a tendency to turn criticism, somewhat unfairly, upon Tyler's original model.

The model has been used by curriculum policymakers in countries such as Hong Kong and Korea as a reason to select and promote innovations, especially imported ones, which are viewed as the most desirable possible goals. This allows official educational policy to focus on the worthwhile nature of curriculum intentions and thus serves to maintain a convenient public facade. Unfortunately, as noted in Section II of the book, the innovation is often wholly unsuited to the local context or the necessary conditions for its implementation, such as resource development and in-service teacher training, are not provided. These problems are a comment on how Tyler's model has been used rather than on its intrinsic features.

Tyler's model related to curriculum planning at a systems level. It is clear that teachers do not plan their teaching primarily with reference to the same variables.

Concluding Comments

In this chapter a number of aspects about curriculum were introduced. Different priorities about what should be taught and how, were very evident in alternative definitions and frames of reference introduced in this chapter. In East Asian countries, particular influences such as political and religious leaders, can determine to a large extent, the curricula which are prescribed for schools. Notwithstanding, planned curricula can differ considerably from implemented curricula and it is these variations (slippages) which are the focus in chapter 2.

Chapter 2

Implementation

Colin Marsh

Introduction

In the previous chapter reference was made to how curriculum is perceived by various individuals and groups. Also, attention was directed to how curriculum planning might occur using the Tyler model as an example.

The focus in this chapter is upon putting curriculum plans into action. This involves gaining an appreciation of the curriculum continuum from planning through to institutionalization; an analysis of the phases that central education agencies typically use with new curriculum packages; a detailed study of the implementation phase; and a survey of implementation factors pertaining to different levels of schooling.

The Curriculum Continuum

As depicted in figure 2.1, there are a number of points on the curriculum continuum. An initial point is a '*plan*' or orientation. This may be based upon a particular theoretical perspective or it could represent a solution to a specific, practical need. The plan provides guidelines about what will be produced — the focus, the range of activities, types of assessment, etc.

The next point on the continuum is *production* of the curriculum package. The package may be very comprehensive, spanning several grade levels and including teacher and student guides, resource booklets and multimedia components. Alternatively it could be a very simple booklet containing general guidelines about a teaching process or content selection.

Adoption is the next point on the continuum. An erroneous judgment by many educators is that once a commitment has been made to purchase or obtain a new curriculum, then effective use will automatically follow. The scores of school storerooms containing little used, outmoded curriculum books is testimony to the argument that adopting a curriculum does not mean that it will be effectively used.

The *implementation* point on the continuum signifies that the school principal and teachers at a school are actively engaged in using a new curriculum. As described in detail in the following sections, it takes a considerable amount of time for teachers to become confident about, and skilled in, using a new

Figure 2.1 The curriculum continuum

Planning and designing	Producing a package	Adoption of the curriculum	Implementation of the curriculum	Institutionalization of the curriculum

curriculum. A typical time period for teachers to become successful implementers is considered to be two to four years. Once a curriculum has reached the point where implementation procedures have become well established and routinized, then *institutionalization* has been reached.

It should be noted, however, that curricula do not stay institutionalized for very long. There are usually pressures from teachers and external forces to make modifications and changes to an existing curriculum and so it is likely that the planning — product — adoption — implementation points of the continuum will start all over again.

Decision-making Phases Used by Central Education Agencies

Although it is difficult to generalize from one country another, there do appear to be some common phases used by central education agencies. The Authority-Innovation Decision-Making Model developed by Rogers and Shoemaker (1971) is a useful illustration. These authors consider that central administration personnel are seen as a *superordinate* group who make major decisions about how a curriculum will be produced and implemented by the *subordinate* group, the school-level teachers and principals. Some authors (for example Marsh and Huberman, 1984; Morris, 1986) argue that the superordinate group can consist of others apart from central education officials. They suggest that other important groups can include textbook publishers who can exert enormous pressures upon what student texts are made available; and university professors who can put considerable pressure on senior education officials in terms of curriculum content and standards.

As depicted in figure 2.2, it is suggested that superordinate and subordinate groups operate within a five stage process.

(A) The first stage, *knowledge*, is clearly the province of superordinate groups as their members are first to receive information about new educational products and techniques from outside agencies and commercial firms. They will process the information in certain ways and perhaps some distortions will occur on the way to the subordinate groups. At this point the decision makers might request more information in the form of documents and papers, and obtain details from experts.

(B) At the *persuasion* stage, a number of dissemination activities will occur within the superordinate group. Officials who have now become familiar with an innovatory technique or product, will be interested in seeking out detailed information, and may initiate feasibility surveys. Some internal lobbying may occur between various 'power élites' over

Figure 2.2   *Authority-innovation decision-making model*

Superordinate group	Ministry of Education/ Head Office	*Others* Textbook publishers, Tertiary institutions
	Knowledge Persuasion Decision	
Functions (demarcation line)		Communication action
Subordinate group		Classroom teachers and principals

their support for a particular innovation. Superordinate decision makers may ask for some information about needs from school personnel to help them in preparing their case, but this tends to be relatively rare.

Other superordinate groups might be involved in initiating moves to adopt and disseminate an innovation, for example, an examination board may promote a new system of criterion-referenced assessment. In this case, similar in-house bargaining will occur, with the likelihood of some spill-over to other decision-making groups such as the head office group, several of whose members might very well be part-time officials on the examination board. Entrepreneurial skill and drive seem to be necessary attributes for getting curricula adopted and it is evident that senior decision makers are not lacking such skills.

(C)   The *decision* stage is the culmination of all formal and informal meetings arranged to persuade participants of the considerable benefits in adopting and implementing a particular innovation. Informally, the decision may have been reached much earlier, but formal meetings and notifications are required to ratify and legitimize the adoption of a particular innovation and the dissemination procedures to be used.

(D)   With regard to these first three stages (knowledge, persuasion and decision), there are few interactions between superordinate groups and classroom teachers. It is only at the *communication* and *action* stages that the decision-making groups disseminate information about its curriculum decisions, and in particular, provide details about how a particular curriculum innovation is to be implemented. Dissemination tactics can take various forms such as personal contacts, in-service days, advisory teacher visits, official pronouncement, news releases and official publications.

Dissemination tactics are also used by those other decision-making groups who are able to wield influence over the teacher/implementer group. For example, examination boards will distribute manuals and handbooks about new syllabuses, moderators may be appointed to visit schools to monitor standards of student achievement, and examiners of a new syllabus might call special meetings of interested teachers to discuss the implications of their new approach.

Textbook publishers undertake similar, but less hierarchical, dissemination activities through their press notices, publicity associated with launching a new publication, visits by travelling salesmen, and the distribution of leaflets, brochures and complimentary copies.

(E)   At the *action* stage, the decision-making groups are not only communicating information about a new curriculum, but in many cases they are specifying it is to be implemented. It is at this phase that various matters about implementation come to the fore and they are discussed in some detail below.

Implementation: Intentions and Reality

The most comprehensive reviews of educational innovations in developing countries (Havelock and Huberman, 1977) paint a very dismal picture of their effects.

> In spite of large scale investment and expectation, few of these innovations appear to make a dent at a national level in the educational or training problems which they were designed to solve. They appear in many respects to be giant pilot projects. Our conclusion was that innovation is not practised up to the level of existing knowledge. Our findings point to a rather dismal picture of international and national efforts to innovate, repetitions of obvious mistakes or omissions.

The World Bank (1980) commented similarly that curriculum development activities had not met expectations and had been thwarted by resistance to change by ill-informed clients, inadequate resources, poor implementation strategies and insufficient monitoring. Adams and Chen (1981) describe educational innovation as 'doleful' and mainly characterized by failure. Similar portrayals are made by Lewin (1981b) with regard to Malaysia, Morris (1986) with regard to Hong Kong and Leung (1989) with regard to the People's Republic of China (the PRC). The problem is not confined to Asian or developing societies for Mann (1976) comments with reference to the American experience:

> ... Most educators realize that the amount and pace of change has fallen far short of initial expectations... Programs were planned, curriculum was developed, teaching/learning units were packaged, teachers were trained, and the results were frustrating, uneven, unexpected, and temporary. With hindsight it is easy to see that designing and disseminating change is not implementing change. What happens inside the school, at the service delivery level, is absolutely related to our success or failure, yet the gap in our knowledge about implementing change in the schools is formidable.

Explanations of this situation have varied between those that explain the problem with reference to the characteristics of the persons who are supposed to use the innovation to those which focus on the characteristics of the innovations themselves.

The first type of explanation uses propositions such as the following to explain why change does not occur, because people are: naturally conservative, resistant to change, lacking in motivation, uncooperative, do not have positive attitudes or do not have a complete understanding of the change. These types of explanation are superficially attractive but wholly unsatisfactory for two reasons. First, they deal with correlations not with causes. A person might have a negative attitude to an innovation because he/she thinks it is impractical or will not benefit the pupils. Consequently he/she does not implement it. It cannot therefore be deduced that he/she has not used the innovation solely because of a negative attitude. Second, they are tautological and therefore untestable propositions. A person who is resistant to change or conservative is defined as someone who does not use an innovation. A person who does use the innovation is defined as someone who is receptive to change or innovative. Merely restating the condition that is being explained is similar to arguing that the cause of unemployment is that people do not have jobs. It is also important to note that people's attitudes towards a practical task, such as a teaching style, are not fixed and are substantially affected by their attempts to use it. As they become more experienced they can develop more positive attitudes. Conversely a positive attitude towards an innovation can be reversed as a result of trying to use it.

In reality people cannot be divided up between those who are willing to change and those who are not. In some situations people are willing to change and in others they are not. It is necessary to look at the conditions which are associated with successful innovations.

Rogers and Shoemaker (1971) identify five attributes of innovations which determine whether or not they are adopted. These are:

- Relative advantage (over the previous practice)
- Compatibility (with existing values, experiences and needs)
- Complexity (is it easy to understand and use)
- Trialability (potential for limited experimentation)
- Observability (visibility of results)

This analysis allows the argument to move away from always blaming teachers for their failure to implement change for it suggests that the problem could arise from the nature of the innovation itself. However, if innovations have to be compatible with existing values and experiences then little real change will ever occur. Hurst (1983) also assumes that teachers make rational decisions whether or not to use an innovation. He argues that they base their decision on seven conditions:

- Communication — is the information on the innovation adequate and accurate, and can they get feedback on their views?
- Relevance — is it perceived to be beneficial to the user or the pupils?
- Effectiveness — will the alleged benefits actually occur?

- Feasibility — is it possible to implement it (are the reasons, time, equipment available?)
- Efficiency — is it the most efficient method to achieve the stated goals?
- Trialability — is it possible to try it out?
- Adaptability — can it be modified in the light of experience?

A teacher has therefore to decide overall whether the benefits exceed the costs of using a curriculum innovation. It must be remembered that a change of behaviour inevitably involves a cost as teachers have to learn something new and sacrifice the style with which they are familiar. This is especially true when teachers are trying to change the style of teaching, which has proved to be the most difficult aspect of the curriculum to change. The aims of subjects, their content and the textbooks used can easily be changed, especially when these are controlled by the government or a central agency. Frequently the same methods have been used to try to bring about changes to the teaching approach that are used to disseminate information on new subject content or textbooks. This relies on the use of official directives and circulars which are the traditional way for a bureaucracy to try to inform people what they should be doing. This allows politicians and civil servants to point to the new policy directive as evidence of appropriate and worthwhile action on their part. Teachers on the other hand have to decide whether or not the benefits of change exceed the anticipated costs. Frequently they find that the innovation is unclear, they do not have the skills to use it or that it is incompatible with other demands, such as the requirements of the public examination. The result is frequently a façade of change — whilst official policies towards the curriculum change there is little change in the classroom, especially in terms of the style of teaching.

This situation is exacerbated by two considerations. First, the failure of innovations is relative to expectations. If one sets very ambitious goals, such as the abandonment of a didactic teaching style and the use of a pupil-centred, inquiry-oriented and problem-solving teaching style then it is likely that failure will be the outcome. Curriculum planners are often under a great deal of pressure to pursue ambitious goals so that they can obtain the necessary resources and satisfy the political need to be seen to have an ambitious and worthwhile project. Second, a great deal of curriculum planning has focused on what ought to be, and little attention has been paid to considering what is the current situation. Curriculum reforms often arise and are justified by an assumption that existing curricula are wholly inadequate and that replacing them with something new and modern will solve the problems. In fact the problems of existing curricula are often the result of factors such as inadequate resources and in-service training. A new curricula introduced in these circumstances is doomed to failure. Successful change will require that new curricula are developed with reference to an analysis of the current situation, not just with reference to what ought to be. This should result in the pursuit of more achievable and modest goals.

Implementation: Practical Issues and Problems

When a teacher is faced with the prospect of implementing a new curriculum, a number of questions are likely to spring to their attention, such as:

How do I do it?
Will I ever get it to work smoothly?
To whom can I turn to get assistance?
Am I doing what is required?
Will I cover the syllabus?
What is the effect on the learner?
Will the students pass the relevant examination?

This emphasis on how to use a new curriculum is a major concern for teachers because as 'craft specialists' they gain most of their intrinsic satisfaction from being successful in using a particular approach and materials with their students. However, the implementation of any new curriculum will take a teacher a considerable period of time as he/she needs to become competent and confident in its use. It is only when a new curriculum is completely accepted by teachers in a school and the activities associated with it are a matter of routine, that the phase *institutionalization* is said to have been reached.

At this stage it is relevant to introduce two approaches to implementation which external curriculum developers consider when preparing teachers' manuals and other instructions for using a curriculum. A majority of packages incorporate explicit instructions, requiring teachers to implement a program along highly specified, tightly controlled lines and in this case it is up to the teacher to maintain *fidelity of use* (for example, curricula developed in Singapore, Japan and the PRC). Less common are innovations which are not supplied with prescriptive guidelines for implementation, either due to the nature of the curriculum, or the context in which it is to be used, or both. These innovations require adaptations and compromises between the intended curriculum as conceived by the developer and that envisaged by each school or teacher. An example would be the Guidelines for Civic Education (EO, 1988) in Hong Kong. In this case *mutual adaptation* between developers and teachers is required during the implementation process. These two approaches to implementation are examined in more detail below.

Fidelity of Use

This is typically a very structured approach to implementation whereby teachers are given explicit instructions about how to teach a unit or course. The instructions to teachers are specified *a priori*, and this means, of course, little provision is made for the various school contexts in which the unit might be used. The basic assumptions are that:

(a) central planning is necessary to eliminate inefficiencies and slippages at the school level;
(b) specialists are needed to produce comprehensive and up-to-date units.

This orientation to implementation, if it is to be successful, requires that the classroom teacher must be thoroughly trained to use the new program or unit. It also appears that the teacher's role is largely that of passive receiver, who will be trained to transmit the content of the new curriculum package and once having received this training, will teach it at a high level of technical proficiency.

Undoubtedly this is the situation for many curriculum packages used in East Asian countries, especially where the content is complex and difficult to master and thereby requires careful sequencing; in subjects where teachers may lack the necessary knowledge or skills; and in subjects or units where appropriate national achievement tests can be incorporated.

Mutual Adaptation

The term 'mutual adaptation' was first used by Dalin and McLaughlin (1975) to describe the adaptation process whereby adjustments are made to the innovation itself and to institutional setting. Some writers argue that mutual adaptation is the only effective way of ensuring successful implementation. For example, House (1979) maintains that implementation is really a political decision and emphasizes the 'personal face-to-face interaction' as a key process. MacDonald and Walker (1976) maintain that implementation really involves 'negotiation' and that there are trade-offs in meaning between curriculum developers and teachers. Although there is always some slippage between curriculum plans and implementation practices, the 'fidelity of use' perspective prevails in most subject areas rather than 'mutual adaptation'.

Because the 'fidelity of use' perspective assumes that implementation practices will occur largely as planned, it is necessary of course, to consider ways in which implementation can be monitored, and even measured. Numerous problems occur when attempts are made to monitor and even describe, levels of implementation. Some of these problems and issues are analyzed in the following section.

Problems of Describing and Measuring the Implementation of a Curriculum

Attempts to describe the implementation of new curricula are fraught with all kinds of difficulties. For example, do you focus upon the curriculum materials, or what the teacher is doing, or what the students are doing? If the intention is to try to do all three things what criteria do you use to select out instances of each, since they are all occurring simultaneously in the classroom? Are there optimal times to examine how a curriculum is being implemented, such as after six months of operation, or a year, or even longer?

Trying to measure degrees of implementation is even more difficult than trying to describe it. Decisions have to be made about what kinds of data should be collected, such as observational data, document analysis or self-report data. Concerns are often raised about who does the measuring and who is to receive the results.

Measuring Student Activities and Achievements

A major reason for producing a new curriculum is to provide better learning opportunities for students, such as higher achievement levels in terms of knowledge and skills. Rarely is it possible, however, for measurements to be obtained

Figure 2.3 CBAM principles

---

1 Change is a process, not an event, requiring time, energy and resources to support it.
2 Change is achieved incrementally and developmentally and entails developmental growth in feelings about and skills in using new programs.
3 Change is accomplished by individuals first. Institutions cannot change until the individuals within them change.
4 Change is a highly personal experience.
5 Change can be facilitated by change agents providing diagnostic, client-centred support to individual teachers.

(Hall and Loucks, 1979; Rutherford, 1983)

---

on student achievements so that it can be stated unequivocally that a new curriculum is superior to the previous one, in terms of particular dimensions. There are so many confounding variables which affect student scores. A single test is unlikely to be suitable for use and to be able to provide valid and reliable comparable data between a new curriculum and the previous one.

The prolonged periods of time needed and the costs involved in developing control and experimental groups make such tasks very expensive, and with little prospect of getting conclusive results.

Measuring Use of Curriculum Materials

In most teaching programs, curriculum materials, especially textbooks, figure prominently in the day–to–day activities of teachers and students. In fact, surveys done of USA schools have revealed that in school, students can spend up to 80 per cent of their time engaged with textbooks (Cornbleth, 1979).

It is clearly important in any study of implementation to gather information about how textbooks and other materials are used. Checklists are a popular way of evaluating curriculum materials and these can range from brief lists of two or three pages using yes/no categories to elaborate inventories of fifteen or more pages using 4 or 5 point Likert scales.

Measuring Teacher Activities

Various methods have been used over the decades to measure teachers' implementation activities, ranging from formal visitations to observation checklists, questionnaires, interviews and self-report techniques. In the USA a number of scholars have focused upon the special problems that teachers experienced in implementing a new curriculum. One group of scholars, Hall *et al.* (1973) at the University of Texas, developed several important instruments (questionnaires and focused interview schedule) over a ten-year period, but they also developed a conceptual orientation to change, named the Concerns Based Adoption Model (CBAM). The major assumptions of this model are listed above in figure 2.3.

It is evident that the focus of the CBAM model is upon the needs, concerns and skills of the *individual teacher*. Worth noting also, are the statements about the time needed to bring about change efforts and that incremental and

Figure 2.4   *The teacher's 'stages of concern' about an innovation*

Stages of Concern	Definitions
6 Refocusing	The focus is on exploration of more universal benefits from the innovation, including the possibility of major changes or replacement with a more powerful alternative. Individual has definite ideas about alternatives to the proposed or existing form of the innovation.
5 Collaboration	The focus is on coordination and cooperation with others regarding use of the innovation.
4 Consequence	Attention focuses on impact of the innovation on student in his/her immediate sphere of influence. The focus is on relevance of the innovation for students, evaluation of student outcomes, including performance and competencies, and changes needed to increase student outcomes.
3 Management	Attention is focused on the processes and tasks of using the innovation and the best use of information and resources. Issues related to efficiency, organizing, managing, scheduling and time demands are utmost.
2 Personal	Individual is uncertain about the demands of the innovation, his/her inadequacy to meet those demands, and his/her role with the innovation. This includes analysis of his/her role in relation to the reward structure of the organization, decision making, and consideration of potential conflicts with existing structures or personal commitment. Financial or status implications of the program for self and colleagues may also be reflected.
1 Informational	A general awareness of the innovation and interest in learning more detail about it is indicated. The person seems to be unworried about himself/herself in relation to the innovation. She/he is interested in substantive aspects of the innovation in a selfless manner such as general characteristics, effects and requirment for use.
0 Awareness	Little concern about or involvement with the innovation is indicated.

(Stages 6, 5, 4 grouped under **IMPACT**; 3 under **TASK**; 2, 1, 0 under **SELF**)

(after Hall, Wallace and Dossett, 1973)

developmental growth are more likely to be the norm for teachers than rapid changes in either teacher attitudes or behaviours.

Two self-report instruments developed by Hall and Loucks (1979) are the Stages of Concern (SoC) and Levels of Use (LoU). These two instruments have been used widely in a number of countries outside of the USA including the UK, Belgium, Australia, Singapore and Hong Kong.

The SoC instrument focuses on teachers' *feelings* as they become involved in implementing an innovation. Hall *et al*. (1979) use the term 'concern' to refer to a 'mentally aroused state about something'. Teachers' concerns will vary both in type and in intensity. At any point in time they might be concerned about several issues but some will be more immediate and cause them more heightened concern than others. For example, teachers might be very concerned about their lack of subject knowledge required to teach a new curriculum.

Hall *et al*. argue that there are a definable set of major stages of concern and that as teachers become involved in implementing an innovation, they will move developmentally through these stages. The seven stages, as listed in figure 2.4, develop from 'early unrelated' to 'self', to 'task' and finally to 'impact' concerns. Individual teachers will progress from lower level to higher level concerns but

Figure 2.5   Two examples of SoC profiles

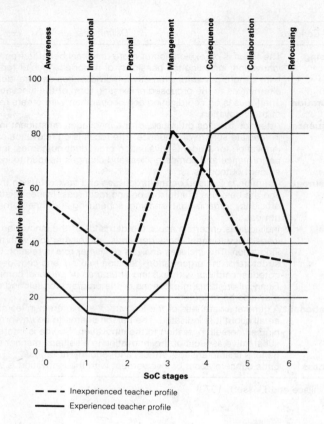

Awareness   Informational   Personal   Management   Consequence   Collaboration   Refocusing

- - - - Inexperienced teacher profile
——— Experienced teacher profile

the progression will depend on the dynamic of each individual. Change agents may be able to reduce certain concerns (for example, personal concerns about using an innovation) but each individual determines for himself/herself whether or not a change to other concerns will occur.

A teacher's intensity of concerns can be depicted on an SoC profile, as shown in figure 2.5. The data for compiling a teacher's SoC profile can be obtained by using an SoC questionnaire, a 35-item Likert scale questionnaire (which was designed and refined by Hall and Loucks (1977) over a five-year period), or by using an Open Ended Statement of Concern instrument.

The broken line in figure 2.5 indicates that this user has mainly Stage 3 Management concerns. The person is probably very concerned about time and organizing and managing the various materials needed in his/her day-to-day lessons. The person is also concerned about students (see Stage 4 score in figure 2.5) but has very little concern about working with others (low Stage 5). It should also be noted that the person does not have intense personal concerns (low Stage 2).

Figure 2.6   Levels of use of the innovation

Levels of use	Definition of use
0 Non-use	State in which the user has little or no knowledge of the innovation, no involvement with the innovation, and is doing nothing toward becoming involved. *Decision Point A Takes action to learn more detailed information about the innovation.*
I Orientation	State in which the user has recently acquired or is acquiring information about the innovation and/or has recently explored or is exploring its value orientation and its demands upon user and user system. *Decision Point B Makes a decision to use the innovation by establishing a time to begin.*
II Preparation	State in which the user is preparing for first use of the innovation. *Decision Point C Changes, if any, and use are dominated by user needs*
III Mechanical use	State in which the user focuses most effort on the short-term, day-to-day use of the innovation with little time for reflection. Changes in use are made more to meet user needs than client needs. The user is primarily engaged in a stepwise attempt to master the tasks required to use the innovation, often resulting in disjointed and superficial use. *Decision Point D-1 A routine pattern of use is established.*
IVA Routine	Use of the innovation is stabilized. Few, if any, changes are being made in on-going use. Little preparation or thought is being given to improving innovation use or its consequences. *Decision Point D-2 Changes use of the innovation based on formal or informal evaluation in order to increase client outcomes.*
IVB Refinement	State in which the user varies the use of the innovation to increase the impact on clients within the immediate sphere of influence. Variations are based on knowledge of both short- and long-term consequences for clients. *Decision Point E Initiates changes in use of innovation based on input of and in coordination with what colleagues are doing.*
V Integration	State in which the user is combining own efforts to use the innovation with related activities of colleagues to achieve a collective impact on clients within their common sphere of influence. *Decision Point F Begins exploring alternatives to or major modifications of the innovation presently in use.*
VI Renewal	State in which the user re-evaluates the quality of use of the innovation, seeks major modifications of or alternatives to present innovation to achieve increased impact on clients, examines new developments in the field, and explores new goals for self and the system.

(after Loucks, Newlove and Hall, 1975)

By contrast, the full line in figure 2.5 reveals a teacher who is mainly concerned about working collaboratively with other teachers in implementing the innovation (high Stage 5 score). This person also has relatively high concerns about maximizing outcomes for students (high Stage 4) but has very low personal (low Stage 2) and relatively low management (low Stage 3) concerns.

The LoU refers to *user behaviour* in relation to implementing an innovation. Eight Levels of Use have been proposed by Hall *et al.* (1973) (see figure 2.6) and

Figure 2.7   Distribution of LoUs for a school staff teaching a mathematics curriculum

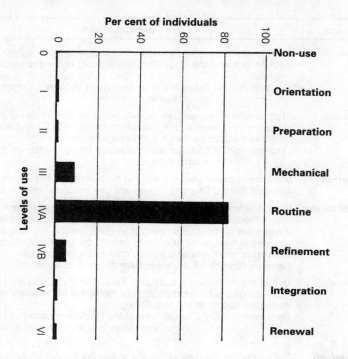

verified through various follow-up studies. It is claimed that a teacher-user progresses through LoU levels as his/her familiarity and expertise with an innovation develop.

LoUs are measured through a 'focused interview' technique (Loucks, Newlove and Hall, 1975). Rather than asking a specific list of pre-determined and pre-sequenced questions, the interviewer uses a branching technique whereby certain decision points during the interview provide cues to initiate a particular set of questions. As with the SoC questionnaire, the LoU interview is generic in nature and can be used for any innovation simply by changing the focus. It is usual for each LoU interview to be tape recorded so that the teacher responses can be carefully coded at a later period, and if necessary, rated by independent coders.

Interviewer skills are obviously important in ensuring successful LoU interviews. Loucks *et al.* (1975) have developed training procedures for LoU researchers to ensure that adequate skills are attained by interviewers and to maintain high inter-rater reliability levels. Results of inter-rater reliability undertaken by Loucks (1976) have been very high, between 0.87 and 0.96.

LoU levels provide valuable guidelines about teacher behaviour associated with implementing an innovation. For example, an LoU III Mechanical Use (see figure 2.7) indicates that such a person teaches a new curriculum in a rather superficial, stepwise process, without reflecting very much, if at all, on his/her students' needs and attitudes. By contrast an LoU IVB teacher is very interested in experimenting with the new curriculum so that students in his/her class make optimal progress with it.

Implementation at Different Levels of Schooling

Although it is possible to make general statements about implementation priorities, it is important to explore the differences between plans and practices which can occur at primary and secondary school levels and between subjects.

There are different rewards and penalties operating for teachers at primary and secondary schools. For example, in primary schools it is usual for the class teacher to be responsible for most, if not all, lessons for a class of students. The teacher has greater flexibility in deciding day-to-day priorities and he/she is able to operate more autonomously with little interference from the school principal. Therefore pressures relating to how particular curricula are implemented are self-imposed to a large extent by the primary school teacher. Due to time constraints, a teacher may not be thorough in terms of planning and/or reflecting upon how he/she implements a specific curriculum. The amount of effort given to implementation by a teacher also depends upon the status of the subject. Clearly, if a subject is emphasized strongly within a society and in a school (for example, mathematics) then each teacher will ensure that implementation strategies are strenuously followed to ensure that his/her teaching is effective.

Of course there can be external controls at the primary school level. A number of countries have introduced basic skills testing at specific primary school grades, such as grade 3 and grade 6, usually in reading and mathematics. Sometimes these tests are diagnostic and student samples are undertaken for within-school use only. In other cases, state-wide tests are used and the results are widely published. In several countries, tests undertaken at middle and upper primary grades are used to determine student placement in streamed classes in high schools.

In these circumstances it is likely that teachers are more concerned about closely following prescribed curricula. Their status as successful teachers is at risk if their students do not perform well in the state-wide tests. It would be folly for them to do anything other than follow a strong fidelity of use orientation.

Secondary schools differ considerably from primary schools in that they are far more subject-centred. Schools tend to be much larger and teachers work with other specialists in particular subject areas. There is little opportunity therefore for teachers to consider the overall development of individual students.

At the lower secondary school grades the emphasis is typically upon wide-ranging introductory units, often multidisciplinary in focus. These subjects tend to be teacher-assessed and there is scope for teachers to introduce their own units without being too concerned about the constraints of external examinations. By contrast, in the senior secondary school classes the emphasis is very firmly upon external examinations, graduation competencies and tertiary entrance criteria. Furthermore, pressures from parents, employers and the students themselves all contribute to a very heavy emphasis upon a fidelity-of-use orientation. In these circumstances, it is critical for the teacher to follow very precisely the content areas prescribed in the curriculum/syllabus. Often a number of students receive additional coaching from teachers and commercial firms to enhance their scores in external examinations.

Colin Marsh

In a number of cases at the secondary school level, curricula developed in the USA and UK have been imported and implemented directly into Asian countries. Morris (1984) notes that these initiatives have occurred in Malaysia, South Korea and Hong Kong and suggests that this has been possible because 'the government departments operate in highly centralized educational systems. Accordingly innovations which conform to the official conceptions of what constitutes a desirable school curriculum are selected and introduced' (p. 43). Notwithstanding, many of these implementation efforts using curricula developed overseas have not been successful and have incurred major problems associated with teacher misuse and lack of training (*ibid.*, Tang and Morris, 1989).

Concluding Comments

In this chapter consideration was given to the numerous problems associated with putting curriculum plans into action. There are various points to consider on the curriculum continuum and the planning aspects are only part of the total picture. Of equal importance are all the activities associated with implementation of curricula. There are various ways of monitoring implementation practices and several approaches were described in this chapter. Finally, implementation issues relating to levels of schooling were considered.

Chapter 3

Assessment

Paul Morris

Introduction

In developing a curriculum it is not sufficient to focus solely on whether or not the aims and objectives are worthwhile nor is it appropriate to determine how the curriculum will be assessed after decisions have been made about the other components of the curriculum. It is important to determine whether it is possible to develop and implement a form of assessment which will reflect the purposes of the curriculum. This requires an understanding of both the techniques of assessment and of the context within which the curriculum will be used. This chapter will attempt to both introduce the key concepts necessary to understand the nature of assessment and identify the major constraints and dilemmas which arise.

Key Terms

The term *evaluation* refers to the identification of the worth or merit of something. Evaluation therefore involves making value judgments. In education, we can evaluate new syllabuses, an educational policy, curriculum resources, curriculum projects, the performance of pupils and so on.

Assessment is the term used to describe those specific actions which are undertaken to obtain information about knowledge, understanding, abilities or attitudes. Assessment provides the information with which evaluation can be carried out. Assessment of pupils usually involves obtaining information about their attainments or attitudes. For example, an examination in physics attempts to assess the pupils' understanding and knowledge of that subject. An assessment can be *descriptive*, such as when a teacher states that a pupil knows all the chemical symbols. It can also be *judgmental*, such as when a teacher states that a pupil is good at chemistry or that pupil is the worst in the class at chemistry. Assessment is always *quantitative* in the sense that it leads to categorizations such as good/bad or to rankings but it need not be numerical. When it is based on individual judgment rather than on systematically gathered data it is often called *qualitative* assessment.

Where a method of assessment provides numerical scores or grades it is called a measurement. Intelligence tests, opinion surveys, multiple choice and aptitude tests are some of the best known examples of means to measure the characteristics or attainment of pupils. Numerical data are easy to manipulate and compare but valid and reliable instruments can only be devised for specific and well-defined characteristics. An assessor will frequently try to augment such numerical data with a range of other data, which are not so easy to reduce to numbers, such as those obtained from observations and interviews. An assessment of pupils' understanding of history could draw upon techniques such as multiple choice tests to provide numerical data. In addition the assessment could be based on observational data such as, contribution to classwork, oral presentation, or the teacher's perception of pupils' interest and enthusiasm. Public assessment usually depends on measurement techniques, but other means can also be used to obtain relevant data.

A distinction also needs to be drawn between *formal* and *informal* assessment. Information about a pupils' abilities can be gathered at a very informal level (for example, during a conversation between a teacher and pupil), or at a very formal level (for example, a public examination), and in a variety of situations between these two extremes. Teachers frequently assess pupils without setting an examination or assigning any marks or grades when they form opinions or reach conclusions about pupils which affect their subsequent interactions.

Why Assess?

The key question now addressed concerns possible reasons for carrying out an assessment. The six major reasons are grading, selection, mastery, guidance, prediction, and diagnosis.

Grading

This involves the assessment of pupils for the purpose of determining and comparing their levels of achievement. So, an examination in which some pupils fail and others pass at different grades or percentages is primarily performing a grading function. This form of assessment places pupils in rank order of achievement and permits comparisons between them. The grades which pupils are given are usually norm referenced which means that they are relative to the grades given to the other pupils who were assessed.

Selection

An assessment which is used to decide which pupils should gain admission to a course or institution or job is performing a selective function. This function is paramount in most societies because of its direct effect on social mobility, especially for people without access to power, influence or wealth. For this reason it has to be seen to be carried out in an unbiased and acceptable way. Public examinations are widely accepted as offering this freedom from bias. Many public examinations, especially those at the end of secondary schooling, perform both a grading and selection function. They grade pupils (pass/fail A, B, C, D etc.), and these grades are then used to select pupils for entry to universities, colleges and many forms of employment. The dominance of this function varies according to the level of the educational system at which assessment occurs. Thus at the primary school level the selective function is usually less predominant than at the secondary level. However in countries such as Japan, where the effects of early selection are long lasting, the selective function is paramount in the assessment of primary school pupils.

Mastery

Assessments can be used to determine what skills or competencies a pupil has mastered. For example a driving test requires a person to be able to demonstrate that he/she can perform a number of skills. An assessment which describes the skills a person can perform and when these are based on pre-selected criterion is an example of a criterion referenced assessment.

Guidance

Here an assessment attempts to help pupils make a decision. Examples are assessments which aid choice of subjects to study, or of career to follow.

Prediction

This refers to assessments which are designed to try to predict how a pupil will perform in later academic studies or in an area of work. Academic or scholastic aptitude tests are the best examples of assessments which primarily serve this purpose. For example, predictive tests can be used to determine whether a pupil is ready to learn to read. They can also be used to assess a pupil's aptitude at mathematics.

Diagnosis

Diagnostic assessments are used to indicate the point at which a pupil has failed to learn something. They help the teacher to identify the difficulties which a pupil is experiencing. Therefore a test which is undertaken to find out which pupils have learning difficulties in English or mathematics so as to provide them with remedial support is serving a diagnostic function.

Some of these functions, such as the grading and selection of pupils, can be viewed as *summative assessment* as they provide a description of the student at the end of a course of study. On the other hand, those which focus on diagnosis or guidance can be viewed as *formative assessment* for they are used to help improve a pupil's future performance.

Public Examinations: Effects

The most widely influential forms of educational assessment are public examinations which primarily serve a selective and allocative function. In societies such as Hong Kong and South Korea, which have wide disparities of income distribution and where a university degree is often a prerequisite for a well paid job, pupils, parents and teachers view success in the public examination as the main goal of education. As a result the perceived importance of the public examination and their limitations serve as both a crucial influence and constraint on the development of all aspects of the school curriculum, especially the teaching style which is used.

The search for qualifications has resulted in examinations in many countries dominating the process of education. Dore (1976) refers to 'the diploma disease' and explains its consequences for pupils in the following terms:

> In the process of qualification, by contrast, the pupil is concerned not with mastery, but with being certified as having mastered. The knowledge that he gains, he gains not for its own sake and not for constant later use in a real life situation — but for the once-and-for-all purpose of reproducing it in an examination. And the learning and reproducing is all just a means to an end — the end of getting a certificate which is a passport to a coveted job, a status, an income. If education is learning to do a job, qualification is a matter of learning in order to get a job.

Dore describes the resulting system as an 'examination hell' in Japan and similar descriptions have been made of Malaysia and Sri Lanka (Lewin, 1984), and Hong Kong (Morris, 1985). Morris, for example, found that despite the promotion of a new pedagogy which involved a movement away from description to more analytical and activity based approaches teaching styles changed little. This was notwithstanding a generally favourable reaction from teachers to the new pedagogy. Although many teachers felt that the new pedagogy was preferable, the pressures on them arising from the school environment and particularly from the pressure to achieve high examination pass rates, was such as to prevent their use. The effect on all aspects of the curriculum of a highly competitive public examination is pervasive. As Lewin (1984) comments:

> In situations where a primary motive in going to school is to be selected for more schooling and acquire qualifications, examinations are likely to exert considerable influence on the curriculum at both design and implementation stages; more than, for example, exhortation, rhetoric and prescription contained in texts and guidebooks. (p. 144)

Because teachers and pupils are influenced by the nature of the public examination then any divergence between the intentions of the curriculum and the examination will result in a gap between plans and practices. It is, therefore, vital to ensure that examinations support and correspond with the educational emphases of the curricula which are used in schools. Somerset (1982, 1984) in his work in Kenya and Nepal has shown that public examinations can be used constructively to bring about changes in the way pupils are taught and the approach to learning which they are encouraged to use. Primary school examination papers were redesigned to incorporate a high proportion of questions requiring the use of intellectual skills other than just the recall of information. Although pupils performance initially declined it subsequently improved as a result of an extensive system of support and feedback to the schools.

Influences on Examinations

Public examinations are often accused of promoting teaching and learning styles which are not consistent with the stated goals of the curriculum the pupils have studied. This accusation is hard to deny because many factors serve to influence and reinforce this by-product of public examinations. These include:

- *Objectivity*: Examiners have a duty to ensure fairness and objectivity, especially when an examination is used to select pupils. This very legitimate concern fosters the reliance on those forms of assessment which do not require a marker to use personal judgment and on forms of assessment, such as multiple choice papers, that are seen to be more 'objective' and unbiased measures of a pupil's performance. A consequence of this can often be an emphasis on assessing pupils' knowledge of trivial facts and information which are easily measured by such forms of assessment. This leads teachers to place the greatest emphasis on memorization by pupils and to ensure that pupils 'know' large quantities of information. Little emphasis is given to encouraging pupils to understand key principles or how to apply them. Although such tests are scored objectively the choice of questions to make up a test is subjective and the suitability of the test for students of different backgrounds is not guaranteed. In fact, boys appear to score higher than girls on multiple choice tests when their scores on other tests are matched.
- *Scale and Efficiency*: The size of some educational systems such as that in the People's Republic of China (the PRC) or Indonesia means that a public examination is a very large scale administrative exercise which can involve millions of pupils. The scale of the operation encourages the use of efficient forms of assessment which minimize the potential for any discrepancy between regions or between markers, and which can be marked quickly. This consideration places a further pressure on examiners to rely on forms of assessment which can be seen to have no obvious bias and which can be easily administered.
- *Teacher Competence*: If teachers are to be involved significantly in the examination process they must have adequate professional training and experience. Particularly in countries which have experienced rapid expansion of schooling such teachers may be in short supply and so it is seen as inappropriate to involve teachers in the design or marking of public examinations. This reinforces the perception of teachers that public examinatons are an assessment of their own competence as well as that of their students and they attempt to align their teaching with the approach which they anticipate will bring the greatest examination success.

- *The Nature and Development of Knowledge*: A society's perception of what constitutes the primary purpose of education and of the status of knowledge can promote the use of some forms of assessment rather than others. As was pointed out in chapter 1, different societies emphasize different educational goals and have different perceptions of how to choose the content of the curriculum and how to present it. If worthwhile knowledge is viewed as a set of known truths and that these are contained in the writings of a prominent religious or political leader then clearly this suggests it can be assessed by determining whether or not a pupil can remember and repeat the key passages.

These considerations make changes in the assessment of pupils and in teaching methods much more difficult to bring about than changes to the other components of a curriculum. One implication of this is that in developing or adopting a new curriculum it is not sufficient only to address the question of whether or not the aims and objectives of a new curriculum are 'worthwhile'. We also need to ask whether it will be possible to develop and implement a form of assessment which reflects the purposes of the curriculum. The answer requires an understanding of the context within which the curriculum operates.

Who Uses Assessment?

The different functions performed by assessment satisfy the needs of different groups or stakeholders in society. Teachers primarily require information about pupils which is immediate and which helps them to plan their lessons and to obtain rapid feedback on the pupils' learning. In contrast governments and employers want information which is impersonal and remote which will allow them to select employees or to evaluate the effectiveness of the school system. Their concern is not about how learning takes place but with how much has been learnt in relative or absolute terms. Figure 3.1 provides a clear indication of the functions and information needs of assessment by different groups.

Many problems concerning assessment and examinations arise because the different stakeholders have very different needs and expectations. If an assessment exercise fully satisfies the needs of one group, such as the universities or employers, it is unlikely to satisfy the needs of parents or teachers. The information is therefore expected to serve too many purposes. In Asian societies which have fairly well established systems of national assessment we can anticipate increasing demands for the use and development of forms of assessment which perform a more formative role.

Who Assesses?

As assessment is primarily undertaken through examinations which are a critical determinant of a pupil's life chances, it is important to identify who controls them. This section will first examine which groups in society most strongly influence examinations. It will then examine the ways in which that influence operates.

Figure 3.1 Assessment needs and purposes of different groups (adapted from Griffin and Nix, 1990)

Group/Stakeholder	Information Need	Purpose/Characteristic
Government	General achievement scores	Summative (remote, formal, administrative)
Employers and universities	Examination scores	
School administrators	Promotion information course data	
	Term test, scores	
Parents	Term report data	
Teachers	Diagnostic test data	
Pupils	Scores and diagnostic data	Formative (instructional, immediate, informal)

Four major organized groups can have an influence on examinations: government bodies and agencies, teachers, the market place (including employers, professional associations, parents) and examination boards. These groups are not always distinct as frequently there are educators in government, administrators in education and so on.

Governments

The control of the government over public examinations depends on the general political climate in a country. In a highly centralized political system where education is viewed as the major means for promoting political consciousness (the PRC) and economic development (Hong Kong, Singapore, Taiwan) it is more likely that the central government will exert a strong control over examinations. In some cases, however, the actual task of setting and marking examination papers is undertaken by an agency or organization which is established but not directly run by the government. This is partly because often governments do not have the expertise or manpower to undertake the task but also because examinations arouse passions if they are perceived to be in any way partisan. In practice most agencies which run examinations rely heavily on teachers to help them set, administer and mark examinations.

Singapore and Bruneidarusalaam rely on local examinations to assess pupils in primary school but switch to examinations run by the Cambridge University Overseas Examination Board to assess secondary school pupils. In Macau there is no single pattern or source of examinations. Pupils can take exams set by the Hong Kong Exams Authority, exams set in China or those used in Portugal. In the PRC examinations are administered by both provincial and central government agencies. The key examinations for secondary school pupils, which directly determine a pupil's career opportunities are more directly controlled by the central government than examinations for primary and middle school pupils, reflecting the need for uniformity across this vast country.

The influence which the government exerts on examinations is sometimes indirect and depends on control of other aspects of the curriculum and of who manages the examination. Thus, many governments determine what should be studied and which text books can be used. They also may determine who will run the agency which sets and administers the examination. These sources of control can allow the government to exert a strong influence on examinations.

Teachers

At the formal level of policy making school teachers have not been a very powerful group in controlling public examinations designed to select pupils. University teachers in some countries have had a much greater control, especially of examinations which select pupils for tertiary education. Thus in Japan and South Korea the final decision on students' admission to university is based on their performance on an examination which is set and marked by the faculty of a particular university.

There are two important ways in which teachers can influence examinations. First, the detailed work of setting papers, devising marking schemes and marking is sometimes done by, or in consultation with, teachers. This is the case in Hong Kong and teachers are therefore able to set questions and award marks which they think are appropriate. Unless governments formulate very detailed curricula and set and mark examinations then there remains a great deal of latitude for manoeuvre and interpretation. Second, teachers in all countries exert an influence on examinations by deciding how much time they will devote to teaching certain topics and which teaching strategy they will use. This is a very powerful, but essentially negative, source of control, for if teachers do not support or are not able to implement an innovation then this will affect how their pupils perform in the examination.

In addition to setting and marking papers, teachers may become involved in committees by being coopted, elected or nominated. In practice it is very difficult for teachers to exert a high degree of influence as it is seldom possible to rearrange their work to allow them to participate fully in committees working intensively over long periods. It should also be noted that the direct control of examinations by teachers has not usually resulted in any radical change of the system.

The Market Place

This source of influence relates to the very vague but important concept of the will or expectations of the society. Many groups of people are not directly involved in education, such as parents, employers, and trade unionists, but sometimes influence examinations. Some examination bodies include members from outside the educational community but their direct influence is usually minimal. This is because they usually lack the knowledge which would enable them to argue successfully with experts and because they join committees responsible for broad policy rather than specific subjects and areas.

The power of such groups is, however, substantial but essentially negative. Employers, professional associations and other external bodies use examination results constantly to help select and promote staff. They do not usually interfere directly because, for their purposes, the system is efficient. If, however, the examination system becomes inefficient or unacceptable then employers will have to find an alternative means to select staff. The continued reliance in most countries on traditional forms of examination is a reflection of their need to maintain public acceptability. Alternatives do exist but unless they can obtain public acceptability they will not become established.

Examination Boards

In practice these bodies are usually established by the government and they have a great influence on the national policies towards assessment although that policy is ultimately determined by the government. These bodies usually employ a core of full time staff who are primarily concerned with the administration of the examination system. They also exert a considerable influence on the outcomes as they are full time employees and have to execute the decisions of the various consultative committees. Prior to 1979 the examinations in Hong Kong were set and marked by a Department of the Government. The task is now undertaken by the Hong Kong Examinations Authority which is an independent organization.

From the above it is evident that usually no single group is able to completely control all aspects of public examinations. In the final analysis the government is usually able to determine the policy of examinations. In times of crisis or when it feels threatened it will do so. Groups outside education can determine the extent of acceptable innovation. The conduct of examinations is governed by policy, but they are implemented by a range of groups which includes teachers and examination board personnel. We noted earlier that the different stakeholders usually have quite different expectations of the purposes of assessment.

What is to be Assessed?

We have defined assessment in the school context as the act of obtaining information about pupils' learning performance. As far as knowledge and understanding are concerned, we want to know how well pupils have learned what we intended them to learn. The central question which arises focuses on what we want the pupils to learn. There is obviously a need to be able to express exactly what it is we want the pupils to know or to be able to do before we can begin to assess their understanding or performance. In other words we need to give careful thought to *what* we want the pupils to learn, *why* we want them to learn it and *how* it should be learned. We will then be in a position to decide how we should assess pupils' learning. Society's views of the primary purposes of an educational system, and what is perceived as the main source of truth, will determine the nature of a curriculum and how it is assessed.

Figure 3.2   Taxonomy of cognitive objectives

Level of Objective	Related Performance
(1) Knowledge Recognition and recall of information.	define, describe, identify, list, match, name, outline, select, repeat.
(2) Comprehension Use of materials or ideas being communicated.	classify, convert, distinguish between, explain, predict, summarize.
(3) Application Use of abstractions in particular and concrete situations.	solve, arrange, compute, deduce, demonstrate, modify, operate, relate.
(4) Analysis This involves the breakdown of a communication into its constituent components or parts so that the relationship between the ideas is made clear.	draw a diagram, differentiate, estimate, infer, order, separate, subdivide.
(5) Synthesis This involves the process of working with parts, elements or pieces and combining them into a structure or pattern.	combine, compose, construct, create, design, formulate, rearrange, revise.
(6) Evaluation Judgments are made on the value of materials and methods for given purposes.	compare, conclude, contrast, criticize, discriminate, judge, justify, support.

The objectives within a given subject typically include mastery of the content of a subject together with more vague objectives such as getting the pupils to develop ways of thinking, intellectual curiosity, imagination and problem solving skills. A number of frameworks have been devised to help educators identify their objectives and how they might be assessed. The most influential of these has been that of Bloom *et al.* (1956) which analyzes educational objectives into three broad categories known as the cognitive, affective and psycho–motor domains. The cognitive domain includes those objectives concerned with the development of intellectual skills and abilities. The affective domain focuses on objectives which describe changes in interest, attitudes and values. The third domain is concerned with physical skills.

We will focus on the cognitive domain, as this is the domain within which most assessment is carried out and the one in which the model has had a world-wide influence. The model provides a taxonomic classification of objectives. That is, in ascending order of complexity, each level of objective includes within it all those below it. An outline of the taxonomy is given in figure 3.2. Achievement of each level permits a new range of performance to be carried out. Comprehension is impossible without knowledge but demonstration of knowledge does not imply comprehension. To demonstrate comprehension a pupil must manipulate knowledge in some way, not just recall it word for word. Similarly, something which is not understood, or comprehended, cannot be applied to a new situation.

The taxonomy draws attention to the fact that a pupil could 'know' or 'understand' a subject in a number of very different ways. One pupil studying 'physics' might have learnt by rote the definition of key concepts and laws. Another pupil in the same class might also be able to apply the ideas, recognize examples of them and be able to explain them to someone else. Another might be able to put the ideas together with other knowledge to invent new ideas. When developing a curriculum, a lesson or an assessment exercise we need to be clear about what objectives we are trying to achieve. The taxonomy provides one way to classify educational objectives which can be stated in terms of observable student behaviour which, in turn, is open to measurement.

This taxonomy has been very influential, especially in Asian societies. This is probably because of its emphasis on cognitive learning and because of its direct applicability to centrally devised systems of curriculum development and assessment. However it, has also been seriously criticized sometimes in its own right and sometimes because of the ways in which it has been used. Four criticisms are especially pertinent:

(i)   It has been argued, most notably by Eisner (1969), that a teacher or a curriculum could have objectives in which the precise nature of the terminal behaviour of the pupils is not predetermined. Eisner calls an unpredetermined objective an 'expressive objective', and argues that even in a subject like mathematics a teacher should use expressive objectives. For example, an instructional objective like 'a pupil will correctly solve a simple equation' could be complemented by an expressive objective like 'pupils will produce their own set of patterns or designs in any mathematical experience of their choice'. Or a student who has learnt to speak a foreign language could be able to satisfy a teacher's predetermined instructional objectives. But a student who can say something new and interesting in that language has not satisfied a predetermined objective.

(ii)   A reliance on prespecified instructional objectives can result in teachers and examiners focusing on those parts of a curriculum which can be easily measured. These fall mainly into three lowest levels of the taxonomy. Broader educational goals such as the development of intellectual curiosity, imagination and intellectual independence could be ignored. The result could be an encouragement of convergent as opposed to divergent styles of thinking.

(iii) The classification of educational objectives into three separate domains is artificial because in practice they are closely interrelated.

(iv)   The order of Bloom's cumulative classification order is questionable. For example, it has been argued that evaluation should run through the whole classification.

Despite these criticisms, the taxonomy has helped to highlight the distinction between knowledge (level 1) and intellectual processes (levels 2–6). The accuracy, sequence and value of the fine distinctions in the second category will remain a matter of debate. However, the distinction has prompted many educators to consider seriously the type of mental activities which they assess in their pupils, and the taxonomy provides a good starting point for this analysis.

Figure 3.3 The appropriateness of types of assessment (based on Jones and Bray, 1986)

	EXTENDED WRITING		SHORT ANSWERS	
	Free writing and essays	Guided responses	Structured questions	Objective tests (e.g. MCQ)
Recalling facts concepts, etc. (course content)	Not appropriate. Use other techniques.	Poor	Useful and appropriate	
Understanding and application of facts, concepts, etc.	Not appropriate	Limited usefulness	Useful and Appropriate	Useful and appropriate, though somewhat limited
Analysis of facts, concepts — making inferences, etc.	Appropriate	Useful and appropriate	Limited use	Not appropriate: too limited
Synthesis and evaluation: creative thinking, generating own problems and solutions	Useful and appropriate	Appropriate training	Not appropriate: too structured and limited	

How to Assess?

This section will review the main features of a variety of currently available assessment methods. Which method is used should primarily depend on the function of the assessment exercise and its relevance to the educational task we are trying to achieve. It should therefore be appropriate to the goals of the course, its context and the style of teaching we have used. Figure 3.3 provides a summary of the appropriateness of four types of assessment for achieving four of the cognitive skills identified in Bloom's taxonomy.

Therefore a multiple choice examination would not seem to be an appropriate way to assess a course which had as its main goal to develop pupils' skills at communication in a second language or to solve problems. Similarly, essay questions might not be appropriate for assessing a course which has been based on students' project work.

The central question which we therefore need to answer in deciding which assessment method(s) to use are: Will it provide an indication of those student abilities or skills in which we are interested? Many forms of assessment are unsatisfactory because they measure objectives other than those which are central to their purposes. For example, tests of intellectual competence such as IQ tests often appear to be assessing a pupil's general knowledge, social experiences, the socioeconomic background of their parents or the pupil's vocabulary.

Another way of distinguishing between types of written assessment is provided by Lee and Law (1988) and illustrated by figure 3.4.

An over-reliance on types of assessment which involve the pupils choosing

Figure 3.4   The types of written assessment

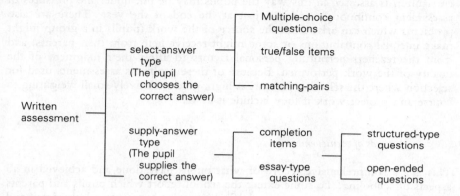

the correct answers can serve to reinforce the importance of convergent thinking with a focus on providing large quantities of information and on those parts of a subject which are certain and provide accepted facts. If a curriculum is attempting to encourage pupils' creativity, expressive skills, fantasy and imagination, then clearly this type of assessment would be wholy inappropriate.

The limitations and effects of conventional forms of assessment have resulted in attempts in some countries to develop alternatives. These are not intended to replace traditional public examinations but they are increasingly used to complement them. The tendency of many nations to import or borrow aspects of curriculum policies from North America and Europe is such that it is appropriate to examine some of the major trends in those countries. One is an increasing use of non-written assessment and of recurrent assessment of coursework, leading to records of achievement and profile reporting. Another is an increasing concern for developing effective forms of formative evaluation. The main features of these developments are described below.

Non-written Forms of Assessment and Coursework Assessment

To try to meet the increasingly diverse goals of school curricula there is increasing use of practical, oral and aural assessments. Fieldwork, laboratory work, oral tests, listening tests and practical tests are all examples of non-written forms of assessment. Assessments based on fieldwork and laboratory work are often used in science. Oral, listening and practical tests are most commonly used in areas such as art, music and languages where learning the subject necessarily involves an increasing mastery of a skill. They can take the form of a set piece of practical exercise, such as a formal oral examination in a language or a continuous assessment of pupils' practical skills.

Coursework assessment often is based on an accumulation of grades or marks for work performed during the year. It may include the assessment of projects in which a pupil or group of pupils undertakes an exercise both within and outside the constraints of formal lessons. Coursework assessment can replace all or part of a terminal examination and allow the pupil to be assessed by a teacher who knows the pupils' strengths and weaknesses. However if a complete curriculum is assessed in this way the pupils may be put under the pressures of assessment continuously and not just at the end of the year. There are also problems which can arise from the source of the work (pupils in a group might make unequal contributions or some might receive help from their parents) and from the teachers permitting personal factors to affect their judgment of the quality of the work performed. Because of these problems assessments used for selection where the selection pressure is high, give a relatively small weighting to course and project work if they include it at all.

Records of Achievement

This is a a comprehensive record of what pupils have done and achieved in all aspects of schooling. To some extent the school report which pupils and parents receive from schools acts as a record of achievement but it often lacks detail and specificity. A comprehensive record would provide assessments of academic performance, involvement in sports and social activities, and personal attributes. Such records could be used for selective purposes or for diagnostic purposes but the range and style of the records should depend on what their function is seen to be. Clearly teachers and prospective employers require different information both in quantity and in kind.

Profile Reporting

This is a particular form of records of achievement and involves presenting the results of public examinations in greater detail so as to provide more information about what a pupil has achieved. The report would therefore not provide a single overall grade or mark but would provide a mark in different areas (for example, heat, light and electricity in physics). It is often used in continuous assessment.

Formative Assessment Procedures

Rating scales have been developed which are designed to help a teacher identify whether pupils are experiencing difficulties in mastering certain skills. Scores obtained by pupils enable a teacher to judge what remedial help and assistance may be needed. A simple example of such a rating scale is shown as figure 3.5.

How Do We Judge Assessments?

Having established what it is we want the pupils to learn, and devised appropriate measures of achievement, the next problem is to determine what criteria we will use to interpret a pupil's performance. The problem is best illustrated by an example: A pupil comes home from school and tells his parents that he has scored 70 per cent on the end of year mathematics examination. At first sight this looks quite good. In fact, his parents are very disappointed, for three reasons. First,

Figure 3.5 An example of a rating scale

Name Date Skill Being Taught				
1 understood the steps involved	1	2	3	4
	Unsatisfactory	Fair	Good	Excellent
2 willing to be involved	1	2	3	4
	Unsatisfactory	Fair	Good	Excellent
3 mastered each sub-skill in turn	1	2	3	4
	Unsatisfactory	Fair	Good	Excellent
4 completed the skills activity	1	2	3	4
	Unsatisfactory	Fair	Good	Excellent

on a trial examination a short time before he scored 90 per cent. Second, they know that most pupils taking the examinations scored more than 70 per cent and third, they know that the minimum mark for promotion to higher form was 75 per cent. Do we judge the student's performance with regard to:

(i)   how well he has done with reference to his own capabilities;
(ii) how well he has done with reference to the other pupils who sat for the examination; or
(iii) how well he has done with reference to a predetermined level of attainment?

The first type of assessment is an example of 'self referenced' assessment, the second is an example of norm–referenced assessment and the third an example of 'criterion referenced' assessment. Most informal assessment is self referenced, but formal assessments are usually based on criteria or norms.

A norm-referenced assessment compares the performance of an individual with that of the group which took the test. Where tests are repeated overtime expectations are developed by reference to the previous performance of others. Tests are constructed with the intention of being equal in difficulty or 'standards' to earlier tests and with the intention that should from a 'normal' or gaussian distribution. This means that a small proportion of scores will be high, the majority will be in the middle range and a small proportion will be low. In public examinations the scores of a large group of pupils are usually aggregated into five or more bands distributed to reflect the pattern shown in figure 3.6.

The scores or grades cannot indicate whether a pupil has achieved any specific objective — they only show which pupil 'knows more' than another pupil.

Figure 3.6   A normal distribution of scores

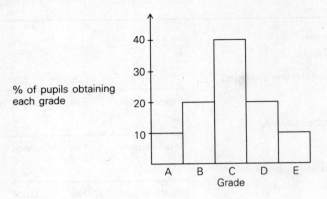

% of pupils obtaining
each grade

Figure 3.7   The possible distribution of scores using criterion referencing

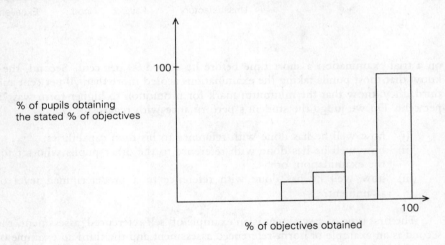

% of pupils obtaining
the stated % of objectives

In contrast a criterion referenced assessment compares each pupils' performance against prespecified levels of achievement or criteria and the results show
how many pupils have or have not mastered certain skills. It is possible for nearly
all the pupils to be successful and the distribution of scores could be as shown in
figure 3.7.

One of the best examples of a criterion referenced assessment is a driving
test. Whether or not a person passes is usually decided by reference to his ability
to carry out a set of tasks to a predetermined level of performance satisfactorily
(for example, a hillstart, emergency braking and a three-point turn).

An assessor who believes in norm-referenced criteria to establish mastery/
non-mastery could produce a quite different test than one who believes in
criterion referencing. An assessor using norm referencing might insert difficult

questions and avoid easy ones that most pupils can answer so as to ensure the distribution shown in figure 3.6 above. An assessor using criterion referencing, by contrast, will ask questions to see if the pupils have understood what they have been taught — the intention is to find out whether they have achieved the objectives. Consequently we can see that the major criticism of norm-referencing is that it does not tell you how much a pupil has learnt. The major criticism of criterion referencing is that it does not make comparisons between groups of pupils, and consequently it could lead to a deterioration in academic standards which are thought to be effectively maintained by failing pupils.

Assessments in the psychomotor domain often lend themselves easily to criterion referenced assessment. In many school subjects there are no obvious criteria to use and artifical or arbitrary criteria for mastery may be introduced such as 'Obtain the correct answer in four out of five problems'. However the focus of criterion reference assessment on whether a pupil can or cannot perform a single task has shifted in recent years. Glaser (1981) who invented the term in 1963, has attempted to emphasize that its purpose should be to

> ... encourage the development of procedures whereby assessments of proficiency could be referred to stages along progressions of increasing competence. (p. 935)

This would require the provision of a map on which pupils' performance could be measured against a set of defined proficiency levels. As Griffin (Griffin and Nix, 1990) explains:

> If the tasks are not ordered along some developing proficiency, the information gained from isolated pieces of criterion referenced assessment information will become trivial and useless in terms of assisting instruction and learning no matter how immediate it is.

Figure 3.8 provides an example of a set of selected key indicators which could be used to describe pupils' proficiency in reading. The levels or bands are derived from the assessments actually used by teachers in their day to day work. They can be used to describe a student's progress in terms of readily observable behaviours

Figure 3.8   Levels of reading proficiency

Compares information from different sources.
Differentiates between main and supporting ideas.
Checks arguments and ideas in a text against experience.
Identifies an author's implied message in a text.
Finds the main idea in a passage.
Identifies key words in a sentence or paragraph.
Identifies words from environment in a story.
Locates own name and other known words in a short word list.

(Griffin and Nix, 1990)

In practice there is usually an interaction between norm and criterion referencing. A teacher who wishes to use criteria to devise a test first has to identify and establish those criteria. One can't wait until pupils have done the test. The teacher will probably select criteria which seem reasonable in the light of past experience with similar groups of pupils studying the topic. Thus the criteria are based on expectations derived from norms. The opposite effect takes place in public examinations. Although each examination of a particular syllabus is norm-referenced, the standards from one year to the next should remain constant so that any particular grade would represent the same level of performance independently of the year.

Norm-referenced and criterion referenced tests are constructed in different ways and are used for different purposes. A norm referenced test should be able to put candidates into rank order in a reliable way that allows for fine discriminations to be made across a wide range of performance. A score of 90 per cent should represent a better level of achievement than a score of 85 per cent, and the same is true of 20 per cent and 15 per cent. The ability of the test to make these discriminations is improved by making it longer and by having many items, each of which can be answered correctly by about half of the candidates. Items which are very easy or very difficult do not discriminate well. By contrast, a criterion referenced test needs to make fine discriminations only at the boundary between mastery and non-mastery. Apart from the elimination of luck or guess work, increasing the length of a test may not increase the reliability of the classification.

It must be emphasized that no test provides scores which are appropriate for selection purposes unless it is both valid and reliable. That is, the test must really be measuring what it is designed to measure and its scores must be accurate and stable. What follows assumes that this is so.

Norm-referenced tests are appropriate for some forms of selection, particularly those where a fixed proportion of a population will be permitted to enter the next stage of schooling. Putting the candidates in rank order permits selection of the top group.

Criterion referenced tests are appropriate for selection by elimination, where those who have not achieved a specific level of mastery are not eligible to continue. An example from athletics would be the minimum qualifying standards to be considered for Olympic events. Criterion referenced tests are also appropriate for monitoring the progress of pupils and for helping teachers to make decisions.

Examinations and Selection: Alternatives

So far we have identified a range of problems and issues relating to the nature and effects of assessment, especially in societies where public examination results are vital determinant of a person's life chances. Specifically it has been argued that (a) there is frequently a divergence between the aim of curriculum designers and assessment practices; (b) for a variety of reasons assessors are encouraged to assess pupils' understanding of trivial information; (c) this has a marked affect on the teaching style which is used, as teachers will adopt a style which is seen to be optimal for the transmission of information. This situation suggests that it might be worthwhile to abolish all forms of public examinations. However we need first to examine what other criteria can be used to select pupils.

Bray (1985) identifies eight criteria, other than examinations, which can be used for selection purposes. These are:

(i) *Quotas*: Many governments have selected which pupils go on to secondary schooling or university by using quotas for certain castes/tribes (India) or for pupils from a province or region.

(ii) *Political Performance*: Pupils have been selected for further education on the basis of their understanding or advocacy of the prevailing political ideology. Such criteria have been used in Tanzania and also in China.

(iii) *Social Class*: The selection of pupils can be partly or wholly based on their social class. In educational systems where pupils of a high social economic class enter élite schools it happens indirectly. In China it operated directly during the Cultural Revolution when pupils from the lower social classes were given priority access to university.

(iv) *Gender*: In some systems female students are either discriminated against or are positively supported. Thus in Iran it is very difficult for girls to get access to secondary education merely because the government has built fewer girls' schools than schools for boys. In contrast, some provincial governments in Papua New Guinea have made arrangements to give girls preferential treatment.

(v) *Religion*: When schools are run by religious organizations they often prefer to take students who already belong to those churches. This can result in the use of selection criteria which favour pupils from some religions.

(vi) *Race and Ethnicity*: In many countries during the colonial period education was provided and selection was based on a pupil's ethnic origins. Thus in Kenya separate schools were provided for Africans, Indians and Europeans and these had very different rates of transition between the different levels of schooling. Similarly in Hong Kong, Singapore and Malaysia different educational systems operated for pupils from different ethnic groups.

(vii) *Wealth*: Where an educational system has schools which are fee paying then access to those schools is at least partially dependent on the parents' wealth. This is the most pervasive of all the criterion, and possibly the most powerful as the parents' wealth affects many other aspects of a pupil's performance, such as access to private tuition, books and an environment conducive to study.

(viii) *Connections, Inheritance, Bribes and Nepotism*: The influence of these essentially personal factors on selection is, for obvious reasons, not officially recognized and very difficult to quantify. However it is evident that in many countries, a pupil's educational and employment opportunities are greatly influenced by who they know. If an individual is related to, knows, or is owed a favour by a person in a position of power, then this can facilitate entry to an élite school (for example, a key point school) or a good job.

Whilst public examinations have a number of weaknesses all the alternative forms of selection also have limitations. The problem is essentially one of scarcity, for many societies have to allocate a small number of places among a large number of applicants.

Public examinations were first developed in seventh century China to select people for the civil service as an alternative to selective systems which favoured people from the higher social classes or those which were based on nepotism, corruption or patronage. Similarly the introduction in nineteenth centry in Germany of the Abitur, the Baccalaureat in France, and the Civil Service examinations in England were also designed to achieve a more equitable and efficient means of selection. The trend accompanied the rise of bureaucratic systems of government which were designed to execute decisions in a uniform, impersonal and predictable way. However, the new system was not without problems. As noted by Matthews (1985):

> This polarization from individuality to generality lies at the heart of the problems which persist in examinations today. The need is to reconcile individual differences in students and their individual curricula with the demand for a common curriculum and some universal form of assessment which will have a common currency and general applicability. (p. 16)

This tension is most evident in the discussions concerning the functions of assessment. The efficient selecting and grading of pupils requires a 'common currency', whilst diagnostic forms of assessment attempt to describe the characteristics of individual pupils.

Examinations: Dilemmas

Before embarking on an analysis of the situation in the specific countries described in the case studies it is appropriate to identify the universal problems or dilemmas which have affected public examinations. Noah and Eckstein (1989) have identified four dilemmas or trade-offs between desirable alternatives in their analysis of examination policies in eight countries. These are:

(i) Many countries have used examinations to select from a relatively small group of school pupils — those who are to gain access to higher education. The introduction of universal secondary education has meant that the examinations are inappropriate for a larger number and variety of pupils. It has proved difficult to widen access to such examinations without devaluing the qualification.

(ii) The desire to provide objective and comparable results has resulted in a greater uniformity of examinations. This has made it more difficult to meet the needs of diverse groups (for example, slow learners, ethnic minorities) and to achieve both breadth and integration in the curriculum.

(iii) Given the powerful influence exerted by examinations on styles of teaching and learning, the development of 'new' and efficient approaches to examinations (especially multiple choice testing) have had an adverse effect. Specifically, the reliance on forms of assessment which require that candidates select 'correct' answers has encouraged pupils to memorize vast quantities of facts. This dilemma was most evident in the two Asian societies (Japan and China) included in the comparison.

(iv) An increasing concern that schools should be accountable to their wider society has resulted in examination results being used as evidence of the quality of schools. This has served to undermine the professional autonomy and status of school personnel which may be a necessary condition for the improvement of schooling.

Concluding Comments

The main problems which affect educational assessment relate to the linked issues of their function, their anticipated audience and their effect on styles of teaching and learning. The central question is whether assessments are intended to be used primarily for selective or diagnostic purposes. If they are primarily diagnostic then employers and other groups in society will find an alternative way of obtaining information which will allow them to grade and select pupils. Clearly diminishing returns will set in if we attempt to use one assessment exercise to achieve all the functions identified. If there is a mismatch between the nature of the assessment and the goals of the curriculum it is the former which will prevail. It is also important to recognize that the nature of public assessment, especially when it performs a selective function, has a marked effect on the style of teaching used and the style of learning promoted by teachers. The various components of a public examination (examination syllabus, examination paper, marking schedule, chief examiner's report) have a more direct impact on what goes on in classrooms and pupils' approaches to studying than any other aspect of the curriculum. We will return to address these issues in Section II of this book when we will examine the nature of curriculum development in specific East Asian countries.

Curriculum Development:
Country Studies

Chapter 4

Curriculum Development in the People's Republic of China

Julian Leung Yat-ming

Introduction

In this chapter, the style of curriculum development used in the People's Republic of China is described with reference to the country's social and political environment. Going beyond the general description, the chapter attempts to analyze the underlying forces of change and continuity that account for the 'confined' system of curriculum development which exists in the PRC. This is illustrated by reference to specific cases of curriculum change. Subsequently, problems associated with the confined system are highlighted and proposed changes are described. Finally, the chapter analyzes China's curriculum development from an international and comparative perspective, but with special reference to third world experiences.

Contextual Background

Size and Imbalances

The People's Republic of China (hereafter called China) is a socialist country which was founded in 1949 by the Chinese Communist Party. Geographically China is the world's fourth largest country and her population, of 1150 million, is the world's largest. She is a multi-ethnic country. Besides the Han-Chinese, who constitute 90 per cent of the population, there are fifty-six national minority groups, each with its own language and distinct culture.

The scale of schooling in China is very great because of its large population and the effect of historical legacies. Prior to 1949 about 80 per cent of the population were illiterate and only 20 per cent of the school age population were enrolled in schools. At present the Chinese government is responsible for a school population of about 220 million pupils from kindergarten to university levels both in the formal and informal system. About 3.5 per cent of China's GNP is spent on education, compared with a median of 4–6 per cent in developing countries. Central government spending on education as a percentage of her total expenditure has increased to 10 per cent in recent years but still remains below the median of 15.5 per cent in developing countries. The distribution of funds is uneven at various levels. Under-investment in primary education at the expense of over-investment in higher education is evident. The ratio of expenditure per pupil at primary, secondary and tertiary level is about 1:2.7:52.3 (*Guanming Ribao Jan*, 1987).

The quantitative expansion of schooling since 1949 has been remarkable: primary provision increased 2.1 times, secondary education 19.2 times and higher education 4.2 times (Tseng, 1986, p. 28). However, there are great imbalances between coastal and inland provinces, rural and urban areas, Han Chinese and national minorities, males and females. On average every Chinese receives five years of schooling but in Tibet the average is two-and-a-half years (Wang and Bai, 1986). The 1982 Census reveals that about one-fifth of China's population is illiterate or semi-illiterate and 80 per cent of them live in the countryside (He, 1986). The national illiteracy rate of the 16–40 age group is 23.5 per cent but in individual counties the rate is 99.3 per cent. The illiteracy rate is as high as 73 per cent among minority groups (*People's Education*, January 1987). According to the All-China Federation of Women, 70 per cent of the country's illiterates are women (*Beijing Review*, 19 September 1983).

The Schooling System

A 6+3+3 structure of formal primary and secondary schooling system shown in fig. 4.1 has existed in China since 1949, although attempts were made to reduce it to a 5+3+2 system during the 'Great Leap Forward' (1958–60) and the Cultural Revolution (1966–76). The present schooling system is a hierarchical, multi-tiered and multi-track one based on meritocratic competition. The schooling system is pyramidal: of 100 children entitled to schooling, ninety-six are enrolled in primary education, fifty-three are promoted to junior secondary school, thirteen to senior secondary and three to higher education (Wang, 1986). The 1985 Education Structural Reform (Jiaoyu Tizhi Gaige) introduced nine-year compulsory education, which is to be implemented throughout China in stages. Local education authorities are allowed to choose between a 5+4 option or a 6+3 option for implementation. There is also a qualitative shift towards technical and vocational education which is expected to account for at least 50 per cent of senior secondary school places.

A keypoint school (chungdian xuexiao) system exists at all levels. Keypoint schools are allocated the best pupils and teaching resources (teachers, funding and equipment) in a particular catchment area. The rationale is to focus resources on the more capable pupils so that they can be prepared for higher education institutions. The keypoint schools are also used as centres of in-service teacher training and for conducting experiments in curriculum innovation. The ratio of keypoint schools is small, about 5 per cent of the entire schooling system, but they generate the majority of university candidates in the highly competitive Unified National Higher School Examination, the enrollment ratio of which averages 26 per cent of the candidates between 1981–1989. Nevertheless, the keypoint school system creates inequalities between schools and intensifies the examination pressure from primary six when selection first takes place.

Figure 4.1 China — the school system

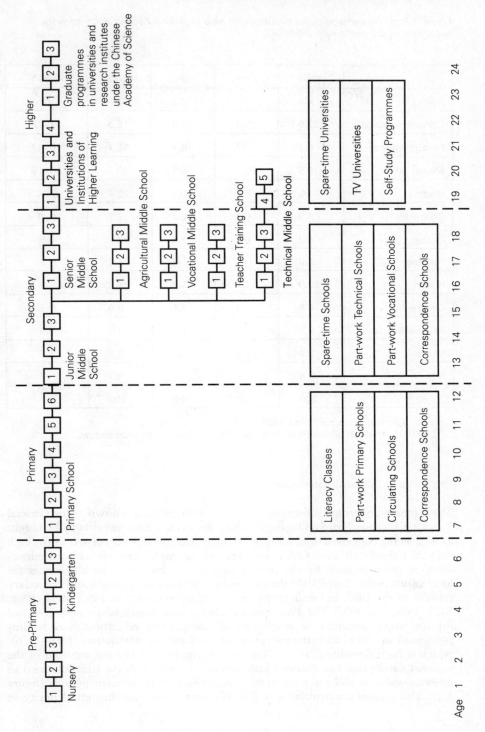

Figure 4.2 (a)   Percentage of the total teaching time by different school subjects in the secondary school curriculum 1954–81

	1954	1958	1963	1978	1981*
Politics	4.4	7.1	6.2	7.2	12
Chinese language	23.0	20.0	21.8	18.3	17–22
Foreign language	6.7	7.7	18.7	15.1	16–17
Mathematics	19.6	20.7	18.1	20.7	16–19
Physics	7.5	8.3	9.4	11.4	5–10
Chemistry	5.9	6.0	6.2	7.2	5–8
Biology	5.0	6.5	3.6	2.2	3.5
Hygiene	1.0	—	—	1.1	1.2
History	10.0	17.7	4.7	4.6	4.5–6.5
Geography	6.7	5.3	3.1	3.6	4–6
Physical Education	6.7	7.1	6.2	7.2	6.9
Music	2.4	1.8	1	0.7	1.7
Arts	2.4	1.8	1	0.7	1.7
	100	100	100	100	

(*Source*:   Chinese Education 1949–1981, PEP)
*   The 1981 timetable allows flexibilities between the arts and science classes.

The National Curriculum

The Chinese government formulates a national curriculum known as the General Teaching Outline (Jiaoxe Dagang). It lists the main school subjects to be taught as well as the suggested allocation of teaching time (in lessons per week) for each subject. Schools all over China are expected to implement the national curriculum as recommended by the central government but there are allowances for local adjustments. Since 1949 the national curriculum for primary and secondary schools in the PRC has undergone seven major revisions, in 1950, 1954, 1961, 1977, 1981, and 1987. The 1987 national curriculum, which is specially designed for the implementation of nine years of compulsory education, was be implemented in 1990. With the exception of the Cultural Revolution (1966–1976), which is now denounced as the 'Ten Year Catastrophe', the organization of the national curriculum has changed little since 1950, although the time allocated to different subjects and the content of subjects shifted at different periods (figure 4.2). The present curriculum is highly academic, stressing theoretical purity in

Figure 4.2 (b)   Percentage of the total teaching time by different school subjects in the
primary school curriculum 1955–81

Year Subject	1955	1963	1978	1981
Politics	—	4.2	2.9	3.7
Chinese language	44.6	48.0	41.2	38.5
Foreign language	—	—	9	4.4
Mathematics	24.4	25.0	24.8	43.7
General Science	3.4	2.2	2.8	4.4
History	2.7	2.2	—	1.5
Geography	2.7	1.1	—	1.5
Physical Education	8.1	6.7	7.7	7.4
Arts	4.0	3.3	5.4	6
Music	6.1	5.6	6.2	7.4
Craft and Labour	4.0	1.7	—	1.5
	100	100	100	100

(*Source*:   Chinese Education 1948–1981, PEP)

those disciplines with the highest prestige, with science seen as supreme. In
Bernstein's terms the curricular organization follows a collection code with strong
framing (Bernstein, 1971). There is little attempt to integrate subjects even at the
junior secondary stage. As a Chinese educator remarked, 'the curriculum stresses
too much on theories, established laws, formula and facts while too little attention is paid to experiments and inquiry. Every pupil is expected to be capable in
all disciplines. This leaves little room for the individual development of pupils.
Their talents and creativity are suppressed' (Qin Xin, 1987).

The Style of Curriculum Development in
The People's Republic of China

Curriculum development in the PRC operates within a highly centralized political system. From an international perspective, China's 'national style' (Becher and
Maclure, 1978) of curriculum development has the characteristics identified with
a 'confined' system as described by Rudduck and Kelly (1976) and exemplified by
Morris (1986). The role of curriculum development is strictly confined to the
central authority which possesses the legal and administrative instruments of
curriculum control. Curriculum development is taken as an integral part of

central planning and consequently is directly linked to overall national development plans. The functions of curriculum development are narrowly vested in the
central agency with only minimal local initiatives. Uniformity of action and
conformity with central decisions, which are hailed as key factors leading to the
success of the Chinese Revolution in 1949, are applied to curriculum development without exception. This led to curriculum uniformity (one syllabus for the
whole country) and the adoption of standardized textbooks. The execution of
policy changes is nationally uniform in conception and application, allowing little
variations to meet local conditions or for adaptation in response to changing
circumstances. However, in reality, the actual implementation of intended curriculum changes often becomes 'cosmetic' and a 'facade' (Lewin, 1981a and 1981b;
Morris, 1982; Guthrie, 1986). For example, physics teachers in China are expected by the official curriculum to follow an inquiry-learning approach based on
laboratory experiments. But the approach is not implemented or partially implemented due to the lack of supporting resources in most schools. The confined
system is also supposed to be self coordinated so there is limited variety of
change agents and innovation actors. In this section, the process of curriculum
development in contemporary China will be described with reference to specific
cases to highlight the unique features of curriculum change in China.

The Administrative Framework of Curriculum Development

The way in which China organizes curriculum development is closely related to
her mechanism of curriculum control. Since 1949 the Ministry of Education
(MOE), which is one of the State Council's seventy-four ministries, has been the
highest authority that governs all educational matters in China. Under the communist system, the primary duty of the MOE is to faithfully execute educational
policies formulated by the Chinese Communist Party. In 1985 the CCP Education Structural Reform replaced the MOE with a new State Commission of
Education (SEdC), which is given a status parallel to the State Commission of
Planning and is empowered to strengthen party and government leadership over
education by (i) monitoring implementation of major principles and policies
concerning education; (ii) making overall arrangements for the development of
education undertakings; (iii) coordinating educational work of various departments; and (iv) providing general plans and guidance of education reform (CCP,
1985).

The Department of Secondary and Primary Education in the SEdC is directly responsible for finalizing the General Teaching Outline (Jiaoxue Dagang),
which specifies the overall curriculum organization and the timetable arrangement for various school subjects. The process of decision-making involves
obtaining approval for what is taken as acceptable knowledge and a negotiation
between subjects over status, resources and territory (Young, 1971; Goodson,
1983). For example, professional geographers proposed a senior secondary school
geography curriculum in 1981 and hoped to raise its status by classifying it as a
science subject in the university entrance examination, which should occupy 6–9
per cent of the total teaching time at senior secondary level. But the 'Big Three'
(mathematics, physics, chemistry) succeeded in securing a higher percentage of
teaching hours (18.5, 9 and 7 per cent respectively) because they claimed that

they were 'foundation sciences'. As a result geography was categorized as an arts subject occupying only 4 per cent of the total timetable (Leung, 1989).

Once the overall teaching outline is finalized, it is the People's Education Press that works out the details of a specific school curriculum as well as producing the teaching materials (jiaocai). The PEP was established in September 1950 upon the belief that nationally unified textbooks had to be written by the most qualified experts to ensure the standards of schools and quality of teaching. In May 1953 Chairman Mao Zedong ordered the Ministry of Education to recruit 150 eminent scholars from different provinces to become full-time editors (writers) to produce primary and secondary school textbooks (Ye, 1985). There are no full-time editors for tertiary textbooks but a branch of the PEP, called the Higher Education Press, is responsible for coordinating outstanding university professionals to produce manuscripts of tertiary texts for publication. This mechanism of curriculum development has remained unchanged since 1950, except during the Cultural Revolution when the PEP was disbanded.

Within the PEP there are different editorial boards responsible for different school subjects. Each editorial board is headed by a chief editor and a group of full-time editors who are university graduates or prominent figures in the curriculum field. Sometimes experienced school teachers and university professionals are seconded for short-term writing projects on specific topics.

There is no divison of labour in curriculum development within the central curriculum development agency. The PEP is engaged in all the main stages of curriculum development from the design of curriculum guidelines to the production of teaching materials. The editorial boards of the PEP are responsible for four tasks. First, they produce the subject-based teaching outlines which are equivalent to the curriculum guides. Before 1985, these outlines merely listed general aims, teaching topics and teaching hours but without specifying key concepts, teaching points and assessment strategies. Second, they produce explanatory notes that inform schools and teachers of the rationales and special emphasis of the specific curriculum. Usually these explanatory notes are sent directly to schools and published in newspapers or academic journals for dissemination. Third, they produce, in teams, the teaching materials (jiaocai) comprising of textbooks (jiaokesu), teaching references for teachers (jiaoxue cankou) and pupils' learning materials such as workbooks, supplementary texts, experiment sheets and an atlas. Fourth, they scrutinize and approve the teaching materials. Fifth, the PEP organizes the printing of the teaching and learning materials. This self coordinated working style existed until 1985 when an independent committee was set up to evaluate and approve textbooks.

The Process of Curriculum Change

Since 1949 the PEP has followed the principle of 'democratic centralism' in developing the school curriculum. In operational terms, this means that the PEP seeks opinions and comments from the widest range of people during the process of curriculum development. Curriculum proposals and draft teaching outlines are circulated widely through a nationwide network to solicit the views of professionals, principals and teachers. Very often there are several revisions before a proposal is finalized. It is impossible to generalize a model of operation as different subjects follow slightly different patterns of development. Nevertheless, a description of the development of the Senior Secondary School Geography Curriculum (SSSGC) described in the following paragraphs may help to illuminate the 'blackbox' of curriculum development in China (Leung, 1989).

The importance of geographical education was denied after 1959 during the Education Revolution as the radical Maoists saw it as educationally worthless. As a result, geography was removed from the senior secondary curriculum and the time allocation for geography was reduced from 6.3 per cent to 1.7 per cent of the total teaching hours in the secondary school years. Then during the Cultural Revolution geography was completely scrapped as a school subject. This was because Jiang Qing, Mao's wife, condemned geography as a 'bourgeois' discipline that encouraged sightseeing and travelling. Geography teachers were forced to resign or teach other subjects. In 1976 geography was first rehabilitated at the junior secondary level. In 1979 the Ministry of Education also planned to restore geography at the senior secondary level. In July 1979 the MOE commissioned the China Geographical Association to call a conference of tertiary level geographers at Wuxi in Jiangsu Province to discuss the possible contribution of geography to China's modernization needs and to suggest how the SSSGC should be organized.

In December 1980 the China Geographical Association was commissioned to hold another conference at Hangzhou on 'Geographical Education at Secondary School Level' to discuss the curriculum (aims, contents, approach and teaching hours) for geography. The majority of the conference delegates were professional geographers (64 per cent), followed by experienced secondary school teachers (23 per cent) and officials from the MOE and PEP (10 per cent). At the Conference three models of SSSGC were proposed by geographers from the higher institutions, namely the earth science model, man-environment model and earth science-economic geography model, each representing a particular school of thought and pedagogical orientation. Trial textbooks and syllabus outlines were produced by the innovators to illustrate their arguments. All the three groups of innovators agreed that the time allocation for SSGC should range between 6–9 per cent of the total teaching time for both the arts and science students.

While the Hangzhou Conference provided a forum for different curriculum interest groups to voice their expectations, final decisions were officially made by the MOE in conjunction with the geography editorial board of the PEP. Eventually in April 1981 the MOE announced that the man-environment model was to be adopted in the SSSGC and the time allocation for it was just 4 per cent of the timetable for arts students. Moreover, SSSGC was to be a subject taken only by arts candidates in the public examination. Then in July 1981 the PEP circulated to schools an 'Explanatory Note on the Outline of Senior Secondary School Geography' which explained the rationale for adopting the man-environment approach as well as outlining the content of the curriculum.

The PEP then proceeded to write textbooks, which took eight months. The writing task was divided between the seven full-time geography editors and one lecturer seconded from a teacher training institute in Beijing. The editors exchanged the manuscripts with each other for comments an suggestions. Individual draft chapters were sent to relevant experts for comments. The chief editor was responsible for the overall editorial work of the two volumes of textbooks. The first edition was ready by March 1982 as a 'trial version' to be implemented in schools in September of the same year. In September 1982, a conference, mainly composed of secondary school teachers and professional geographers, was called at Xiamen to solicit post-factum comments on the trial textbooks. Feedback from the delegates, together with other suggestions collected from other channels, were taken into account when the PEP revised the textbook.

It can be seen from the innovation process of SSSGC that both the range of participants and the level of participation are very limited. Two main groups of innovation actors can be identified in the innovation process. The first group is the *superordinate-legitimized* innovators. They are the officials of the Ministry of Education, People's Education Press and local education bureaus who are mandated to make the final decisions on the timetable arrangement, approach and content of the curriculum. Their source of power arises from their unassailable position of passing legislation and issuing directives which have to be strictly followed. For example, in June 1982 the MOE issued a circular called 'On Offering Senior Middle School Geography' to local education bureaus, requesting them 'to take serious consideration of the new curriculum'. In the circular, a sentence was quoted from Premier Zhou Zheyang's Government Report, which said that 'schools at various level must strengthen the teaching of Chinese history and geography, this is a major aspect of inculcating patriotism among pupils'. The circular then reminded readers that 'the implication of this statement must be thoroughly interpreted by education departments at various levels and schools'.

The second group of innovation actors is the *subordinate non-legitimized* innovators and there are two sub-groups defined by role status. The dominant sub-group comprises geography professionals from tertiary institutions. They dominate the debate and discussions by virtue of their status in the academic community, expertise in the relevant area and practical access to 'world trends' in geographical education. Yet their influence is nominal and consultative as they do not have any real decision-making power. The second sub-group comprises experienced teachers who participate in the innovation process to give 'representational consent' (Havelock and Huberman, 1977) to various proposals.

The clear distinction of roles and duties between the superordinate and subordinate group of innovation actors, together with the shifting pattern of participation, excludes the possibility of collaborative curriculum work between different groups of curriculum stakeholders in the form of an ad hoc curriculum development committee or team as practised in many countries. A 'convectional' pattern (Archer, 1979) of conflict resolution is displayed. Controversies arising in academic forums are passed upward to the power center (MOE and PEP) to be arbitrated and the decision is transmitted downwards as policy-directed changes. A charismatic approach to curriculum decision-making (Lewin, 1988) based on the insights of individuals in influential positions with particular strong beliefs is exhibited. After all, it is the arbitration of the chief editor of the PEP who decides on the final curriculum. The arbitration is based of the chief editor's dual role as an official following the party line and as a professional geographer supporting the man–environment paradigm of geographical education which is perceived as beneficial for China's development needs.

The Features of Curriculum Change

The case of SSSGC is unique because it represents a displaced secondary school subject attempting to justify its academic value and fight for a place in the national curriculum. It also involves heated debates between different schools of geographers. The development of other school subjects is generally incremental in nature. There is greater consensus among the curriculum stakeholders as a paradigmatic shift is not involved. For science subjects, like physics, the curriculum development process is just a matter of updating the curriculum by ad hoc committees comprised of top scientists and PEP editors who work together to revise the syllabus with reference to imported foreign textbooks (Cheng, 1984). For the more ideologically laden subjects like politics and history there is a strict control by the Chinese Communist Party to make sure that the official views are adopted. Sensitive issues are screened by the most senior political leaders. For example, it is reported that Deng Xiaoping gave specific guidelines to PEP history editors on how controversial political issues between 1949 and 1976 were to be introduced to pupils (Pu, 1985). For the skill-oriented subjects like Chinese language and English, some arguments in pedagogical approaches and selection of reading materials are involved in the development process. But since these arguments are not antagonistic in nature they are resolved by allowing local variations. For example, as Lai (this volume) illustrates, there are several versions of Chinese language texts produced by different schools of Chinese language professionals as well as the official texts produced by the PEP.

Another central feature of curriculum development in the PRC is that the central concern of curriculum change focuses more on changes in curriculum content than on pedagogical strategies and the teacher's role perception. During different periods since 1949, the change of curriculum content includes (a) the strengthening the elements of political indoctrination, such as patriotism and fostering a socialist outlook by pupils; (b) the modernization of curriculum content to replace outdated and traditional content; (c) the reappraisal of knowledge to bring about subject integration and coordination; and (d) the introduction of entirely new content areas into the curriculum. Few curriculum innovations are designed to encourage teachers to move away from the traditional expository methods of teaching and towards the use of enquiry-oriented learning or promotion of experiential learning situations. Curriculum innovations do not usually require the teacher to reappraise his/her perception of the teachers' role or to readjust his/her personal relationship with pupils. Teacher-centredness remains the underpinning principle of curriculum change although the official rhetoric may call for more pupil-centred approaches.

Curriculum research is undertaken by the Curriculum and Teaching Research Materials Institute was established in 1983 to carry out research on pedagogy, curriculum development and evaluation. It publishes a monthly journal called *Curriculum, Teaching Materials and Teaching Methods* (*Kejing, Jiaocai* and *Jiaofa*) which is widely circulated in China. The Central Institute of Educational Research also conducts curriculum research on experimental curriculum projects in different types of schools in China. Teacher training institutes usually have research teams concerned with pedagogical methods which are considered as vital to curriculum implementation at the grassroots level. Every school subject is supported by at least one nationwide journal on teaching methods and many provincial or regional journals. On the surface curriculum research is vigorous but the main emphasis seems to focus on exchanging views on pedagogical approaches and describing foreign practices based on a translation of textbooks and journals. Little is done to devise a curriculum model that best fits China's contextual characteristics through scientific systematic research (Jiang, 1988).

Textbook Production and Distribution

All textbooks cover teaching materials for only one semester so there are two books per year per subject. Textbooks are purchased by pupils at a price which is kept low by a large state subsidy. The government also takes strong measures to guarantee the printing of textbooks for all pupils. The nationwide distribution of primary and secondary school textbooks is handled by the New China Bookstore (Xinhua Shudian) which is a book wholesale agency. The annual estimation of print runs are submitted by provincial education bureaus to the China National Publishing Administration, which allocates a printing quota to the PEP printing houses in Beijing and different provinces. Printed textbooks are delivered by Xinhua Shudian to its retail bookstores for schools to collect. This complicated system usually works well and ensures the availability of textbooks before each semester starts.

Forces of Curriculum Change and Continuity

Having described the characteristics of top-down, power-coercive and confined system of curriculum development in the PRC, it should be pointed out that there is no attempt to impose on it a pejorative label, or to infer that a more centralized system leads to bureaucratic stagnation in curriculum development whereas a decentralized system leads to innovative developments (Becher and Maclure, 1978; Watson, 1979; Lauglo, 1986). Indeed, such generalizations are simplistic for, as Rudduck and Kelly (1976) argue, there is little evidence to indicate a close correlation between centralization and decentralization and the form and effectiveness of curriculum development. A similar view is shared by Marsh and Huberman (1984) who argue that both the 'top-down' and 'bottom-up' approaches are appropriate under specific conditions.

What seems more important for a deeper understanding of curriculum development in the PRC is to examine the forces of curriculum change and continuity shaping the course of curriculum development in China. The literature on curriculum change has richly documented how curriculum reforms are generated by various socioeconomic and political expectations. For example, the Schools Council (1973) identified five major forces of curriculum change: scientific and technological advance; educational research; social change; changes within the education system; and new special education needs. In many developing countries the driving forces behind curriculum change and renewal often have a different character due to the importance of historical (post-colonial development), sociopolitical (nation-building) and economic (modernization) reasons. A number of dominant forces of change are identified in the literature on curriculum development in developing countries. These include (a) the need for national cohesion and identity through political education and citizenship education; (b) the indigenization of curricula to make them more appropriate to national characteristics; (c) the transplantation of western curriculum packages because these are perceived as 'advanced knowledge' and shortcuts to acquisition of modern skills; (d) education for self-reliance; (e) education for basic needs and literacy; (f) the vocationalization of school curriculum for better integration of schooling and employment; (g) responding to the priorities of donors; and (h) education for rural development and community development (Coombs, 1980; Dove, 1980; Lillis, 1984; Lewin, 1985; Hawes, 1985).

In this section, six main underlying forces which have shaped both the process and product of curriculum change in the People's Republic of China are examined. They are: political struggle and the contradictions of leadership, the needs of modernization, the Chinese perception of curriculum, traditional teaching methods, teacher professionalism and examination pressure.

Political Struggle and the Contradictions of Leadership

Seen from a conflict-oriented perspective, curriculum change is a political process substained by arguments connected to sources of justification found in cultural, political, economic, social and religious conditions (Kirst and Walker, 1971; Lawton, 1980; Lewin, 1985; Reid, 1988). Chinese education is widely recognized as 'existing in one of the more highly charged political environments among the nations of the world' (Fraser and Hawkins, 1973). Since 1949 China's political leaders have been embroiled in bitter political struggles between different hegemonic groups, namely the radical Maoists and pragmatic modernizers represented by Liu Shaoqi, Zhou Enlai and Deng Xiaoping. Lofstedt (1980) has observed that the controversies among the Chinese leadership regarding education stem from fundamentally different sets of basic value systems and definitions of problems than from actual evaluation of the performance of the educational system. In effect the education system becomes merely an arena for the resulting political struggle, or 'struggle of the two lines' in the Chinese political jargon.

The result of this leadership contradiction is a zero-sum pattern of educational development which is manifested by a perpetual swing between two models of education described by Chen (1974) — the 'revolutionary' and 'academic model'. In a nutshell, the revolutionary model is a Maoist legacy which sees education as a powerful tool for consolidating proletariat dictatorship by reproducing citizens loyal to the Chinese socialist revolution. The major impact of this model on curriculum development includes the combination of productive labour and book knowledge, discrediting theoretical knowledge, the abolition of selective examinations and, most importantly of all, the politicization of the school curriculum for promoting a selfless and 'serve the people' ideology. For example, the official guidelines on curriculum development in 1960 were 'to follow Mao Zedong Thought as the guiding principle; to develop pupils' communist world outlook and morality; to sweep away bourgeois thinking and to strengthen education against imperialism' (People's Education Press, 1982). At the zenith of the Cultural Revolution the school curriculum degenerated into the crudest forms of anti-intellectualism. What was taught in schools comprised mainly the thought of Mao Zedong and simple scientific knowledge related to basic agricultural and industrial production.

In contrast, the 'academic' model has a strong connection with the pre-1949 education system. It stresses the acquisition of advanced knowledge by pupils through a differentiated system of formal schooling and meritocratic competition. Accordingly, the school curriculum has a strong orientation to essentialism and pragmatism, reflecting an emphasis on the value of scientific knowledge and technological know-how. The importance of political indoctrination is not ignored, but played down to a minimal level that does not affect pupils' learning.

The Needs of Modernization

Education has an explicit role to play in Chinese history. In imperial China the study of Confucian classics was used for fostering moral virtue and selecting scholar-officials to serve the Emperor. The development of modern education as an agent of transformation and modernization began in 1860 after China's door was forced open by Western powers. Since then western learning (xixue) was seen as complementary to traditional Chinese learning for the attainment of prosperity and strength (fuchang) so that China could resist foreign aggression. This substance-application principle (Chinese learning for substance, western learning for practical application) consistently manifested itself in curriculum changes in contemporary China under different governments. After the downfall of the Qing Dynasty in 1911 the notion of 'substance' was transformed from Confucianism to republicanism and militant nationalism. In parallel the 'application' aspect was enriched by a belief generated by the May Fourth Movement in 1919 that 'science could save China'. Prior to 1949 China searched for a national system of modern education based successively on a Japanese, American and Franco-German model.

After 1949, the 'substance-application' principle was metamorphosed into the 'red and expert' dichotomy. In the course of China's socialist development, education is expected to perform the dual task of supplying both the political capital and technological manpower for China's national development needs. The first Constitution of the Peoples' Republic of China in 1954 stipulated that 'the state develops socialist educational undertakings and works to raise the scientific and cultural level of the whole nation ... in order to wipe out illiteracy and provide political, cultural, scientific, technical and professional education'. However, the notion of modernization was to be completely divorced from westernization and capitalism. From 1952 onward the Russian model of education was transplanted into China because the authoritarian and centralized model minimized regional differences and favoured the consolidation of political power and the diffusion of socialist dogma (Bastid, 1987). The Russian curriculum model was taken as beneficial to China's development needs because its strong notion of early specialization, the importance given to mathematics and science and its rigid pedagogical approach, enabled the rapid production of specialized manpower for China's Four Modernizations, which were first identified in the early sixties as the comprehensive modernization of agriculture, industry, national defence and science and technology by 2000 AD. Although Sino-Russian relationships deteriorated in the late 1950s and did not fully recover until 1989, the Russian mode of education was firmly established in China.

When the dialectics of red-and-expert is applied to curriculum development the dichotomy of serving permanent revolution (redness) and manpower development (expertness) becomes sharply antagonistic. When 'redness' was magnified by the Maoist radicals the school curriculum was used overwhelmingly for political indoctrination rather than the transmission of objective knowledge. For example, during the first 'education revolution' launched by Mao in 1958 the geography curriculum 'only reports the achievements of socialist construction; it accuses capitalist countries for exploiting natural resources, and describes economic depression and unemployment in the West. It denies the rational aspects of industrial location and management in capitalist countries. Anything in socialist countries is good but anything in capitalist countries is bad' (Chen, 1985).

When China emerged from the ferment of the Cultural Revolution she found her science and technology 'falling twenty years behind the advanced countries' (Deng Xiaoping, 1977). In particular, the educational system was expected to supply the 800,000 qualified workers who were required to launch the modernization programmes. As a result, the greatest concern of the Chinese leaders was to restore the academic model of education to enable China to catch up with the outside world. To modernize the school curriculum, the Chinese government organised a 'blitz' textbook writing team composed of 200 scholars in August 1977 to upgrade the primary and secondary textbooks. They stayed in a hotel in Beijing and worked for a full year to rewrite textbooks with reference to imported materials from the USA, UK, West Germany and Japan (Tang, 1985). The 'modernized' school curriculum generally reflected a stress on academic excellence which was often beyond the average ability of the majority of pupils.

Perceptions of the Curriculum in China

The Chinese term for curriculum is 'kecheng' which first appeared in the sixth century, AD. The term carries with it a strong literal sense of a course, or something to be achieved at the terminal point of learning. It therefore fits in well with the 'means-end' conception of curriculum of Tyler (1950), but not with a concern for the interrelationship between the four key curriculum elements.

Since 1949 the arrangement and selection of curriculum knowledge has been subjected to fluctuations that stemmed from power struggles and the red-expert dichotomy described in the last two sections. The present official perception of the school curriculum in the PRC is an eclectic mixture arising from the political expectations of the Chinese Communist Party and the pedagogical considerations on teaching and learning. Chen (1985), representing the PEP, explains that the school curriculum is

an aggregation of the party's and country's educational policies, educational objectives at various school levels, physio-psychological features, new levels of scientific development and the knowledge, skills, thoughts, behavior and habits to be mastered by pupils. The school curriculum must bear unique features of socialist New China so that it really produces all-round people in morality, knowledge and physical development — a new generation with ideals, morality, culture and discipline... We must use dialectical materialism and historical material-ism as our guiding principle on curriculum building ... the combination of education and labour is a fundamental policy in our country, and curriculum must reflect this combination.

The 1985 Education Structural Reform gave the school curriculum the new task of 'training before employment', the rationale for which was to equip pupils with employable skills in schools which allowed them to obtain employment (Wu, 1986).

One unique feature of the Chinese perception of curriculum is the over-emphasis on content at the expense of other key curriculum elements, namely objectives, teaching-methods and assessment. As described in part two, the production of teaching materials (jiaocai) for all levels of schooling is excep-tionally important in the process of curriculum development. Furthermore, teaching materials become synonymous with textbooks (jiaokeshu). Their im-portance even supercedes curriculum guides. Such a feature develops from and is reinforced by a range of philosophical and practical forces. Great importance is accorded to textbooks as a major type of learning material. As Warming (1982) remarks, textbooks command attention because they do not only provide the basic source of information but also transmit culture, reflect values and serve as springboards for the intellectual development of individuals and nations. In many developing countries textbooks are viewed as a cost-effective tool for upgrading academic achievements in poorer schools with less qualified teachers. The availa-bility to pupils of high quality text materials is considered a key factor for improving pupils' knowledge of science, mathematics and language (Neumann, 1980; Heyneman *et al.*, 1984). But many developing countries are severely con-strained by finance and the lack of professional expertise and other sociopolitical obstacles in the production and provision of textbooks to school learners (Pearce, 1982; Altbach, 1983).

In the PRC textbooks are also considered as efficient 'for educating millions of Chinese youths to become successors of the socialist revolution' (Zhang, 1985). They are the 'physical foundation of teaching and learning' as they provide 'crucial sources for pupils to obtain knowledge systematically and the foundation stone for more advanced studies ... also a pre-requisite for good teaching if teachers use them properly' (Wu, 1986). The establishment of the People's Education Press as a centralized agency for producing standardized textbooks reflects the belief of the Chinese leadership that high-quality instructional mate-rials contribute to effective learning and student achievement. In the production of textbooks, the PEP follows two basic criteria. The first is efficiency of words, which means that the texts are to be written in precise words. The second is academic excellence, which means that the updated information must be in-cluded. As a result, textbooks in China stress the organization of academic information in an encyclopaedic manner. They are adult-centred and written in a very scholarly language. Pupils' exercises reinforce knowledge recall rather than the acquisition of skills and attempts to extend pupils' intellectual abilities.

Traditional Pedagogy

China inherits a dogmatic Confucian pedagogical tradition which has fused effectively with the Soviet mode of instruction. The resulting hybrid pattern of teaching and learning is textbook-based and teacher-centred. It is geared to implement the syllabus which is usually content-overloaded. In 1985, the Chinese vice-premier Wan Li criticized the traditional teaching method in very strong words, saying that

> the traditional educational thoughts and teaching methods of our coun-
> try are very backward. Contents are fixed, can't be questioned, can't be
> elaborated, can't be suspected. In examinations answers are given
> according to a fixed format and contents. The kind of educational
> thoughts and methods produce ren-cai (qualified manpower) only cap-
> able of wei-shu (following the book) and wei-shang (listening to super-
> iors). They lack creativity and progressive spirits.

Pan (1986) succinctly outlines the distinct features of the orthodox teaching methods practised by the majority of teachers at all levels in China. Too much emphasis is put on the transmission of theoretical knowledge, the rigid separation of subjects, classroom spoon-feeding, teacher dominance, uniformity and external motivation (parental and social expectations). But too little attention is paid to learning psychology, the acquisition of practical and social skills, internal motivation, pupil participation and differences between the abilities and needs of pupils.

The strong commitment to a teacher-centred approach confines curriculum innovation to changes in subject matter rather than an attempt to extend teachers' pedagogical repertoire. Many teaching journals in China publish good examples of teaching, most of which are concerned with how efficiently the lesson can be taught (i.e. teaching more content in a shorter time period) rather than how pupils' intellectual abilities can be expanded.

Teacher Professionalism

A shortage of qualified teachers is an acute problem in China. In 1983, about half of all primary teachers and one-third of secondary school teachers were unqualified (World Bank Report, 1984). An official from the State Planning Commission warned that the implementation of nine-year compulsory education would be seriously undermined by the high percentage of unqualified teachers in the primary (37 per cent) and junior secondary (73 per cent) levels. She stated that 15 per cent of the teaching force in primary and secondary schools were incompetent and incapable teachers who should be removed from the teaching force (Wang, 1988). There is a concern that low teacher professionalism will undermine the implementation of nine-year compulsory education and induce juvenile delinquency.

The low professionalism of Chinese teachers is a major cause of the poor representation of teachers in the confined system of curriculum development. Moreover, teachers are perceived by the government as passive adopters of the official curriculum. Their primary role is to follow faithfully the pre-specified teaching every subject. These 'teacher-proof' handbooks are thick manuals produced by the PEP or writing teams from teacher-training institutes. The purposes of the handbooks are mainly to develop teachers' subject knowledge and to advise on lesson planning and classroom teaching strategies. The unqualified and inexperienced teachers rely heavily on the handbooks to help them understand the texts which they use in their teaching. They view the handbooks as survival guides.

Without a highly professional teaching force, it is unrealistic to expect radical curriculum development approaches in China along the lines of school-based innovations or widespread involvement of teachers in curriculum development as advocated in the Western literature (Shipman, 1974; Fullan and Pomfret, 1977; Young, 1979, Connelly and Ben-Peretz, 1980; Leithwood *et al.*, 1982; Robinson, 1982). There is some truth in the advice of Jennings-Wray (1984) that developing countries should not be swayed by the rhetoric of teacher involvement in all stages of the curriculum change process, especially in contexts where the status of the teaching profession is at a low ebb, and where official policy has traditionally viewed teachers as receivers of 'pre-packaged' curricula.

Alongside the low level of teacher professionalism, there is also a strong element of conservatism amongst many experienced teachers in China who serve as the 'backbone' (Gugan) of the teaching force. They are known as 'supergrade' (Teji) teachers in the career structure. The majority of them were educated in the 1950s and 1960s and they are firmly committed to the teacher-centred approach and early specialization. As a result, it is difficult to introduce curriculum innovations that challenge the superiority of the teacher or weaken the compartmentalization of knowledge. For example, the State Education Commission has tried to introduce integrated science and social studies in junior secondary schools but these projects are viewed with suspicion and resisted by many teachers (Huo, 1988).

Examination Pressure

Assessment is an important component of curriculum development. In chapter 3 the rationales and techniques of assessment have been described. Nevertheless, external public examinations exert a powerful backwash effect on teaching and learning in schools when only a minority of pupils completing the secondary school cycle can continue into the tertiary cycle (Dore, 1976; Lewin, 1981b, Oxenham, 1984; Somerset, 1985). The backwash effect of examinations on the school curriculum is particularly strong in the current Chinese education system that stresses stiff competition for the selection of outstanding candidates. In China it is publicly acknowledged that the university entrance examination is the 'conductor's baton' that orchestrates teaching and learning in schools, although in reality 80 per cent of the secondary pupils have no access to tertiary education. The Chinese describe this severe competition vividly as 'a million horses and soldiers crowding to cross a narrow bridge'.

Other than the excess of demand over supply, several other factors reinforce the 'examination hell' (Dore, 1976) in China. First, the present Chinese leadership values academic qualification in allocating jobs in the state controlled labour market. University degree holders, representing only 1 per cent of the entire working population, can easily gain access to privileged and secure jobs in the government or state factories. Therefore, university entrance examinations are seen as the most important springboard for jumping to the top of the social pyramid. Second, the reputation and material rewards of a school are measured by its performance in the public examination. Successful schools with high university enrollment rate are praised in the mass media and their successful experiences are reported in teaching journals for diffusion (Lu, 1986). In the rural regions, successful university candidates are congratulated by musical bangs and firecrackers because they bring glory to the village clans. Third, the keypoint school system reinforces examination competition because keypoint schools at various levels recruit only the pupils who perform best in the public examination.

Curriculum development is constrained by examination pressure in several ways. The national curriculum is already monolithically structured and academically oriented. Streaming in the senior secondary level is based entirely on the six subjects required by the university entrance examination.* To promote curriculum diversification, the State Education Commission has encouraged schools to offer optional courses but not many schools are willing to sacrifice time on the 'non-examination subjects'. Even if options are offered they are those that supplement the examination subjects, such as additional mathematics, calculus and computer science (Da, 1988). Some keypoint secondary schools, like the Shanghai East China Normal University attached No. 2 Middle School, even offer first year university courses in physics and mathematics for their top students and ask for exemption credits after university admission (Leung, 1989). The vocationalization of the school curriculum also meets resistance from parents. Above all, teachers attempt to match their teaching styles to examination requirements. They drill the pupils with past examination papers and mock examination questions which are produced by profit-seeking publication houses and readily available in the market. Even the local education bureaus take part in question-spotting and preparing a 'sea of items' (Tihai) for schools. The SEdC repeatedly asks schools not to over-emphasize passing rates in public examinations and not to over-drill pupils. But their pleas have met with little success.

Problems and Solutions

So far the main features and the underlying forces accounting for the confined curriculum development style in China have been described and analyzed. This unique style of curriculum development in China stems from the specific socio-political 'conditions of change' (Ball, 1987), in contemporary China as well as the deep structure of the Chinese culture, namely, teacher and textbook-centredness. In view of China's physical vastness and the regional imbalances in development, the system produces a national curriculum which is supposed to be a universal standard of achievement across China. It has also successfully accomplished

* All candidates are required to take six subjects, three of which are compulsory: politics, foreign language and Chinese. Arts candidate take history, geography and mathematics. Science candidates take physics, mathematics, chemistry (half paper) and biology (half paper).

the tremendous task of producing the basic teaching materials for the school population of 220 million. At the same time, the system has produced three crucial problems which are recognized by the Chinese educators who are attempting to make further improvement.

First, it is accepted that post-1976 curriculum modernization has been over-concerned with borrowing advanced scientific knowledge from the developed world and is narrowly focused on the selection of university candidates. Emphasis on standardized official syllabuses and textbooks has ignored local variations. In 1983 the MOE decided to split senior secondary school mathematics, physics, chemistry into two versions: an original version A for capable pupils and a watered-down version B for lower ability groups. In 1985 the SEdC modified the teaching requirements of four junior secondary school subjects (mathematics, physics, chemistry and foreign language) by reducing the teaching content and lowering examination requirements (Ma Li, 1985). The 1981 national curriculum was viewed as 'divorced from the realities in the majority of regions and schools in the country. Haste makes waste — neither can teachers teach well nor pupils follow' (Yang, 1986). The 1981 national curriculum is also criticized for restricting the all-round development of pupils because it focuses narrowly on a small number of academic subjects (Jiang, 1988).

The second problem is concerned with the relevance of the school curriculum for the vast majority of rural school children. Hu Yaobang, the former CCP General Secretary, openly pointed out the irrelevance of the school curriculum for rural children. He was concerned that fundamental knowledge such as basic abacus, functional literacy and basic soil science were neglected. The curriculum was both examination and urban oriented. Those who could not enter universities gained no employable skills. (Hu quoted in Wang, 1986). It was decreed by the SEdC in 1988 that curriculum development must be oriented to 80 per cent of pupils in the countryside (He, 1988).

The third problem is related to the extent of coordination between the main educational agencies involved in curriculum development, evaluation, teacher training and resource allocation. It is clear that the lack of explicitness and clarity in the curriculum guides has undermined the translation of curriculum goals into action. On the other hand, textbooks are written without reference to actual classroom realities in terms of the availability of resources and time. They are crammed with information and written in a condensed language. As a result, teachers are compelled to follow a 'filling the lesson with information' (man tang guan) teaching approach which is openly acknowledged as undesirable but is in practice prevalent and inevitable. As a result of curriculum development being equated with textbook production, assessment objectives and strategies are not given due consideration in the curriculum development process. They are left to ad hoc examination-paper setting teams that work under the SEdC. Teachers are bewildered by the lack of any clear-cut guidelines and of constructive feedback from examination results. They, therefore, rely on past examination papers and question-spotting to anticipate the examination. Teacher training institutions pay more attention to teaching their students subject content rather than equipping them with adequate skills required to overcome teaching constraints in schools. For example, teachers are not given enough exposure to educational technology which might enable them to produce indigenous teaching materials.

Since 1985, a number of measures have been taken to try to make curriculum development more effective. First, it is planned to view curriculum development as a form of 'system engineering' (Ye, 1987). This will entail the SEdC declaring nationally standardized curriculum guides that clearly state the general aims and more detailed instructional objectives, teaching points, basic concepts and skills. Based on these official curriculum guidelines, both the PEP and local educators will produce teaching materials that will be scrutinized and approved by a newly-established National Evaluation Committee for Primary and Secondary Textbooks. The committee, with various sub-committees, is composed of scholars, teacher trainers, psychologists and experienced school teachers. The criteria for the evaluation of textbooks are that: (a) the materials must be suitable for the needs of the pupils; (b) they must take into account social, economic and cultural differences between regions; (c) they must cater for the all round development of pupils (Currin, 1987). Schools could then choose the approved textbooks they think are relevant to their local needs. It is hoped that the devolution of curriculum control will encourage greater participation in curriculum innovation and local initiatives. At the same time it will overcome the lack of flexibility induced by the previous practice of having just one set of standardized textbooks for all school subjects except Chinese language.

Second, it is planned that a research development dissemination approach to curriculum change will be used. This will be compatible with the existing mandatory and top-down approach of curriculum development. The Central Institute of Educational Research has been assigned to undertake thirty-two experimental projects in curriculum diversification and integration in different sites in China (Shi, 1988). Efforts have been made to improve the vertical relationship between different levels of schooling and the horizontal relationship between subjects. The purpose is to avoid repetition, inconsistencies and linkage gaps. The main focus of attention is to make the core curriculum for nine-year basic education more balanced and relevant. Special attention has been paid to updating knowledge, relating theory and practice, training for work and developing thinking skills (Jiang, 1988; Shi, 1988).

Third, the public examination system and the methods of assessment will be changed to reduce the negative backwash effect on curriculum development. With more specific curriculum guides provided for different subjects, it will be easier for examiners to set test items which are based on clearly pre-specified skills and pedagogical approaches even with the existence of several versions of textbooks in the country. It is hoped that the existing heavy reliance on textbook based information recall can be reduced. Moreover, it has been proposed that an independent examination agency be set up to monitor the Unified National Higher School Examination. The national public examination will only test pupils' basic numerical and language skills, leaving the other subjects to be examined at the provincial level by local examination agencies which award school leaving certificates to secondary school graduates. The new practice has been piloted in Shanghai, Nanjing and Guangzhou since 1987. It is expected to be gradually introduced nationwide because not every province is ready to conduct examinations independently.

Concluding Comments

From a comparative perspective, it can be seen that the pattern and problems of curriculum in post-1976 China bear a close resemblance to those experiences of other developing countries in Asia, Africa and Latin America (APEID, 1976, 1977; Lewin, 1985; Saunders and Vulliamy, 1983; Woodhouse, 1984; Lungu, 1985; Magendzo, 1988; Ogundere, 1988). The following features have been highlighted: there is a highly centralized and confined system of curriculum development but there is an absence of an effective coordinating mechanism and the required institutional supports (a) are not adequately developed; (b) have a high degree of élitism in the decision-making process about appropriate forms of knowledge and participation in curriculum planning; (c) have an abundance of curriculum changes aimed at achieving an immediate political or economic impact; (d) changes are mainly applied to an academic, subject-centred curriculum; and (e) the transplantation of the façade of foreign trends is viewed as a shortcut to modernization.

From the brief retrospective survey made in the previous sections it can be seen that since 1978 curriculum development in China has been undergoing a gradual transition from a highly confined system to a more profuse system. The prerequisite conditions favouring such a direction of change are based on the relative political stability and economic prosperity within China as well as the willingness of the central government to devolve power to the local government to activate grassroots initiatives for increasing productivity and overcoming local problems. Moreover, the Chinese leadership is more tolerant to the influx of Western ideologies.

However, the crackdown on the pro-democracy movement in June 1989 and the subsequent leadership change have swung the political pendulum back to the Stalinist model of central planning and tight political control. In the field of education, the SEdC has called for stronger emphasis on political education to combat the tide of 'bourgeois liberalization'. Primary and secondary teachers were asked to teach their pupils about class struggle and imperialist subversion. English language teachers have been asked to pay greater attention to ideological education by introducing to pupils reading materials that would promote patriotism and collectivism (Wen Bo, 1990). The recent 'leadership contradiction' will definitely have its impact on educational and curriculum development in the PRC. What is not clear is whether the change will result in yet another rerun of the destructive zero-sum game that has been played since 1949.

Chapter 5

Curriculum Dissemination in the People's Republic of China

Winnie Y.W. Au Yeung, Lai

Introduction

Education in China has always been perceived and used as an important means of transmitting the prevailing political ideology. This means that the content and purposes of education have to be in line with the prevailing political ideology. It also implies that as political ideology changes, corresponding changes in education must take place.

This is confirmed by Deng Xiaoping who in a speech made at the National Education Working Conference on April 1978 stated that:

> the urgent task of the educationalists was to get rid of the negative influence of the Gang of Four in promoting anti-revolutionism and anti-socialism. Education must serve to restore and promote the quality tradition of revolution.

He also quoted Mao's statement:

> the promotion of political ideology is the responsibility of all departments ... but teachers and principals in schools bear particular responsibility.

In the pre-1949 period the education system was more élitist and primarily served the function of preparing people for employment in the civil service. Since the founding of the PRC in 1949, attempts were made to make education more accessible to the masses. It was in 1956 that plans were made to achieve compulsory primary education in seven to twelve years' time (China Education Yearbook Editorial Board, 1984). However, the extent to which this has been achieved is in question.

Changes in political ideology took place much more frequently since 1949. As a result, educational, especially curriculum, changes occurred more frequently. In the case of Chinese Language, six major curriculum reforms were launched between the period 1949 and 1976, and these were closely associated with major shifts in political ideology.

These reforms were launched in 1951, 1956, 1958, 1961 and 1963 respectively. The 1951 reform was aimed at eliminating the influence of the Kuomingtang, the 1956 reform was a result of the Pro-Russian influence, the 1958 reform was a result of the Anti-Russian Campaign, the 1961 reform was in support of the Great Leap Forward Movement, and the 1963 reform was a result of the launching of Anti-Revisionism.

The role of education as the vehicle for promoting the prevailing ideology frequently necessitated rapid and hasty curriculum changes as new leaders emerged and others were disgraced. This resulted in problems in the dissemination of changes such as difficulties associated with the provision of information about the new syllabus, editing of teaching materials, and providing support at the teacher training level. These problems have resulted in a number of difficulties for schools attempting to implement the changes.

This chapter initially describes the structure of the education system and then analyzes the strategies of curriculum dissemination adopted in the PRC to promote the 'new' secondary school Chinese Language which was introduced in 1978. This is undertaken by means of an analysis of both the agents and components involved in the process of curriculum dissemination.

The Historical Background

After the death of Mao Zedong in September 1976 and the fall of the Gang of Four in October of the same year, a series of education reforms were introduced by Hua Kuofeng and Deng Xiaoping as the PRC attempted to open up and make up for the loss resulting from the Cultural Revolution. In the 1978 Constitution of the NPC, Article 13 stated that:

> the State devotes a major effort to developing education in order to raise the cultural and scientific level of the whole nation. Education must serve proletarian politics and be combined with productive labour and must enable everyone who receives an education to develop morally and physically and become a worker with both socialist consciousness and culture.

As far as the Chinese Language curriculum was concerned, a new curriculum was introduced for primary and secondary schools, aimed at educating a new generation who could contribute to the Four Modernizations of the country (Chen, 1987). The primary feature of the new curriculum was a continued emphasis on inculcating a socialist ideology. A secondary purpose, which had been neglected since the onset of the Cultural Revolution, was to develop students' linguistic skills.

The Portrayal

Literature on curriculum reform in the PRC displays a number of weaknesses. First, many of the accounts such as those by Cowen and Mclean (1984) and Lofstedt

(1984) who wrote about the developments of Chinese education in the 1970s tend to portray the situation as homogeneous and monolithic. Second, much of the literature relies on official sources and portrays the system as highly centralized, top-down and homogenous.

Price (1976) in describing the formation of education policy in the PRC, stated that:

> ... No study must ignore the role of the Chinese Communist Party, with its small groups active in every organization of any size. This is connected vertically with the Central Committee in Peking through provincial, municipal (city) and lower level committees, and it has a propaganda Department which is specially concerned with education. In addition to this there are government organs, both Revolutionary Committees of various kinds, and also branch organs of the central ministries. But for the question which concerns us here the Communist Party's role is decisive, in mobilizing people to carry out centrally formulated policies and more generally in organizing political education. (p. 70)

His article on Chinese curricula (1981) further restates his view that the Chinese education system was of the 'top-down' variety and centrally controlled. He opined that:

> ... Future curriculum developments are unclear. Educators are not powerful change agents. It is the leaders of the Communist Party who hold the strings of power in education and outside and will certainly continue to do so ... (p. 87)

The picture which emerges is of a politically motivated and centrally initiated curriculum which is implemented in schools. It should be noted however that within the central government, the lack of cooperation and the competition between the various departments and curriculum agents results in a great deal of complexity, adaptation and confusion. The result is that a diversity of messages are sent to the schools and teachers about what is required of them. The resulting problems of implementation have been identified by Leung (1989) with reference to the secondary school Geography curriculum. Zhang (1984, 1985) in proposing means to reform the secondary school Chinese Language curricula also discussed the conflict between the aims and objectives prescribed by the different agents and parties.

The Structure of the Education System

The organizations which make up the educational system are shown in figure 5.1.

In order to understand the process of curriculum dissemination in the PRC, it is necessary to understand the role of the different institutions in the administrative structure. These are shown in figure 5.2.

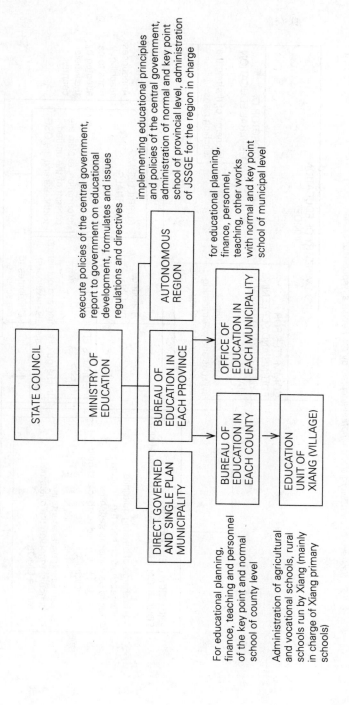

Figure 5.1   The educational administration structure of the People's Republic of China

STATE COUNCIL

MINISTRY OF EDUCATION

execute policies of the central government, report to government on educational development, formulates and issues regulations and directives

AUTONOMOUS REGION

implementing educational principles and policies of the central government, administration of normal and key point school of provincial level, administration of JSSGE for the region in charge

BUREAU OF EDUCATION IN EACH PROVINCE

DIRECT GOVERNED AND SINGLE PLAN MUNICIPALITY

OFFICE OF EDUCATION IN EACH MUNICIPALITY

for educational planning, finance, personnel, teaching, other works with normal and key point school of municipal level

BUREAU OF EDUCATION IN EACH COUNTY

For educational planning, finance, teaching and personnel of the key point and normal school of county level

EDUCATION UNIT OF XIANG (VILLAGE)

Administration of agricultural and vocational schools, rural schools run by Xiang (mainly in charge of Xiang primary schools)

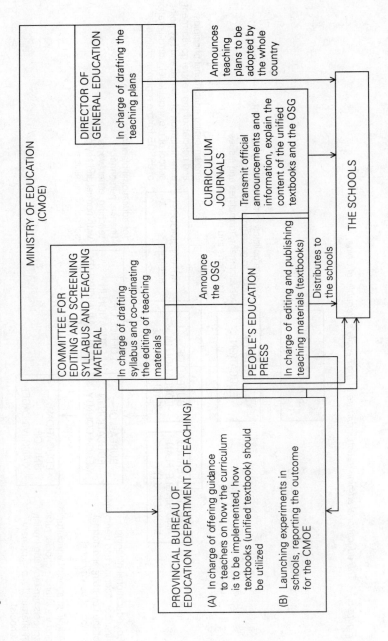

Figure 5.2   Strategy of curriculum dissemination adopted by the People's Republic of China

The Central Ministry of Education (the CMOE)

The CMOE, which is the highest educational decision making body in the PRC, is directly under the jurisdiction of the State Council (guowuyuan). Its task is to execute the policy of the government, to report to the government on educational development, to seek government approval for policy measures, and to formulate and issue regulations and directives governing the work of primary, secondary and higher education. The CMOE also initiates laws and directives that govern educational work in the whole nation. It is, however, responsible only for the overall policy. The local government and corresponding organs at provincial (sheng), prefectural (diqu), municipal (shi), county (xian) and local district or village (xiang) levels have their own educational bureaus. The regional educational authorities are under the direction of both the local government and the CMOE in terms of funding and curriculum design. As far as the dissemination of the Chinese Language curriculum is concerned, the CMOE is responsible for the following:

(i)   drafting the official Syllabus Guide;
(ii) instructing and coordinating the PEP to edit and publish the textbooks;
(iii) allocating the teaching hours;
(iv) answering queries concerning subject-based matters.

In June 1985, the CMOE was reestablished and became the State Education Commission (the SEdC). The structure and role remained very much the same, especially within the departments taking care of primary and secondary education.

The Provincial Bureaux of Education

The Provincial Bureaux of Education takes the major responsibility for administering education policies, they are the most important agent in the dissemination of subject curriculum. Their relationship with the CMOE is most appropriately described by the following statement:

> The CMOE issues general directives, but the actual planning as well as the implementation are responsibilities of the provinces. (China Education Yearbook, 1984, p. 163)

The Provincial Bureaux and Municipal Offices of Education are mainly responsible for the following:

(i)   distributes education funds;
(ii) monitors the staffing situation, i.e. to allocate new graduates to teach in schools, to work out the staff student ratio etc;
(iii) conducts junior and senior secondary school entrance examinations as well as the subsequent admission exercises;
(iv) prepares the syllabus and textbooks for the prevocational and agricultural secondary schools.

87

The Provincial Bureaux of Education (Lofstedt, 1984) are in charge of middle technical schools, middle normal schools in the province, and key secondary and primary schools which do not come under the leadership of the lower levels. They also run some higher education institutions. This confirms the comment made by senior SEdC officials that they are shouldering the major responsibilities in administering education policies.

A Provincial Bureau of Education comprises about six or seven divisions. As far as the dissemination of curriculum for normal secondary schools is concerned, the Department of Teaching Research (Jiao Yan Shi), which is sub-divided into subject-based sections, is the main agent responsible for subject-based curriculum dissemination matters. This involves sending out instructions on how the text-books should be used, what teaching strategies should be adopted, the kind of supplementary materials to be utilized, and the extent to which these materials should be used etc. Overall the Provincial Bureaux shoulder the main responsibility for disseminating educational policies.

The Municipal Office of Education

In general, the Municipal Education Offices are under the administration of the Provincial Bureau of Education. Their relationship with the Provincial Bureaux is similar to that of the counties and xians. As far as the dissemination of curricula change is concerned, they are instructed by the Provincial Bureau of Education. The resources are also supplied by the Provincial Bureaux. Apart from not having to attend to the vocational and agricultural secondary schools, their work is basically very similar to that of the bureaux but they are concerned with educational issues in an municipal district within a province.

There are some municipalities which are under the direct governance of the central government, such as Beijing, Shanghai, and Guangzhou. This is a result of the economic status of those municipalities.

Shanghai and Beijing are categorized as 'Direct Governed Cities'. This means they have an administrative system which is independent from their respective provincial government which is directly under the governance of the central government. Furthermore, Shanghai has its own university entrance examination. The universities in Shanghai have allocated a significant percentage of vacancies for senior secondary graduates from Shanghai.

The other category of municipality is the 'Single Plan City' (Danlie Shi). Guangzhou is one of them. It is also under the direct administration of the central government. Apart from the financial funding which is allocated by the Guang-dong provincial government, Guangzhou is independent in all other matters related to education.

The structure and function of these Municipal Offices of Education are almost identical to those of the Provincial Bureaux of Education. Their relationship with the Bureau of Education of the province with which they belong geographically, is a parallel one. That is, they do not have to report to the Provincial Education Bureau on their working policy, they are not funded via the Provincial Bureau of Education. They communicate directly with the CMOE concerning administrative matters.

In the case of the Teaching Research Departments of the Municipal Office of Education, they are responsible for:

- (i) administering the junior secondary and senior secondary school entrance examinations;
  - (a) producing the examination syllabus guide annually to specify the scope and content to be examined;
  - (b) coordinating the setting and marking of the examination papers;
- (ii) holding in-service talks for serving teachers and to organize demonstration lessons/public lessons for teachers;
- (iii) organizing extra-curricular activities and open competitions for students;
- (iv) collaborating with individual schools to conduct school based curriculum reform projects such as trying out new approaches in teaching and piloting teaching materials.

It is important to note that the availability of such services and the frequency of conducting these activities are at the discretion of individual offices, thus variations of practice are substantial. Furthermore, the role of the key personnel in the Education Office is not clearly defined as explained by an Education officer of the Guangzhou Education Office:

There is no formal channel as to how the officers of the Teaching Research Department liaise with the SEdC ... The scope of the work of the Teaching Research Officers have never been clearly defined. They do observe lessons in schools but there are no official regulations concerning their authority to monitor classroom teaching. Usually they can offer suggestions for improvement, but the teachers are not obligated to abide by their suggestions ... The focus of work of the Teaching Research Office is not specified by the Central Government; individual offices can decide their focus and frequency of activities such as the number of demonstration lessons, number of school visits and lesson observation and the number of open competition for students.

However, it would be incorrect to assume that the duties of Bureaux and Offices of Education of equal status are identical, nor is it accurate to assume that the division of labour between the bureaux and offices of different provinces are identical. A senior official of an Education Office explained that the work of the Education Offices varies with the administrative system.

The County Bureau of Education

The County Bureau of Education takes care of education matters in a county which is in terms of area and population, much smaller than a municipality.

Interviews by the author in 1987 confirmed the accuracy of Lofstedt's (1984) protrayal of the role of the County Bureaux:

The County Education Bureau is responsible for the general primary and middle schools in the county town, and the key middle schools in the same town. It also shares the responsibility for the general middle schools in the rural areas and the primary schools in the country side with the xiang level government. (p. 68)

As far as the dissemination of the curriculum is concerned, they are responsible for organizing in-service forums and seminars for the teachers to familiarize them with curriculum changes. The other duty is to communicate messages from the Provincial Bureau of Education concerning the implementation of the curriculum.

However, Guangzhou and Shanghai, which are both directly under the central government, have a similar role and status as that of a Provincial Bureau of Education, their Municipal Offices are not directly in control of the County Offices. The County Offices are under the direct control of the respective Provincial Bureaux.

It is therefore difficult to generalize about the curriculum dissemination system in the PRC since the practice varies from region to region. The variations of practice in disseminating the curriculum are mainly due to two factors: first, the difference in the economic and administrative status of the municipality which could be either under the direct governance of the central government or under the provincial government, and second, the status of the schools, which could be national key point schools, provincial key point schools, municipal key-point schools or just ordinary schools.

The Schools

There are many categories of secondary schools in the PRC. The vast majority of pupils attend grammar type schools. There are ordinary non key-point secondary and the key-point secondary schools. The ordinary non key-point secondary schools are administered by different levels of Education Offices according to their geographical location, i.e. whether they are situated in municipalities, counties or xians. The key-point secondary schools (KPS) are also under different levels of administration according to their status. Within the same municipality, there are some KPSs that are directly under the administration of the CMOE — the National KPSs, while others are under the provincial Bureau of Education — the Provincial KPSs. There are also KPSs that are under the Municipal Education Office — the Municipal KPSs. KPSs at county and xian level also exist. The majority of them are under the administration of the local education office but there are some under the administration of the Municipal Office or even the Provincial Bureau of Education. However, these are exceptional cases.

The existence of the different administrative channels for the different types of key-point secondary schools, (the National KPSs, the Provincial KPSs, the Municipal KPSs, the County and Xian KPSs) and the ordinary non key-point schools makes the operation and monitoring of curriculum dissemination very complex. For example, the Guangdong Provincial Bureau of Education can undertake direct dissemination of curricula directives to the Provincial KPSs located in Guangzhou city, whereas curricular directives have to go through the

Municipal Education Office to reach the ordinary non-key point schools and the Municipal KPSs which are also situated in the same city, or even the same district.

The above is a brief and generalized picture of the administrative structure of the PRC with reference to the organizations involved with dissemination of school curricula. The following section will focus on the process of dissemination and the role of the dissemination agents.

Curriculum Dissemination

The channels and processes of curriculum dissemination in the PRC are perhaps one of the most bureaucratic and complex in the world. As a result, the education system suffers from policy intentions which frequently become a façade and have little effect on classroom practice.

The processes of curriculum dissemination among PRC educators reflect this essentially bureaucratic perspective. In a course book on Curriculum Studies for Normal University students, Chen (1988), a prominent scholar in the study of curriculum, does not devote any chapter to discuss and explain the concept and practices of dissemination in curriculum development. Neither does he outline the basic models of curriculum dissemination. He states that the personnel and organizational structures involved in the development and implementation of a curriculum, includes the following:

(i) the Head of the Central Education Administration Office, for his permission and endorsement;

(ii) the Screening Committee members, who are made up of well-known scholars coopted by the Central Education Administration Department, for their expertise knowledge on the subject matter;

(iii) the scholars and experts who were involved in drafting the curriculum initially;

(iv) the editors of textbooks.

Curriculum change is therefore viewed primarily as a top-down project. The personnel in the central administrative arena are perceived as the key agents in bringing about the change. The role of the sub-ordinate groups as users of the change (Rogers and Shoemaker 1971) is neglected.

The comments made by Chen (1988) concerning the current Chinese approach to curriculum development are illustrative. He states that:

> From the above, it can be seen that the personnel involved in the development of the curriculum is not a monolithic group. It includes experts from all subject areas, education researchers, officials of education administration departments and professional textbook editors. It is only through the cooperation of these people that an appropriate set of teaching material is produced. (pp. 265–6)

The above statement clearly indicates that according to the Central Education Authority, the development of a curriculum is the task of a superordinate group and ends with the production of teaching materials. In the PRC, the task of disseminating curricula is left to the People's Education Press (the PEP), the publishing house which is also the national curriculum development agency, and the Bureaux and Offices of Education. The strategies adopted are very much subject to their preference and discretion. This practice is a result of the assumption that in a country with a highly centralized administrative system, policy from the central government will naturally and unquestionably be implemented.

This is also reflected in the structure of the education system in the PRC, which is basically geared towards the distribution of financial and human resources as well as the political impact of the projects. There is little concern with the means to achieving the ends — for it is assumed that the ends will be achieved automatically if the intention and objectives of the project are made clear. As far as curriculum dissemination is concerned, it is assumed that once the syllabus guide is published and the textbooks are available, the students will naturally acquire the sort of knowledge specified.

Another significant feature is the relationship between the curriculum and the teaching materials. The term curriculum literally means the teaching materials — to be more specific, the textbooks. Thus the work of curriculum dissemination means the work of distributing the textbooks and informing teachers how they should be utilized. It is taken for granted that the editors of textbooks will take care of such activities. This probably explains why responsibility for the dissemination of curricula information is left to the editors at the PEP. However, as these editors work full time producing textbooks, and as there are no explicit rules and regulations governing their role in the dissemination of curriculum information, the extent to which these editors contribute to dissemination is questionable. Further, it should be noted that there is an absence of an establishment similar to that of an Inspectorate to take care of dissemination.

The Dissemination Agents

An understanding of the process of dissemination can be obtained by an analysis of the introduction and dissemination of a specific innovation. Figure 5.3 shows the main components used to disseminate changes to the Chinese Language curriculum during the period 1977–1987. The function and relationship of these components namely, the Official Syllabus Guide, the examination, the textbooks and the subject-based journals are discussed below (see figure 5.3). Although there are sometimes other dissemination agents such as professional associations and other interest groups it is argued below that the four listed above are the most relevant.

Prior to analysing the role of these components, it is necessary to identify the alternative perspectives on the aims and objectives of Chinese Language education which exist.

Aims and Objectives of Chinese Language Education

Since the establishment of Chinese as an independent subject in 1903 under the Kweimou System, the aims and content of the subject have been controversial.

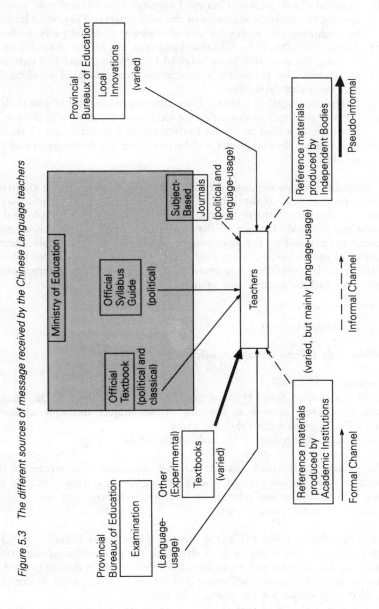

Figure 5.3   The different sources of message received by the Chinese Language teachers

The central issue revolves around the different perceptions of the purposes of Chinese language education. The three main alternative orientations are:

(a) Political ideological — Chinese Language education should aim at promoting the political ideology of the ruling party. This could be achieved by including the works by and of eminent political party leaders.
(b) Literature-cultural — Chinese Language education should aim at enhancing the student's knowledge of Chinese literature and culture. This is achieved by including a substantial proportion of classical literary works in the curriculum.
(c) Linguistic-usage — Chinese Language education should aim at developing the student's communicative skills and be able to make use of the language as a tool to obtain knowledge and information. This orientation implies that emphasis will be placed on the development of linguistic skills.

These three different perceptions directly affect the content of the curriculum.

Since the founding of the PRC in 1949, Chinese language has always been perceived by the party leaders to bear the responsibility to promote and reflect the prevailing political ideology of the communist party. However, a consensus has never been reached by the government, academics and the public concerning the priority of the different orientations. Consequently as we will see the orientation promoted by the central government is subject to reinterpretaton and adaptation by various groups and agencies.

The Major Agencies

The syllabus (the Official Syllabus Guide — the OSG)

The functions of the OSG
The OSG is a subject-based syllabus guide produced by the CMOE. It contains the aims, objectives, as well as content, of the subject and it is assumed that teachers will implement the OSG faithfully.

The official description of the role of the OSG is:

> The reform of teaching material is the important component of the content of education reform, the Teaching Outline (the OSG) is the basic reference for the editing of teaching materials and for guiding teaching. (SEdC, 1986, Preface)

Since the founding of the PRC, the People's Education Press (the PEP), the national publishing house has been in charge of the production of the OSGs; the editors of the different subject areas draft the OSG which is then approved by the Committee for Editing and Screening Syllabuses and Teaching Materials. The PEP is also responsible for the printing of these OSGs.

It is surprising to find that there is very limited information on the overall content of the OSG compared with the massive amount devoted to the content of school textbooks, lesson plans and teaching approaches. Comments in the OSG focus on the nature and/or balance of the prescribed texts and they are written by the editors of the PEP. Huang's (1980) article on the changes made in the 1980 OSG was the only piece of work on the OSG located. Others, such as Liu (1981) wrote about the 'spirits' of the curriculum. The PEP Secondary School Chinese Language Editional Office (1981) focused on explaining how the pre-scribed texts should be used. Tien (1983) one of the senior editors of PEP also wrote about how the articles on language knowledge should be utilized. The large amount of writing attempting to explain the nature and teaching require-ments by these officials is a good indicator that the OSG is not self explanatory. It probably also confirms the information gathered from interviews that the OSG has little influence on the implementation of the subject curriculum.

Another indication that the OSG is not perceived as an important document is that in the official *Education Yearbook 1949–1981*, there is no section devoted to the OSGs. The existence of the OSG was mentioned under the chapter on Teaching Materials, a chapter which took up sixty-two pages out of 1103 pages of the entire volume.

The OSGs are descriptions of the intended curriculum. The 1978 and 1980 reforms to the Chinese Language curriculum indicate that the OSGs only provide overall guidance and a framework for the editing of the unified textbooks. However, the OSG did not achieve its intended outcome for the unified text-books did not adhere to the OSG's guidelines. This includes differences in the list of prescribed texts as well as the emphasis on political ideological education. Furthermore, the textbooks were, for the teachers, the important source of information on the content of the curriculum.

Two editions of the OSG for Secondary School Chinese Language were produced in 1978 and 1980. The 1980 edition was substantially different from the earlier edition in a number of ways. The sections of the OSG that underwent drastic changes and amendments were: reference to politics and Chairman Mao; emphasis in the aims of language education; the means to conduct political ideological education in the language lessons; the content of the teaching mate-rials (the prescribed texts); the sequencing and arrangement of the teaching materials; the teaching of writing; and issues related to the qualifications of the teachers.

Overall these changes amounted to a major redefinition of the nature and purposes of the subject. Its role in 1978 was to reaffirm the role of Chinese Language in the transmission of political ideology, which had priority over the development of language skills. The 1980 version elevated the development of language and communication skills as an equally important objective as the promotion of politics. The 1980 version stressed that the dual roles of the subject were:

> to develop the students' skills in making use of the language appropriate-ly, to develop their reading and writing skills of the Standard Modern Chinese and the ability to read simple Classical Chinese. In the course of developing these skills, attention should be paid to elevate the students' socialist awareness and to develop the behavior of the proletariats and the moral qualities of communism. (SEdC, 1986, p. 388)

The shift in the emphasis on the role of Chinese Language from the promotion of political ideological education to its development as a tool for communication was a reflection of the drive to achieve the Four Modernizations.

The changes occurred within a very short period of time, (less than two years) and created problems for teachers if they wished to reflect the requirements set forth in the OSG as will be seen in the subsequent section. Materials were not available, examinations were not modified and little in-service support was provided. The result was that whilst official policy changed it took many years for it to have any impact in the school. In brief the policy changes, whilst directly linked to political changes, did not result in a major and immediate change in the curriculum implemented in schools.

The drastic changes made within such a short period of time meant that teachers were given different messages about the 'how' and 'what' of Chinese language teaching. Whilst the official role of the OSG was to determine the content of textbooks, its role was at best unclear in the case of Chinese Language because the textbooks were produced prior to its publication and there was substantial inconsistency between them.

Relationship with public examinations
Interviews revealed that examination guides were viewed by both teachers and students as more important than the OSGs. The examination guides have actually taken over the role of the OSGs in many aspects, especially in guiding and influencing the 'what' and 'how' of classroom teaching.

The OSGs did not have any influence over the public exams as evidenced by the examination syllabus Guide for the Senior Secondary School Entrance Examination (the SSSEE) (Guangzhou Education Office, 1986). Its focus differed considerably from that of the OSG. In practice teachers tend to rely on the SSSEE to determine what they should teach and this is frequently inconsistent with the OSG. The main difference is that the examination syllabus guide emphasizes the type of language skills to be examined and the list of prescribed texts from which questions on literature and linguistic knowledge will be set. The emphasis is linguistically oriented, with some elements of literature. The assessment of pupils' knowledge of politics is never mentioned.

Thus the OSG cannot be regarded as a document which reflects the content and substance of the Chinese Language curriculum. Further, it has a limited role in providing guidance on the implementation of the curriculum.

Examinations
Examinations have always been one of the most active and effective agents in disseminating curricula. This is particularly so in China, where examinations have been used as a means to select officials to serve the imperial government since the Han Dynasty. In the PRC, the analogy of the public examinations to teaching and learning as the 'conducting rod' (Zhihui ban) of the conductor to an orchestra is commonly accepted.

Secondary school students have to sit for public examinations twice within the six years of secondary schooling. The first public examination they have to sit is the Senior Secondary School Entrance Examination (SSSEE) which is held at the end of junior secondary Form 3. The aim of this public examination is to select students into senior secondary schools. The second public examination is the Unified University Entrance Examination (the UUEE) which is held at the end of senior secondary Form 3. For those students who intend to seek senior secondary schooling, they must sit for the SSSEE. For those who intend to pursue tertiary education, they must sit for the UUEE. Consequently, the SSSEE has a much larger enrolment of students than the UUEE.

Each Provincial Bureau or Municipal Office of Education is responsible for the administration of the SSSEE for the region under its administration. For example, the Municipal Education Office of Guangzhou is in charge of setting the examination paper for Guangzhou city and its suburbs whereas the Provincial Education Bureau of Guangdong is in charge of the SSSEE for the rest of the municipalities, counties, villages etc. in Guangdong province.

The UUEE is administered by the CMOE Committee on UUEE. The Committee members include administrative officials responsible for the technical aspects of conducting the UUEE as well as subject specialists who set and mark the examination papers. The subject specialists include university professors, experienced secondary school teachers and editors of textbooks. They are coopted on a yearly basis. Confidentiality of the examination papers is enforced by putting the subject specialists together in a place where they cannot contact the public, or even their families without special official permission. The duration of their 'retreat' is normally from the time they start to design the examination papers until the examinations are over.

The Senior Secondary School Entrance Examination — the SSSEE
Analysis of the nature of the SSSEE in Guangzhou, Shanghai and Beijing in 1985 and 1987 reveals that the content and style of the SSSEE for the same year set by the different municipalities differed considerably. Data from the analysis of the SSSEE of the three municipalities reveal three essential differences.

First, the style, format and cognitive skills examined in the SSSEE differed considerably in different places. The Guangzhou papers adopted multiple choice items extensively while the Shanghai nad Beijing papers adopted filling in blanks. The Guangzhou papers placed less emphasis on factual questions and focused on examining the students' ability to make use of the language. An analysis of examination guides and model answers reveals that the most obvious difference between areas is the degree of emphasis on the ability to think and express oneself within the communist party line. The Beijing papers and the marking scheme contain more political elements while the Guangzhou papers had the least. The three cities are, therefore, emphasizing different goals and purposes, and teachers are receiving different messages about the nature of the curriculum. Changes in the structure of the papers, styles of questions and content were also evident from year to year within the same municipality.

Second, a comparison of the papers of Shanghai and its nearby regions reveals that the influence of the practice of big cities on other places is not evident. i.e. the SSSEE of individual education administrative unit has its own characteristics.

Third, a comparison of the focus of the SSSEE papers and the aims and objectives set forth in the Official Syllabus Guide reveals that the SSSEE has only adopted a small percentage of the recommended/prescribed content of the OSG as well as the prescribed content of the official textbooks. The focus of the SSSEE papers are on language knowledge and language skills.

Winnie Y.W. Au Yeung, Lai

Overall in the SSSEE papers, only a small percentage of the questions were based on the prescribed texts listed in the Official Syllabus Guide. The rest of the questions were mainly examining the language skills which were not explicitly specified in the OSG. The majority of the SSSEE papers did not include any explicit assessment of political elements which was a central goal of the 1980 OSG.

Examination guides have been produced every year for the SSSEE by the relevant Office/Bureau of Education in charge of conducting the SSSEE, and their content is very language usage oriented. This is contrary to the balance suggested by the OSG. Thus the SSSEE, instead of assisting the dissemination of the official curriculum, has been redefining the aims and objectives of the subject.

As a result of this dissonance, the CMOE has, since the mid-1980s, instructed those in charge of setting the papers to increase the coverage of the prescribed texts included in the unified textbook to enhance conformity of the papers, and at the same time to highlight the status of the unified textbooks. However, the content of the subsequent SSSEE papers still remains very much linguistically oriented. Diversity of the content and structure of the SSSEE papers is still evident.

The Unified University Entrance Examination (the UUEE)
The Unified University Entrance Examination, which is held at the end of the three years of senior secondary education, is 'the' examination which is perceived by educators all over the country as an indicator of the focus and direction of secondary education. Comparatively speaking, the UUEE syllabus bears much closer relationship to the OSG and the official textbooks than the SSSEE. The number of prescribed texts listed in the OSG which are to be examined in the UUEE is much more than that to the SSSEE. (In the 1983 UUEE paper, 40 per cent of the marks were allocated to questions set on the prescribed texts.).

The UUEE emphasizes the literature and linguistic knowledge of the prescribed texts, which are only partially covered by the unified textbooks. As a result, experimental textbooks which focus on the development of language skills and include a large number of exercises on the linguistic and literature aspects of the essays are utilized extensively by students. These experimental textbooks were edited and published by normal universities, such as Beijing Normal and East China Normal, as well as by teachers and regional Education Offices, such as the set published by No. 15 Middle School of Anshan City in Liaoning Province. Some schools use one set of experimental textbooks as 'the' set of teaching materials while the majority of schools use the experimental textbooks side by side with the unified textbooks.

In addition, the considerable amount of supplementary materials on sale for preparing students for the UUEE focus on drilling the students' language skills, and indicates that the official textbooks do not provide enough information and exercises to prepare students for the UUEE. In other words, the requirements of the UUEE are much more than the content of the unified textbooks.

Thus it is appropriate to say that the UUEE is not disseminating the official curricular messages as reflected in the OSG and the unified textbooks. This claim is further supported by the fact that the political elements present in the UUEE papers were no more than that in the SSSEE. The 1985 and 1987 UUEE papers have no trace of political elements which is not in accordance with the emphasis of the OSG.

Textbooks

In China, textbooks are considered to be the main component of the subject curriculum. This is particularly so for Chinese Language. The official textbook is made up mainly of prescribed texts, i.e. essays, prose and poems selected from the works of famous authors/academics of different periods. The list of pre-scribed texts in Chinese Language is very often perceived as having equivalent status as the syllabus. Similarly in Hong Kong in the 1950s and 1960s the index of teaching materials was the only official document produced by the Education Department concerning the Chinese Language curriculum. Thus, the content of textbooks is a central agent for dissemination and a good indicator of the content as well as the aims and objectives of the subject curriculum.

By looking into the relationship between the OSG and the official textbooks for secondary school Chinese Language, it is clear that the content of the official textbooks does not reflect the nature, aims and objectives of the OSG. A com-parison of the prescribed texts listed in the OSGs and the content of the Unified textbooks (the official textbook) published by the People's Education Press, as in the case of books 3 and 4 for Junior Secondary Form 2 reveals that the textbooks have included only about two-thirds of the texts listed in the OSG. The one-third of texts not included are mainly of a political ideological orientation.

This reflects the difference in the perception of the aims of a Chinese Language education among the officials in the CMOE, who approved the OSG and the editors of the PEP, who edited the unified textbooks. The respective proportion of prescribed texts with political-ideological, literature-cultural and language-usage orientation, clearly indicates that the CMOE was politically oriented and the PEP felt the curriculum should be oriented towards language-usage.

Officially, there is only one set of textbooks used in the schools in the country — that is, the officially published unified textbooks. It is stated by the CMOE that:

> The country unified the supply of teaching materials for primary and secondary schools. The PEP has been responsible for editing and pub-lishing. In 1977–79 the CMOE, based on the 10-year Programme guide-line established the education system for primary and secondary schools and produced one set of teaching material to be used by the whole country ... the set of teaching material for the 6-year programme to be used in the whole country is scheduled for completion in 1985. (China Education Year Book, 1984, p. 483)

In reality there are many sets of 'experimental' textbooks in use. The content of these experimental textbooks is different from that of the Unified Textbooks. Most of them are also trying to redefine the aims and objectives of language education to reduce the emphasis on political ideological education. Some of these 'experimental' textbooks have replaced the official textbooks, others are used side by side with the official textbooks. Such practices are particularly common in key-point schools and those 'normal' schools with high academic standards.

In 1981, the People's Education Press announced the publication of a set of Chinese Language textbooks for key-point secondary schools. The content of this set of textbooks also differs considerably from that of the Unified textbooks. The most obvious difference is the emphasis on classical literature. As far as the content of the prescribed text is concerned, the key-point school textbooks adopted less than 30 per cent of the prescribed texts. Secondary Form 2 in 1980. Only about 25 per cent of the prescribed texts are included by both the Unified Textbooks and the key-point school textbooks.

Interviews with PEP editors reveals that the discrepancies between the OSG and the official textbooks have arisen because the content of the OSG is lagging far behind in terms of political development and the means to achieve such ends. It is considered to be too politically oriented and its ideals are difficult to achieve in the classroom. In order to ensure the Unified Textbooks are fulfilling the responsibility to reflect the current political situation, the editors have to change the contents of the official textbooks from time to time. This is done by substituting the writings of the disgraced political leaders with those by political leaders in power. In addition, in order to make the Unified Textbooks more relevant to the SSSEE, the PEP editors have to develop a set of textbooks attempting to strike a balance between its political and educational roles.

The fact is that a considerable number of schools are using linguistically-oriented sets of textbooks in preparing students for the SSSEE and their students manage to do very well indicates that the SSSEE was not actually reinforcing the expectations of the OSG.

Overall, both the Unified Textbooks and the experimental ones, were attempting to redefine the aims and objectives of language teaching. This redefinition effectively resulted in the development of a less politically and more linguistically/communicatively oriented curriculum.

Further, from 1978 up till the mid-1980s, the content of the unified textbooks changed every year. A number of prescribed texts were removed and replaced by others. The changes were mainly politically oriented. In order to be online with the prevailing political ideology, the content of the textbooks has to be amended as political ideologies keep changing. The other reason for these constant changes is that the textbooks are compiled in a hurry, and in many cases the curricula have not gone through sufficient piloting. Thus when errors are identified in the course of teaching, or when the texts are found not suitable for teaching, amendments and substitutions are made.

The frequent changes made to the unified textbooks not only undermines the status of the OSG, it also creates problems for the dissemination of the curriculum. The common saying that 'every year a new set of teaching material comes into existence, turning every teacher into a novice again' is a good indicator of the consequence for teachers. At best it has been difficult for teachers to keep up with these changes.

Curriculum journals

A major source of nationwide dissemination is by curriculum journals.

Two types of journals exist, the subject-based journals and curriculum journals. Their original function was to transmit curriculum policy changes from the CMOE to teachers. The majority of subject-based journals are published by the PEP in collaboration with the universities and teacher training institutions. This is the case for Chinese Language, Maths, Physics and English.

Curriculum, Teaching Material and Teaching Methods (*Kecheng, Jiaocai, Jiaofa*) published by the PEP from 1981 under the auspices of the Curriculum and Teaching Material Research Institute is the curriculum journal for all subject disciplines.

The division of work between the two types of journals is that the latter is responsible for publishing all the major official announcements concerning the changes made to the different subject curricula while the former is responsible for explaining and illustrating in detail the various changes and requirements, as in the case of Chinese Language.

However, the circulation of subject-based journals is limited. In the case of secondary school Chinese Language, the number of full-time teachers teaching the subject is about 700,000, and yet the total number of the four key subject-based journals published per issue has been less than 100,000. The circulation number of the CTMTM is also only about 30,000. As a result, the effect of these journals on disseminating curricula information is problematic.

Initially, these journals were intended to disseminate official messages about changes to the subject curriculum. However, the circulation number dropped drastically. In the case of the Chinese language journals — *Secondary School Chinese Language Teaching*, dropped from 150,000 copies in the early 1980s to less than 30,000 in the mid-1980s. This was due to two reasons. First, the growing number of schools using other sets of textbooks. Second, public examinations were reintroduced and became the 'conducting rod' of teaching, the focus of the journals switched to examinations so as to increase the circulation. As a result, these journals are now more involved in disseminating information about the examinations, which, as we have seen, do not correspond with the emphasis or approach specified in the OSG and the officially produced textbooks.

The People's Education Press (the PEP)

As noted above, the PEP is the national publication and printing house for the PRC. It is also the central curriculum development agency. It is directly controlled by the CMOE. Apart from being responsible for editing the textbooks for primary and secondary schools, the PEP shoulders the responsibility for screening all textbooks even though a new department — the Department for Screening and Approving Teaching Materials for Primary and Secondary Schools was set up in 1987 to screen teaching materials.

The PEP editors also consider that they have the responsibility for looking after the dissemination of curricular information as explained by senior officials of SEdC in an interview with the author in 1987:

Members of staff in the editorial section of PEP go out to different provinces to visit schools, Bureaux and Offices of Education to collect comments on the textbooks and to find out how the textbooks are utilized.

The purpose of these visits is:

... to answer questions on the content of the textbooks, discuss with members of the Teaching Research Section on the structure and design of the textbooks, and to collect data on the mistakes and errors located. Such data will be made use of in subsequent revision of the textbooks and as reference for the content of articles to be contributed to the subject-based journals. Furthermore these editors also conduct in-service training for the teachers upon request, but the frequency of such activities is low.

Thus the visits, in service education and published materials provided by the PEP centred on the need to provide teachers with more information on the content of the official textbooks.

The Subsidiary Agencies

Other agencies involved in dissemination belong to two main categories — the academic institutions and the non-academic institutions.

The academic institutions
These include normal universities and teacher training colleges. They are primarily engaged in the publication of teaching plans for secondary schools. Beijing Normal University and East China Normal University have been publishing teaching plans for secondary school Chinese language teachers since the early 1980s. They also play an active role in the development of secondary school curriculum. For example, Beijing Normal University was asked by the PEP to edit the four-year junior secondary course Chinese Language textbooks as the PEP was busy with the production of the five and six year course secondary school Chinese Language textbooks. BNU thus had an officially recognized role in the development of the curriculum.

The non-academic orgainzations
These agencies are non-profit making. They produce materials to:

... assist secondary school teachers, to strengthen their ability, to prepare lessons, to study the teaching materials and to raise the quality of teaching. (People's Progressive Party Library, 1983, Preface)

The People's Progressive Party Library is one of these organizations. It is a voluntary establishment based in Beijing under the People's Progressive Party, the majority of whose members are engaged in education. The dissemination of their publications, such as *Index to Secondary School Language Teaching Reference Materials* (autumn, 1983) is mainly restricted to the membership. The content of their publications is based on the OSG and the Unified Textbooks and thus follows closely official curriculum policy. These publications are welcomed by the teachers. Although the circulation of this publication is limited, it is one of the few that is disseminating the messages of the OSG and the Unified textbooks.

Problems with Curriculum Dissemination

In a large country such as the PRC, curriculum dissemination is logistically not an easy task. This is especially so with the dissemination of a centrally planned curriculum.

As the section on textbooks has shown, the content has been amended every year before the mid-1980s. The work of disseminating information on curricular changes in the PRC is therefore an ongoing exercise. Every year the officials in the Bureaux and Offices of Education have to identify the changes made in the Unified Textbooks and to inform teachers of the nature of these changes and the means to cope with them. But the teachers are primarily concerned with changes to the public examination.

The two major problems in the dissemination of curricula information are, first, those related to the supply of teaching materials, specifically the textbooks and second, those related to the dissemination of curriculum information, such as how the textbooks should be utilized and the methods of implementation.

As for the supply of teaching materials — an official document in 1979 (SEdC Office, 1986) confirmed that there have been cases where textbooks arrived after the school term had begun. Furthermore, in some subjects the target of 'each student having his her own copy has not been realised. The situation has been basically overcome in the mid-1980s but the problem still occurs from time to time. Textbooks often arrive just a few days before the new term starts, leaving very little time for lesson preparation.

The teachers find this particularly irritating. In an interview with the author, a teacher in Guangzhou made the following comments:

> ... Up till today, the problem with the textbook supply bothers the language teachers very much. As the teachers were used to the fact that part of the content of the textbook will change every year, we are very anxious to have an adequate amount of time to prepare the lessons. Teachers frequently complain about the textbooks coming late. Very often we managed to get hold of the new copy a day or two before the new term ...

The late arrival of the textbooks from the publishers means that the officers of the Bureaux and Offices of Education, who are responsible for disseminating information about the curriculum to the teachers, are also receiving the textbooks late. Without the textbooks at hand, it is impossible for them to locate the changes made and to identify the aspects that need explanation and elaboration. Thus, during the years when the new curriculum was introduced and the subsequent years when the content of the textbook was amended drastically, the late arrival and shortage of textbooks was detrimental to the effective dissemination of changes and the implementation of the intended curriculum.

There were also times when the textbooks that were ready for use in the new term were abandoned. The reason for this was a political one. For example in 1980–81, immediately after the stepping down of Chairman Hua Kuofeng, a notice was sent to the New China Book Store (Xinhua Shudian) to stop distributing the Chinese Language textbooks for the spring term. The schools were informed by the CMOE that they should select appropriate essays to replace the prescribed texts temporarily. It was confirmed by PEP editors, school teachers and education officers that the action was taken in order to stop the use of essays written by and about Hua Kuofeng which praise his contribution to the country and the Communist Party. Comparison of the content of the Unified Texts for 1979 and 1981 confirms that the essays written by Hua were deleted and the way he is addressed was amended to 'Comrade Hua' instead of 'Chairman Hua'.

The Dissemination of the 1987 Curriculum

In the spring of 1987, the SEdC formally announced a new curriculum for all the primary and secondary schools. The new syllabus for eighteen subjects was also announced. This new curriculum was effectively another revision of the subject syllabus of the 1978 full-time ten-year programme for primary and secondary schools. The subjects have undergone major amendments are: primary school Chinese language, junior and senior secondary school Chinese Language, secondary school Russian, secondary school Physics, Chemistry, History and Geography, and senior secondary school Algebra.

According to official statements, the reasons for the introduction of the 1987 curriculum were, first, that the content of most of the textbooks were outdated and could not meet the needs of the students. Second, the content of some subjects was found to be too difficult. Third, the need for the inclusion of new subjects, such as world history.

As far as the strategy of curriculum dissemination is concerned, the OSG and the Unified Textbooks were again used as the main means to disseminate the new policy. This approach was identical with that used for the 1978 curriculum.

In addition, the SEdC requested university professors and experienced teachers in Beijing and Shanghai to publish different sets of teacher's guides for all subjects for use as references by the teachers. These teacher's guides serve as a new component in the dissemination of the official curriculum.

Another new feature incorporated in the 1987 curriculum reforms a decision by the SEdC to allow the publication of alternate sets of textbooks for each subject. These alternate sets of textbooks can be edited by any educational institution such as universities, Municipal Offices of Education or even schools. However, these textbooks must be trialled in schools before they are submitted to the Textbook Screening Committee for approval. The presence of these alternate sets of textbooks indicates that the central authorities have recognized that the PEP texts do not serve as the sole texts. However the screening mechanism will ensure central control of alternate texts in ways which did not previously exist. This policy change implies that the strategy of dissemination of curricular information in the PRC is changing from that used for the 1978 curriculum reform.

Concluding Comments

This chapter reveals that the CMOE was not wholly in control of curriculum development in the PRC. Apart from coordinating the PEP to design the OSG and to edit the unified textbooks and to arrange for delivery of textbooks to the schools, the CMOE has delegated the other duties of disseminating curricular information to the Bureaus and Offices of Education which resulted in a great deal of variation in practice. This was evident in the control of examinations, experimental textbooks and supplementary texts.

The overall strategy adopted has been one that is top-down and bureaucratic. Changes to the curriculum are both politically motivated and centrally initiated. However, the size and complexity of the system results in major discrepancies between official policy and actual practice. In reality the components of the curriculum which directly affect teachers and pupils are examinations, textbooks and syllabuses. They frequently emphasize different goals than those promoted by the central government and its agencies. This situation has been exacerbated by the logistical problems of distributing textbooks and disseminating information about curriculum changes.

Chapter 6

Curriculum Development in Hong Kong

J.A.G. McClelland

Introduction

Hong Kong is constitutionally a colony of the United Kingdom, and will remain so until 1997, so a similarity between its education system and that of the UK is to be expected. Equally, given that the vast majority of the population is Chinese and speaks Cantonese, a dialect of Chinese, some contrasts are also to be expected.

It has been typical of territories under British administration that:

relatively small numbers of highly academically oriented schools have developed and flourished, preparing an élite for university study;

the majority have been established by voluntary agencies;

development of appropriate schooling for the rest of the population has lagged far behind, often at the express wish of influential local people or in response to their unwillingness to make use of what they perceive as second class provision;

the élite schools have operated through the medium of English and no alternative route to the 'glittering prizes' has developed through the medium of the mother tongue or tongues;

the curriculum has been dominated by matriculation requirements and, where public examining has been localized, great care has been taken to maintain a notional equivalence with the standards of the General Certificate of Education (GCE) examinations in England and Wales. Adaptation to local circumstances has usually meant the substitution of local and regional topics for UK-oriented topics in otherwise highly derivative syllabuses;

the tertiary sector has started off very small and so highly selective but has suffered from 'creaming' as the children of wealthy families and the highest achievers have continued to study abroad.

Figure 6.1   *Attendance at school by age and stage*

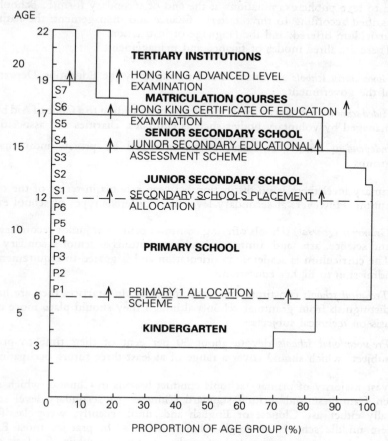

Typically, the deficiencies of the system have been well documented by reports and reform has been passionately advocated by many but inertia, disagreement about exactly what reforms may be needed and lack of resources, have conspired against coherent developments.

All of these typical features can be found in Hong Kong.

Schooling in Hong Kong

A general picture of schooling in Hong Kong is provided as figure 6.1. International schools, schools operated by the English Schools Foundation, which cater mainly for the children of expatriates, special schools and institutions offering craft or technician training courses are not included. Compulsory and free schooling begins at age 6 and continues for nine years. In practice, most children attend kindergarten and most continue for two years beyond the compulsory period to take public examinations at the end of secondary form 5. Schools can be classified according to three criteria: finance and management; the nature of the curriculum offered; and the language of instruction.

There are three modes of finance and management:

Government schools are financed and managed by the Education Department of the government.

Aided schools are financed by the government according to a Code of Aid but are managed by voluntary bodies such as churches, charities and associations.

Independent schools are financed and managed by private individuals or groups.

At primary level there is no distinction between schools in terms of the official curriculum. However, at secondary level three different types of school exist:

Grammar (general) schools offering common courses at junior secondary level and science, arts, and commercial subjects options at senior secondary level. The curriculum is academic in orientation and is geared to requirements for admission to higher education.

Technical schools constitute one small minority. In practice, they are hard to distinguish from grammar schools although they should place more emphasis on technical subjects.

Pre-vocational schools devote about 50 per cent of their time to practical subjects which should cover a range of at least three future occupations.

The vast majority of primary schools conduct lessons in Chinese, which means spoken Cantonese and written standard Chinese. At secondary level schools officially either use Chinese or English and, until recently, were classified as Chinese middle schools or Anglo-Chinese schools. In practice most English medium schools use a great deal of spoken Cantonese while, for lack of appropriate textbooks in Chinese, many Chinese medium schools use textbooks written in English.

Principals of schools at all levels have a great deal of authority and responsibility for the curriculum. This is often exercised in such a way that teachers feel themselves to be presenters rather than implementors, adaptors or developers of the curriculum.

Kindergarten

All kindergartens are private and many are profit-making: teachers are very poorly paid and only a minority have professional qualifications or schooling beyond junior secondary level, although the situation is improving year by year. Typically there is a strong emphasis on reading, writing and arithmetic, rote learning strategies are encouraged and children are routinely given homework. Failure to give this emphasis is reported to lead to diminished popularity with parents. To a large extent an emphasis on rote learning and on written rather than oral expression is built into the process of becoming literate in Chinese. The typical class size is around thirty-five but one of eighty has been recorded.

Although the Education Department (see below) does not take direct responsibility for kindergartens, they are given advice on the curriculum and are monitored by advisory inspectors. The officially recommended curriculum involves themes and activities with an emphasis on learning through play.

Primary Schools

About 7 per cent of primary pupils are enrolled in government schools, 84 per cent in aided, and 10 per cent in private schools. There are many more primary schools than there are buildings to accommodate them so it is usual for two schools to share the same premises, each operating a restricted day. These are known as bi-sessional schools. The typical class size is above forty.

Primary school teachers are expected to hold a Certificate from a College of Education but it is possible for schools to employ untrained teachers. Most of these, known as permitted teachers, are employed by private schools. There is no establishment for graduates. Training takes either three years following secondary 5 or two years following secondary 7. In recent years it has become increasingly difficult to recruit students to colleges leading to fears that the quality of teaching may deteriorate. Calls for an all-graduate profession have been resisted on the grounds of cost: graduates and certificate holders are placed at different points on the master pay-scale. In spite of this many teachers enrol on BEd courses overseas. Recently some BEd courses have been approved for school principals and teachers of children with learning difficulties, so it is possible that moves towards graduate status for primary school teachers will gather momentum.

The recommended number of periods of forty minutes to be devoted to different subjects at P5 and P6 is set out in table 6.1. The recommended teaching method is termed the activity approach but, in most classrooms, a great deal of the time is taken up by didactic teaching and seatwork. In part this is because the size of a typical classroom and the number of pupils it must accommodate makes it very difficult for a full range of teaching methods to be used, as was pointed out in chapter 2. According to official figures for 1990, less than 40 per cent of primary schools adopt the activity approach. This figure is likely to be optimistic if it is taken to mean that the approach is fully implemented.

Secondary Schools

About 6 per cent of secondary school pupils are in government, 68 per cent in aided and 24 per cent in private schools. Technical and pre-vocational schools together account for about 9 per cent of the total enrollment. Secondary schools do not share premises but many have more classes than teaching rooms. They may use temporary classrooms or 'floating' classes, taking advantage of rooms vacated for physical education, etc. Junior secondary school places are bought by

Table 6.1   Recommended distribution of teaching at primary 5 and 6

Subject	Periods
Chinese	9
English	9
Mathematics	6
Social studies	3
Health education	2
Science	2
Music	2
Art	2
Craft	2
Physical education	2

the government in private schools for those who cannot be accommodated in existing government and aided schools. In 1989 bought places accounted for just over 13 per cent of the total enrollment. The typical class size is around forty in forms 1 to 5. The maximum number of pupils permitted to occupy a standard classroom is limited by regulation to forty-five.

Compulsory schooling ends at age 15 which should be reached in form 3. Up to 90 per cent of those completing form 3 continue to form 4 while about 25 per cent of those completing form 5 continue to form 6.

At form 6 class size is more variable but forty is not uncommon. Because about one-third leave at the end of the year, class size at form 7 is smaller, particularly in the most reputable schools, which suffer proportionately the highest loss.

It is expected that all pupils should progress through the system at the same rate, but schools are permitted to retain up to 5 per cent of any year group at any stage. Although the number of over-age students is not identical to the number who have repeated a year, it is a good approximation. At all levels it is very close to what would be predicted if every school retained the permitted numbers. Although intended for slower learners, the policy is widely practiced by schools, including those which attract high achievers. Relatively low achievement in such a school often leads to a request to be permitted to repeat the year, so it is not necessarily a source of resentment.

One side effect of repetition of years is that many of those who do not progress to form 4 leave before entering form 3. Statistics for enrollment show that over 10 per cent of a year-group entering form 1 do not enter form 3 two years later. Having been held back at least once, they reach 15, the age at which they are permitted to leave, while in form 2 or even earlier. Although the pull-through from form 3 to form 4 is around 90 per cent the actual proportion of a year-group remaining to form 4 is rather smaller at around 80 per cent.

The permitted establishment in secondary schools is 70 per cent graduate and 30 per cent non-graduate teachers. The non-graduate teachers are expected to teach primarily at junior secondary level, that is, forms 1–3, and also to take subjects such as physical education at all levels. Graduate teachers are expected to obtain a postgraduate certificate in education from a university but can be recruited directly. Without a professional qualification, promotion is restricted.

Transitions

Entry to primary 1 is based on an allocation scheme mainly taking into account locality and parental preference. As schools at all levels of the system vary widely in popularity some are chosen much more frequently than others. Such schools may operate an unofficial screening policy based very much on the candidate's proficiency at language and mathematics. This is one reason why kindergartens promote conventional learning and why parents demand it of them.

Entry to secondary schools is managed through a Secondary Schools Places Allocation Scheme. Pupils take three internally set and marked tests, one in P5 and two in P6 covering all the subjects in table 6.1 except physical education. The weightings given to subjects are the same as the recommended number of periods per week except that mathematics is given a weighting of 9. All pupils also take an academic aptitude test and scores on this test are used to scale the internal test scores for an entire school. The scaling procedure preserves the rank order of students within a school but modifies both the mean score for the school and the spread, or dispersion, of the scores. On the basis of their individual scaled scores, all pupils in a district are divided into five roughly equal bands. Starting from the top, pupils within bands are assigned to schools according to their stated preferences. Superimposed on this is a nominated schools system in which some secondary schools are permitted to reserve up to 25 per cent of their places for pupils from one or more nominated primary schools. To a large extent the result of the allocation exercise is that popular schools attract the highest achievers and, through this, retain their reputations. Prevocational and private schools are usually the least popular.

The transition from S3 to S4 at the end of compulsory schooling is managed through a Junior Secondary Education Assessment System. Like the previous scheme, this is based on scores on internally set and marked tests adjusted by a scaling procedure, and on stated preferences. About 70 per cent of pupils going on to S4 remain in the same school. Most schools operate three blocks of subjects at S4, designated science, social science or arts, and commercial subjects. In general this is the sequence in which boys rank their preferences while girls are more likely to reverse the first two. Science tends to recruit the highest achieving boys, social science the highest achieving girls and the rest gravitate to commercial subjects. The wide difference between schools in overall levels of achievement at entry means that a pupil unable to gain entry to science subjects at one school may have a much higher level of achievement than one accepted into the science group in another school.

Entry to form 6 is based on the results of the Hong Kong Certificate of Education Examination and on stated preference. Entry to tertiary education occurs at the end of S6 for the Chinese University of Hong Kong but at the end of S7 for the other universities, polytechnics and colleges which award degrees. It is planned that the system should be standardized to the more widespread method in the near future.

Decision Making in Hong Kong

An outline of the decision-making process in Hong Kong is shown as figure 6.2. Two of the advisory bodies have only indirect links with decisions affecting

Figure 6.2   Decision making related to education in Hong Kong

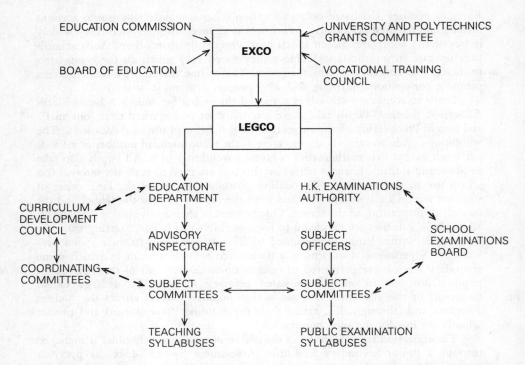

schools and so will not be mentioned again: the University and Polytechnics
Grants Committee whose members are appointed by the Governor to advise on
the development of higher education; the Vocational Training Council, with a
combination of official and appointed members, which advises on technical
education and industrial training.

Educational policy is formulated by an Executive Council (EXCO) consisting of the Governor, senior civil servants and invited persons of high standing.
Technically, responsibility lies with the Governor. Policy initiatives are debated
and modified by a Legislative Council (LEGCO), most of whom are appointed
by the Governor, with a minority elected through functional constituencies.
EXCO is advised by two bodies. The Education Commission has been established to investigate in depth areas where policy initiatives are required, and
to publish reports giving policy recommendations for public comment. Its
non-official members are appointed by the Governor. The Board of Education
similarly includes invited members of educational and other institutions.

The Education Department (ED) is headed by a Director, who is a senior
civil servant. The Director is advised by a Curriculum Development Council
(CDC) whose thirty-six non-official members are appointed by the Director.
The hierarchy of committees reporting to the CDC is shown in figure 6.2.
Coordinating committees monitor the overall curriculum for kindergarten, primary, secondary, sixth form, technical and special education, and the provision of
textbooks. Subject committees are responsible for developing teaching syllabuses

and, where appropriate, liaising with the corresponding Hong Kong Examinations Authority (HKEA) committees.

Because the flow of information is controlled by officials, figure 6.2 shows a relatively peripheral role for the Council and the coordinating committees. Formally, policy documents written by ED officials and recommended syllabuses and guidelines are promulgated under the title of the CDC. In practical terms, the appointed members of the Council have very little formative influence on their contents.

Curriculum Development

Curriculum development in Hong Kong has followed a typical British territory line. To a very large extent the output of the CDC has derived very directly and visibly from UK models. The major exceptions have been in areas unique to HK, where misgivings expressed by members of LEGCO have been translated into ED initiatives in the areas of civic education (1985) and sex education (1986), and in Chinese language and Chinese history. In the case of the Chinese subjects no viable UK model exists while it would have been politically unacceptable to borrow explicitly from either the People's Republic of China or from Taiwan.

The CDC produces recommended teaching syllabuses for all subjects at all school levels. Through its Textbook Coordinating Committee it provides lists of acceptable textbooks. Not surprisingly, these faithfully follow each recommended syllabus in scope, sequence and approach. Local authors and publishers are free to write and put on sale whatever they wish, within the normal restrictions on publishing, but they are well aware that failure of a title to appear on the recommended list is the kiss of death for profitability, so they adjust their sights accordingly. The requirement to use 'acceptable' materials was spelt out in Regulation 92 of the Education Regulations, 1971, governing schools, which stated *inter alia* that:

92 (1) No instruction may be given by any school except in accordance with a syllabus approved by the Director.

   (6) No person shall use any document for instruction in a class in any school unless particulars of the title, author and publisher of the document and such other particulars of the document as the Director may require have been furnished to the Director not less than 14 days previously.

A 'document', according to the Education Ordinance:

... includes any account, counterfoil, textbook, exercise book, pamphlet, publication, poster, drawing, sketch, film, filmstrip, slide, gramophone record, and other printed, written or recorded matter, whether relating to school management, teaching or recreation or to any other activity of, or in connection with, a school.

Also placing restrictions of a more specific kind was Regulation 98 which includes

98 (1) No instruction, education, entertainment, recreation or pro-
         paganda or activity of any kind which, in the opinion of the
         Director, is in any way of a political or partly political nature and
         prejudicial to the public interest or the welfare of the pupils or of
         education generally or contrary to the approved syllabus, shall be
         permitted upon any school premises or upon the occasion of any
         school activity.

In May 1990 it was announced that these restrictions would be lifted and it
remains to be seen how this will affect perceptions of freedom on schools.

In describing its own role in the nature and process of curriculum an official
CDC document states (1987a):

> Schools in HK have almost unlimited freedom in the choice of subjects
> comprising their curricula, of syllabuses for the individual subjects and
> of textbooks and resource materials to support the syllabuses. . . . Pro-
> vided a syllabus is educationally sound, balanced in its content and
> approach and suited to the needs of the pupils with whom it will be
> used, approval is normally given. . . . Provided the books are well pro-
> duced and are not objectionable in any way, the schools are free to use
> them in preference to those on the lists. (p. 3)

No data are provided to indicate the frequency with which requests are received
and permission granted. Later in the document it is:

> admitted that . . . a system of 'guided participation' has developed . . .
> with the ED acting as a catalyst for change. (p. 7)

While acknowledging that it is a widely held view, it denies that:

> heavy government involvement in schools is responsible for the con-
> servative nature of HK schools and that curriculum innovations are
> initiated, conducted and led by the ED — 'It is always the ED steering
> the course and manning the helm'. (p. 7)

It may be that schools have been aware of their freedom but have chosen not to
exercise it or it may be that they have been more impressed by the wording of
the Regulations than by assurances that the powers would be used positively.
Either way, the flavour of many classrooms is well captured by a local teacher
who writes (Tsui, 1988):

> Although students do not finish the recommended work for one year
> they are moved on to the next year's material as though it had not only
> been completed but mastered. Students need to be liberated from the
> tyranny of textbooks which cater to a purely theoretical continuity
> [embodied in the recommended syllabus] rather than to their actual
> needs. . . . What binds us is not the ED but our own submissive mental-
> ity that deifies whatever comes from above, a Chinese cultural trait.
> (p. 29)

Given that, in practice, the vast majority of schools adopt the recommended syllabuses and their associated textbooks, curriculum development is assimilated to modification and adaptation of existing syllabuses and to the introduction of official syllabuses for new subjects. As the CDC (1987a) describes it:

> New subjects or major revisions of existing subjects are now generally introduced into the curriculum by means of pilot schemes conducted by the Advisory Inspectorate on behalf of the CDC. (p. 4)

Revisions of existing syllabuses are the responsibility of the Subject Committees. These include teachers and members of tertiary institutions as well as officials, and proposals are circulated to schools for comment. However, non-official members are appointed as individuals, not as representatives of their institutions or associations, work with materials which are routinely marked 'restricted', and have no control over the flow of information to and from the committee. As the officials are bureaucrats with a vested interest in continuity and absence of controversy, radically new or different ideas put forward by committee members or as comment on proposals are likely to be sidestepped, eliminated, or diluted.

The limitations of these arrangements are acknowledged as follows:

> ... there is now a need to consider whether the general strategy for curriculum development, the present organization of the CDC and the resources available to support curriculum development adequately serve current and perceived future demands.... With the general improvement of standards in schools, the upgrading of teacher training and the steady development of professionalism among teachers, consideration should now be given to the greater encouragement of school-based curriculum development in order that schools will have the means to cater for their specific needs. It is also important that more teachers should be drawn into the process of planning, implementation and evaluation of the curriculum within their own schools rather than, as at present, merely serving as members of CDC committees, valuable though their contribution has been.... A change of direction appears to be worth consideration. (p. 7)

However, the commitment to devolution may be judged in the light of current proposed procedures (CDC, 1990) for completely new examination syllabuses, which are as follows:

1 A proposal is received by CDC, from whatever source.
2 CDC officials conduct a survey in schools and other relevant institutions to establish need and to estimate likely uptake.
3 A small group of officials, drawn from CDC and HKEA, forms a provisional Joint Nuclear Subject Committee (JNSC) to draw up aims, objectives and a rough outline syllabus.
4 Following approval by the HKEA Board and the CD Council (which may or may not include any subject specialists) an official JNSC is formed to produce a draft syllabus, setting out the content only.

5 Following approval by the HKEA Board and the relevant CDC Coordinating Committee, the draft syllabus is sent to schools and relevant institutions for comment.
6 The draft is revised by JNSC if thought necessary in the light of comments received.
7 HKEA and CDC Subject Committees are formed, one to add examination rubrics, the other to devise a teaching syllabus for the content.
8 Following further approval as in step 5, both syllabuses are published.

As can be seen, the development of the syllabus will be at an advanced stage before the subject committees are formed so members will face an uphill struggle to make substantial modifications while root-and-branch surgery will be virtually impossible. The possibility of cooperating with a wider body of teachers through, for example, subject associations has not been simply overlooked: many offers have been made in the past but have been explicitly rejected. Once again, an opportunity to broaden the input to syllabus development has been missed, giving the quoted statement of commitment to wider participation a hollow ring.

Further evidence of inward-looking mentality is provided by a report on language teaching (Hong Kong Government, 1989) commissioned by the ED in which proposed solutions to the problems facing Hong Kong schools are almost exclusively located within the ED and its constituent Institute for Language in Education. The notion that other agencies might have something to offer has barely received 'lip-service'.

It should be apparent that contradictory impressions exist concerning the role of government, as put into practice through the ED. As was noted in the Llewellyn Report (1982):

> Education has not fared badly [financially], in relative terms, ... but expansion and increased policy commitment do not seem to have created what might be called a 'joint enterprise' spirit in the education community. Rather, there is a 'we-they' attitude prevalent in the educational enterprise ... There is a pervasive feeling that responsibility for, and knowledge about, what is happening lies elsewhere; but no-one is sure where this is, or who holds the master plan. There is, in short, a noticeable lack of mutual trust and understanding.... The education system seems over-administered in terms of minute bureaucratic surveillance of regulations yet under-planned in terms of strategic goals and the know-how to attain them. (pp. 15, 16)

In fact, government influence is weak in areas where it might well be strong and strong where it might well be weak. It might well be stronger in the areas of language of instruction and the choice of subjects offered by a school. It is left entirely to principals of schools to decide upon the language of instruction to be used and upon the range of subjects to be offered. Parental choice is overwhelmingly for schools claiming to teach through the medium of English and offering an academically oriented set of subjects. Principals of schools have no official protection from this pressure and so bow to it even when it is patently obvious that it is not in the best interests of pupils. However, once a subject has been chosen, the pressure to follow the recommended syllabus, acting through the recommended textbooks, in-service courses, advice, and the absence of more than one examination target in any given subject, is intense.

It bears emphasis that 'following the recommended syllabus' cannot be taken to mean more than covering the topics listed in the syllabus in the given sequence and at more or less the recommended speed. It does not necessarily mean that teachers adopt the recommended strategy for teaching the material nor that they attempt to address the broader aims which accompany syllabuses.

In this respect, the initial experience of most teachers is not helpful. A study of the induction of 129 teachers at secondary level (Cooke *et al.*, 1990) shows that the overwhelming majority received no official course nor advisory visits and very little help within school other than through general orientation. Most did not receive their timetables until about two weeks before teaching commenced, most were given a full workload with no concessions for their inexperience: few were observed teaching or given advice based on their performance. It would be hardly surprising if they relied heavily on the official syllabus and adopted highly didactic teaching methods.

Although the pressure to adopt the content of a recommended syllabus is strong, the pressure to implement its strategy and aims is weak and the support which teachers might need to achieve successful implementation is generally not available. Advisory inspectors have too great a load to be able to offer meaningful and sustained advice to individual teachers, official in-service courses usually either focus on minor changes to syllabuses and their assessment or on verbal explanation of the rationale, and access to resources to enrich teaching is limited.

The lack of influence on choice of subjects gives rise to two negative trends. When the CDC responds to a perceived need for courses of a less academic orientation or which cover a gap in the experience of pupils by introducing a new subject or syllabus, there is no requirement on schools to adopt it. Although a very wide range of syllabuses is available at senior secondary level, many of them have very low rates of adoption. The other trend, exemplified recently by a proposed new course in environmental studies, could be termed 'upward drift'. What is originally envisaged as a course for lower academic achievers or as non-examinable becomes re-defined as academic and examinable so that it will appear more attractive.

The problem is acknowledged in another (and much less self-congratulatory) CDC document (1988) in which curricular provision is analyzed in terms of Areas of Experience (DES, 1985):

> The relative weighting to be allocated to each area of learning and experience in terms of its component subjects is usually decided by schools themselves and normally schools do make an effort to offer their students a balanced curriculum at the senior secondary level. However, it is noted that in recent years, some schools tend to specialize at too early a stage disregarding the fact that the students at this level should maintain contact with all the elements of learning and experience while exercising some choices of subjects. The problem of designing a curriculum which caters for a wider ability range has to be tackled in the coming years. Though certain attempts have been made in the past.... further thought still needs to be given to this aspect of curriculum development. (p. 10)

The early specialization which is deplored is one of the few prevalent examples of schools visibly failing to follow ED recommendations. Rather than following three years of general courses in science and social studies followed by two-year examination syllabuses, many extend the examination syllabuses downwards, reversing the pattern. This is an adaptation to examination pressure as schools attempt to prepare a range of pupils wider than those for whom the examinations were designed.

Examinations and Examination Pressure

As was pointed out in chapter 3, assessment can be used for a variety of purposes, one of which is selection. In what follows, assessment used for selection to different courses, institutions or levels of schooling will be termed examination.

In Hong Kong there are both public examinations and school-based examinations. Public examinations are administered by the HKEA, described above, and generally take the familiar form of unseen papers taken by all candidates simultaneously. Papers are set by professionals, supported by officials, on the basis of published examination syllabuses and are marked by panels of subject teachers. Internal examinations are set and marked by teachers in a school. Where they are used for purposes wider than those of individual schools they are subject to a scaling procedure as described under *Transitions*.

A pupil proceeding through schooling in Hong Kong from kindergarten to S7 must face many examination hurdles. Although it is officially discouraged, they may undergo tests and interviews to gain access to favoured kindergartens and again for access to favoured primary schools. At P5 and P6 they take internally set and marked examinations together with an academic aptitude test whose combined results determine access to secondary schools. A further internal examination at S3 determines access to senior secondary schooling. Public examinations follow at the end of S5 and S7. In addition, yearly internal examinations precede promotion or retention while, in schools which practice streaming, they also determine the stream into which each pupil is channeled.

It is possible that internally set and marked examinations administered within the normal school setting are less temporarily stressful than public examinations and it can be argued that they have greater potential for curricular validity, given that those who set the papers are in a position to know the actual experience of their pupils. However, it is not at all clear that they reduce examination pressure on pupils nor on teachers as this is more dependent on the consequences of success or failure than on the mechanics of the testing procedure.

If all primary and secondary schools in Hong Kong were roughly equivalent in terms of facilities and resources it would not matter unduly which one a pupil attended. It is only where wide discrepancies exist, or are perceived to exist, that access to the school of choice becomes a matter of acute concern. To this can be added the effect of the severe constriction in the flow of pupils (figure 6.1) from 100 per cent in S1 and 80 per cent in S4 to 22 per cent in S6 and 15 per cent in S7 which, by itself, would be likely to promote a sense of urgency in pupils and teachers. The pressure to be in the best school at all times is high, as the consequences of failure are serious. Expectations of salary and conditions of employment rise markedly with the educational level attained by pupils in Hong Kong so their aspirations have a sound economic basis.

It is possible to view voluntary extension of schooling in different ways, which lie along a spectrum. At one end is the view that pupils remain in school because they aspire to higher education. The public examination is the barrier to be surmounted so it is the duty of the schools to prepare their pupils for this ordeal regardless of their probability of success. Provided that a school provides a suitable range of subjects and presents them in accordance with recommended methods, no blame attaches to it for the failure of individual students. Limited facilities mean that schools must manage access to specific groups of subjects but this can be accepted on pragmatic grounds.

At the other end of the spectrum is the view that pupils remain at school because they are not yet mature enough, nor knowledgeable enough, to go out to work at any but the most unrewarding tasks. The duty of the school in this case is to diagnose their current needs and to offer them a curriculum within which they can find a range of useful and achievable learning tasks. Access to experiences must be managed actively by the school and teachers must make their own decisions in the light of their knowledge rather than presenting centrally devised syllabuses.

It appears to be the case that parents in Hong Kong fall closer to the first than to the second end of the spectrum, valuing conventional book-learning and the conventional examination success to which it is directed, to the virtual exclusion of all else. They appear to attribute differences in achievement more readily to differences in attitude than to differences in aptitude.

Principals of schools and teachers are drawn towards the first end, whether or not this fits well with their professional judgment, because they know that their school's reputation and, hence, its ability to recruit high-band pupils, is more intimately associated with its examination results than with other measures of success such as helping less academically oriented students to achieve their potential. If a school were not to prepare its lower achieving pupils for public examinations in subjects needed for entry to higher stages, this would be interpreted as condemnation without a trial. The need to prepare students stretches well back from the examination years, distorting earlier schooling.

Where schools practice streaming it is quite common to find that all streams progress in parallel through the same material, using the same textbooks, the only concession to differences between streams lying in the range of exercises to be carried out and in the omission of some 'difficult' topics by the teachers of lower streams.

Limited access to higher education itself affects the nature of the examination syllabuses. If an examination is to discriminate accurately between high achievers it must be relatively difficult. In an easy test high achievers would all do very well and have more or less the same score. For an examination to be difficult and yet to have curricular validity means that the associated syllabus must be demanding.

These factors combine to put both teachers and pupils under examination pressure. As the Llewellyn Report (1982) expressed it:

Student motivation and application verges on the fanatical, by Western standards. (p. 56)

The Language of Instruction

It is not possible to do justice to this issue in a few sentences. It is a problem of popular perception rather than of educational rationale and has a strong economic basis. Ability to use English is seen as valuable for entry to higher education, for emigration and for access to better paid jobs. Attempts to set up a Chinese medium alternative route through school and university have foundered on the unwillingness of local parents to send their children to such schools. From this three negative results flow: teachers in nominally English medium schools adapt to their students' inability to cope with the demands of learning in a second language by providing basic statements in English with discussion and elaboration in Cantonese; the Chinese University of Hong Kong is forced to recruit most of its undergraduates from the Anglo-Chinese schools; the limited demand for Chinese language secondary school texts does not stimulate provision of up-to-date and attractive books.

As the Chinese medium system was set up on a 5:1:4 year basis, while the English medium system follows the UK with 5:2:3 years, recruitment to CUHK from English medium schools takes place in the middle of the two-year matriculation programme, causing resentment within the schools and perceptions of 'poaching' in those institutions which recruit one year later. (The fact that much larger numbers of the more academically successful students leave at the same stage to go abroad is seldom mentioned.)

The effect on student learning of mixed mode teaching is not self-evidently bad, although this is commonly claimed to be the case. As yet, no unequivocal evidence is available either way. It may be that there is an interaction between the effects of existing achievement, motivation and mode of instruction such that some groups gain advantage while others are at a disadvantage. However, the existing disparity, in many schools, between what is claimed — English medium instruction — and what is delivered points to an urgent need for reform and rationalization.

As pointed out above, the HK government, through the ED, has been unwilling to dictate language policy to schools, and its most recent report proposes to advise, but not to require, schools to place students unequivocally in one medium or the other. The existing freedom of schools to switch officially to Chinese has not been exercised very often due to the undeniable fact that such a decision leads to a reduction in the popularity of the school, which, in turn, is reflected in the academic achievement or 'band level' of those applying to enter it. It would be unrealistic to suppose that the new advice would make much difference unless it were accompanied by meaningful incentives.

The reality of this pressure on schools was illustrated most poignantly in June 1990. One outspoken principal of a highly reputable school, who is also a member of the Legislative Council, had changed the medium of instruction in his school from English to Chinese in a blaze of publicity intended to encourage others to follow suit. In view of the decline in popularity which followed, the school staff voted to return to the previous system and the principal found himself with no alternative but to resign.

An Example of Curriculum Development

Some of the strengths and weaknesses of curriculum development in Hong Kong can be illustrated through the history of development of the Junior Secondary Science syllabus. This will be described under three headings. *Initiation* refers to the way in which the idea arose and was accepted: *development* refers to the process leading to adoption of the syllabus: *evaluation* refers to any process whereby information was obtained relating to the decision to publish the recommended syllabus or to its actual implementation in schools.

Initiation

In 1970, schools offered science at the first three forms of secondary school either as an amalgamated general science course or as three separate sciences. As many students changed schools between form 3 and form 4, this led to problems of articulation. At the same time countries worldwide were following the lead of the USA and UK and reconsidering secondary school science. The Director of Education decided to invite a visiting expert from the UK in 1971 and 1972 to survey the situation and to provide advice. The advice received was to develop a local version of the Scottish Integrated Science programme. (For this reason the syllabus is widely called 'integrated science' although the term does not appear in its official title.)

The Scottish programme had two central features requiring changes in typical Hong Kong teacher behaviour: the integrated material was to be taught by individual teachers rather than being broken up into segments to be taught by subject specialists; and the students were to learn through a process of guided discovery. Local adaptation initially was envisaged as redistribution of the two-year course over three years, with the addition of some new topics. A CDC inspector was sent to Scotland for a year to experience the programme in its original context.

Development

It was decided, by CDC, to mount a three-year pilot scheme, beginning in 1973 at form 1 level, and adding forms 2 and 3 in successive years. Twenty schools were invited to participate, while a further six volunteered and were accepted. The invited schools were supplied with apparatus and materials, and a three-week intensive course was mounted in July, 1973, designed and run by four experts from UK and attended by fifty-three individuals. These included lecturers from the colleges of education and subject officers from the ED, participating schools being represented by one or two teachers each.

In the first trial the original worksheets from Scotland were used but, as feedback rapidly indicated problems with the level of language and with the local availability of specified materials, a rewriting team was established. A further team was added to translate the materials into Chinese.

Two reports were published (ED, 1974, 1975) covering the first and second years of the trials. Before the end of the third year of the 'pilot scheme' it was decided to publish the syllabus and to recommend it to all schools, after which adoption increased until, in 1979, it was reported as having reached 93 per cent of schools. During this period, to 1979, in-service courses were provided for teachers and for laboratory technicians from time to time. These consisted of briefings about the aims and objectives of the programme and workshops in which some of the recommended student activities were carried out. However they lacked three characteristics of in-service courses which are widely agreed as being necessary to effectiveness; modelling by experienced teachers, practice at delivery, sustained on-site coaching. In 1979 it was decided that in-service courses were no longer needed and they were discontinued.

Evaluation

Evaluation of the first year form 1 trial was carried out by the science subjects section of the Advisory Inspectorate, in other words, those responsible for the innovation. Following agreements reached at the initial in-service stage, information was gathered in three ways: direct observation of lessons and conversations with teachers during school visits; by questionnaire to participating teacher; and by multiple choice 'progress tests'.

In the report (ED, 1974) no information is provided about the number or distribution of visits. A recommendation that, in future, visits should include two lessons per month per school together with a whole-day visit to each school, suggests that the initial schedule was less than this. No observation schedule or other means for gathering consistent data is reported. Difficulties mentioned by teachers are reported, with frequencies given for schools. All schools included 'inadequate laboratory facilities'.

The questionnaire asked for a variety of information and opinion and the most salient findings were that teachers:

(i) overwhelmingly agreed with a statement that 'a stage-managed discovery approach with 40+ students is impossible';
(ii) overwhelmingly agreed that supplementary material was needed in addition to the worksheets;
(iii) mainly agreed that they had difficulty maintaining discipline during practical sessions.

In a separate item, teachers were asked to assess their own behaviour by placing a tick against one of a set of statements. About two-thirds chose the vaguely worded 'some discussion and some questioning by the teacher'. Confirmation by systematic observation would have been helpful.

Multiple choice tests were administered in December, March and June to cover only the sections taught in the intervening period. That is, there was no summative test for the year. Results are reported for only nineteen schools as others did not return all results or 'do not follow the curriculum closely'. The forty-item tests were designed on a specification grid with recall, comprehension, application, higher abilities on one dimension and knowledge of the empirical world, ability to observe objectively, ability to solve problems and to think scientifically, vocabulary and grammar of science, on the other. Items were submitted by teachers and supplemented by inspectors where cells in the grid were not filled. Items reclassified in the same way by 60 per cent of the teachers were taken to be valid. Neither item analyses nor estimates of reliability are provided. The tests are within-group only and are not mutually comparable because of non-overlapping content, so no conclusions can be drawn about the success of the course in comparison to any other.

In the second year evaluation was by multiple choice tests only (ED, 1975) and no report has been written of any further classroom observation nor of any attempt to obtain opinion systematically from teachers and students. For purposes of analysis of results, a 10 per cent sample was formed at form 1 by taking every tenth name from class lists while at form 2 a 10 per cent sample was formed by choosing two schools. Mean scores overall and in three of the categories listed as the second dimension of the specification grid (not enough items could be devised for 'vocabulary and grammar of science') were around 60 per cent and this was taken to indicate the success of the programme. A minor curiosity is that the mean score for items classified as application was higher than that for recall and that this was interpreted as indicating that the programme moved students away from rote memorization. As the categories were explicitly derived from Bloom's taxonomy (see chapter 3) this is a quite odd conclusion.

No evaluation of the third year of the programme has been reported. The facts that teachers, in the first year of trials, found their laboratories to be inadequate and that they believed the central methodological feature of the innovation to be impossible to practice counted for little against the ability of pupils to obtain mean scores around 60 per cent on home-made multiple choice tests.

The only evaluation to have been carried out which addresses the question of classroom processes is a small-scale study by Hung (1988). Classrooms were observed using the Science Teaching Observation Schedule (Eggleston *et al.*, 1975) and interviews were conducted with teachers and with students. The picture which emerges is of highly didactic instruction interspersed with laboratory activities carried out as confirmatory demonstrations rather than as investigations. Insofar as this is representative of schools using the syllabus the content has been adopted but the associated processes have not been implemented. In addition to this, as pointed out earlier, many schools do not continue the integrated programme into the third year but channel science teaching into three separate subjects.

The introduction of the Junior Secondary Science syllabus does not represent an isolated and unrepresentative case. Very similar characteristics have been reported for other syllabuses: geography (Speak, 1988); social studies (Wong, 1985); economics (Morris, 1983). If anything the development of the science syllabus comes across as the most thorough job. The common pattern is of top-down decision making, imitation of overseas developments, tight focusing on syllabus development, and confirmatory or pseudo-evaluation (Madaus *et al.*, 1983), with adoption rather than implementation as the target.

School-Based Curriculum Development (SBCD)

Another perspective on curriculum development in Hong Kong can be obtained from the recent initiatives in the area of SBCD. As quoted above, the CDC, in 1988, viewed the introduction of SBCD in Hong Kong as timely and, in 1989, a project scheme was introduced with the stated intention of encouraging schools to take more responsibility for their curriculum. At first sight this would seem to be an exciting new initiative, 'breaking the mould' and introducing the thin end of a wedge between syllabus development and curriculum development. (This distinction is not clear in Chinese as both terms are usually translated to the same four characters.) The degree to which this is true can be judged, again, by considering initiation, development and evaluation of the scheme.

Initiation

Ideas about SBCD have a long history but they have achieved prominence in the educational literature relatively recently. No doubt this trend would have influenced official thinking in Hong Kong even if it had not been reinforced by comments in the Llewellyn Report (1982) that 'every effort must be made to encourage innovation at the school level which, after all, is where the real work is being done'. In line with common practice, a high CDC official was sent to UK for a year to develop expertise, setting in train a process in which it becomes increasingly difficult to avoid affirmative action. Reputations are put at stake. By 1987 a Project Scheme had been devised which, it was claimed (CDC, 1987a):

> ... would enable talented teachers with a flair for curriculum development to become fully involved in the curriculum process, making SBCD possible on a formal basis ... More importantly, it would help in the long term to raise the professional standards of teachers generally. (p. 14)

The existing system is described in the same document as follows:

> ... the ED encourages schools to adapt the CDC syllabuses rather than to implement them in an unmodified state since no document can provide all the material required or anticipate all the learning experiences necessary to cater for the wide range of ability now existing in the school system.... In order to assist schools to achieve the desired flexibility of approach, the ED offers many curriculum-related activities which are designed to help teachers interpret syllabuses according to the needs of their students.... the syllabuses, curriculum material and support services ... are intended to provide the raw material for the teaching of a subject, but how that raw material is shaped is entirely at the discretion of the individual schools. (p. 3)

It bears emphasis, in view of what follows, that this quotation sets out activities and tasks which teachers may be expected to perform as part of their normal professional duties. To carry them out a teacher would have to gather and select resources appropriate to the intended modification or adaptation of the syllabus.

As the description of the project scheme was elaborated (CDC, 1987b) a more limited interpretation emerged, both in terms of scope:

> ... appropriate modification and adaptation to the centrally devised curriculum to meet the different needs in schools is considered necessary.... It is considered appropriate for the projects to aim primarily at new approaches to teaching the syllabuses or guidelines on different aspects of education recommended by the CDC.

and in terms of control:

> [Advisory inspectorate] posts would be required for the supervision of the school-based projects. It is envisaged that project advisors would undertake this work at each school level, assuming responsibility for initiating and planning projects, establishing criteria for the selection and award of grants and monitoring progress. (p. 13)

In the first proposed budget about 75 per cent of the cost of the scheme was devoted to salaries for these new inspectors. This was not approved, with the result that the role of the advisory inspectorate was less intrusive at the planning stage, except at kindergarten level.

Most damaging to the notion of devolution of responsibility to schools was a decision to pay teachers for their time. To enable payments to be made within the regulations, it was necessary to stipulate that teachers should sign an undertaking to the effect that all work on a project would be performed outside their normal hours and would not interfere with their normal duties, a quite astonishing contradiction of a central tenet of SBCD. This should have signalled clearly that the sorts of curriculum development to be undertaken in projects were different from teachers' normal duties. However, in view of the marked similarity between what they were expected to do as a matter of course and what they were being paid to do as project work teachers could be forgiven for beginning to view enrichment of the curriculum as something requiring extra payment.

Another paper (CDC, 1987c) set out the general principles for the award:

> As the scheme is ... to encourage the development of school-based curricula, it may, in general, include projects
> (a) on new teaching approaches to specific topics in the CDC syllabuses or guidelines;
> (b) on new topics or areas of studies as alternatives to certain aspects of the CDC syllabuses or guidelines;
> (c) on teaching/resource materials aiming to meet the specific needs of a target group of pupils in areas within the framework of the curriculum recommended by the CDC.
> The projects may lead to the production of simple teaching materials such as a set of worksheets for a specific teaching topic for a particular level or multi-media teaching packages which normally include a teachers' guide, teaching materials or suggestions for learning

activities and a number of audio-visual aids such as slides, cassette tapes, overhead transparencies etc.

Development

In 1988 details of the scheme were circulated to all schools and meetings were held to explain the rationale and operation to principals. Two committees were established to receive proposals and to select those to support. An Executive Committee consisting only of officials evaluates the proposals and advises an Advisory Committee which contains two of the same officials and a number of lay members. In the first year of operation, this Advisory Committee began with a Chairman and five others drawn from the Main Committee of the CDC. It proceeded to coopt four further officials representing the sixth form, secondary, primary and kindergarten levels. The influence of officials on decisions is therefore exceedingly high.

In the first year of operation, 1988/89, forty-nine applications were received and thirty-five were accepted at kindergarten (two), primary (seven), secondary (nineteen) and special school (seven) levels. One involved resource sharing between twenty-four schools and the Institute of Language in Education, a constituent of the ED, one involved teachers from two schools, while thirty-three were located in individual schools. In two schools two projects were supported. From the Directory published by the ED (1990) it can be seen that the projects followed the guidelines for an award, quoted above, very closely. Although it is sometimes difficult to determine how resources were developed, many projects appear to have involved the gathering and selection rather than the creation of materials. The most popular areas were related to art, environmental issues and computer applications. Only two projects involved teachers from more than one subject area and only one makes any reference to catering for students of different abilities.

In the second round, seventy-seven applications were received, of which sixty were successful. From the list of titles it appears that they were quite similar to those supported in the first round.

Support for project designers has taken the form of an orientation programme and visits to schools by inspectors. The orientation programme for the first year group consisted of briefing on the concept of SBCD, the teachers' role, and the technicalities of the scheme, together with discussions with subject inspectors. Two rounds of visits were made, one by inspectors from the Curriculum Development Section and one by subject inspectors.

A display of completed projects was held in November 1989 and it is intended that resources considered to be particularly useful and generalizable should be reproduced and made available to schools free of charge.

Evaluation

Information on the projects was gathered in three ways: through the reports of inspectors following their visits; through a standardized interim progress report filled in by project designers in March followed by a final report in June, through inspection of the final products.

Other than asking for written comments from the designers no attempt has been made nor suggested to check out the effectiveness of the resources in terms of student learning nor to sample student opinions. If resources are used by other schools, no suggestion has been put forward to monitor their transferability. There appears to be an assumption that, if they look good, they are good.

A small-scale study has been carried out (Lo, 1990) involving nineteen of the projects in the first round. Insofar as this is a representative sample it suggests that, at kindergarten and primary levels, the initiators were superiors, whether inspectors or principals, while at secondary level the projects took over work which was already in progress or represented the personal enthusiasms of the designers. The resources developed or used were almost exclusively gathered rather than created or were available commercially. Visits by inspectors, as reported, focused more on how to organize the final display of the project than on issues of design and implementation.

Concluding Comments

When Northern Ireland had a limited form of self-government within the UK its legislation followed that of the parent government in what was called a 'step by step' policy: only on a few local issues was there any real divergence. One of its critics described it as 'a body of people who, individually, can do nothing and, collectively, can decide that nothing can be done'. It is tempting, but it would be uncharitable, to draw an analogy with the CDC. It would be even less charitable to interpret the School-Based Curriculum Project Scheme as an attempt to embrace the rhetoric of SBCD without relinquishing any of the control over the curriculum which would be necessary for SBCD to flourish.

In fact, the government of Hong Kong has accomplished a great deal in a short period. The influx of people which helped to raise its population from little more than half a million in 1945 to nearly six million in 1990 has necessitated very extensive programmes of expansion in all sectors. Free primary education for all was reached in 1971 and this was extended to junior secondary schooling by 1979. The very large pull-through to senior secondary level means that schooling effectively was extended for five years rather than for three. To provide buildings, resources and teachers, with an adequate curriculum, was a massive undertaking. Given that teacher training could not keep pace with the expansion so that large numbers of untrained teachers had to be recruited, a centrally devised set of syllabuses and recommendations for their presentation made a great deal of sense.

One side effect of the rapid expansion has been that officials in the ED have been required to turn their attention to whatever has been the most pressing problem of the moment and to adopt a variety of roles. Members of the Advisory Inspectorate have been faced with a very heavy workload including visiting schools for purposes related both to quality control and advice about implementation of syllabuses, organizing and teaching in-service courses, servicing committees and engaging in curriculum development. Just as the expansion of schooling meant that many teachers had little or no training, so the expansion of the ED meant that many inspectors were in the same position with respect to the specific demands of their multiple tasks, for example the production of

127

guidelines on civic and sex education. Quite apart from the bureaucratic inertia which is a feature of government departments worldwide it is very understandable that such officials should be reluctant to initiate or to foster rapid or radical change to the curriculum and that they should seek to adopt models and materials from elsewhere.

In 1990 the problems associated with accommodation and with teacher training are within sight of solution. What remains, and is recognized as the pressing problem, is development of the curriculum to meet the educational needs of the entire range of the school population. Official statements suggest that such development will be devolved increasingly to schools and teachers and the removal of some of the more restrictive regulations should facilitate this process. At the same time within the Education Department, a proposed reorganization of the CDC should permit officials to concentrate more fully on specific tasks. Officials with a full or main commitment to curriculum development might well perceive the potential value of drawing experienced and innovative teachers into the process, more readily than those for whom curriculum development is a peripheral activity.

At present the widespread features of curriculum development in Hong Kong, as illustrated by the development of the Junior Secondary Science syllabus and the introduction of the School–Based Curriculum Projects Scheme, are that it is top–down and product oriented, sensitive to international trends and developments but still generally derivative from UK models, geared towards adoption of syllabuses and resources, takes implementation as unproblematic, and views systematic and independent evaluation of classroom behaviours and outcomes as superfluous.

Chapter 7

Curriculum Development in Singapore

Khoon Yoong Wong

Introduction

We have got where we are because we paid the price for excellence. It is up to you to decide whether you want to stay on track in pursuit of excellence, or to go for a more relaxed system, which means accepting lower standards of achievement and less rewards. (Lee Kuan Yew *Straits Times*, 28 February 1990)

Singapore has developed an efficient, albeit a highly competitive, educational system that demands a high standard of academic performance among its school children. The many changes to educational policies and curriculum have been justified in achieving the goal of preparing its limited human resources to strive economically in a technological and commercial environment. Many of these changes are perceived by the general public and educators as inevitable though somewhat disconcerting. An observer commented that Singapore 'has continually experimented with its educational system to such an extent that neither teachers nor students can keep track of educational policies from one year to the next ...' (Altbach, 1985, p. 25).

This chapter describes the Singapore education system and policies with particular attention to the nature and implementation of various curricula for the Singapore students. The curricula are under constant revision, and the process of curriculum revision will be illustrated with a case study involving the mathematics curriculum. Research findings about curriculum innovations are likely to be responded to differently by various stake-holders, for example, the teachers, the curriculum planners, and the politicians. Three recent research studies will provide examples of these differences.

About Singapore: Basic Information

Singapore is a small nation consisting of the main island of Singapore (area 570.4 sq km) and over fifty small islands and reefs (total area of 636 sq km). It is situated to the south of Peninsular Malaysia to which it is joined by a causeway.

The climate is equatorial with high daily average temperature (23°C to 30°C) and high humidity (over 70 per cent) throughout the year.

Singapore is a young republic celebrating its twenty-fifth anniversary of nation building in 1990. Its population of 2.65 million is made up of people of various ethnic groups: Chinese (76 per cent), Malays (15.1 per cent), Indians (6.5 per cent) and others (2.4 per cent) identified as Caucasians, Eurasians, Japanese and Arabs. People below 15 years of age (near the end of secondary schooling) form 23.1 per cent of the population. In the 1980s, the population increased at an average annual rate of 1.2 per cent, but this is expected to dip to 0.6 per cent in the 1990s.

The ethnic groups have provided a colourful variety of languages, religions, customs and festivals to the nation. At the same time, this variety has necessitated careful planning and implementation of various national policies (including educational ones) to ensure racial harmony while meeting the diverse needs of these ethnic groups. The constant challenge is to create a distinct identity of a Singapore nation.

The official languages are Malay, Chinese (Mandarin), Tamil, and English. English is the language of administration and the language of instruction at all educational levels. Malay is the national language, but most non-Malay students do not learn it in schools. The Chinese are encouraged through active campaigns to use Mandarin in place of various dialects such as Hokkien, Cantonese, and Teochew. These campaigns, though serving to make Mandarin a more common language among the Chinese, have nevertheless given rise to a sense of unease among the minority groups.

In 1988, the general literacy rate of the population aged 10 years and above was 87.2 per cent. This is a great improvement over a similar rate of 37.5 per cent in 1980. This achievement is attributed to the success of the bilingualism policy.

The major religions in Singapore are Buddhism, Taoism, Islam, Christianity, and Hinduism. Smaller religious groups also exist for the Sikhs, Jews, and Jains. The Constitution of the Republic guarantees freedom of worship to all. Many Chinese who call themselves Taoist or Buddhist actually practise a mixture of the three main Chinese beliefs: Confucianism, Taoism, and Buddhism. According to the 1980 census, 56 per cent of the population were Buddhists and Taoists, 16 per cent were Muslims, 10 per cent were Christians, and 4 per cent were Hindus. Recently certain religious groups have mounted active missionary campaigns that are perceived as threatening to the security and harmony of the nation. The Maintenance of Religious Harmony Bill is being debated in the Parliament with the aim of setting up an inter-religious body to regulate religious activities to ensure harmony in a secular state. The government has also abolished the study of religious knowledge as a compulsory subject in secondary schools from 1990, on the ground that students should not be segregated in school lessons on the basis of religion. These developments show very clearly the constant need to modify educational practices to take heed of sensitive issues arising within a multi-religious society.

Singapore comes from the word 'Singapura' which means Lion City. Early references to Singapore mentioned a settlement called Temasek ('Sea Lion') on the island. According to legend, Sri Tri Buana, a ruler of Palembang in the twelfth century, landed at Temasek one day while seeking shelter from a storm.

He saw an animal which he took to be a lion and called the place 'Singapura'. A small settlement was established and it was under the rule of various local chieftains for the next 400 years. In the early nineteenth century, it came under the rule of the Sultan of Johor.

In 1819, Sir Stamford Raffles signed a treaty with the Sultan of Johor to establish a trading station on the island. In 1826, it became, together with Penang and Malacca, a member of the Straits Settlements. Endowed with a deep, well sheltered harbour, it quickly became the entreport centre of the region. The thriving commercial activities attracted large numbers of immigrants from Malacca, Indonesia, India and China. Eventually the Chinese became the largest single ethnic group of the population.

In 1946, Singapore became a Crown Colony separated from the Federation of Malaya. Throughout the 1950s, there were strikes and riots instigated by the Communists and left-wing political groups. In 1959, it became a self-governing state with Lee Kuan Yew as the first Prime Minister. In 1963, Singapore was merged with Malaya, Sarawak and Sabah to become Malaysia. However for the next two years, inter-communal and Kuala Lumpur-Singapore acrimony became very intense and in 1965 Singapore was separated from Malaysia to become an independent nation.

In 1967 when Britain decided to withdraw its forces from Singapore, the government decided to implement National Service for all Singapore males as an important solution to build up a credible defence force with minimal costs. All males reaching the age of 18 are required to undertake full-time national service which lasts two or two-and-a-half years, depending on rank. The military training ensures that the national servicemen are tough, well trained and motivated to defend the nation. Teachers play an important role in getting across to their pupils the message that total defence of Singapore is the responsibility of every citizen. Learning about total defence (military, psychological, civil, economic and social) thus forms an important component of the informal curriculum of secondary schooling.

Education System: A Historical Perspective

This section provides a brief sketch of the development of the Singapore education system. More details can be found in Doraisamy (1969), Soon (1988) and Commentary (1989).

In late 1800s, the education of boys was provided by small vernacular schools run by the Chinese and Tamil communities and religious study for the Malays was conducted by Muslim religious schools called madrasahs. Gradually the colonial government established English schools to produce diligent clerks to work for the East India Company. Missionary schools were also established by individuals or Christian societies. However, the English-based education was to serve an economic or religious purpose rather than wider educational or social objectives.

In the post-war period, the colonial government continued to build English schools and encouraged parents of all races to send their children to these schools. The curriculum in these schools was designed to provide skills that were marketable for commercial and administrative activities. On the other hand, Chinese education provided by the vernacular schools became politicized with its graduates facing poor career prospects. Faced with high unemployment and labour unrest in the mid 1950s, the government offered the Chinese schools grant-in-aid status. This assistance produced a stabilizing effect on the political front and paved the way for the government to determine the curriculum in Chinese schools at a later stage.

In 1958, the government made primary education freely available to every child of school-going age. Pupil enrolment increased rapidly from 315,000 in 1959 to 522,000 in 1968, a 66 per cent increase within a decade (Soon, 1988), and an accelerated school building programme could not cope with this increase. Schools have to be conducted in two sessions (morning and afternoon) to maximize the use of limited resources. Only in 1986 increasing affluence and concern for quality education led to the decision to convert all secondary schools to single sessions. The first step has been taken in 1990 when the Education Budget provided funding for all Secondary 1 classes to become single session by 1994. However, it will take much longer and more money to convert all primary and secondary schools to single session. Single sessions are considered important because given the extra curriculum time the schools can offer a wide variety of activities to their pupils to enrich their educational experiences. Even in a compact society like Singapore that is relatively prosperous, financial constraint can be a limiting factor for curriculum implementation.

Another landmark in Singapore education was the recommendation of the bilingualism policy in 1956 by the All Party Report on Chinese Education. The policy stipulated that English should be the medium of instruction while pupils could continue to learn their mother tongue. English was chosen because of two main reasons. First, it is an international language and competence in English is essential for survival in a commercial society that depends on trading with the outside world. Second, English is not the native language of any ethnic group so that its neutral status would allow for greater social cohesion to build a nation out of various racial groups. However, the study of English has exposed pupils to Western thinking and social behaviours, some of which are found to be unacceptable in the various traditional cultures. Thus, the government was faced with the problem of raising the standard of English (particularly in Chinese schools) and at the same time trying to preserve cultural heritage transmitted traditionally through a vernacular education. Various measures were taken to resolve this problem:

1966: mathematics and science to be taught in English in Chinese primary
     schools
1969: civics in English schools to be taught in the mother tongue
1970: history to be taught in the mother tongue from primary 3

These changes to the school curriculum have not been able to resolve in a satisfactory way the problem of bilingualism and cultural heritage even up to the present time.

By the late 1970s, the education system was seen to be failing to meet the social and economic needs of the nation. This prompted a study in 1978 of the education system undertaken by the then First Deputy Prime Minister, Dr Goh Keng Swee. The Goh report examined various weaknesses of the education system and the following two areas had a direct impact on further curriculum development:

(a) Ineffective bilingual policy contributing to low literacy levels, especially in English; for example, more than 60 per cent of the pupils failed in one or both languages at the Standard 6 and 'O' level examinations; only 11 per cent of the national servicemen could understand communication in English at a reasonable level.

(b) High educational wastage with attrition rate of 29 per cent at primary level and 36 per cent at secondary level; this wastage was particularly evident in failure to achieve thet expected standards, premature school leaving, repetition of grades, and unemployable school leavers.

The many changes recommended by the Goh report have led to a new education structure that is usually referred to as the New Education System (NES). Two major recommendations that formed the cornerstone of the NES throughout the 1980s have also elicited the most controversial public reactions. They are:

(a) streaming according to ability; and
(b) greater emphasis on English with some reduction in the standard in the mother tongue.

These issues will be discussed later in the chapter together with the nature of the present new education system. However, it is necessary at this point to describe the roles of the various agents involved in curriculum decisions.

The Agents of Curriculum Decisions

The agents refer to institutions or individuals that have input into curriculum decisions and implementation. In Singapore five major agents can be identified: politicians, the Ministry of Education (MOE), the Curriculum Development Institute of Singapore (CDIS), the teacher training institutes, the schools and teachers. Their roles in curriculum matters are briefly described below.

Since its independence, Singapore has been ruled by the Peoples' Action Party in a Parliament that has minimal opposition. Although this has provided for strong leadership, especially in times of economic and political crisis, it has also led to a passive attitude among the public and many professionals that the political masters have all the answers and that their thinking will always prevail. The politicians have exerted decisive influences in educational policies, particularly those pertaining to moral values and languages, since these matters have significant ramifications in promoting social cohesion and national identity. Examples of the political influences include the Goh report mentioned earlier, the Ong report on moral education (1979), and the recent decision about independent schools initiated by the Minister for Education (see later section). Curriculum relating to academic disciplines like mathematics and science seldom attracts the attention of the politicians. The politicians play their role during debates in the Parliament. There is also a government Parliamentary Committee on Education that collects feedback from various sources about educational issues and raises these issues with the ministers.

The Ministry of Education is headed by a Minister for Education and two ministers of states for education. Within the Ministry of Education, the main agents engaged in curriculum decisions are the Curriculum Planning Division and the Research and Testing Division. The Curriculum Planning Division designs, reviews and revises the syllabuses of all school subjects and monitors the implementation of these syllabuses in all the schools. The Research and Testing Division conducts public examinations and research projects on educational issues. The system is a highly centralized one with major decisions coming from the Ministry to the schools in a top-down manner.

The Curriculum Development Institute of Singapore was formed in 1980 to develop instructional materials and to train teachers to use these materials in in-service courses and school-based workshops. The materials include textbooks, workbooks, teacher guides, and various audio-visual materials such as slides, cassettes, and educational games. Many of these materials are of very good quality and they present formidable competition to commercial educational publishers in a relatively small market. Nearly all the primary schools use the CDIS materials. At secondary level, in addition to the CDIS materials, some schools also use textbooks that are produced by commercial publishers, but these must be approved by the Ministry of Education.

Teacher training is provided by the Institute of Education and the College of Physical Education. Primary teachers are trained in a two-year certificate programme while secondary teachers are graduates who undertake a one-year postgraduate diploma in education. Both types of teacher trainees receive a bursary while under training and they have to serve the Ministry after graduation. The Institute of Education also conducts many in-service courses to upgrade the skills of teachers in areas that are crucial for providing quality education in schools, for example, career guidance, process skills in science, mixed-ability teaching in mathematics, and innovative methods to teach English and Chinese. In a recent move to improve the quality of teacher training, the Institute and the College will be amalgamated to form a National Institute of Education which will be affiliated to the second university to be formed in 1991.

While teacher training is the phase when trainees learn to interpret the intended curriculum and to acquire basic skills, the actions of the classroom teachers largely determine the nature of the implemented curriculum. In Singapore, teachers teach either in the morning or afternoon session, five days a week. Quite often, however, they have to come back in the morning or afternoon and on Saturdays to supervise extra-curricular activities and to attend meetings. Their classes are relatively large (about thirty-five) and the classrooms are often dusty and noisy from passing traffic. The teachers have to prepare their pupils to obtain good grades in public examinations within an overloaded curriculum made even more difficult by the double sessions. Recently teachers have been called upon to perform multiple roles: a subject specialist, a disciplinarian, a career guidance officer, a counsellor, and an administrator who should be computer literate. This makes teaching a very stressful profession that is not a favourite career choice among school leavers despite its relatively good salary. The conditions of work and the multiple roles are likely to constrain the teachers in attempting to fulfil the aims of the intended curriculum, and in some cases might lead to a negotiation of these aims to fit the limiting environment (see later section on Specific Instructional Objectives for an example of this effect).

The scope of the responsibilities of these agents of curriculum decisions is summarized by the basic statistics given in the next section.

Basic Statistics

Schooling is not compulsory is Singapore. In 1988, the pupil enrolment ratio (number of pupils aged 6–17 years old divided by population of the same age group) is 93.7, which is a great improvement over the similar ratio of 79.1 in 1978 (*Straits Times*, 25 March 1990).

The following tables give a summary of the basic statistics of the Singapore education system as in 1989 (*Education Statistics Digest*, 1989).

Table 7.1   School, enrolment, teacher, and principal by levels (1989)

	Pre-primary	Primary	Secondary	Junior college	Total
School	39	203	167	18	427
Enrolment Male	2773	135429	86689	12193	237084
Female	2161	122261	84166	14510	223098
Teacher Male	0	2852	2901	539	6292
Female	232	7146	4764	968	13110
Principal Male		125	81	11	217
Female		75	56	7	138

Notes: (1) Secondary schools include pre-university centres.
(2) Junior colleges also include four centralized institutes.
(3) Schools include government, government-aided and independent schools.

Females make up about two–thirds of the total teacher population, especially at the lower levels. As a consequence, there are insufficient male teachers to provide suitable role models to the male pupils. Various advertising efforts have been used to recruit males into the teaching profession, but the result is not encouraging.

Girls outnumber boys in the arts and commerce tracks, while boys out-number girls in the technical track. Roughly the same percentages of boys and girls enrol in the science track.

Table 7.3 shows clearly that with the exception of the results for PSPE (terminal examination for the monolingual pupils at primary level), the results of the other public examinations have shown a dramatic increase in percentage passes over the past ten years. This has been used to show that the streaming policy is successful in upgrading the standard of education at various levels.

Table 7.2   Enrolment in various tracks by level (1989)

Track	Sex	Sec 3	Sec 4	Sec 5 N	Pre-U	JC	Total
Arts	M	5276	5401	1717	654	1365	14413
	F	9074	9914	3506	1040	3512	27046
Commerce	M	1307	1159	515	1528	1621	5930
	F	2347	2532	1155	3415	4222	13671
Science	M	7609	7120	463	410	8708	24310
	F	6911	7073	609	199	5255	20047
Technical	M	5695	7134	3105			15934
	F	630	774	392			1796

Note: Pre-U include pre-university centres and centralized institutes.

Table 7.3   Results of national examinations: 1978, 1984 and 1988

Year		PSPE	PSLE	GCE 'N'	GCE 'O'	GCE 'A'
1978	No. sat		55181		22428	8766
	% pass		74.4		62.1	59.0
1984	No. sat	2814	49174	14149	34346	8787
	% pass	87.5	85.5	30.0	79.7	65.2
1988	No. sat	2223	43222	13861	37614	12931
	% pass	56.4	86.5	75.8	89.1	72.5

Note: PSPE and GCE 'N' level were first offered in 1984.

In 1990, the education budget is S$2100m, about 15.4 per cent of total government spending. This is a sizeable proportion of the annual budget.

We shall now return to an examination of the New Education System and the nature of the present school curriculum.

The New Education System

The primary objectives of the education system in Singapore are to:

(a) offer every child an equal opportunity to excel to the limit of his/her ability;

(b) prepare the child for the process of life-long learning to cope with rapid changes in technologies;

(c) instil in every child proper moral values so that he/she will grow up to be a useful and loyal citizen. (Ministry of Education, 1989)

These objectives are to be realized through streaming of pupils into different courses and the offering of various programmes in the school curriculum. The structure of the education system with streaming is shown in the following diagram.

Figure 7.1   *A structure of the New Education System*

	Age	Courses		
Pre-primary (informal)	3	Nursery		
	4	Kindergarten 1		
	5	Kindergarten 2		
Primary	6	Primary 1		
	7	Primary 2		
	8	Primary 3		
		(P3 exam, school-based)		
	9	Primary 4 Normal	P4 Extended	P4 Monolingual
	10	P5 Normal	P5 Extended	P5 Monolingual
	11	P6 Normal	P6 Extended	P6 Monolingual
		(PSLE)	P7 Extended	P7 Monolingual
			P8 Extended	P8 Monolingual
			(PSLE)	(PSPE)
Secondary	12	S1 S/E S1 N		(vocational)
	13	S2 S/E S2 N		
	14	S3 S/E S3 N		
	15	S4 S/E S4 N		
		(O Level) (N Level)		
		S5 N (O Level)		
Pre-university	16	Junior College 1/Pre-U1		
	17	Junior College 2/Pre-U2		
	18	Pre-U3		
		(A Level)		
Tertiary		Universities, polytechnics or education institutes		

Informal education at pre-primary level begins with nursery classes for 3-year-olds followed by two years of kindergarten. The kindergartens are run by the People's Action Party (about two-thirds of the pre-school population with 210 centres), the People's Associations and private entrepreneurs. There is no standard curriculum at this level and facilities and methods of teaching vary from centre to centre. Many parents concerned about streaming at Primary 3 want their children to have a head-start at the pre-primary level with serious learning (reading, writing, and arithmetic) rather than to enjoy themselves with plays only. This is typical of the Singapore syndrome called *kiasu-ism* which means fear of losing out in any situation. In an editorial entitled 'Easy on the Child' (*Straits Times*, July 23 1986), it was lamented that

> parents who are easily overwhelmed by the spirit of competition may well lose their sense of proportion and put undue pressure on their children to perform, even at the age of five.

It suggested quite rightly that parents should consider pre-primary education as a means 'to give the child a taste of what it is like to be in school, and nothing more' (*ibid.*). There is no evidence that this advice is accepted by those highly anxious parents.

Formal education begins at 6 years old. In the first three years, all primary school pupils take the same course that emphasizes language learning (English and mother tongue which might be Chinese, Malay, or Tamil), mathematics and moral education. At the end of primary 3, pupils are streamed on the basis of school based assessment into three different courses:

Normal course (about 90 per cent) of three years of upper primary education;

Extended course (6 per cent) of five years of upper primary schooling to complete the same Normal course; and

Monolingual course (4 per cent) of five years of upper primary schooling in basic literacy and numeracy.

Pupils in the Normal and Extended courses take the Primary School Leaving Examination (PSLE) and those who pass this examination proceed to secondary school. Pupils in the Monolingual course study a non-academic curriculum and sit for the Primary School Proficiency Examination (PSPE), after which they can enrol in the Vocational and Industrial Training Board (VITB) for pre-vocational training or join the workforce.

The average class size is thirty-six for the Normal stream and twenty-five for the Extended or Monolingual stream. The smaller class size for the weaker pupils is to allow teachers the opportunity to give their pupils more individualized attention.

Streaming at the end of primary 3 was first introduced in 1980. The objective is to maximize the pupils' potential in learning by providing different courses that allow them to learn at their own pace. While streaming is an easy way to cater for individual differences (certainly practised informally when pupils are put into different classes according to performance), implementing it at a national level at an early age (about 8 or 9 years old) has evoked strong emotional responses from parents and educators. Several arguments have been advanced against streaming. First, early streaming is not fair to those who develop slowly, especially in the cognitive areas. Second, pupils who are streamed to a lower course (for example, Monolingual) would have reduced opportunity to change to a higher level of education (which has advantages in terms of career advancement). Third, there is social stigma associated with the lower courses. Lastly, errors in streaming cannot be entirely avoided and the cumulative effects are likely to be very demoralizing for the pupils in the long run.

Proponents of streaming argue that without a flexible system to cater for pupils' different abilities, the weaker pupils will fail in an academic curriculum while the above average pupils are not stretched to their full potential. According to Soon (1988) the attrition rate at PSLE for the first group under NES was 8 per cent, dramatically lower than the pre-NES attrition rate of 29 per cent. Educational wastage has been minimized as less than 1 per cent of the total school population below 16 years left school without having at least ten years of education (*ibid.*, p. 29).

The second stage of streaming begins when pupils enter secondary 1. On the basis of their PSLE examination result, these pupils are divided into the Special (top 5 per cent), Express (next 57 per cent) or the Normal[1] (last 38 per cent)

stream. Lateral movement across streams is permitted under special circumstances at the end of secondary 1 or 2.

At secondary 3, pupils opt for one of the four tracks: arts, science, commerce or technical. The curriculum for most subjects is dictated by the Cambridge GCE 'O' Level syllabuses. At the end of the fourth year, the special and Express pupils take the Singapore-Cambridge GCE 'O' Level examination, while those in the Normal stream take the Singapore-Cambridge 'N' Level examination. About 75 per cent of the Normal pupils will go on to secondary 5 and take the GCE 'O' Level examination.

The average class size at secondary school is twenty for the Special stream and thirty-five for the Express or Normal stream. Teachers have constantly argued for smaller class sizes for the weaker Normal pupils but this does not seem to have received favourable support from their political masters.

It can be argued that the success of streaming at the secondary level is also justified using performance in public examinations, which 'provides a fairly objective and reliable measure of academic attainment' (Soon, 1988, p. 29). In the pre-NES years, the percentage of pupils who obtained three or more 'O' level passes was around 60 per cent. This percentage increased steadily during the NES years to about 90 per cent in 1985. In spite of this academic success the social stigma of belonging to a Normal class is not easily erased. The normal pupils have been described as slow in learning, with poor power of retention, lack of discipline, lack of motivation and concentration and weak in English ability. Unfortunately, even some teachers feel that they must be less than competent to be asked to take these classes.

After completing secondary education, those who qualify enter junior colleges (two years) or pre-university or centralized institutes (three years) for further academic study. At the end of the course, they sit for the Singapore-Cambridge GCE 'A' Level examination. Those who do well in this 'A' Level examination can join the National University of Singapore or the Nanyang Technological Institute for degree courses, or the polytechnics (there are three) and various institutes for diploma courses. Students who do not qualify for the 'A' Level course may join the polytechnics or various institutes to acquire vocational skills or seek employment.

Adult education has been given an important role in continually upgrading the academic skills (especially literacy in English and numeracy) and occupational competence of workers. For example, in 1988, the Vocational and Industrial Training Board trained more than 100,000 workers in three programmes named BEST (Basic Education for Skill Training), WISE (Worker Improvement through Secondary Education) and MOST (Modular Skills Training Scheme) (for details, see Law, 1989).

The School Curriculum

The standard curriculum is developed and its implementation monitored by the Ministry of Education. Three basic components of the curriculum are:

(a) bilingualism with English as the medium of instruction at all levels and the mother tongue being taught as the medium to promote traditional values and moral education;

(b) a balanced curriculum that includes language, mathematics, science, aesthetics, and physical education;
(c) extracurricular activities that provide healthy recreation and that culti- vate desirable social attitudes among the pupils.

Academic excellence is prized and rewarded. This results in keen competi- tion among pupils for grades and so makes school life highly stressful. In addition to school lessons, many pupils also attend tuition classes conducted by tutors mostly in private homes. Private tuition is a lucrative business and many parents as well as teachers see it as a necessary 'evil' that gives those pupils who can afford tuition a competitive edge in academic performance. While there is no research to measure the degree of this success, too much time spent on book learning, reading and working on the computer has produced serious health problems. It was reported (*Straits Times*, 15 September 1988) that at primary 6, 50 per cent of boys and 56 per cent of girls wore spectacles and at seondary 4, 56 per cent of boys and 64 per cent of girls also wore spectacles due to defective eyesight. Recently a pilot project has been introduced which teaches primary pupils how to massage their eyes in an attempt to alleviate this problem.

Just as streaming is the distinctive feature of the educational structure, the bilingual policy that has existed due to historical developments and present-day necessity forms the crucial aspect of the school curriculum. As indicated in an early section, the Goh report found that poor ability in English had contributed significantly to low literacy levels. To make bilingual education more effective, the report proposed that the more able pupils will learn English and their mother tongue at the 'first language' level (i.e. at a fairly competent level) while the average pupils will learn English at the 'first language' level and their mother tongue at the lower 'second language' level. The very weak pupils should become literate in one language only (in effect this means English) rather than being illiterate in two languages. Unlike streaming, this pragmatic policy did not generate much public controversy at the time of implementation. The success of the bilingual policy under streaming has again been measured by percentage passes at public examinations. For instance, during the pre-NES years, less than 40 per cent of pupils passed in one or both languages at PSLE or the 'O' level examination. However, in 1985 the percentage passes in English and a second language at PSLE were 90.2 per cent and 98.7 per cent respectively (Soon, 1988). The percentage passes in English at 'O' Level improved significantly from 40 per cent in 1980 to 67 per cent in 1989, the latter percentage being comparable to that of English children sitting for the same paper in England (*Straits Times*, 17 March 1990).

Although academic performance might be a reasonable indicator of the success of a curriculum, curriculum practices can produce quite unexpected effects in the wider social context. As pupils learn most of their subjects in English they invariably subscribe to Western values and social behaviours that might not be consistent with traditional cultures. The study of the mother tongue takes up much less time compared to studies involving English and so it has not fulfilled its objective of helping the pupils to understand and retain desirable traditional values. In 1989, there was a sizeable emigration of professionals and one of the perceived factors was the difficulty of learning Chinese even at the lower level. On the other hand, some educationists who are unhappy with the low standard of Chinese language argue for measures to raise its standard. Faced with this dilemma, the government has allowed ten primary schools to teach Chinese at 'first language' level, and proposes to set up a centre for research into bilingualism (*Straits Times*, 17 March 1990). At this stage similar problems relating to the study of Malay and Tamil as a second language have not been adequately debated in public.

Subjects and Levels

The school year begins in January and ends in mid-November. There are four school terms of ten weeks each. For weekdays, morning sessions are from 7.30 am to 1 pm, and afternoon sessions from 1.20 pm to 6.30 pm. A school day usually begins with the singing of the national anthem (in Malay) and taking the Singapore Pledge (in English).[2] Pupils normally stay back after school on two days per week for extra-curricular activities or remedial classes. Saturday mornings are also used for extra-curricular activities or school-based workshops for teachers.

The curriculum times for various subjects are decided by the Ministry of Education. Minor adjustments however can be made by the schools to suit their needs and constraints. Changes to the curriculum structure and times are also initiated by the Ministry of Education from time to time to ensure quality education.

The following tables illustrate typical curriculum times at specific levels. These times are slightly different at different year levels and for different streams.

Table 7.4 Curriculum times (no. of hours per week) of subjects at primary 4

	Subject	No. of hours per week
Examination subjects	English	6.5
	Second language	4
	Mathematics	3.5
	Science (from P3)	2.75
	Social studies (from P4)	1.5
	Art and crafts	1
Non-examination subjects	Moral education	1.5
	Music	1
	Physical education	1
	Health education	0.5
	Assembly	0.5
Total (per week)		23.75

In addition to the bilingual policy, moral education is seen to be important in helping pupils to develop desirable social behaviours and loyalty to the nation.

Pupils in the Special stream (the top 10 per cent) can take the second language at first level. Classes in these languages are conducted in air-conditioned language laboratories or audio-visual rooms. Class size is kept small to allow teachers to give individual attention to these pupils.

Table 7.5   Curriculum times (no. of hours per week) of subjects at secondary 1

	Subject	No. of hours per week
Examination subjects	English and literature	5
	Second language	4
	Mathematics	3.5
	General science	4
	History	1.5
	Geography	1.5
	Technical (boy) or home economics (girl)	2
	Art and crafts	1.5
Non-examination subjects	Moral education	1.5
	Music	1
	Physical education	1.5
	Assembly	0.5
Total (per week)		27.5

English continues to be the main language of instruction. The study of literature in English is to enhance literacy in the language as well as to understand the nature of human conditions.

The content for the Normal stream (lower ability group) is slightly less than that for the Express or Special stream. Teaching is also carried out at a pace suited to pupils' ability levels. Faced with various learning problems of the Normal pupils, teachers are constantly looking for innovative techniques to deal with these problems. Many secondary 5 Normal pupils complain that too many of the 'O' Level topics are crammed into one year. Recent curricular revisions attempt to address these problems, and one such revision involving the mathematics curriculum will be described later on in this chapter.

Pupils in the upper secondary level are given electives in addition to various compulsory subjects. They may choose from 1 to 4 elective subjects. Most pupils take about 6 to 9 examination subjects. Some pupils are allowed to offer a third language (usually French, Japanese or German). The curriculum for a secondary 3 Normal course is given below.

Table 7.6   Curriculum times (no. of hours per week) of subjects at secondary 3 Normal

	Subject	No. of hours per week
Examination subjects	English	5.5
	Second language	4
	Mathematics	4
	Electives (1 to 4)	9
	Religious knowledge	2
Non-examination subjects	Music	1
	Physical education	1.5
	Assembly	0.5
Total (per week)		27.5

Although mathematics and science form the key components of the curriculum for most secondary pupils, there are two special programmes that cater to the needs of pupils who want to excel in the aesthetics: the art elective programme and the music elective programme. Both are four year courses leading to examination at the GCE 'O' Level.

At junior colleges, pupils can select from combinations of different subjects. The typical allocation of instructional times is given below.

Table 7.7   Curriculum times (no. of hours per week) of subjects at junior college

	Subject	No. of hours per week
Examination subjects	General paper	4
	Second language	4
	Electives (about 3)	15
Non-examination subjects	Moral education	1
	Physical education	2
	Assembly	1
Total (per week)		27

Changes and Innovations

The previous section describes the current curriculum structure at various levels. However, some changes will be effected in the near future, whereby the education system will be used as a means to tackle problems arising from conflicts and challenges in the society at large. The following five changes related to curriculum development are briefly described below:

(a) Moral education and religious knowledge
(b) Move towards independence for the principals
(c) Pastoral care and career guidance
(d) Gifted education programme and the search for creativity
(e) Computer education for a high tech society

Moral Education and Religious Knowledge

The importance of moral education was outlined in Goh's report (1980). At the same time, Ong's report (1979) suggested three important aspects to be included in moral education: character development, social responsibility, and loyalty to the nation. In 1981, the Ministry of Education appointed a team to examine various relevant issues about moral education (Eng, 1981), which resulted in the development of the current programmes.

From primary 1 to 6, pupils are taught moral education in a programme in their mother tongue called 'Good Citizen'. An estimate indicates that this provides pupils with about 360 hours over the six-year period. The emphasis is on instilling good social behaviours and loyalty to the country.

In secondary 1 and 2, the moral education programme, 'Being and Becoming', is conducted in English. Pupils in secondary 3 and 4 take religious knowledge, which is the study of one of the following: Bible Knowledge, Buddhist Studies, Hindu Studies, Islamic religious knowledge, Sikh Studies, and Confucian Ethics. Up to 1989, attendance in religious knowledge classes was compulsory and schools had to set examinations in this subject. In 1988, concern about excessive individualism, crass materialism and undesirable influences from certain Westernized practices led to a debate about core values and the development of a national ideology (a similar approach has been adopted much earlier by Malaysia in its Rukunegara and by Indonesia in its Pancasila). At the same time, evangelical activities of certain over-jealous religious groups were perceived as threatening the social harmony in a multi-racial society. The teaching of religious knowledge has had the unforeseen effect of segregating pupils along religious lines during these lessons. This segregation is unlikely to help promote better understanding among pupils from various religious groups. Thus, in 1989, the government decided to phase out religious knowledge as a compulsory subject with effect from 1990 and to replace it with a new civics programme.

The new civics programme for secondary schools is to be worked out by a team consisting of professionals from the Curriculum Development Institute of Singapore, the Schools Division, the Institute of Education, and some school principals. The programme will emphasize the four principles spelt out in the President's Parliamentary address in 1989: placing society above self; upholding the family as the basic building block of society; resolving major issues through consensus; stressing racial and religious tolerance through harmony (*Straits Times*, 25 February 1990). This new programme is to be implemented in 1992 and will be taught in English.

The success of a moral education programme is difficult to evaluate and research is lacking in this area. At a personal level, pupils' school life as in the case for adults in Singapore, is governed by many rules. For instance, a girl of 13 wrote in the Teen Page of *Straits Times* on 20 February 1990:

> When I was in primary school, there were only six rules for me to follow ... Now, in secondary school, there are forty general rules ... twenty-six laboratory safety rules ... fifteen technical workshop rules, fourteen Home Economics rules and twelve library rules. I can't believe that I have to observe so many rules.

Move Towards Independence for the Principals

While pupils are having to cope with various school rules, some school principals are talking about too much control over school administration by regulations and instructions from the Ministry of Education. This centralized control is seen as stifling initiatives of the principals and leading to a lack of identity in the schools. Partly in response to this criticism, the Minister for Education, in December 1986, invited twelve principals from key secondary schools to join him on a study tour of selected public and private schools in the United Kingdom and the United States that were considered 'excellent' in providing sound all-round education for their pupils. This led to the publication of a report in February 1987 entitled *Towards Excellence in Schools*. The principals involved in the study tour made eleven key recommendations:

1 Give principals more freedom to run the school their way.
2 Let the principals choose their teachers and other key personnel.
3 Continue to admit pupils (into independent schools) based on their grades.
4 Keep enrolment around 1000 to 1200 pupils per school.
5 Bring the teacher-pupil ratio down from the current 1:24 to 1:15.
6 Introduce pastoral care and career guidance to ensure the total development of pupils.
7 Give principals more flexibility to decide the curricula for their pupils. Give pupils more time and facilities to take part in extra-curricular activities. Raise the standard of art, music and drama.
8 Make all schools single session, starting from secondary schools.
9 Give schools more ancillary staff to support the work of the teachers and the principal.
10 Government should provide financial aid to ensure pupils who qualify for entry into independent schools but who cannot afford to pay will not be penalized.
11 Involve parents and alumni in the activities of the school.

The report generated a lot of debate and discussion among parliamentarians and the general public. The main outcome was to allow certain well established schools to 'go independent' and to charge school fees according to the schools' budget and development. Within two years, five schools became independent with more schools planning to do so in the future.

The content of the curriculum is already fixed by public examination syllabuses, so there is little scope for change in this area. However, enrichment activities are provided to enhance the learning of the required content. In addition, some independent schools are trying to change the ways of implementing the curriculum. For instance, one independent school plans to teach elementary mathematics at secondary 3 and additional mathematics at secondary 4 instead of teaching both subjects concurrently in two-year levels as being done at the present time. The rationale is that elementary mathematics should provide the foundation for the more difficult additional mathematics. In addition to this, subjects that require a lot of memorization such as geography will be taught at secondary 4 close to the time for public examination (based on the recency effect of memory) so that pupils need to spend less time for revision, compared to learning the subject over a two-year period. The success or otherwise of this experiment will be known only in two years' time.

In the midst of much heated debate about finance (to attract good teachers by giving them more pay, bonuses and professional development and to pay for more and better facilities), a moral issue raised by a parliamentarian is worth noting here. Speculating on the product of excellence, he had the following thought about the pupil from an independent school:

> He will be spoonfed with excellence and then will leave the school expecting the best treatment from society since he is such a privileged

person ... It is his right to expect this since he has the ability to do well in examinations. He is less likely to want to talk about his obligations and debt to the society that raised and supported him. (*Straits Times*, 20 March 1987)

Once again this raises the important, but unresolved, issue of how a curriculum can be designed to provide a balanced academic attainment with social obligations in a prosperous but materialistic society like Singapore.

Pastoral Care and Careers Guidance

Another outcome of the current debate on excellence is the introduction of a new pastoral care and careers guidance programme in many secondary schools.

In the 1970s, careers guidance was provided by some schools on an ad hoc basis but it was considered of little significance to the overall academic curriculum. In 1979, the Careers Guidance Unit at the Ministry of Education was disbanded. In 1985, the National Productivity Council argued that the lack of careers guidance in schools would have deleterious effects on the productivity of the future workforce. The need for careers guidance is also supported by some research findings. For example, in a survey conducted among 1380 secondary pupils in 1987 (Tan, 1988), it was found that about 57.5 per cent of the students had no job preference and 30.7 per cent preferred professional jobs. There was a marked disdain for blue collar jobs. There was no sex stereotyping among pupils in job preference. About a third of them anticipated tough competition from others as the main hindrance in fulfilling their career goals.

However, it was the principals' report on 'Excellence' that provided the necessary impetus for introducing a new pastoral care and careers guidance programme into the school curriculum. This programme has two components: pastoral care to provide a nurturing climate in which pupils can experience success that fosters self esteem, and careers guidance to help pupils to understand their aspirations for career and to study towards the relevant educational requirements.

The model of pastoral care which has been approved is described in the document entitled *Pastoral Care and Career Guidance in Singapore Schools: A Fresh Approach*. It is part of the curriculum at secondary level, but unlike most other subjects the content of this curriculum will not be prescribed by the Ministry of Education. Each school shall develop with the involvement of parents its own programme to meet local needs. Support is provided by guidance officers from the Ministry of Education, the establishment of a careers library and the development of an expert system about local careers information. In-service training is provided for key teachers but it is expected that eventually most teachers will be trained to play an active role in integrating careers education with the academic curriculum. The risk, according to Watts (1988), is 'the substantial gap between the teaching and learning methods which are currently used in the traditional "academic" parts of the curriculum, and those which are appropriate to the "pastoral" curriculum' (p. 34). However, with suitable training and appropriate action research, it is feasible for teachers to integrate both teaching styles to meet the academic and pastoral needs of the pupils.

Gifted Education Programme and the Search for Creativity

Faced with a shortage of talent and practising the principle of meritocracy, the Singapore education system has devised a special programme to identify and nurture creative and talented pupils from an early age. The Gifted Education Programme was first implemented in 1984 in two primary and two secondary schools. In 1989, there were three primary and three secondary schools catering for the more than 1000 pupils from primary 4 to secondary 4. There is little published material about the programme and the following description is based on a recent article by its project director (Tan, 1989).

The main objectives of the programme are:

(a) to develop the pupils' intellectual ability by equipping them with the tools for self-directed learning and by developing higher level thinking skills;
(b) to educate pupils towards social responsibility and civic awareness.

Pupils are selected at the end of primary 3 using locally developed tests on language ability, numerical ability and general ability. A second selection is taken from the top 4–5 per cent of primary 6 pupils. These selections are open to the whole cohort so that every child is given a chance to be selected for the programme. At each level, it was found that boys outnumbered girls by 2 to 1.[3]

These gifted pupils are placed in special classes taught by teachers who are specially trained to use teaching approaches that emphasize pupil participation, group work and learning through discovery. Classes are kept small (about twenty-five) to ensure the effectiveness of the innovative teaching methods and to give more individual attention to the pupils. The curriculum provides enrichment to the topics covered in the regular syllabuses since the gifted pupils have to sit for the same public examinations as the other pupils. Pupils are trained to do library research, to conduct experiments and investigations, to collect data through survey and interview, and to write research reports. Talks by outside experts cover topics like artificial intelligence, cancer research, star gazing, and creative writing. Field trips and excursions are organized to help pupils to see the applications of what they have learned in the classrooms. Camps are planned to enable them to develop social and leadership skills.

Feedback about the programme involved an analysis of results of public examinations and pupils' responses. The gifted pupils were allowed to take more subjects in the public examinations than other pupils and their performance was very good. In general, they liked the flexible curriculum, the faster pace and more in-depth treatment of the content. All agreed that such a programme should be available in Singapore. Some of those who completed their secondary 4 level also took part in a Science Enrichment Programme launched in 1988 to provide students gifted in science and mathematics to participate in research activities under the guidance of scientists from the National University of Singapore.

While special provisions are made to nurture the talent of the few intellectually gifted pupils, there is a need to foster creativity and problem solving skills among the majority of pupils to enable them to face new challenges in their future careers. In a speech to the Nanyang Technological Institute on 'Economic Change and the Formulation of Education Policy' on 22 July 1986, the Minister for Education argued that a sound grounding in the basics (English, mathematics, science) is the pre-requisite to teach pupils how to think logically and to impart to them the habit of life-long learning. A 'bottom-up' approach from principals and teachers to the Ministry was more likely to succeed in promoting creativity and innovation in schools (*Straits Times*, 23 July 1986). The call for creativity was enthusiastically endorsed by several principals. However, while discussing the types of 'creative programmes' to be implemented in schools, the editorial of *Straits Times* on 24 July 1986 noted:

> In a highly competitive system like ours, it would be wishful thinking to believe that grades would play second fiddle to creativity. Our teachers and principals — not to mention the students themselves — are not likely to devote sufficient attention to creativity if they feel that grades might suffer. Parents, too, will not be happy if they find that creativity comes with a high price tag.

A year later, it was suggested that

> Teaching in schools should move away from rote-learning to encourage more creative work ... And for creativity to thrive, Singaporeans should learn to tolerate those who appear to have 'deviant' and 'undisciplined' behaviour. (*Straits Times*, 18 September 1987)

On 21 March 1989 a Member of Parliament, who was also a lecturer at the National University of Singapore, complained that Singapore's top students were exam-smart but could not think for themselves. He wanted the teaching approach adopted for the Gifted Education Programme to be extended to a larger group of pupils in primary and secondary schools.

In order to put the creativity policy into action, the Ministry of Education examined several thinking programmes developed in Western countries and decided to adopt the CoRT (Cognitive Research Trust) programme based on Edward de Bono's lateral thinking method. The programme seeks to teach pupils to think more widely and to see things in a different way before they are taught to do critical thinking. It is designed for pupils from ages 9 to 19 and for all ability groups.

The programme was first introduced in 1987 to fourteen secondary schools and two years later about forty-five schools were using the programme. Initially, the lessons were conducted during English periods or special lessons. Currently, the Ministry of Education is preparing to integrate some of the thinking skills (such as PMI, CAF) into various academic subjects such as mathematics, science, geography and moral education. The CoRT programme is quite popular but its effectiveness has yet to be determined. There is also a continuing search for other thinking programmes that might be adopted for pupils of different abilities.

At the primary level, some principals adopt the 'bottom-up' approach by initiating thinking programmes for their pupils. For example, the Henry Park Primary School developed in 1986 a project to promote higher cognitive skills among selected primary 4 pupils through activities in problem solving. Primary 4 pupils were chosen because they would not have to sit for public examinations for the next two years. A handbook was published documenting its development and evaluation. Activities were carried out outside curriculum time. At the end of the two year project, the pupils indicated that they enjoyed the Thinking Skills lessons, they were found to be more confident in presenting their ideas, and they had developed better observation skills in science lessons. There is no evidence from this study to support the stance that creativity lessons lead to lower grades.

A key component of any thinking skills programme is the ability to use resources effectively to access relevant information to answer research questions. This skill is traditionally perceived as part of a learning skills programme. In 1987, the Ministry of Education conducted a series of workshops for teachers to teach learning skills to secondary school pupils. As these skills are acquired, pupils develop metacognitive insight into the ways they learn and think. Thus, they are able to cope with their school work and examinations more confidently thereby maximizing their learning experience while at school. The skills also equip the pupils to become more independent learners in their adult life, thus preparing them for the rapid changes in their future working environment. These learning skills are to be taught by all subject teachers so that the skills can be applied across the curriculum. The author has been actively involved in preparing materials that integrate certain learning skills into the mathematics curriculum. These materials are disseminated through training workshops.

Computer Education for a High Tech Society

Over the past ten years, Singapore has developed a sophisticated electronics industry that not only attracts sizeable foreign investment but also exposes its people to advanced technology for career, education and leisure. To ensure that pupils are computer literate, the Ministry of Education implemented the Computer Appreciation Club programme for all secondary schools in 1981.

From 1981 to 1983, the Ministry of Education supplied to each secondary school three sets of computer systems for the use of Computer Appreciation Club activities. Teachers are trained in simple programming (in BASIC or LOGO) and in the use of application software (word processing, graphics, spreadsheet and data management) so that they can conduct computer club activities for their pupils. Enthusiasm for joining computer clubs is generally high but due to limited computer resources only about 11 per cent of the school pupils are club members. Activities are conducted outside curriculum time and they include lessons, talks, workshops, competitions and excursions. In a recent survey (Wong *et al.*, 1989), it was found that on average, each club member spent about 2.6 hours per week on club activities, while each teacher spent about 5.1 hours per week supervising these activities.

In addition to the Computer Appreciation Club programme, the Curriculum Development Institute of Singapore also implements a Computer Awareness Course for schools that have the necessary resources to conduct the course. Pupils are given lectures about computer and have hands-on experience in using application software and writing simple programs. This course provides a systematic way of helping pupils to become computer literate. Classes are also conducted outside curriculum time.

Using the computer as an instructional tool is still in an early phase of development in Sinagpore. Various CAI software programs are being piloted on a small scale in some schools. In 1988 English teachers were trained to use a simple word processor in the technique of process writing. The author has written several Logo microworlds for teaching mathematics topics such as statistical simulation, geometric transformations, and graphing in Cartesian, polar and parametric coordinates. Use of these microworlds is part of the training programme for heads of mathematics departments and graduate mathematics teachers.

Principals, teachers and pupils are generally very enthusiastic about computer based instruction. However, the main problems in implementing such a programme at the school level are the lack of computer facilities (a computer laboratory rather than just a few computers placed in isolated classrooms or resource room) and the difficulty of deploying all the computer literate teachers (about eleven per school) to take charge of computer education programmes (Wong *et al.*, 1989). In response to this need, the Ministry decided in 1987 to supply each secondary school with twelve IBM compatible computers. Since 1989, more than one-third of the secondary schools now have their computer laboratories.

Although computer education has been vigorously promoted in the secondary schools and junior colleges, the Ministry of Education has not given similar support to computer education in the primary schools. Primary schools that are keen to introduce computer literacy to their pupils need to find their own funds, but financial support from various institutes (such as the Turf Club) has been very encouraging. In the spirit of *kiasu-ism*, parents who can afford to do so are sending their children to computer classes as early as 5 years of age.

The impact of computers on curriculum implementation is affected by the development of the School Link Project. This project involves a computer network linking microcomputers in schools (primary and secondary) to a central computer system at the Ministry of Education. The project covers the following seven aspects of educational administration:

1 Pupil Management System
2 Financial System
3 Office System
4 Questions Bank System — School Item Pool
5 Time-tabling System
6 Library System
7 Inventory System

These systems are expected to cut down the time spent by teachers when carrying out administrative chores so that they will have more time to prepare interesting lessons to improve the quality of their instruction. The School Item Pool is of particular interest to classroom teachers. It is a system designed to allow teachers to prepare test items according to tables of specifications, to edit the items and to lay out items in the test paper before printing. Using this system, teachers can prepare test papers that have a professional appearance in a more efficient and less time consuming manner. The system also allows schools to share pools of items among themselves.

The above sections describe various innovations intended to produce 'excellence in education' for the Singapore pupils. Although informal feedback suggests that these innovations generally achieve the intended objectives, systematic evaluation of these changes should be initiated and the evaluation results published so that there is more informed debate about curriculum development among the various agents or stake-holders of curriculum decisions. The following sections look at three recent research studies that throw some light on the impact of curriculum innovations.

Research

Curriculum development should be informed by systematic research findings. Similary, curriculum implementation needs to be assessed using appropriate quantitative and qualitative methodology. In Singapore, educational research is conducted by the Research and Testing Branch of the Ministry of Education, lecturers and postgraduate students in the Institute of Education, members of the Educational Research Association, Singapore, and other interested bodies. Most of the research by the Ministry of Education has implications for curriculum development and evaluation but the research findings are generally not available to outside researchers. Research studies by other agents are published in the Singapore Journal of Education and Teaching and Learning under the auspices of the the Institute of Education. School-based projects conducted by teachers (probationary teachers are required to conduct such projects of their own choice as part of the requirements for tenancy in their appointment) are encouraged with funding from the Ministry of Education as a means to enhance the quality of instruction in the schools. Unfortunately, the results of these school-based projects are seldom published.

In the following sections, three research projects are discussed to show their relation to curriculum in general. The projects are:

(a) Survey on the Writing and Use of Specific Instructional Objectives (SIO)
(b) The Cognitive and Social Development of Pre-School Children in Singapore
(c) Children's (English) Language and Reading Development

Survey on the Writing and Use of Specific Instructional Objectives (SIO)

All over the world teachers are trained to understand the importance of instructional objectives for their lessons. These objectives also form the basis for designing test items so that pupil learning can be assessed in a fair and meaningful way. Among the various schemes of instructional objectives available, that of Bloom's taxonomy (1956) is probably the most widely used one. Learning about Bloom's taxonomy is an important part of teacher training in Singapore.

In 1983, the Curriculum Branch and the Testing Branch of the Ministry of Education introduced a project requiring teachers to write specific instructional objectives (SIOs; based on Bloom's taxonomy) for their lessons as a means of improving the quality of teaching.

During phase I (1983–1985), workshops were conducted by the Ministry of Education for 116 secondary teachers. Later, these teachers, functioning as the resource persons in their schools, conducted school-based workshops for their colleagues. At the initial stage, SIOs were written for English, mathematics and science lessons, to be followed by lessons in other subjects.

For phase II (1986–1988), workshops were conducted to show how SIOs could be used for effective testing, in particular to design tables of specifications based on SIOs.

In 1986–1987, the Singapore Teachers' Union conducted a survey among 450 experienced secondary school teachers on how they used SIOs. The overall feedback was not encouraging. About a third of the teachers in the survey found the writing of SIOs 'an unpleasant task which they have to do unwillingly' (p. 20). Of those teachers who wrote SIOs, 54.7 per cent did not use them to prepare lesson plans. Despite this the policy requiring teachers to include SIOs in their schemes of work was implemented. To help teachers to complete this unpleasant task, textbook publishers and the CDIS have recently included SIOs as supplementary materials for the teachers.

According to Mager (1962), tests should be based on SIOs, or else 'they are at best misleading; at worse, they are irrelevant, unfair, or useless' (p. 4). However, 64.4 per cent of the teachers in the STU's survey felt that most SIOs dealt with recall of facts and it was difficult to write SIOs for higher order skills. Only 38.7 per cent used SIOs in constructing their test items. In fact, many teachers construct test items by modifying questions from past year examination papers and assessment guidebooks rather than using SIOs. Once the test items are constructed, they are 'fitted' into the tables of specification so that they satisfy the assessment guidelines laid down by the Ministry of Education. Through experience, teachers find that using this approach enables them to gauge more adequately the ability of their pupils against the standard required by public examinations.

The above research study shows that curriculum policy from a central authority might still be enforced even in the face of adverse research findings. It also demonstrates the tenacity of teachers who have to cope with unpleasant curriculum innovation yet maintain the expectations on them, in this case, to produce good examination results. The consequence is a distortion of the aims of the curriculum planners. Indeed, the real impact of this innovation on classroom learning remains unknown to the planners and more research needs to be conducted in this area.

The Cognitive and Social Development of Pre-School Children in Singapore

This is a large-scale research funded by the Bernard van Leer Foundation of the Netherlands and administered by the Institute of Education, Singapore. It is coded as the IE-BVL Project and since its inception in 1983 has cost more than a S$1m.

The project covers three phases (see Ko, 1987; Lee, in press).

In phase I (1983–1986), data were collected among more than 3000 preschoolers on their cognitive and social skills. Several Piagetian tasks on language, mathematics, cognition and social development were administered individually in English (in some cases, in the child's preferred language). Strong evidence was found that few children could master two languages effectively at the same time. Not surprisingly, children who spoke a certain language at home tended to perform better in that language. Although Ko (1987) suggested that parents should play an important role, it is not clear whether it implies that most parents should speak English at home, since English is the main language of instruction.

Phase II (1986–1989) attempted to upgrade the English skills among children in non-private kindergartens through training teachers to use more effective teaching strategies.

The project is entering phase III (1989–1992), during which time the study will focus on cooperation between parents and teachers and the relative effects of parental involvement in their children's education. It has been suggested that while school activities should concentrate on literacy and numeracy, home activities should focus on proper social upbringing rather than to reinforce reading and writing.

This ongoing research has generated a lot of activities that involve preschoolers, teachers, parents and the community at large. It should have a beneficial impact on curriculum content and practices not only at pre-primary but also at lower primary level.

Children's (English) Language and Reading Development

Because English is such an important component in the Singapore curriculum, it has been the subject of many research projects. One such project is the Children's Language and Reading Development (Ng; 1987) conducted by lecturers from the Institute of Education.

The project began in March 1983 in twenty-four randomly selected primary schools involving 628 primary 1 to 3 pupils. The reading skills of these pupils were measured progressively. At the early stage, the Ministry of Education requested recommendations on teaching strategies for English. The project was subsequently enlarged to encompass observations of classroom activities in reading and interviews with teachers about reading instruction issues. The key finding was that lower primary pupils had restricted use of English since they learned English as an accumulation of discrete skills through repetitious drill in word recognition, punctuation and grammar.

As a result of this project, the Reading and English Acquisition Programme (REAP) was introduced in 1985. Materials were developed to allow pupils to acquire communicative use of English through listening, speaking, writing and reading activities. Teachers were trained in the use of these new materials. Evaluation in 1987 showed postive results in favour of the experimental group.

To summarize, these three projects show how research might provide useful information about the effects of curriculum practices in schools. Research studies should not only evaluate these effects but also provide impetus to future directions for curriculum development. In Singapore there is a need to be more open in disseminating research findings, especially those conducted for policy-makers. Small scale school-based projects by teachers can have direct impact on practices at a micro-level and the synthesis of these studies could point to significant features common to the whole system. This synthesis is lacking at the present time.

When relevant research about classroom practices is lacking, any curriculum development will have to rely on the experiences and reflection of those called upon to develop the curriculum. The next section describes such a case study involving the revision of the mathematics curriculum.

Revising the Mathematics Curriculum: A Case Study

The previous sections describe the nature of the standard school curriculum and recent innovations to school programmes to cope with challenges arising from political, economic, social and educational changes. Although global factors for curriculum changes are readily identified, the above discussion does not analyze the process of decision-making at the functional level. To understand the nature of this process requires an ethnographic approach involving persistent observation and questioning at the key stages of decision-making. However, in Singapore (and probably elsewhere too), decisions about education policies are made at a high level, involving directors of key divisions in the ministry, ministers for education and possibly the cabinet. It is impossible for researchers to gain access to this intricate process and to study how it actually functions.

It is, however, possible to describe how curriculum development has taken place at a lower level. This case study attempts to document *from a personal perspective* a process of revising mathematics syllabuses as part of an evaluation exercise carried out by the Ministry of Education.

Curriculum development involves more than just planning a syllabus. Producing a relevant syllabus that meets certain education objectives is a necessary step towards making a curriculum meaningful to the teachers and of significance to the pupils.

Mathematics is a compulsory subject at the primary and secondary levels. The Ministry of Education issues its own syllabus for primary schools. This syllabus covers topics in numbers, mensuration, geometry, statistics and simple algebra. For each topic, the syllabus describes the instructional objectives, lists the main concepts and learning outcomes, and provides sample exercises. Teachers normally use the textbooks, workbooks, and audio-visual materials produced by the Curriculum Development Institute of Singapore. However, teachers are expected to adapt the content to match the needs of their particular class of pupils.

At the secondary level, all pupils take the (elementary) mathematics course. At secondary 3 and 4 the more able pupils also take the additional mathematics course. Both courses are based on the 'O' Level syllabuses offered by the Cambridge Local Examination Syndicate. The syllabus for the weaker Normal pupils from secondary 1 to 4 is a sub-set of the topics included in the 'O' Level syllabus. The revision described below involves only the primary mathematics syllabus and the elementary mathematics syllabuses for the Normal and 'O' Level courses. The Ministry of Education has no intention of changing the content of the additional mathematics syllabus.

The Cambridge 'O' Level mathematics syllabus has undergone several changes in the past thirty years. In the 1950s, the syllabus (called syllabus A) covered topics in a compartmentalized fashion, such as arithmetic, algebra, and geometry (Euclidean). During the 1960s, many of these topics were integrated into a single subject called syllabus B. When modern mathematics were in vogue in the 1970s, pupils learnt about sets, axioms, transformations in the new syllabus C. Teachers generally taught these modern topics in the traditional chalk and talk way rather than using the discovery approach advocated by proponents of the modern mathematics movement. In the early 1980s, some educators were worried about the lack of basic numeracy skills as a consequence of the modern mathematics syllabus (perhaps an unfair conclusion) and it became clear that a combination of traditional and modern topics was needed. This gave rise to syllabus D which is the current one studied by all Singapore secondary school pupils.

In 1981, the Ministry of Education produced a mathematics syllabus for the Express and Special streams by arranging the topics in syllabus D into a four-year programme. At the same time, a sub-set of the topics in syllabus D was selected for the weaker Normal pupils for the 'N' Level examination.

In January 1988, the Curriculum Development Division of the Ministry of Education set up a Mathematics Syllabus Review Committee to review and revise the mathematics syllabuses in use since 1981. The Committee included mathematics inspectors, project directors of the primary and secondary mathematics projects at the Curriculum Development Institute of Singapore, officers from the Testing Branch, and a mathematics educator (the author) from the Institute of Education. Teachers were not represented on the Committee.

The terms of reference included: to study the adequacy of the syllabuses in meeting the needs of the pupils and to revise the syllabuses to reflect if appropriate recent trends in mathematics education. From the anecdotal feedback provided by the inspectors and teachers, the following areas require attention and revision:

(a) The Primary 1 content is too simple since much of it has already been covered in kindergartens. Topics at other levels should be adjusted so that the demand on pupils at each level is more balanced.

(b) Some topics in the secondary syllabus are too difficult for the weaker pupils (for example, vectors) or lack real applications. These topics should be deleted and replaced by other topics to help motivate these weak pupils. Besides, there should be a balance between process and product in mathematics learning.

(c) The teaching method is very traditional with teacher-centered instruction and pupils practising a lot of exercises in a rote manner. Understanding of mathematics concepts and problem solving is sacrificed at the expense of mastery of skills. Teachers blame this on an overloaded syllabus and the pressure to prepare pupils to excel in public examinations that test skills rather than understanding. Learning by discovery is seen as time consuming and more teaching time is needed to correct pupils who 'discover' the wrong things.

(d) Modern technology (for example, computers and calculators) should be used in mathematics learning and teaching, especially when these tools are readily available in Singapore.

These issues are not unique to Singapore as they are still being debated among mathematics educators all over the world. Some key findings such as the Agenda for Action (Shufelt and Smart, 1983) on problem solving and the Cockcroft Report (1982) on investigations and communications of mathematics ideas were used by the Review Committee. At the initial meetings, the Committee decided to carry out several activities. These included:

(a) To design questionnaires to obtain feedback from schools and teachers about the current syllabus and suggestions for change.
(b) To hold discussions with teachers and pupils, including observations of some lessons.
(c) To analyze pupils' performance in public examinations.
(d) To review recent mathematics curricula in other countries: United Kingdom, Australia, New Zealand, United States, European countries (for example, Hungary), Japan, Malaysia, Hong Kong, China, and to take note of syllabus changes offered by Cambridge, in particular the GCSE examination.
(e) To obtain feedback from tertiary institute (the University and polytechnics) about the adequacy of the syllabuses as preparation for future studies.
(f) To obtain feedback from employers about the requirements of mathematics for various careers, and in relation to this, to obtain the percentage of pupils leaving schools and entering the workforce at each level.

These activities sought to provide sufficient information and ideas that were essential for decision-making. Most of these activities were completed with the exception of talking to pupils and employers. The Committee members did not observe any lesson; instead, routine classroom observations by the inspectors and the mathematics educator were cited whenever appropriate. Although the Committee members were familiar with psychological theories of learning and teaching mathematics (from a Western perspective), they were unable to use any significant local studies to support their decisions.

The school questionnaires, sent out in March 1988, sought views of teachers on the coverage of topics at each level, including estimates of instructional time for each topic. Teachers were also asked to indicate the ease with which pupils learnt various topics, and the importance and nature (dull — interesting) of these topics. The data were analyzed and used for discussion.

Meetings with a small sample of primary and secondary mathematics teachers and mathematicians of the University and polytechnics were held in April and May 1988. During these meetings, many teachers indicated that they were against the use of calculators at the upper primary levels (the calculator is already being used in upper secondary levels), arguing that its use at the primary level would lead to lower mental arithmetic ability and 'laziness' in thinking. Some teachers were not sure about the 'process' aspect of mathematics learning and requested in-service training if this were to be included in the revised syllabus. When asked, most teachers did not suggest new topics, probably fearful that this would add to an already overcrowded syllabus. At a later stage, the committee decided to include new topics such as nets of solids and tessellations that would encourage pupils to develop visual ability, an aspect found to be missing in the current syllabus. The importance of visual ability has only been recognized recently by the mathematics education community, in particular with respect to the debate about dual hemispheric learning.

After some deliberations, including examination of overseas research on the effects of calculators on learning, the Committee recommended its use at the upper primary level as a tool to enable pupils to engage in problem-solving activities. To allay the fear of loss of mental ability, it suggested that schools should periodically administer speed tests on mental computations and estimation techniques. Unfortunately, this proposal was later rejected by the Curriculum Development Committee.

Teaching methods became a major discussion point since it was felt that not enough teachers were using innovative techniques that will make mathematics learning enjoyable and meaningful (for example, use of concrete materials and games) to the unmotivated pupils. In particular, teachers should allow more discussions and conduct practical work during mathematics lessons. To help teachers realize this curricular objective, it was decided to produce a teacher guide that included samples of how these techniques can be carried out to promote mathematical thinking (the process aspect). The role of the computer as a learning tool was noted but due to the constraint imposed by an external examination, it was decided not to examine how the introduction of the computer into the classroom might affect the content, for example, the use of symbolic manipulator on the learning of algebra.

Examination requirements are a constant constraint to curriculum development and implementation in most systems around the world. The new Cambridge GCSE examination was discussed with a Cambridge representative who was in Singapore at that time. The GCSE examination attempts to assess the process aspect through coursework and through the inclusion of special items that require the application of problem solving heuristics. Coursework was found to be unacceptable for several reasons: it is subjective assessment, it requires a lot of teacher time and effort, and its reliability and validity is subject to controversy. However, it was decided that the examination format should reflect the new emphasis of the revised curriculum. The details of the new format, including examination guidelines and sample test items, will be undertaken by the Testing Branch at a later stage.

After about one year of deliberations on the details of the syllabuses, it was time for the Committee to write the overall aims and specific objectives. It might seem strange that the details were worked out in advance of the aims. However, during meetings, the Committee members had frequently referred to the aims and objectives of the current syllabuses, and discussions alternated between general aims and specific content. In many sessions different interpretations of these widely accepted aims were hotly debated, although these interpretations and negotiations of meanings are rarely included in official documents.

Besides elaborating the aims and objectives, the Committee felt the need to devise a framework that would describe the philosophy of the revised curriculum. The framework according to the Committee, must be able to integrate the following aspects about mathematics learning and teaching:

understanding of concepts
mastery of essential skills
acquisition of mathematical processes
promotion of positive attitude towards mathematics
metacognitive insight about one's thinking and learning

These aspects should support the development of problem solving ability that enables pupils to apply this ability to real and realistic decision making. After much discussion of various pictorial models, the following pentagonal model was accepted as an appropriate compromise.

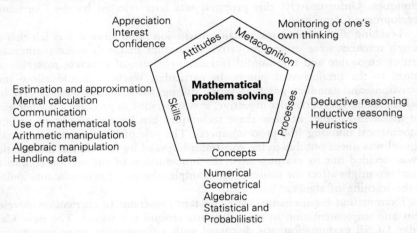

Appreciation
Interest
Confidence

Attitudes

Metacognition

Monitoring of one's own thinking

Mathematical problem solving

Skills

Processes

Estimation and approximation
Mental calculation
Communication
Use of mathematical tools
Arithmetic manipulation
Algebraic manipulation
Handling data

Deductive reasoning
Inductive reasoning
Heuristics

Concepts

Numerical
Geometrical
Algebraic
Statistical and
Probablilistic

The draft was submitted to the Curriculum Development Committee and was accepted in February 1989. In August 1989, feedback about the draft was obtained from a random sample of twenty-six primary and twenty secondary schools. The overall response from teachers was that the content was adequate and appropriate, but training was required for the new topics (nets and tessellations). Modifications were made after taking this feedback into account, and the final version was approved in January 1990. Schools were briefed in August 1990 and commercial publishers will be given copies of the syllabuses. Teachers will be trained beginning in 1991. The revised curriculum will be implemented in 1992 for primary 1, 2 and 4 Extended and secondary 1.

Concluding Comments

A school curriculum can be defined in terms of its aims, content and resources, teaching and learning strategies, and assessment practices. However, it also exists within a broader context involving the physical, political, cultural, economic, and social environments that define and constrain its role in educating the populace. Given its compact size, Singapore has, over the past three decades, developed a centralized education system that is efficient and capable of responding quickly to unforeseen changes to ensure that its children will survive in a technological environment.

The aims of the school curriculum in Singapore are geared towards econo-mic survival by exploiting to the full the potential of each pupil. Means to achieve this aim include streaming to reduce educational wastage, the develop-ment of specific programmes such as the Gifted Education Programme and CoRT, and providing vocational training for the non-academic pupils. The majority of the pupils still take an academic curriculum that is based on Western notions of academic discipline and they are assessed by rigorous public examina-tions modelled on the Cambridge system. This approach coupled with the pivotal role of English and the exposure to Western influences has led to the cultural dilemma of how to preserve some elements of traditional values in the onslaught of materialism. Hence, the teaching of mother tongue and moral education (and until 1989 religious knowledge) is made compulsory for all pupils to learn about their cultures and to inculcate acceptable social behaviours in a multiracial society. That this approach has not been very successful is evident from the recent debate about bilingualism and a new civics programme.

Teachers, and especially the younger graduates, are generally well trained in the academic subjects and the pedagogy. However, they tend to use a teacher-centered approach rather than discovery learning or group work that require the pupils to take a more active role in learning. They argue that a didactic approach is necessary to cope with overcrowded syllabuses for large classes within a double session constraint and the pressure to produce good grades in public examina-tions. The teachers themselves have gone through similar examinations in their younger days and they tend to believe what has worked for them should also work for their pupils. The Ministry of Education encourages teachers to experi-ment with innovative teaching methods through an extensive in-service pro-gramme that requires each teacher to complete at least one in-service course every three or four years of teaching. It also provides financial grants for teachers to conduct school-based projects that should have an impact on the school curriculum.

Textbooks have to be reviewed and approved by the Ministry of Education. The official Curriculum Development Institute of Singapore produces textbooks, teacher guides and other audio-visual materials for most subjects and this presents a serious challenge to private publishers within a small market. The CDIS materials are often backed up with workshops for the teachers, a service which private publishers find hard to emulate. In addition to textbooks, teachers rely heavily on past year examination papers and guidebooks to prepare lesson plans (teaching to the examination requirement) rather than using taxonomies of instructional objectives. Similarly, instructional objectives are seldom used in constructing test papers.

Debates about key educational policies are often initiated by politicians in the Parliament. In addition to three ministers in charge of education, a government Parliamentary Committee on Education helps to collect feedback from various sources about educational issues. Final decisions are made after internal consulta-tion within the Ministry of Education and at the cabinet, after which major policies are submitted to Parliament for approval. When a policy is implemented, it is unlikely that the Ministry will withdraw the decision even in the face of public controversy (for example, streaming) or research findings (for example, survey on SIOs).

Curriculum implementation is facilitated through an efficient administrative system that makes use of a sophisticated computer network called the School Link. The system is intended to reduce the time and energy spent by principals and teachers on administrative chores so that they can use this time to improve on the quality of instruction. This perceived saving in time has yet to be substantiated.

Teacher salaries are equivalent to other professions in the civil service. However, teaching is a very demanding job in a less than favourable environment: large class size, examination pressure, dusty and noisy classrooms. Teachers are often called upon to perform an ever increasing number of roles: a subject specialist, a disciplinarian, a career guidance officer, a counsellor, an administrator who should be computer literate. Hence, it is not surprising that teaching is not a favourite career choice among pupils and their parents. For the past three years, the Ministry of Education has launched TV commercials to attract eligible candidates (especially males) into the teaching profession. It has also announced plans to improve on the facilities provided to teachers and pupils. These attempts should benefit the schools in particular but the survival of the nation will depend on the effort being successful.

Notes

1 Note the different meanings of 'Normal': in primary schools, most pupils take the Normal course, in secondary schools, the Normal course is for the slow learners.
2 We, the citizens of Singapore, pledge ourselves as one united people regardless of race, language or religion to build a democratic society based on justice and equality so as to achieve happiness, prosperity and progress for our nation.
3 Tan suggested that 'male dominance' also prevails at the lower intellectual spectrum.

Chapter 8

Curriculum Development in South Korea

Se-Ho Shin and Kyung-Chue Huh

Introduction

The population of South Korea was about 42 million in 1989, and the total number of students was about 11 million, or 25 per cent of the whole population.

The Koreans are a homogeneous race who speak one language. Both shamanistic rites and ancestor worship have deep roots in the customs of the Koreans, but these have been blended with Confucianism, Buddhism, Taoism, and more recently with Christian beliefs. Thus, the primary trait of Korean culture is to be found in the synthesis of these external influences on the native mold. Similarly, a primary trait of curriculum development is the extent to which it has reflected external influences. In this chapter the nature of the educational system, the school curriculum and the processes of decision-making are analyzed. Subsequently the problems affecting the curriculum are discussed.

School System in South Korea

A ladder-type school system of 6–3–3–4 is currently in use in Korea, as stipulated by the Education Law, promulgated in 1949. Article 81 of the Education Law provides for the establishment of the types of schools shown in Figure 8.1.

Curriculum Development: A Historical Review

Since the establishment of the government of the Republic of Korea in 1948, the school curriculum has been revised five times as of 1990. Kim *et al.* (1987) described the five curricula in terms of five broad phases, namely (i) subject-matter centered; (ii) life-centered; (iii) discipline-centered; (iv) humanistic-oriented; and (v) future-oriented curricula. Even though these categorizations do not completely match with the contents of the curricula, it is convenient to use these terms in describing the history of curriculum revision (or development) in South Korea.

The first revision of curriculum was made in 1955 which was ten years after

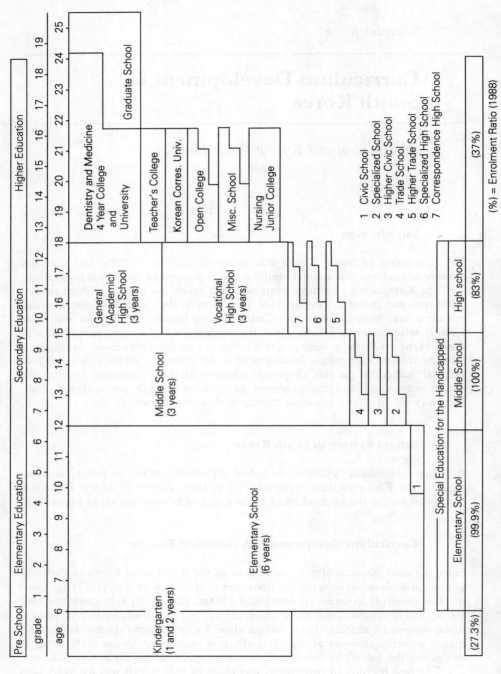

Figure 8.1 The current school system in South Korea

Korea ceased to be a Japanese colony. This was a turbulent period which witnessed many historic events such as three years of American military administration, the establishment of the Korean government, and the outbreak of the Korean War. Schools did operate during the war but without a unified and well constructed national curriculum. Thus teachers relied on curricula which they made themselves.

From 1945, the year when Japanese colonization of Korea ended, up to 1955, all levels of school were managed on the basis of syllabuses that were temporarily constructed by the American Military Administration. Korean educators of that time were, of course, eager to construct new curriculum relevant to the needs of the Korean people, but their wishes had to be postponed because of the outbreak of the Korean War.

In 1955, at the end of the war, Korean educators began to revise the temporarily made syllabuses and constructed a new curriculum which was the first designed by Korean educators. At this time, John Dewey's ideas were in great vogue and a leading and influential figure in the field of Korean education was Dr Chen-suck Oh, who was one of John Dewey's students. His progressive educational ideals, which emphasize children's lives and interests, were popular among educators and an effort was made to construct a school curricula which reflected the spirit of Dewey's progressivism.

However, the resulting curriculum is better regarded as one which focused on subject-matter beacuse it was actually developed on the basis of traditional subject boundaries. This is the reason why the first revision is termed a subject-matter centered instead of a child-centered curriculum.

The second revision occurred in 1963. Around this time, there were major political changes such as the April 19 Students' Revolution, which resulted in the collapse of the First Republic, the establishment of the Second Republic, the May 16 Military Coup, the collapse of the Second Republic, and the beginning of the Third Republic. With this turmoil, the military government of the Third Republic felt a need to revise the national curriculum to reflect their political philosophy. Curriculum specialists at that time were still influenced by the educational ideas of John Dewey and the key concepts of his theory were the cornerstones of the second revision. At this time, the Ministry of Education (MOE) officially defined the curriculum as 'the total amount of experiences that the students undergo by the guidance of school'. Thus, the second revision is called an 'experience-centered' or 'life-centered' curriculum.

The revised secondary curriculum consequently emphasized life experiences as the basis for the selection of content and localism as the principle of curriculum management. The curriculum also stressed anti-communism and moral education in response to the political philosophy of the Third Republic.

The third major change was made in 1973, ten years after the second revision. The third Republic regime changed its characteristics in October 1972, which was called 'October Yoo-shin' (make things new). The main characteristics of the new Third Republic were an emphasis on economic development, the pursuit of a strong anti-Communist policy, and an emphasis on the inculcation of a 'national identity and national spirit'. From a curricular point of view, this resulted in an increased importance for subjects such as science, technology, national ethics and national history. Overall this resulted in a move towards a more 'discipline centred curriculum' that was advocated by Brunerians in the

1960s in the USA. Following Bruner the 'structures' and 'basic concepts' of each subject were emphasized and 'discovery and inquiry' were promoted as the main teaching methods. For example, the concept of set was introduced into the first grade mathematics in primary school, and the science textbook focused on problem solving. In addition, moral education was included as a new subject in the curriculum and Korean history was emphasized more than in previous curricula. The moral education curriculum emphasized national identity, anti-communism and the validity of the 'October Yoo-shin' doctrine of the government.

In 1981, the fourth curriculum change was carried out by the government of the Fifth Republic that started in 1980. This revision was characterized by the fact that the whole process of curriculum change was entrusted to a professional curriculum research institute, namely the Korean Educational Development Institute (KEDI). This resulted in the introduction of integrated subjects in lower grades in elementary school. This revision was directed toward achieving a 'humanistic oriented curriculum'.

Even though the fourth curriculum has been named a humanistic oriented one, it is difficult to identify a leading curriculum theorist or any leading curriculum theory which influenced this change. But the reasons that Korean curriculum scholars call the fourth change a humanistic one are that the curriculum emphasized the education of the whole person and the integration of subjects.

Finally the fifth revision occured in 1987–88. Unlike the former revisions, the fifth occurred in a politically stable climate and was an attempt to adjust the curriculum to the future needs of society. During this period Korea hosted the Asian Olympics and the 24th World Olympic Games (1988 in Seoul). As a developing country increasingly involved in world events, there was a very strong demand that students should learn the things that are specially needed in future. This led to the fifth revision which was similar to that of fourth but focused more on the needs of an information society of the future.

The fifth change cannot be easily associated with any single leading curriculum scholar. Some curriculum specialists thought that some parts of the new curriculum were made in preparation for the future and this was to an extent true. For example, mathematics and science were emphasized (by increasing the number of instructional periods) in preparation for the future challenges. Computer education was also given emphasis; some chapters of 'practical art' (an elementary school subject) were allocated to computer education and a new subject, 'information industry', was established in the upper-secondary school curricula. This was done to meet the needs which it is anticipated will arise in a future information society.

Processes of Curriculum Development in South Korea

The most salient characteristic of curriculum development in South Korea is that the mode of decision-making is highly centralized (Cheng, 1990). The intended curriculum is determined at the national level and thus, all schools in Korea follow the same national curricula. In this section, the form and content of school curricula and the procedures by which they are developed are described. The description is based on the most recent revision, i.e. the fifth revision.

Forms of School Curricula

It is very easy to understand the formal curriculum of Korean schools because they are basically the same across the nation. There is only one kind of primary school curriculum and one kind of middle school curriculum. The 'primary school curriculum' published by Ministry of Education (MOE) describes what subjects are taught, in what ways they should be taught and the time allocated to each subject in primary schools.

Although the details are somewhat different depending on the school level, the forms (or structures) of school curricula are basically the same. School curriculum for each level of school is compiled as a book (or a pamphlet) which consists of two parts: 'General guidelines' relating to the whole school curriculum, and 'Specific guidelines' concerning each particular subject-matter curriculum. The general guidelines consist of four parts: (i) guiding principles; (ii) the curriculum goals of each level of schooling; (iii) subject-matter organization and time allotment; and (iv) guidelines for curriculum management. The 'guiding principles' are the same regardless of the school level, whilst the General guidelines differ depending on the level of school. The contents of these are as the following.

The 'Guiding Principles'

The 'guiding principles' are, as their name suggests, the general guidelines for the curriculum at all levels of schooling. They describe why the school curricula should be changed, the direction of change and what the model of the ideal human is towards which our students should be educated. The guiding principles of the fifth revised curriculum are as follows:

Education aims to enable all citizens to perfect their characters, foster independence, develop better citizenship and thereby to devote themselves to development of the democracy and contribute to realization of an ideal of human co-prosperity.

To realize this aim, Korean education has concentrated its efforts on developing mentally and physically strong Koreans, who love their nation and its culture, who think scientifically with a passion of truth-investigation, and who are aesthetic, responsible, cooperative, and hard working.

During the last four decades, school curricula have been revised several times. The curricula needed to be revised again in order to meet the challenges raised in a highly industrialized, information-intensive society, which is the result of a rapidly increasing amount of knowledge and scientific technology. Those challenges include a need to respond objectively to an ever-changing international situations and to ensure the type of environment where Korean citizens can lead happy and harmonious lives, resulting in south-north unification.

In response to these challenges, this fifth revision of the school curricula is constructed with an emphasis on cultivating students as well rounded persons: physically fit, intellectually independent, creative, logical, and sensitive towards other people and the environment, as well as morally responsible.

1 Healthy person
   (a) Strong body
   (b) Tenacious will
   (c) Elegant taste
   (d) Rich emotion
2 Independent person
   (a) Self-confident
   (b) Autonomous decision-making ability
   (c) Progressive pioneer spirit
   (d) Strong awareness of national identity
3 Creative person
   (a) Basic learning skills
   (b) Scientific investigative abilities
   (c) Rational problem solving abilities
   (d) Aptitude for original thought
4 Moral person
   (a) Proper values
   (b) Awareness of human dignity
   (c) Sense of good citizenship
   (d) Concern for the well-being of others

As an example of the form and content of the school curriculum in Korea, the goals and organization of the primary and high school curriculum are presented below.

The Primary School Curriculum

Goals
The goals of elementary school education, constructed on the basis of those prescribed in the 'Educational Act' and the 'Guiding Principles' of school curriculum construction, are as follows:

   (i)   To develop physical and mental strength and to foster sound health and safety habits.
   (ii) To observe basic etiquettes and self-discipline necessary for daily life, as well as developing concern for one's neighbours.
   (iii) To foster nationalism.
   (iv) To acquire basic language skills, developing the ability to effectively express oneself.
   (v)   To understand basic concepts concerning social and natural phenomena; encouraging scientific investigation and problem solving.
   (vi) To appreciate beauty and to creatively express oneself.

(vii) To acquire basic life skills, emphasizing frugality and the need for self-support.

Organization and time allotment
1 Organization
(a) Elementary school curricula consist of subject–matter and extra–curricular activities.
  (i) The subject–matter includes nine areas: moral education, Korean language, social studies, mathematics, science, physical education, music, visual arts, and practical arts. The lower-grade curriculum includes four integrated areas of subject-matter, such as 'We are the First-Graders', 'Daily Life', 'Inquiring Life' and 'Pleasant Life'.
  (ii) Extra–curricular activities are composed of 'childrens' association activities', 'Club activities', and 'School events'.
2 Time allotment
  (a) Time allotment by subject area is shown below.

Subjects	Grade		1	2
Subject Areas	Korean language	We are the First Graders	210 (7)	238 (7)
	Mathematics		120 (4)	136 (4)
	Daily life		120 (4)	136 (4)
	Inquiring life		60 (2)	68 (2)
	Pleasant life		180 (6)	238 (7)
Extra-curricular activities			30 (1)	34 (1)
Total			790 (24)	850 (25)

Subjects	Grade	3	4	5	6
Subject areas	Moral education	68 (2)	68 (2)	68 (2)	68 (2)
	Korean language	238 (7)	204 (6)	204 (6)	204 (6)
	Social studies	102 (3)	102 (3)	136 (4)	136 (4)
	Mathematics	136 (4)	136 (4)	170 (5)	170 (5)
	Science	102 (3)	136 (4)	136 (4)	136 (4)
	Physical education	102 (3)	102 (3)	102 (3)	102 (3)
	Music	68 (2)	68 (2)	68 (2)	68 (2)
	Visual arts	68 (2)	68 (2)	68 (2)	68 (2)
	Practical arts		68 (2)	68 (2)	68 (2)
Sub total					
Extra-curricular activities		68 (2)	68 (2)	68 (2)	68 (2)
Grand total		952 (28)	1020 (30)	1088 (32)	1088 (32)

1   The numbers in the table assigned to each subject show the total number of instruction hours in the 34 weeks of a school year. The numbers in parentheses indicate hours per week.

2   In case of first grade, the integrated subject, 'We are the First Graders', is taught for the first four weeks in March, the numbers assigned to the other subjects and extra-curricular activities are the instruction hours that are to be taught during the remaining 30 weeks.

3   One hour means an instruction period of 40 minutes. However, each school can adapt the allotted time to the conditions of weather, season, pupils' developmental stage and the characteristics of the subject content to be taught.

4   Instruction hours assigned to extra-curricular activities in grades 2 and 3 can be adjusted depending upon each school's situation.

The High School Curriculum

Goals

The goals of high school education, constructed on the basis of those prescribed in the 'Educational Act', and the 'Guiding Principles' of school curriculum construction, are:

(i)   To develop physical and mental strength, as well as cultivating a mature self-image and good character.

(ii) To understand the concept of human dignity and the value of democracy, to cultivate the desire to contribute to national development, and to encourage concern for the welfare of all human beings.

(iii) To acquire basic verbal and mathematical skills which encourage further learning, as well as logic and creative thinking abilities, and to apply these skills practically.

(iv) To understand basic principles of natural and social phenomena, encouraging the development of information processing and scientific investigation skills.

(v)   To develop an appreciation of aesthetic and creative abilities through the provision of opportunities for aesthetic experiences; and to make effective use of leisure time.

(vi) To choose the future career best suited to an individual's aptitude and ability, while constructing the academic and professional basis for that career.

Organization and time allotment

1   Organization

(a)   The high school curriculum consists of a range of subjects and extracurricular activities.

(i)   The subjects are composed of general subjects and specialized subjects. General subjects include fourteen subjects, such as: moral education, Korean language, Korean history, social studies, mathematics, natural science, physical education, military exercises, music, visual arts, written Chinese, foreign languages, and industry-home economics and free optionals.

(ii) General subjects and specialized subjects consist of compulsory subjects and electives.

(iii) Common compulsory subjects are given to all students whatever school they attend, whether academic, vocational, or other special high school.

(iv) The curriculum of academic high schools is divided at grade 12 and above, into three courses of study: humanities and social sciences, natural science, and vocational.

(v) Vocational high schools are divided into the following: farming, engineering, commerce, marine-fisheries, and domestic-practical arts. The curriculum is composed of general subjects, specialized compulsory subjects, and specialized electives, according to each specialized area or course.

(vi) Special high schools are divided into the following: science, athletics, and arts. The curriculum is composed of general subjects, specialized compulsory subjects, and specialized electives, according to each specialized area course.

(b) Extra-curricular activities consists of four areas: classroom activities, club activities, student council activities, and school events.

2 Time allotment

The number of units for each subject in the high school curriculum is as follow:

Subject Areas	Subjects	General subjects				Specialized Subjects
		Common Compulsory	Electives by course			Compulsory and Electives for Vocational and Special H.S., and for Vocational Course of academic H.S.
			Humanities Social Science Course	Natural Science Course	Vocational and Specialized H.S. and Vocational Courses of Academic H.S.	
Moral education	National ethics	6 ¦ (6)				
Korean language	Language Literature Writing Grammar	10 ¦ (10) ¦ (4)	8 6 4	8 4	)) 4)	Subjects for Farming, Engineering, Commerce, Marine and Fisheries, Domestic Affairs and Practical Arts, and Other Courses.
Korean history	Korean history	6 ¦ (4)				
Social Studies	Politics and Economics Korean geography World history Social culture World geography	6 ¦ (4) 6 ¦ (4)	4 4 4	4	))) 4))	
Mathematics	General Mathematics Mathematics " I " II	8 ¦ (8)	10	18	) 6)))	

Subject Areas	Subjects	General subjects				Specialized Subjects
		Common Compulsory	Electives by course			Compulsory and Electives for Vocational and Special H.S., and for Vocational Course of academic H.S.
			Humanities Social Science Course	Natural Science Course	Vocational and Specialized H.S. and Vocational Courses of Academic H.S.	
Science	Science I	10	(8)] Select 1			)
	" II		(8)	8		)
	Physics			8		) 4
	Chemistry			8		)
	Biology			6] Select 1		)
	Earth science			6		)
Physical education	Physical education	6	(6)	8	8	4
Military exercise	Military exercise	12	(12)			
Music	Music	4	(4)] Select 1			)
Arts	Arts	4	(4)			) 2
Written Chinese	Written Chinese			8	4	4
	English I	8	(8)			8
	English II			12	12	
Foreign language	German French Spanish Chinese Japanese			Select 1 10	Select 1 10	))) 6))
	Industrial-engineering Home economics			Select 1 8	Select 1 8	)) 4)
Vocational Education and Home Economics	Farming Engineering Commerce Marine and fishery Domestic affairs Information industry			Select 1	Select 1	
Free optionals			2	2	2	
Number of unit to be taken						Vocat'l H.S. 82–122 Special H.S. Vocat'l Course in 50–100 Academic H.S.
Extra-curricular activities		12	(12)			
	Total			204–216		

1 One unit refers to 50 minutes per week during one semester (17 weeks).
2 The number in parenthesis refers to the number of criterion units pertaining to Vocational High Schools and Special High Schools.

The Fifth Curriculum Revision

As already stated, the procedures of curriculum decision-making in Korea are very centralized; thus, key decisions about curriculum policy are determined by the MOE. However, as criticism of the centralized system of decision-making have increased, the MOE is trying to change the approach to decision-making. The MOE still decides whether to change the curriculum or not, what to change, and how to change. However, since the fourth revision the MOE has entrusted KEDI with a substantial role in the process of curriculum revision and development. It is therefore essential to look at the different roles performed by the MOE and KEDI in order to clearly understand how school curricula have developed.

Division of Tasks

Figure 8.2 shows the procedures, major tasks, time scale, and the institute involved in the fifth curriculum revision. It can be seen that the tasks of policy-making (for example, basic work plan, basic direction of revision), reviewing and finalizing the draft confirmation and promulgation of a new version of the curriculum were performed by the MOE, whilst the research and development were undertaken by KEDI.

One thing to be noted here is that figure 8.2 describes the curriculum development processes of kindergarten, primary, and middle school. High school curricula were developed in the same manner but one year later.

Curriculum and Textbook Revision

The task of curriculum revision (or development) undertaken by the MOE also involves textbook revision, the provision of teacher's guides and teacher training. This is a complicated job which takes a long time. The complexity is exacerbated when the revision involves various school levels.

The schedule for textbook revision in kindergarten, elementary, middle and high school, which was made by MOE, is presented in figure 8.3.

KEDI: Research Team Organization

It is also necessary to understand how KEDI proceeded with the task of providing basic research and the actual development of curriculum drafts. The tasks and the sequence in which they were performed was shown in figure 8.2. In this section, the way KEDI organized research is described.

To proceed with the curriculum development plan that was depicted in figure 8.3, KEDI organized a Curriculum Research and Development Team. This team was mainly composed of staff from KEDI, but also included many resource persons such as personnel from schools, universities and other concerned professionals, some of whom joined as the members of the advisory

Figure 8.2 *Work plan of the fifth curriculum revision*

Procedures	Major tasks	Period	Institution in charge
Policy-making	• Basic plan to revise the fifth curriculum • Work plan • Establishment of the direction of revision	1985. 6 1986. 2	MOE
Basic research	• Analysis of the relevance and effectiveness of the current curriculum • Needs assessment • International comparative study of curriculum • Analysis of the research trend of curriculum and subject education • Research on elementary integrated curriculum • Study on the improvement of the textbook system	1982 1986. 6	KEDI
Development of the fifth curriculum draft	• General guidelines – Organization Principles – Educational objectives – Organization and time allotment – Management guidelines	1986. 1 1986. 6	KEDI
	• Specific guidelines – Teaching objectives of subjects and extra-curricular activities – Cautions in teaching	1986. 1 1986.12	
Deliberation of the draft	Deliberation of General guidelines	1986. 7 1986. 8	MOE
	Deliberation of Specific guidelines	1973. 3 1987. 5	
Confirmation and notification	• Final substitution of the Draft • Final Deliberation • Notification	1987. 6 1987.11	MOE

Figure 8.3 *Plan of the fifth curriculum and textbook revision*

Time	The Fifth Revision					
School Year	'86	'87	'88	'89	'90	'91
Kinder-garten	Curriculum Development Deliberation and Notification — Teacher's guide Development	Teacher Training Piloting Application				
Elementary School	Curriculum Development Deliberation and Notification — Teacher Training Textbook Development — Piloting Textbook Application					
Middle School	Curriculum Development Deliberation and Notification — Teacher Training Textbook Development — Piloting Textbook Application					
High School	Curriculum Development Deliberation and Notification — Teacher Training Textbook Devleopment Piloting Application					
Special School	Curriculum Development Deliberation and Notification — Teacher Training Textbook Development — Piloting Textbook Application					

professorial team. The kind of team organization of KEDI for developing the fifth revised draft for school curricula is shown in figure 8.4.

The KEDI team also worked in close connection with other organizations. The cooperative relationship of KEDI with its related organizations is depicted in Figure 8.5.

The MOE decided the scope and objectives of curriculum revision after discussion with the Council for Education Reform which provided the ideology and directions on which the revision was based. This body of seventy eminent persons was established in 1987 by Presidential Decree. It provided a broad plan

Figure 8.4   Team organization to develop the fifth revised draft of school curriculum

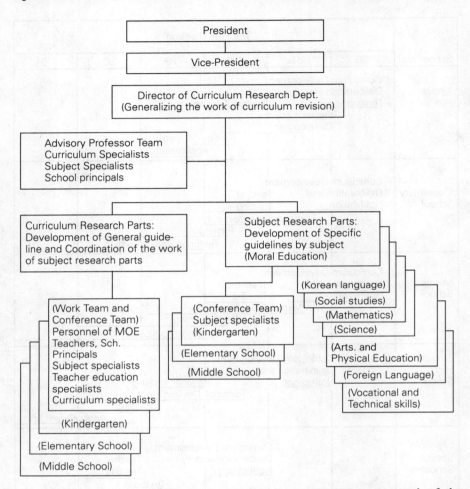

for educational reform and was disestablished in 1989. The personnel of the Council have participated in various activities to elicit views from a wide cross section of the community. Institutions of teacher education (Colleges of Education, Teachers' Colleges) and related personnel of Universities and College participated actively in the many tasks related to curriculum revision. In addition, KEDI was assisted by parents, academic societies and other social organizations that expressed concern over the fifth curriculum revision.

Issues and Problems in Curriculum Development in South Korea

An analysis of issues and problems in curriculum development in a country is highly subjective for it is obviously dependent on both the focus and the criteria selected by the analyst.

Figure 8.5   Relationship between KEDI and related organizations

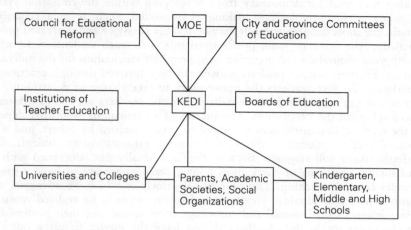

Five broad issues and problems are identified. These are the problems of : (i) the centralized mode of curriculum decision-making; (ii) the discrepancy between 'general guidelines' and 'specific guidelines by subject'; (iii) the lack of curriculum materials; (iv) the low level of teachers' professionalism in curriculum development; and (v) the influence of college entrance examinations on the curriculum.

The Curriculum Decision-making Process

The system of centralized curricular decision-making is mandated by Article 155 of the Education Law. In the past, decisions regarding education were monopolized by a minority élite class who decided educational content. This group consisted of religious leaders, the governing class in power, and a group of scholars. Nowadays, equality of educational opportunity necessitates a change of the method of determining educational content. Participation by concerned citizens has increased. This trend is especially apparent in countries practising free democracy. Many policies promoting school-based curriculum development are examples of this trend.

Before criticizing the effects of a centralized mode of curriculum decision-making we need to examine in depth this mode in the light of the nature of our free democratic ideology, and the influences of such a method of decision-making on education. It is important to note that a centralized system is not without any merit. It is effective in the following ways: to realize a national will in education, to manage nation wide school affairs uniformly, to protect schools from the heterogeneous needs and pressures of many factions in society, and to forbid the egoistic permeation into schools of the educational industries, particularly publishing companies.

However, the above justification is only possible if one assumes that the democratic system is immature and inadequately developed. A mature democratic society copes with these problems by allowing autonomous managerial decisions and the spontaneous participation of concerned people, rather than by

175

utilizing the authority of an élite. A reliance on centralized educational decision-making may prohibit democracy from developing within the education system for when curriculum decision-making is one-sided, such as in a centralized system, the most dangerous result may be teacher passivity and decreased professionalism. The teachers' main professional role is to teach students well, which presupposes their ability to prescribe an appropriate curriculum for the individual student. Further, teacher professionalism can be improved through practice and experience. To give teachers the opportunity to take charge of determining the curriculum can stimulate professionalism, because teachers are the professionals who implement the curriculum. The success of a curriculum eventually depends on the teacher. If a curriculum is limited or predetermined by others, and if the teachers' role is reduced to simply transmitting information to students, their professionalism will stagnate. Because they are usually not concerned with the fundamental problems of curriculum policy, teachers are apt to have a passive attitudes towards teaching. The educational principles which we advocate, such as autonomy, individuality, creativity and so on can only be realized when we view teachers as professional and encourage them to enhance their professionalism. In order to do this, teachers should have the power to carry out their professional role. The quick way to do this is to give teachers the right to determine one part of the curriculum. This may require reforms to the present system, but, assuming that teachers know the best method to teach students, they should be allowed to not follow precisely the official curriculum but have the discretion to reorganize and adapt it.

Realizing the critical problems which resulted from the centralized system, and in view of the socio-political atmosphere which emphasizes democratization, the government is preparing for a drastic change of the whole educational system. One change envisaged is to move from a centralized curriculum decision-making system to a decentralized one. Koreans are now preparing for this development with great hope but also with some degree of uneasiness.

The Discrepancy Between 'General Guidelines' and 'Specific Guidelines'

The official curriculum in South Korea is composed of two basic parts: the 'General Guidelines' and 'Specific Guidelines by subject'. The General Guidelines, as has already been indicated, include (i) guiding principles; (ii) goals of curriculum; (iii) organization and time allocation of subjects; and (iv) guidelines for curriculum management.

The general guidelines describe the ideal human characteristics to which all levels of school education should be directed, the educational goals of each level of schooling, the scope and the range of subjects to be included in school education, and the general rules or guidelines for managing the school curriculum.

The subject specific guidelines includes: (i) the subject-specific objectives; (ii) objectives and contents by grade; and (iii) guidelines for instruction and evaluation. These guidelines therefore provide a detailed description of the objectives, contents, and evaluation method for each school subject.

In general, especially, in the cases of the fourth and fifth curriculum revision, the general guidelines were developed first by the education-curriculum specialist, while the subject specific guidelines are developed later by subject-matter specialists. This two-step developmental process and the differentiation of the work between two groups of people causes serious problems of consistency in curriculum development.

The most serious and salient problem is the appearance of a gap between the 'spirit' of the general guidelines and the actual subject-matter curriculum. The core of the problem is that the intentions specified in the general guidelines are not faithfully reflected in each subject-specific curriculum. It is often the case that the general guidelines say one thing and each subject-matter curriculum says another. In the case of the fifth revision, the general guidelines mandated that subject-specific curricula should emphasize the enhancement of human character-istics such as bodily and mental health, independence, creativity, and morality. Each subject-specific curriculum was constructed with reference to its own academic tradition, however, disregarding the demand of the general guidelines. These two elements of the curriculum are therefore poorly connected which means that it is difficult to translate broad goals into operational realities.

This phenomenon is a long standing one. From the first revision to the fifth, the problem has haunted the educational system like a ghost. The problem is evident, but we don't understand clearly why it happens and how to deal with it. The gap has been ascribed to the power conflict between education-major special-ists and subject-matter specialists. The former group, who comprise persons who have specialized in the study of education as graduates and undergraduates, play a pivotal role in the process of national curriculum reform as they take on the role of coordinating and controlling the revision process. Others argue that the Korean school curriculum has developed on the basis of two incompatible cur-riculum theories. According to Cho and Huh (1988), the general guidelines were constructed on the basic of a life-centered curriculum theory, whereas the subject-specific curriculum guidelines were developed on the basic of a discipline-centered curriculum perspective.

At any rate, this problem remains unsolved, and will emerge again as a serious problem in the sixth revision of the curriculum. For the sake of both the efficency and consistency of school curriculum, it is necessary that this problem is solved.

The Lack of Curriculum Materials

Textbooks and teachers' guides are the main materials available to teachers. Whilst the official School Curriculum promulgated by the MOE is removed from the school, the textbooks are heavily used by teachers and pupils because internal and external assessment is limited to the content of the approved textbooks.

The first problem is that textbook publication is under the strict control of the MOE and the second is that the development and provisions of various forms of curriculum materials is severely neglected. As textbooks are seen as the prepared and assessed curriculum for teachers and students it is natural that the development of texts should be under the tight control of the MOE. The present textbook publishing system distinguishes between first class and second class texts, with no obvious difference between the quality of the books in each category.

Teaching in schools is driven by the textbook and the method by which textbooks are published, disseminated and managed is a major factor determing the teaching and learning style used. As schools can only use government designated or confirmed textbooks, these constitute the authoritative definition of the subject and encourage a one-sided, textbook-centered teaching style. The contents of the textbooks also serve as the absolute criteria for educational evaluation. The solution to the problem of whether textbooks should be produced or selected by a public institution or government is dependent upon the type of society and the goals we are trying to achieve (Shin, 1990). It is obvious that, although texbooks are merely one sort of curriculum resource, as long as they are published and managed by public authority, textbook-centered education will not be changed, and the achievement of a flexible education system which stresses independent thought will not be realized.

In relation to this, we cannot overlook the attendant problem of reference books, which explain and supplement the contents of textbooks, and which are proliferating. As long as textbook-centered education continues, students will continue to need reference books, and the publishing companies will continue to produce them. As a result students have become dependent upon textbooks and rote learning which stifles the possibilities of nourishing their independence and creativity.

The next problem of textbook-centered education is that curriculum materials for students are limited to one official textbook. Other resources, such as video programs, slides, and tape recording materials for teachers and students are not provided as an integrated set for each subject, grade and semester, at the time of the curriculum revision. Limiting the development of curriculum materials for students to only one textbook per subject may inhibit learning by making it difficult to respond to the differing needs and requests of students. In addition, in comparison to the extensive use of a range of media throughout society, the provision for education is far behind. The inadequacy of the textbook publishing system may be one of the reasons that students are not satisfied with textbooks and increasingly depend on reference books.

At the very least, educational publishing companies should develop qualitatively better curricular materials rather than just publishing reference books which supplement the textbooks. The schools should be able to decide which curricular materials they adopt. A fundamental change such as this may be the means for reducing the uniformity and inflexibility of the Korean educational system.

Teacher Professionalism

Teacher passivity and a low level of professionalism were previously mentioned as a possible consequence of the centralized system of curriculum control. As with the tenets of the self-fulfilling prophecy with regard to the effect of expectations on students' performance, teachers will also only achieve what is expected of them. If we believe that teachers are professionals, and give them the means to act professionally, they will meet those expectations.

The success or failure of a curriculum is completely dependent upon the teacher's understanding and utilization of that curriculum. It is self-evident that curriculum revision does not succeed without the participation of teachers. There have been cases of innovative new curricular programs which were developed at great expense, but were completely unsuccessful. This reinforces the importance of teacher participation in educational development.

It is important then that curriculum revision must reinforce a teacher's desire to innovate, as well as address and offer solutions for practical problems experienced by all teachers. It may be far sighted and more effective if we have teachers develop revised drafts of school curricula at local levels, and then synthesize these inputs to develop a national level curriculum.

In the past, in-service teacher training has been provided only after the curriculum was revised. The teacher training program is an important aspect in the success or failure of a new curriculum and should be a major concern. Issues related to curriculum revision should be presented to teachers to allow them to air their concerns and give them an opportunity to participate in the developmental process. After the new curriculum is confirmed and promulgated, a far reaching teacher training program should be planned and implemented.

Curriculum problems should be presented to teachers so that they come to think that the problems are theirs. Teachers must have an understanding of the curriculum, and should be equipped with the ability to identify and solve problems. It is important, therefore, that a cooperative working relationship be established amongst the curriculum development authority, professional research institutions, and teacher education institutions.

The Influence of College Entrance Examinations

Finally, the most serious and comprehensive problem in curriculum development in Korea is that the school curriculum is under the total influence of the College Entrance Examination (CEE). This is the case not only with high school education but also with middle school and even elementary school education. The CEE is administered by the National Institute of Education Evaluation which was established as an autonomous body in 1985 by the Ministry of Education.

On the surface, the CEE might seem to have nothing to do with the curriculum of schools. In practice it exerts a far-reaching influence on the way the curriculum is implemented.

It is no exaggeration to say that the CEE determines everything in schools which is related to the curriculum. Splendid goals and objectives described in the official 'curriculum' are either totally disregarded or distorted. Principals, teachers, parents and even the students teach and learn only for the purpose of obtaining entrance to a college. Subject content, teaching methods, and evaluation practices are all determined with reference to the CEE. Subject content, which seems valuable from an educational point of view, is not taught if it is not tested in the CEE; teaching and learning methods that are viewed as not effective in preparing pupils for the CEE preparation are not used; and evaluation is undertaken not for getting information about the degree of accomplishment of educational objectives but for obtaining information about how well the students are prepared for the CEE. The format of the examination also exerts a powerful influence on teaching and learning styles. The only form of assessment used in the CEE is multiple choice questions which encourage pupils to memorize large quantities of discrete information. There is no encouragement or need for them to try and grasp the overall or deep structure of the subjects they study.

In this sense, CEE-centered school education nullifies all the expected effects of educational innovation. The school curriculum is managed to reflect the demands of the CEE. Subjects such as music, drawing, and physical education are not taught or disregarded so as to devote time to other subjects that are important in the CEE. Extra-curricular activities are usually displaced with supplementary lessons designed to prepare pupils for the CEE.

Examination-centered education is the most critical of the educational problems in South Korea. The problems ensuing from CEE-centered education permeates through all areas of education (including curriculum management and curriculum development), making all the educational practices move in an undesirable direction. Currently, many innovations are being prepared and proposed for solving this problem. Though no method which guarantees success has been proposed yet, we expect that CEE system will be revised in the near future, in ways which allow the normal operation of secondary level school curricula.

Chapter 9

Curriculum Development in Macau

Mark Bray and Philip Hui

Introduction

The education system of Macau has been long neglected by comparative educationists and other academics. This has been chiefly because Macau has seemed small and idiosyncratic, very different from other parts of Asia and apparently with few instructive messages for neighbouring and other countries.

Such views have arguably been unfortunate and misguided. Macau is certainly very different from other parts of Asia, but through this fact can provide illuminating contrasts. Study of education in Macau can also contribute to a broader understanding of historical and contemporary colonialism, of the forces of change in a *laissez-faire* system, and of the advantages and constraints imposed by the small size of a territory.

In order to provide a context for discussion of schools and curricula, this chapter commences with an outline of Macau's socioeconomic background. It then describes the features of the various school systems operating in the territory, before turning to specific features of the curricula in those schools.

Analysis of curriculum development in Macau requires description of a diverse array of school systems and their curricula. The diversity and accompanying complexity have developed as a result of colonial neglect of education for the local population. It is in this sense that Macau is unique within Asia, for only recently has the government abandoned an extreme *laissez-faire* type of policy. Among the specific topics considered in this chapter are language in the school curriculum, the longstanding absence of a territory-wide examination system, and the nature and impact of higher education.

Background

History and Politics

Macau takes 1557 as the year of its foundation. At this time, after several unsuccessful attempts dating back to 1513, Portuguese traders finally secured from the Chinese authorities rights of settlement in the territory. Some constitutional specialists argue that the arrangement was a lease rather than a cession

(Afonso and Pereira, 1987, p. 185). However, the Europeans were allowed considerable autonomy, and an 1887 treaty brought explicit recognition of Portuguese sovereignty.

Macau had confirmed itself as the keystone of the Portuguese trade-empire soon after its establishment. Portuguese trade of spice, silk, porcelain and silver was virtually unrivalled during the period 1570 to 1640. Almost all China's foreign trade passed through Portuguese hands, and Macau was among the world's foremost entrepôts.

Macau also played a major religious and cultural role. In 1576 the territory was made the centre of a diocese which included all of China and Japan. The church established many schools, one of which became a university in 1594 and taught theology, humanities, Greek, Latin, rhetoric and philosophy (Pires 1987, p. 16). Teixeira's (1982) historical account shows that Macau well deserved its appellation 'The City of Schools'. Macau was a major conduit through which Western education and science entered China, Japan and Korea.

After the mid-seventeenth century, Macau's fortunes declined. Portugal proved unable to hold her empire together, and competition for East Asian trade became increasingly intense. The foundation of Hong Kong in 1842 was a particularly serious blow, for its far superior port took over the strategic significance that Macau had previously enjoyed. Macau became little more than an inward-looking backwater.

After the end of World War II, the Nationalist government in China wished to repossess the territory. However, the Chinese authorities were unable to force the issue, especially after civil war broke out. Even after the Communist victory in 1949 the issue was not pressed. During the Korean War Macau was used for smuggling raw materials and munitions into China. The People's Republic of China therefore came to consider Macau more valuable as a Portuguese colony than as an integral part of China (Edmonds, 1989, p. xxiii).

The Indian takeover of Portuguese Goa, Damao and Diu in 1961 must have left many people wondering how long Portugal would hold on to the territory, especially since China expressly supported the Indian stance. As the 1960s progressed, tension with the Chinese government mounted.

The outbreak of China's Cultural Revolution in 1966 led to violent riots in the territory and to vigorous anti-Portuguese propaganda both locally and in China itself. Unexpectedly, however, as soon as the Portuguese announced that they did intend to leave, the Communists immediately altered their stance (*ibid.*, p. xxv). It may be assumed that the Chinese authorities were conscious of Macau's valuable role as an outlet for external trade, and again found it more useful to retain Macau as a foreign port than to repossess it.

Eight years later, Portugal itself experienced a revolution. The new government had a very different view of world affairs, and immediately set about decolonizing its African territories. In Asia, East Timor was unilaterally seized by Indonesia, and matters would perhaps have been more simple for Portugal if China had similarly seized Macau. However, the Chinese continued to view the Portuguese administration of Macau as an asset for foreign trade, and maintained their refusal to reassert sovereignty.

Finally, in 1987 the Portuguese and Chinese governments agreed that Macau would revert to China in 1999. This will be two years after a similar resumption of sovereignty in Hong Kong. Like Hong Kong, Macau is expected to remain a

Special Aministrative Region for at least fifty years after the transition. Meanwhile, Macau is officially regarded as a Chinese territory under Portuguese administration.

Geography and Population

The territory of Macau consists of a small peninsula plus two adjacent islands. The total land area is just 17 square kilometres, and the surrounding territory belonging to the People's Republic of China (PRC) is easily visible from many points.

According to official figures, the 1986 population was 426,000 (Macau, 1987, p. 1), though as noted by Edmonds (1989, p. xv) a figure exceeding 500,000 would probably have been more accurate. Over 90 per cent of the population is Chinese by race. Two significant minority groups are a small cadre of Portuguese and a mixed-race group known as the Macanese (Zepp, 1987, p. 125). Many of the Portuguese are descendants from long-established families, though others have been recruited on short-term contracts to assist with administration, education and other social services.

A considerable proportion of Macau's food and other daily necessities is imported each day across the Chinese border. Macau also has excellent communications with Hong Kong, which is only 38 nautical miles to the east and is easily reached by jetfoil, hydrofoil and ship. The significance of the links with Hong Kong is demonstrated by the extent of the traffic. For example it was reported that in August 1989 1.35 million passengers travelled between Macau and Hong Kong (*Sunday Morning Post* [Hong Kong], 15 October 1989). This figure represented nearly three times the total population.

Economy

Macau's economy compares well with others in the region. In East Asia, Macau ranks fifth in per capita Gross Domestic Product (GDP), after Brunei Darussalam, Japan, Singapore and Hong Kong (Cremer, 1989, p. 221). The territory ranks sixth in hospital beds, second in medical doctors, sixth in infant mortality rate, second in life expectancy at birth, and fifth in private cars per 100 persons (*ibid.*). Imprecise as these comparisons are — for instance because of different statistical measurement concepts — they nonetheless show that Macau has regained at least some of the prominence which the territory once enjoyed in the region.

Official figures placed the 1986 GDP per head at US$3962 (Macau, 1987, p. 1). Manufacturing contributes about a third of GDP, with textiles, toys and artificial flowers holding the greatest share of export markets (Feitor 1987, p. 139). Recent years have also brought major growth of the tourist industry, part of it linked to gambling in the casinos. Cremer (1989, p. 227) reports that of the 4.5 million tourists coming to Macau in 1985, 85 per cent were gamblers. The direct and indirect contribution of the gambling sector to Macau's GDP was estimated at 15–20 per cent, and taxation on the gambling industry provided nearly half of the government's total revenue.

Figure 9.1   Structure of school systems, Macau

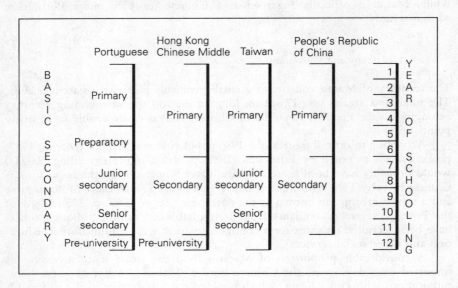

Education in Macau

In the late 1980s, the Macau authorities embarked on a series of major education reforms (Rosa, 1990; Macau, 1990). The chief stimulus for this activity was awareness that in 1999 sovereignty over the territory would revert to China. From the local viewpoint it was clear that considerable preparation was needed to ensure that the citizens of Macau could view their future with confidence; and from the Portuguese viewpoint it seemed desirable to depart from the territory with a sense of accomplishment and honour. The impetus for reform may also be traced to certain key individuals, and it was facilitated by the improved economic performance of the territory during the 1980s.

Subsequent sections of this chapter will comment on some aspects of the reforms, including efforts to strengthen linkages between the various types of schools, to expand and adapt the system of higher education, and to introduce a system of local examinations. Meanwhile, it is desirable to describe the pre-reform situation of the late 1980s.

Macau has never had a single, distinctive education system. Instead it has an uncoordinated collection of systems, imported from Portugal, the People's Republic of China, Taiwan and Hong Kong. The number of years in the primary, junior secondary and senior secondary cycles varies according to the model. The Portuguese model follows a 4+2+5+1 pattern, the (former) PRC one is 6+5, and the Taiwan one is 6+3+3. Hong Kong has two main models of schooling. The one borrowed by Macau is the Chinese Middle School system with a 6+5+1 structure (Alves Pinto, 1987, pp. 20–1; Macau, 1989a, p. 17).

The structure of these four basic types of system is shown in Figure 9.1. However, even the categorization into four basic systems is to some extent a

Table 9.1   Number of schools, by type and level, 1987/88

Level/combination	System of Curriculum						
	Taiwan	PRC	Hong Kong	Portuguese	Luso-Chinese	Other	Total
Pre-school	4		2	2			8
Pre-school and basic	21	10	6	2	3	1	43
Pre-school, basic and secondary	8	2	1	1			12
Basic	2			2			4
Basic and secondary	2	1	4	1	1		9
Basic and secondary-technical-professional		1	1				2
Secondary	4	2		1			7
Secondary and teacher training						1	1
Secondary and higher			1				1
Teacher training				1			1
Nursing school				1	1		2
Higher			1			2	3
TOTAL	41	16	16	11	5	4	93

Note: The original table referred to the 'Anglo-Saxon' rather than the Hong Kong model. 'Hong Kong' seems a better descriptor, since the model was adopted from there rather than directly from the United Kingdom.
Source: Macau (1989a). p.40.

simplification. Table 9.1 shows a bewildering total collection of combinations. The existence of these different systems reflects the haphazard way in which education in Macau has been allowed to develop, and has major implications for the curriculum.

Another striking aspect of education in Macau is the distinction between official and private schools. The former comprise only 12 per cent of the total. The vast majority of schools are private institutions run by religious bodies, social service organizations, commercial enterprises and individuals. A small number of private schools operate a curriculum which parallels that of the official Portuguese schools (table 9.2), but the curriculum of the majority is very different from that in official schools. The nature of differences will be explained below.

Table 9.3 provides similar data on the institutions existing in 1989/90, classified by the medium of instruction. The overwhelming majority of institutions used Chinese as the medium of instruction (except when teaching other languages as classroom subjects). All these institutions were private. Sixteen institutions, which were also all private, were called Anglo-Chinese schools. These institutions were comparable to the Anglo-Chinese schools of Hong Kong (Fung, 1986, p. 316), and used both English and Chinese as media of instruction. The third category was known as Luso-Chinese. These fifteen institutions, which were all operated by the government, taught in Chinese but included Portuguese as a subject. The remaining institutions taught exclusively in Portuguese. Among the eleven institutions in this category, four were official and seven were private.

Table 9.2   Schools, teachers and pupils in Macau, 1987/88

		OFFICIAL	PRIVATE With parallel curriculum	PRIVATE Without parallel curriculum	TOTAL
Pre-primary:	Schools	8	1	54	63
	Teachers	48	6	359	413
	Pupils	819	74	13,595	14,488
Primary:	Schools	9	2	63	74
	Teachers	122	35	920	1080
	Pupils	2311	330	29,028	31,669
Secondary:	Schools	3	2	26	31
	Teachers	101	44	624	769
	Pupils	811	270	12,768	13,849

Source: Direcção dos Serviços de Educação, Macau.

Table 9.3   Number of institutions, by medium of instruction, 1989/90

School Type	OFFICIAL Schools	OFFICIAL Pupils	PRIVATE Schools	PRIVATE Pupils	TOTAL Schools	TOTAL Pupils
Chinese	—	—	128	58,380	128	58,380
Anglo-Chinese	—	—	16	6672	16	6672
Luso-Chinese	15	2672	—	—	15	2672
Portuguese	4	1959	7	945	11	2904
TOTAL	19	4631	151	65,997	170	70,628

Note: Some figures in this table (for example, for the number of Luso-Chinese schools) show wide variation from table 9.1. This may be partly a function of the different years to which the figures refer, but it also appears that table 9.3 has used a different definition of 'school'. For example it seems that the institution teaching at basic and secondary levels was considered one institution for table 9.1 but two (or even three?) institutions for table 9.3.

Source: Macau (1989b), pp. 4, 23.

Schooling in Macau is voluntary, though fewer than 4 per cent of children aged 6 to 14 are thought not to attend school (Chiu, 1987, p. 5). Introduction of compulsory schooling was among the reforms considered in the late 1980s (Macau, 1990, p. 25). If and when compulsion is introduced, Macau will be brought more into line with the majority of countries in the region.

The government does have an Education Department, but until the late 1980s it was almost entirely concerned with the official schools. No laws or regulations existed to control operation of the private schools. The institutions were free to devise their own curricula, recruit their own teachers, determine their own conditions of service, and decide on the size of classes.

Macau's principal post-secondary institution is the University of East Asia. It was founded in 1981 as a private, commercial enterprise, but in 1988 was purchased by the government and is now run by a non-profit foundation.

Schools and School Curricula

Major questions surround the relevance of school curricula in Macau. They arise particularly from the colonial origins of the official system, the multiplicity of other imported models, and the lack of local textbooks. This section comments on both official and private schools, and presents the broad features of each sub-system. A subsequent section of the chapter presents profiles of six institutions to illustrate the broader points made here.

Official Schools

The official schools comprise about 12 per cent of the total, and contain about 7 per cent of the enrolments. The Portuguese (as opposed to the Luso-Chinese) schools are really European institutions operating in Asia. Their students use Portuguese textbooks, and learn about Portuguese history, geography and botany. Their students also follow the Portuguese assessment system; and because the authorities are afraid of long-distance telephone calls revealing the questions, students also sit examinations simultaneously — even if it happens to be 4.00 pm in Portugal and midnight in Macau!

Pupils in the Portuguese schools are required to learn two foreign languages. English, French, German and Chinese are offered, among which English is the most popular and Chinese is the least popular. Apart from this optional course in Chinese, the curriculum contains very little of relevance to Macau or the wider Asian setting. Most of the students proceeding to higher education go to Portugal, though a few study in other European countries. Until 1988 no students from the Portuguese schools had entered the University of East Asia.

It might seem remarkable that such schools still exist in the late twentieth century, for they seem to embody all the negative aspects of colonial education so strongly criticized elsewhere (for example, Gifford *et al.*, 1971; Altbach and Kelly, 1978; Watson, 1982). Two points may be raised in partial defence. The first is that the government does also run the Luso-Chinese schools which use Chinese as the principal teaching medium; and the second is that many pupils in Portuguese schools are from Portuguese families — either longstanding residents or working in Macau on short-term contracts. To reinforce that latter point, it might be argued that the schools are conceptually little different from the international schools in Hong Kong and elsewhere, which primarily cater for children of expatriates and which follow British, American or other foreign curricula (Fung, 1986, p. 316).

These considerations could amount only to a partial defence, however, particularly during the period up to the mid-1980s. Until 1985 the Luso-Chinese schools operated only at the primary level, and they occupied a very small place within the system. In 1985/86, for example, Luso-Chinese schools contained just 1.8 per cent of total enrolments (Macau, 1989b, p. 23). Second, although Portuguese children might have been the majority in the official Portuguese schools, many pupils were either mixed-race or fully Chinese. And the difference between the official schools in Macau and the international schools in Hong Kong is that the former were the *only* schools run by the government. Whereas the international schools in Hong Kong were considered outside the main system, the official schools in Macau, at least from the government viewpoint, *were* the main system.

A further difference between Macau's official schools and Hong Kong's international schools concerns their links with employment in the bureaucracy. One basic requirement for any post in the Macau government is a knowledge of Portuguese. But in the mid-1980s the only institutions which could provide that fluency at the secondary level were the three official schools or the two (smaller) private schools which operated a parallel curriculum. Local families who wished their children to have access to government posts therefore had very little choice. The government of Hong Kong certainly did not look to its international schools for a supply of recruits in the same way that the government of Macau looked to its official schools.

The nature and role of the official schools must therefore be ascribed to the perceptions of the Portuguese and Macau governments. The colonial authorities have looked after their own narrow interests, and have neglected the broader interests of the people they have governed. In the past, this could partly be blamed on the poverty not only of Macau but also of Portugal. However, this is not a complete explanation, for one may look at the proportion of budgets as well as at absolute expenditures. In 1975, the Macau government spent only 2.2 per cent of its budget on education. By world standards that figure was very low. World Bank statistics (1980, p. 67) show that at that period the average for industrialized countries was 15.6 per cent, and that for developing countries was 15.1 per cent. In Hong Kong the 1975 figure was 20.7 per cent (Cheng, 1990, p. 28).

Despite this low overall government expenditure, however, in financial terms the official schools were well endowed. Teachers in official schools received salaries and fringe benefits which were three to four times higher than those of their counterparts in private schools. Also, the facilities of official schools have generally been much better than those of private schools, and average class size has been much smaller. The relative luxury of the official schools has caused considerable resentment from the private institutions.

However, this picture has begun to change. In 1984 the Governor himself admitted that the territory's social system had 'undoubtedly been characterized by enormous inertia' (Macau, 1984, p. 4), and the government began to look for ways to subsidize private schools. In 1989 the government paid private schools 500 patacas (US$62.5) per month per teacher. By that year the proportion of the government budget allocated to education had risen to 7.6 per cent (Rosa, 1989, p. 2), and it was projected to reach 12 per cent in 1990 (*Macau Daily News*, 30 November 1989). This dramatic rate of increase brought Macau more into line with other countries in the region.

Private Schools

Private institutions comprise the vast majority of schools in Macau. Most are operated by religious and social service organizations rather than as profit-making enterprises. No formal apparatus exists to coordinate the schools.

Among the private schools existing in 1987/88, two taught in Portuguese with a curriculum parallel to that of the official schools. However the majority of private schools taught either in English or in Chinese, and many did not even teach Portuguese as a subject. This reflected the impact of market forces. Apart from official business in Macau, the Portuguese language is of little use in the region. For commercial and daily activities, Chinese and English are much more valuable. Parents recognize this, and the schools follow the demands of the market.

The actual nature of the curriculum depends very much on the preferences and background of the sponsors of individual institutions. Clergy of different nationalities may be found in the church schools, and they bring with them the educational traditions of their home countries. Likewise, many of the schools following the Taiwanese model import the curricula and instructional practices of that country; and similar comments apply to the left-wing schools linked to the PRC. The schools may celebrate the national days of Taiwan or the PRC, and they seek to send their graduates to higher education institutions in those countries.

One problem common to all private schools concerns textbooks. Because Macau has a small market, commercial publishers have been unwilling to sponsor textbooks which are specifically designed for Macau pupils; and because the government has been concerned only with its own official schools, no local textbooks have been published by the government. Private schools therefore have to use imported books. Most books come from Hong Kong, though some come from Taiwan and China. The books are of limited specific relevance to Macau, with the result that pupils in private schools tend to know much more about these external places than about their own society. Thus pupils using Hong Kong textbooks learn about the Hong Kong currency, the Hong Kong transportation systems, and the Hong Kong system of government. Their teachers may be able to use this information to stimulate discussion of Macau, but such extension of concepts is not always easy and cannot be taken for granted.

An additional problem with textbooks arises at the kindergarten level. The textbooks developed for Hong Kong use a thematic approach, but Macau kindergartens generally use a subject-based approach. Because the kindergarten teachers in Macau have no curriculum guidelines, they are generally left to follow their own instincts and inclinations. The result in many institutions is far from satisfactory, with teachers following one set of methods in an ad hoc way but using textbooks designed for another.

Finally, it should be mentioned that at primary and secondary level average class sizes in private schools are between fifty and sixty pupils. Since in addition most teachers are untrained, it is not surprising that most instruction is teacher-centred. Considerable emphasis is placed on rote-learning and memorization, and the activity methods employed in some Hong Kong schools and in many Western countries are rarely found in Macau.

Profiles of Curricula in Six Secondary Schools

These schools have been selected to match the main categories identified above. The profiles presented here focus on the Portuguese official schools, the Luso-Chinese official school, a left-wing (PRC) private school, a Protestant private school following the Hong Kong model, a Catholic private school following the

Taiwan model, and a Catholic private school following the Hong Kong model. The profiles are based on visits to the schools in 1990. To draw out the curriculum differences, the profiles pay particular attention to the teaching of history and geography.

The Portuguese Official Schools

The main elements of the curriculum in Portuguese official schools were described above and require little elaboration. The Portuguese official schools all follow a common curriculum. History and geography are core courses in grades 7 to 9, and are also compulsory in the arts stream from grade 10. All textbooks are imported from Portugal, and the schools follow Portuguese assessment procedures. The majority of teachers are Portuguese. They are generally well-qualified and well-paid. Most teachers are on secondment from Portugal and spend only a few years in the territory. This restricts their familiarity with the local Chinese culture.

The Luso-Chinese Official School

Macau has only one Luso-Chinese official secondary school. It developed from the primary system, commencing secondary operation in 1985. The school has thirty-six periods a week, of which Portuguese takes six and English takes five. Other classes are conducted in Cantonese.

Among the thirty-six staff, twelve are Portuguese and the remainder are local Chinese. All are degree holders, having obtained their qualifications in Portugal, the PRC, Taiwan, USA and Hong Kong. Some have professional training. Conditions of service are comparable with those in the Portuguese official schools.

History is taught in grades 7 to 9, and is allocated three periods a week. The content is divided into Chinese history and world history. Geography is allocated two periods a week in grades 7 and 8, but is not taught in grade 9. The students use Hong Kong textbooks, and do not learn anything about Portugal that would not be taught to students in Hong Kong.

A Private School Following the PRC Model

Hou Kong secondary school has been taken as an example of a left-wing institution following the PRC model. Most of the teachers are from the PRC, and some have received teacher-training in the PRC. The students sit PRC examinations.

Students in junior middle 1 to 3 have two periods a week for Chinese history. This covers the spectrum from ancient to modern times, and includes some important incidents in contemporary China. Elements of Macau history are also taught in form 3. Students in senior middle forms 1 to 3 have two periods a week for ancient and modern world history. The geography syllabus has parallels. Students focus on the geography of the world, and of China, Hong Kong and Macau.

The textbooks for Chinese history are imported from the PRC. They are therefore written in simplified characters, and reflect the official ideology of the PRC government. Textbooks for world history are imported from Hong Kong. They are written in complex characters, reflect prevailing ideologies in Hong Kong, are more colourful, and are superior in layout and printing quality. Materials for Macau history are prepared by the teachers themselves.

A Protestant Private School Following the Hong Kong Model

Pui Ching Secondary School has been taken as an example of a Protestant private school following the Hong Kong model. Among the private schools, Pui Ching pays the highest teachers' salaries. It is therefore able to attract good staff. With regard to higher education, the school aims for its students to go either to the Chinese University of Hong Kong or to universities in the USA.

In this school, Chinese history is taught from forms 1 to 5 and is allocated two periods per week. The curriculum focuses on both ancient and contemporary history, and follows the Hong Kong Certificate of Education Examination syllabus.

Students in forms 1 to 3 also have to study world history, which is allocated one period per week. Students in forms 4 and 5 have the option of continuing with some study of world history. The syllabus focuses on four countries with ancient civilizations and on the USA, UK, USSR and France. Portugal is not mentioned.

Similar comments apply to the geography syllabus. Junior classes cover regional geography which includes China, Hong Kong and Macau, and senior classes cover humanistic and natural geography. The head geography teacher is conscious of the desirability of studying Macau, and has prepared a book for internal use. Apart from that, all books are imported from Hong Kong.

A Catholic Private School Following the Taiwan Model

The Sacred Heart Canossian College (Chinese Section) is a Catholic private girls' school following the Taiwan model. Its teachers follow rather traditional methods, placing great emphasis on rote learning. The school is primarily oriented towards higher education in Taiwan, though it does also use textbooks from Hong Kong.

Chinese history is taught is junior middle forms 1 to 3 and in senior middle forms 1 and 2, using the Hong Kong syllabus and textbooks. In senior middle 3, however, the students use the Taiwan syllabus and textbooks. Similar comments apply to world history.

In geography lessons, junior middle forms 1 to 3 follow the Hong Kong syllabus, though they also spend some time on Macau geography, using materials prepared by the principal. Senior middle forms 1 to 3 follow the Taiwan syllabus.

Mark Bray and Philip Hui

Table 9.4   Number of teachers by place of birth, 1987/88

Place of Birth	Number	Per Cent
Macau	1109	41.2
Portugal	344	12.8
People's Republic of China	840	31.2
Hong Kong	145	5.4
Others	239	8.9
Unknown	14	0.5
TOTAL	2691	100.0

Source: Macau (1989a), p. 45.

A Catholic Private School Following the Hong Kong Model

Yuet Wah Secondary School contrasts with Sacred Heart by following the Hong Kong model more closely. It is a Catholic boys' school with both Chinese and English sections. The Chinese section follows a 3+3 model, while the English sections follows a 5+1 model. Most graduates from the Chinese section go either to the University of East Asia (UEA) or to Taiwan. Graduates from the English section go either to UEA or to such countries as Canada and Australia. They sit the General Certificate in Education (GCE) Advanced Level examination.

Chinese history is taught throughout the Chinese section, following the Hong Kong syllabus and using Hong Kong textbooks. World history is taught in forms 1 to 3 of the English section, and in senior middle 3 of the Chinese section. Geography follows a comparable pattern, also using Hong Kong textbooks. Like other schools in the private sector, pupils learn almost nothing about Portugal.

The Nature of the Teaching Force

Some comments on the teaching force were made in the previous section, but deserve elaboration. The backgrounds, nationalities and skills of teachers have considerable influence on what and how they teach.

As already indicated, many of Macau's teachers are imported. This is especially true of the official Portuguese schools, where almost all staff are Portuguese. Church and other private schools employ more Macau teachers, but also recruit large numbers from the People's Republic of China and elsewhere. Table 9.4 shows that in 1987/88 only 41.2 per cent of teachers had been born in Macau. As many as 31.2 per cent had been born in the PRC, though not all were recent migrants. Teachers from Hong Kong formed only 5.4 per cent of the total, chiefly because Macau salaries and job opportunities compared poorly with those in Hong Kong. Many of the teachers in the category labelled 'others' were Taiwanese and non-Portuguese Europeans. The local staff were concentrated in the lower levels of the system, while the Portuguese and PRC staff were concentrated in the secondary schools. The majority of Hong Kong citizens were found in the post-secondary sector.

Table 9.5 shows that in 1987/88, many teachers were untrained. This was most clear in the primary schools, where 50 per cent of teachers had only

Table 9.5 Teachers and their qualifications, by level, 1987/88

	Secondary		Primary teacher training		Primary teacher training in progress		Tertiary		Tertiary level teacher training in progress		TOTAL	
	No.	%	No.	%	No.	%	No.	%	No.	%	No.	%
Pre-primary	123	28	275	61	39	9	9	2	—	—	446	100
Primary	563	50	301	27	177	16	88	8	—	—	1129	100
Secondary	133	16	1	—	—	—	626	75	75	9	835	100
TOTAL	819	34	577	24	216	9	723	30	75	3	2410	100

Source: Rosa (1989), p. 5.

secondary education. At the secondary level, 16 per cent of teachers had only secondary education, and only 9 per cent of teachers were in the process of gaining tertiary-level teacher training.

To some extent the high proportion of untrained teachers is again attributable to the small size of the territory, for the authorities have found it difficult to establish institutions of sufficient size to gain economies of scale (Bray and Hui 1989). However, teacher training institutions have not been completely lacking. Since 1952 the Roman Catholic church has operated a one-year full-time course for pre-primary and primary teachers, and the government has run a small programme for teachers of Portuguese. In addition, in recent years 266 primary teachers have received training on a three-year part-time correspondence course run by the South China Normal University (Chiu, 1987, p. 8).

In order to improve the situation, the Macau government has been keen to train teachers through the University of East Asia. In 1987, a special in-service programme was launched for twenty-four pre-primary and forty primary teachers. Two years later, three-year full-time pre-primary and primary teacher training courses were launched for sixty form 5 leavers. Like other courses at the University, the programmes are partly operated through mobilization of external resources. In 1987 a core of nine trainers was recruited from Hong Kong, and in 1989 the Dean of Education was recruited from the South China Normal University in the PRC. Visiting lecturers have been employed for some additional specialist inputs.

Recognizing that urgent needs also exist in the secondary schools, the university has decided to set up a four-year, full-time BEd programme through which form 6 school leavers can be trained as teachers of English and Chinese. The plan also anticipated development of programmes for teachers of other secondary school subjects, particularly science and social science. However it will be impossible to provide specialist training for every subject, so some teachers must either gain training outside the territory or manage without any training.

In the long term, moreover, the programmes will face a logistic problem that is familiar in most small countries. The present proposals are economically feasible because the untrained teachers form a large pool. The original training plan estimated that by 1995 all teachers in Macau would have been trained. Though provision would still be needed for a few new entrants and for further upgrading of existing staff, the current programmes would no longer be economically viable. In this respect the fact that most of the university staff are outsiders on short-term contracts becomes advantageous, though conflict exists between this feature and the government's localization policy.

The Language of Instruction

Issues surrounding the language of instruction in Macau schools are particularly complex and controversial. As implied above, they have major importance not only for pedagogy but also for social and economic matters.

A pertinent contrast may again be drawn between Macau and Hong Kong. In the latter, language issues seem to cause interminable debate and considerable passion (for example, Cheng *et al.*, 1973; Johnson, 1983; Kwo, 1987; Lord and Cheng, 1987). Yet while Hong Kong's problems may seem complex and intractable, they pale by comparison with those in Macau. In Hong Kong the basic questions are whether schools should teach in English or in Chinese, and if the latter whether in Cantonese or Putonghua. Macau faces the same questions, but must add the question of Portuguese. The citizens of Hong Kong are at least fortunate that the colonial language is useful in regional and international contexts. No such claim can be made for the colonial language of Macau.

As already mentioned, knowledge of Portuguese is a basic requirement for all government posts. For those who do not wish to enter the civil service, however, Portuguese has little practical value. Advocates of mother tongue education opt for schooling in Cantonese; some of the schools linked to Taiwan and the PRC permit teachers to use Mandarin; and parents who want their children to gain advantages in international commerce press for English. With regard to the last point, it is not insignificant that even the government publishes its economic bulletins and similar materials in English as well as in Portuguese and Chinese.

The 1987 Sino-Portuguese Agreement did ensure some continued place for Portuguese, stating that in the Macau Special Administrative Region that would exist for fifty years after 1999. Portuguese as well as Chinese could be used in the Executive and Legislative Councils and in the law courts. However, the new political era brought by the signature of the Sino-Portuguese Agreement has also brought a marked shift towards Chinese. Work commenced on translation of the laws and other key documents into Chinese, and the hard line previously adopted by the colonial regime was markedly softened.

Nevertheless, two major complications remained. The first, explained in more detail below, was that the principal language of the University of East Asia remained English. Local students who wished to study at the university therefore required competence in English rather than in Portuguese or Chinese.

The second complication was that in the late 1980s the Portuguese government, aware that sovereignty of Macau was finally going to revert to China, realized that this was the last real chance to spread the Portuguese language in East Asia. Since 1978 grants had been available to encourage private schools to teach Portuguese. In 1987 the financial inducements were revised and these grants were given more prominence. In 1988 the government declared that Portuguese would become a compulsory subject in all private schools, though it later retracted this proposal in the face of strong opposition from the two main education associations (Lo, 1989, p. 11).

Moves were also made to strengthen the Portuguese presence at the University. Initiatives were given top-level support in 1989 when the President of Portugual, Dr Mario Soares, visited the territory. He noted that 'to some of the Portuguese who are living in Macau the attempts to spread and defend the Portuguese language have been a failure', but continued that 'there is sufficient reason to support that from now on we need double effort' (Soares, 1989). Part of this effort included provision of grants of 5000 patacas (US\$625) per class per year to schools which included Portuguese in the curriculum.

From a long-term perspective the renewed effort seems a waste of time and money, for the role of Portuguese seems already on the decline and it will inevitably decline further after 1999. However, it appears that the Portuguese authorities are still prepared to give precedence to their own cultural and political inclinations rather than to the practical needs of school pupils in Macau.

Examinations

Until very recently, another unusual feature of the Macau system was its complete lack of territory-wide examinations. This again reflected the *laissez-faire* attitude of successive governments and the fragmented nature of the education system. Students in government schools followed the Portuguese assessment system, while students in private schools either sat foreign examinations or sat no external examinations at all.

The chief factor which permitted Macau to exist without a territory-wide examination system was its small size. Whereas larger countries have to establish national examinations in order to allow employers to compare different job applicants, employers in Macau could find out most of what they needed to know from personal contacts. Applicants to the civil service sat a written Portuguese language test, but were otherwise selected on the basis of reference letters and interviews.

To some observers, the lack of examinations might have appeared a blessing. Chapter 3 in this book has discussed what Dore (1976) called the 'diploma disease'. In many societies, Dore points out, the process of education has become distorted by the demands of public examinations — 'the examination tail has come to wag the education dog'. From this perspective, it might appear that schools in Macau had greater freedom to pursue broad educational goals than did schools which were dominated by public examinations and the diploma disease.

Yet this situation was not without problems, especially for the younger schools which complained that they had no yardstick against which to prove their ability and compete with the prestige of older institutions. The lack of an examination has also meant that students who wished to study or gain employment abroad were unable to present standardized credentials.

Many schools would have liked to get round this difficulty by entering their students for Hong Kong examinations. However, the Hong Kong Examinations Authority is prohibited by its Ordinance from operating outside Hong Kong. Thus the only Macau students able to sit these examinations are those who hold Hong Kong identity cards. A few schools have therefore opted for examinations set by the University of Cambridge Examinations Syndicate (UK), a practice which was at one time encouraged by the University of East Asia (Mellor, 1988, p. 17). However, use of external examinations always raises questions of relevance and control. Examinations set in Cambridge might not match the precise needs of Macau, and the 'washback' effects of an examination set in Europe might be particularly questionable. Similar comments apply to examinations set in Taiwan and the PRC.

Major change in the situation was brought in 1990, when the UEA for the first time held an entrance examination open to all schools in the territory. The examination comprised one paper 'in the language which shall be the medium of instruction' (i.e. for most students English, but for some Chinese or Portuguese), and one paper in mathematics. Individual faculties were permitted to set additional papers in specific subjects. The existence and nature of the examination is not without controversy, for it is bound to have considerable effect on the curricula of secondary schools, and it is set by a tertiary institution rather than by an independent body comparable to the Hong Kong Examinations Authority.

However, the examination is likely to help unify the system, and will help schools which want an academic yardstick against which to establish their reputations.

The Nature and Impact of Tertiary Education

Partly because of Macau's unusual history and circumstances, and partly because the territory has a small population, the tertiary education sector differs markedly from that of other East Asian countries. As well as being significant in itself, the distinctive nature of tertiary education also has major implications for lower levels of education. This has already been noted above with reference to the language issue.

Origins and Philosophy

The first section of this chapter noted that a university was founded in Macau in 1594. That institution ceased to function in 1762, when the territory was again left without local provision of higher education. Only since 1981, with the foundation of the University of East Asia (UEA), has Macau again had a tertiary institution of its own.

Mellor's (1988) account of the origins of the UEA observes (p. 1) that the University of East Asia 'does not conform to any of the known patterns of universities'. His remarks refer chiefly to the structure of the institution; but they might equally refer to its origins and philosophy.

The University was established primarily as a commercial venture. Its founders had identified considerable unsatisfied demand for education in Hong Kong, and were keen to tap that demand. Hong Kong law prohibited establishment of private universities in the territory, and there seemed little prospect that the law would be changed. Macau had no comparable prohibition, and its authorities were much less antagonistic to the concept of a private university. Macau therefore seemed a good site, within easy reach of Hong Kong and also with its own tertiary education needs. The businessmen proposing the institution felt that additional demand might be found among Chinese communities in Malaysia and elsewhere. This desire to have international appeal in part explains why the institution was called the University of East Asia rather than the University of Macau (*ibid.*, pp. 3–6).

Since the university was a commercial venture, its principal objective was to secure financial profit; and since it existed primarily to tap demand from outside Macau its principal working language was English rather than Portuguese. The staff were mainly recruited from outside Macau, and the courses were primarily oriented to non-Macau students.

In 1988 the main body of the university was purchased by the government, and the institution is now run by a non-profit foundation. The change of ownership of course brought a change in philosophy and outlook. However, the influence of the original philosophy and mode of operation remains strong.

Table 9.6   Enrolments in the University of East Asia, by college, 1981–88

	1981	1983	1985	1987	1988
Curricula for Degrees and Diplomas					
University College	47	162	1196	1031	1352
Graduate College		348	1166	535	1756
Open College (i) in Chinese		2016	1395	2059	2449
(ii) in English		1964	1683	1689	1983
Polytechnic College*		200	170	161	215
Sub-Total	*47*	*4690*	*5610*	*6465*	*7755*
Junior College Curricula	113	120	416	388	574
TOTAL	160	4810	6026	6863	8329

*   called the College of Continuing Education until 1985
Source: Mellor (1988), p. 184.

Structure

The UEA was originally composed of several constituent colleges, each of which had a distinctive function. University College provided the basic degree courses; a College of Continuing Education provided extra-mural courses for adults and a diploma course in computer studies for school leavers; a Graduate College catered for postgraduate studies; and an Education Programme provided teacher training.

The UEA also had a Junior College. This body offered pre-university courses, and was comparable to what in other countries would be called a sixth-form college (*ibid.*, p. 18). It provided a link between the university and the schools, and was necessary because of the fragmented nature of the Macau education system. Finally, an Open College operated courses using distance teaching methods. The Open College principally operated from offices in Hong Kong rather than Macau.

After the government's purchase of the main body of the university, the structure of the institution was changed. The Open College was not purchased, though it retained the right to offer UEA degrees. The Open College merged with the Graduate College to become the East Asia Open Institute, and continued its main operations in Hong Kong. The remaining parts of the university were reorganized into a set of faculties along the conventional British pattern.

In 1990, the university also changed the basic length of its degree courses from three to four years. In part, this change resulted from the need to facilitate and attract direct entry from local secondary schools so that the UEA could become the normal first choice for Macau school leavers. The change also brought the university into line with the dominant models in Portugal, the PRC and North America, and it enabled the UEA to strengthen the quality of its programmes and thereby to facilitate recognition both locally and abroad.

Enrolments

Table 9.6 shows enrolments by college in the period 1981–88. As well as indicating the relative sizes of the colleges, the table shows the impressive growth

Table 9.7   Enrolment in the University of East Asia, by origin, 1986/87

	Macau	**Hong Kong**	**China**	**Malaysia**	**Other**
University College	107	164	720	4	7
Graduate College	52	1530	—	123	34
Open College (i) in Chinese	170	1362	—	5	9
(ii) in English	60	1738	—	—	—
Polytechnic College	90	125	—	1	6
Junior College	245	152	56	133	26
TOTAL (number)	724	5071	776	266	82
(per cent)	10.5	73.3	11.2	3.8	1.2

Source: Mellor (1988), p. 187.

of the university. By 1988 the institution had 7755 students. The vast majority (85.8 per cent) studied on a part-time basis.

The origin of the students, shown in table 9.7, is also of considerable interest and importance. In 1986/87 only 10.5 per cent of the students came from Macau. By far the largest number came from Hong Kong, though significant numbers were also recruited from China and Malaysia. Only in the Junior College did Macau students comprise the largest group, and even there they represented only 40 per cent of the total.

Examination of the origins of the student body helps one understand why Mellor (1988) described the university as having 'an almost excessively international flavour' (p. 32). It has also had major implications for the curriculum. It is doubtful whether at this point in history any other territory in the world had a tertiary education sector with this extent of foreign domination.

Following the 1988 change of ownership of the university, however, the government made deliberate efforts to increase the proportion of Macau students. The separation of the Graduate College and the Open College markedly reduced the enrolment, but significantly tilted the balance in favour of Macau. Figures for 1989/90 showed an institution with just 1648 students compared with 8329 two years previously; but 73.9 per cent of the students in 1989/90 were from Macau compared with about 10 per cent two years previously.

Courses

As noted above, one effect of the initially strong desire of the UEA founders to attract large numbers of students from outside Macau was that English was made the principal medium of instruction. Partly because staff and courses were already in place, this feature was retained despite the 1988 change of ownership. A few courses are taught in Cantonese, and can therefore be followed by students from Hong Kong, Macau and southern China. In the early years of the university, no courses were taught in Portuguese. As part of the government's attempt to strengthen the Portuguese legacy in East Asia, in 1987 a Centre for Portuguese Studies was established 'to contribute to the academic programmes of the University ... by promoting the study of Portuguese culture' (Mellor, 1988, p. 107). The government's acquisition of the main body of the university in 1988 strengthened the potential for further inputs of Portuguese. However, they are not likely ever to become dominant.

The desire to attract non-local students also has implications for the content of many courses. The programme in business law, for example, focuses exclusively on the Hong Kong legal system; and the Chinese Law Diploma programme deals entirely with Chinese law. The University does run a course in Portuguese law (which is the law used in Macau), but it has encountered recruitment problems because of the shortage of potential applicants with adequate competence in Portuguese.

Another problem arises from the profit-making motive with which the university commenced. Course development is a costly and time-consuming activity. In these circumstances, it seemed appropriate in some cases simply to purchase courses from other institutions. Such purchases had the additional benefit of facilitating negotiation to secure external recognition.

The most obvious examples in which courses were purchased from other countries were in the Open College. UEA staff did design some of their own programmes, but the majority of courses were originally prepared by the Open University (UK), Massey University (New Zealand), Athabasca University (Canada), and the Royal Melbourne Institute of Technology (Australia). The UK Open University materials include such topics as seventeenth century England, the Enlightenment, and European nineteenth century novelists. The vast majority of Macau's population are Chinese in race and culture, and generally find it difficult to identify with European topics of this sort.

In addition, in the early years the courses of the University of East Asia, like those of many other private universities, were almost exclusively oriented to the arts, humanities, social sciences and business studies. The Open College did offer a small number of science courses, but they were heavily theoretical in content, and lacked laboratory work. To some extent, this was a function of the size of the territory as well as of the fact that the UEA commenced as a private institution, for in territories with small populations it is often impossible to gain sufficient economies of scale to permit instruction in specialized subjects (Bray and Hui, 1989; Bray, 1990). In 1989 the university did commence programmes in engineering, but it will never be possible to cover a full range of subjects. Although the UEA certainly broadens access to higher education, Macau citizens will still have to go elsewhere for in-depth study of science, medicine, dentistry, etc.

Concluding Comments

Despite the long history of the territory, the education system of Macau has been the focus of very little academic research. This is regrettable, for it has many interesting features. Even if to a considerable extent Macau is distinctive and idiosyncratic, the contrasts with other countries and territories may be illuminating.

This chapter has drawn particular attention to the *laissez-faire* nature of the education system, to the constraints imposed by small size, and to the impact of Portuguese colonialism. Especially instructive contrasts may be made between Macau and Hong Kong. The latter is also a colony, and is also due to revert to Chinese sovereignty at the end of this century. However, Hong Kong has twelve times as many people, has a much larger higher education sector, and has been a British colony rather than a Portuguese one. Despite its much shorter history,

Hong Kong is also in many ways much more advanced. Macau learns a great deal from Hong Kong, but Hong Kong learns little from Macau.

The topics about which Macau is currently learning from Hong Kong (among other places) include compulsory education, curriculum development and a territory-wide assessment system. The Macau government is also introducing subsidies for its private schools. That could lead to an aided sector resembling that in Hong Kong, where, as in Macau, only about 10 per cent of schools are owned by the government but where there is a large aided sector separate from the private sector. If the Macau government does move in this direction, undoubtedly it will also impose increasing controls on the private schools. Morris (1990) has criticized the extent to which curriculum innovation in Hong Kong has relied on a top-down, power-coercive mechanism. Macau has had the opposite problem of being too *laissez-faire*, and has been greatly in need of a much clearer set of central policy initiatives which are designed to identify the nature, purposes and assessment procedures of the curriculum.

If proposed reforms go ahead, it seems likely that Macau will belatedly develop a much more distinctive education system with its own identity. The fact that all the schools rely almost exclusively on foreign textbooks, and that very few materials are available to help Macau students to understand their own society is both regrettable and extraordinary in an era of word-processing and low-cost printing.

It is also remarkable to reflect on Mellor's (1988, p. 17) observation that a 1980 meeting called by the University of East Asia to consult secondary schools on the University's proposed entrance requirements was the first formal meeting to which all secondary school heads had ever been invited. This indicates that the authorities had failed to make use of the advantages of small size, for it was far easier for them to call a meeting of secondary heads than it would have been for their counterparts in Singapore and Hong Kong, let alone Indonesia or China.

Now that the reform is underway, however, it appears that the advantages of small size are being capitalized upon more effectively. Thus a meeting to discuss reform proposals was called in October 1989, and in proportional terms had a far higher attendance of educators than could ever be contemplated in a larger education system. Likewise, in 1988 the authorities embarked on a survey of the education system (Macau, 1989a) which produced a far greater level of detail than would have been possible in a larger system. It is planned to conduct a similar survey every year as part of a programme to achieve much more effective monitoring of the system. The reform plans of the late 1980s have already brought major changes, and the prospects for coherent educational development are now brighter than ever before.

Chapter 10

Curriculum Development in Indonesia

R. Murray Thomas

Introduction

The complexity of curriculum development in Indonesia is related to the nation's size, cultural diversity, governmental structure, and educational history.

Geographically the nation occupies the world's largest archipelago of more than 13,000 islands, with nearly 1000 of them inhabited. The islands spread across the seas south of continental southeast Asia for 1888 kilometers (1180 miles) north to south and 5110 kilometers (3194 miles) east to west, making the country broader than the United States. With an estimated 180 million inhabitants by 1990, Indonesia is the world's fifth most populous nation, exceeded only by China, India, the Soviet Union, and the United States. Therefore, the offerings of the country's education system are expected to serve a large and growing population that is distributed across a wide expanse of land and sea.

The country's geographic character — thousands of widely dispersed, mountainous islands — has made social interaction among the region's peoples difficult, thereby promoting the evolution of many separate cultures. For example, more than 350 indigenous languages exist today. This diversity poses problems for educators charged with the task of developing curricula adjusted to learners from varied cultural backgrounds.

Prior to World War II, the archipelago was controlled by Holland as its Netherlands East Indies colony until the Japanese military ousted the Dutch in 1942. When the war ended, Dutch efforts to regain control of the colony were frustrated by the native Indonesians' intention to establish a self-governing republic. However, it required more than four years of revolution against the Dutch before the citizens of the Republic of Indonesia could peacefully pursue their own destiny. Among their ambitions was that of extending educational opportunity throughout the entire populace.

Since 1949, the country has been ruled under a parliamentary system that in recent years has been dominated by a single political party with a former army general as the nation's president. Against such a historical background, the nation's educational leaders over the past four decades have sought to retain the most useful aspects of the colonial education system while, at the same time, adopting new practices suited to the needs of a self-governing southeast Asian democracy.

During the latter decades of Dutch rule, schools were officially under the jurisdiction of the colonial department of education, obliged to abide by regulations issued from the department. Under the Republic of Indonesia, public secular schools and non-Muslim private schools became the responsibility of a Ministry of Education and Culture, while Islamic schools were administered under a Ministry of Religion. Several other ministries managed a small number of institutions designed for training specialized personnel. This same administrative structure continues in place today.

The history of Indonesian education can be pictured as a stream into which several tributaries have fed over the centuries. The oldest variety of education was an informal type that took place in the home and community, with the young learning their language, customs, and occupations from parents and neighbors. Nearly 2000 years ago, education in a formal sense was introduced by Hindu and Buddhist scholars to the feudal princely states were spread throughout the archipelago, although such education was limited primarily to the aristocracy. Then around the thirteenth century AD, the Islamic religion, brought to the islands by traders, began to exert a strong influence. Unlike Hindu-Buddhist education, Islamic teaching was directed at the entire citizenry, with the result that today an estimated 88 per cent of the nation's inhabitants are Muslims. In the sixteenth century, ambitious Portuguese, Spanish, Dutch and English commercial entrepreneurs began establishing a growing list of settlements in southeast Asia, with the Dutch finally gaining control over most of the Indonesian islands. These Westerners brought both Christianity and European-type schools to the region. Whereas the curriculum of Muslim institutions was dominated by religious topics and the Arabic language, the subject-matter in European schools was primarily secular. Today the subject-matter in three-fourths of the nation's educational institutions — the non-Islamic schools — is almost entirely secular. Furthermore, in recent decades secular studies have made regular inroads on the traditional Muslim curriculum (Thomas, 1988b).

With this introductory sketch of the Indonesian educational scene as a backdrop, we turn now to the nation's present-day patterns of curriculum construction.

Three Dimensions of Curriculum-Development Analysis

A convenient way to perceive Indonesian curriculum development is in terms of three interrelated dimensions: (i) school types and levels; (ii) agents in the curriculum-development system; and (iii) the specificity of the agents' proposals. The following description of these dimensions provides the conceptual scheme to be used throughout the remainder of the chapter for describing the Indonesian case.

Dimension 1: School Levels and Types

The word *levels* in this context refers to the steps on the educational ladder that learners ascend with the passing years. In Indonesia, as in most countries, the steps begin with the nursery school and kindergarten, then advance through elementary, secondary, and tertiary institutions. Beyond the typical age-level of university students there are also adult-education programs designed to upgrade older learners' literacy and occupational competence.

The phrase *types of education* refers to differences between programs that are at the same level on the ladder. From the viewpoint of curriculum development, the two most significant ways that types differ are in their goals and their sponsorship. An example of differing goals is found in the array of programs for secondary-school students. For instance, in the general or college-preparatory upper-secondary school there are three tracks (science-mathematics, humanities-languages, social sciences), each with its own objectives and subject matter. Parallel to the college-preparatory schools are separate senior-secondary institutions offering several kinds of specialized vocational training.

There is also diversity in types of sponsorship. For instance, at the primary level there are secular public schools conducted under the auspices of the Ministry of Education and Culture, Christian and Buddhist schools operated by private religious foundations, public Islamic schools (*madrasahs*) under the Ministry of Religion, and private Islamic schools (*pesantrens*) conducted by individual Muslim scholars.

Figure 10.1 pictures typical levels and types. We should note, however, that figure 10.1 has intentionally been much simplified in order to make the level-and-type relationship easy to comprehend. The actual array of types in the Indonesian education system is far too complex to display in a single diagram.

Dimension 2: Agents in the Curriculum-Development System

The word *agents* refers to groups or individuals that may take part in curriculum decisions. Such agents form an administrative hierarchy that (i) begins with the nation's parliament at the top; (ii) descends through a series of educational organizations, such as bureaux and departments of the Ministry of Education or of private-school foundations; and (iii) finally arrives at the individual school and the classroom teacher.

The interaction among these agents in determining the contents of the curriculum can differ from one subject-matter field to another, depending upon such conditions as the political significance of the particular field and the kinds of expertise deemed important for making decisions about that field. The effect of such conditions on the curriculum-development process is illustrated later in the chapter.

Dimension 3: The Specificity of Agents' Proposals

Different agents in the hierarchy can delineate the curriculum in different degrees of specificity. To illustrate this point, we can consider what various educators mean when they speak of *curriculum* and of their role in curriculum development. Most of them intend *the curriculum* to mean what teachers are expected to teach, with this expectation cast in a printed form called the *recommended curriculum*. However, other educators use the term curriculum to mean what classroom teachers actually do teach. In preferring this second definition, they are recognizing that often there is a discrepancy between the contents of a printed course of study and what teachers ultimately offer their students in the classroom. For

Figure 10.1   *Levels and types of Indonesian schools*

				AGES OF STUDENTS															
3	4	5	6	7	8	9	10	11	12	13	14	15	16	17	18	19	20	21	22+

Secular Schools - - - Ministry of Education and Culture

kindergarten	6-year general primary school	3-year lower secondary	3-year upper secondary	higher education
		general	academic	universities
		business	business	institutes
		technical	technical	academies
		home economics	home economics	polytechnics
			teacher education	higher schools
			others	

Islamic Schools - - - Ministry of Religion

kindergarten	6-year primary madrasah	3-year lower secondary madrasah	3-year upper secondary madrasah	higher education
			4- or 6-year teacher education	universities
			5-year madrasah	institutes

pesantren

instance, teachers can give brief treatment to some topics, then embellish others in great detail, thereby departing somewhat from the recommended curriculum. Or they can deviate even more by omitting certain topics entirely and adding others of their own choosing. Thus, when curriculum refers to the learning fare that teachers actually provide for their students in the classroom, the term means *the taught curriculum* (what the teacher presents) or *the experienced curriculum* (what the students receive).

Not only is it useful to recognize a difference between recommended and taught curricula, but it is also helpful to identify different degrees of specificity within the recommended-curriculum category. For example, in the Indonesian education system we can profitably distinguish among the following varieties of recommendations, which range from the most general at the top to the most complex at the bottom. The recommended curriculum, as issued by any particular agent, is comprised of one of these varieties of contents:

Variety 1: **Subject titles** — This level is comprised of no more than the titles of general subjects or topics, such as mathematics, Indonesian language, social science, music, health education, and the like.

Variety 2: *Subject titles, and* **general objectives** — General subjects, plus their constituent general objectives are listed. For instance, under the subject of mathematics there can be such general objectives as the mastery of addition, subtraction, multiplication, and division of whole numbers and fractions.

Variety 3: *Subject titles, general objectives, and* **instructional objectives** — General subjects, general objectives, and the instructional objectives that comprise the general objectives are provided. For example, in the area of Indonesian language, the general objective 'mastery of oral reading and comprehension' can be followed by such instructional objectives as 'student applies phonics rules in pronouncing the following new words met in a reading passage: berusaha (try), mempersilakan (invite), sembahyang (to pray)'.

Variety 4a: *Subject titles, general objectives, instructional objectives, and* **one sample method** *and material for each of* **a few lessons** — This is the same as variety 3, with the addition that several of the objectives include one illustrative example of an instructional method and a material (such as the identification of a textbook passage) that teachers can use in pursuing such objectives.

Variety 4b: *Subject titles, general objectives, instructional objectives, and sample* **alternatives** *of methods and materials for* **a few lessons** — This is the same as variety 4a, except that several methods and materials, rather than just one, are proposed as resources from which teachers can choose. For the example of oral reading in variety 3, suggested alternative methods and materials might include:

Methods — (i) students take turns reading aloud to the teacher; (ii) students are divided into pairs and read aloud to each other; (iii) each student takes a turn reading aloud into a tape recorder outside the classroom while the rest of the class engages in silent reading. Materials — (i) textbook entitled *Melancong di Bali* (Sightseeing in Bali); (ii) stories written by the teacher or students about visits to areas of Indonesia.

Variety 5a: *Subject titles, general objectives, instructional objectives, and one sample method, material, and* **evaluation** *technique for* **a few lessons** — This level is the same as variety 4a, plus one evaluation technique, such as one set of test questions or one homework assignment.

Variety 5b: *Subject titles, general objectives, instructional objectives, and sample* **alternative** *methods, materials, and* **evaluation techniques** *for* **a few lessons** — This option consists of variety 4b, plus several evaluation resources, such as alternative test items, rating scales, check lists, or homework assignments.

Variety 6a: *Subject titles, general objectives, instructional objectives, and a* **single** *method, material, and evaluation technique for* **every lesson** — This is the same as variety 5a, except one method, material, and evaluation technique is furnished for every objective in every lesson that is to be taught.

Variety 6b: *Subject titles, general objectives, instructional objectives, and* **alternatives** *in methods, materials, and evaluation techniques for* **every lesson** — This option extends variety 6a to include more than one method, material, and evaluation approach for *every objective* in *every lesson*.

Variety 6b, therefore, is the most specific and complete formulation of a recommended curriculum, furnishing the teacher precise guidelines as well as the exact instructional materials for pursuing each objective. Whereas Variety 6a does not provide for differences among pupils in learning styles or among teachers in their skills, variety 6b offers options that permit teachers to adjust instruction to such differences.

It should be apparent that the above list is illustrative rather than exhaustive. Other permutations of general and specific objectives, of methods and materials, and of evaluation devices can be constructed to produce additional varieties of recommendations. For instance, variety 4a assumes that both the actual reading material to be used by the students — a textbook — and an accompanying teacher's guidebook are provided as the recommended curriculum. However, in perhaps all education systems it is often true that only a textbook is furnished without an accompanying instructor's guidebook, so it becomes the teacher's responsibility — unaided by an instructor's manual — to devise the method for using the textbook.

Although our list of varieties is not definitive, it is nevertheless sufficiently complete to guide our discussion. In the following pages, the discussion is organized according to levels and types of educational programs. Then, within each program, the agents and the degree of specificity of their curriculum proposals are described. The description of each program also includes mention of problems and of forces that have influenced the program's development.

The sequence of educational levels begins with the two forms of education that are most widespread — elementary and secondary schooling — then proceeds to pre-school education. (Curriculum development in higher-education institutions, which typically takes place within each faculty or department, is not treated in this chapter.) Finally, an example of an experiment in curriculum development is offered to illustrate the level of sophistication that educational planners in recent years have brought to the process of curriculum innovation.

Elementary and Secondary Education

The standard twelve-year pattern of pre-university education to which virtually all Indonesian schools conform consists of six years of elementary, three years of junior-secondary, and three years of senior-secondary schooling. (The nation's fifth five-year national-development plan for the period 1989–1994 called for the extension of compulsory basic education through grade 9. However, by 1990 the specific nature of this plan, along with its curriculum provisions, had not been developed.) For the purpose of explaining curriculum development in these institutions, it is convenient to view the nation's secular and Islamic schools as separate, parallel systems, with the former conducted under the Ministry of Education and Culture (hereafter referred to as the Ministry of Education) and the latter under the Ministry of Religion. The following discussion addresses the main line of curriculum development for secular and for Islamic schools.

Secular Elementary and Secondary Schools

By the latter 1980s there were more than 140,000 six-year secular elementary schools in Indonesia enrolling over 27 million pupils (*Statistik Persekolahan — Sekolah Dasar*, 1986, p. 1). The schools operated under several types of sponsorship. Most were public (93 per cent), in that they were built and funded by provincial or local governments. A small number (7 per cent) were private, operated either by religious groups (Christian, Muslim, Buddhist, Hindu) or by secular foundations, often with some financial aid from the government. The number of general secular secondary schools exceeded 25,000, with a total enrollment of around 9 million students. Another 400,000 students attended over 1000 technical secondary schools (*Europa Year Book*, 1988, p. 1381; *Statistical Yearbook*, 1988, pp. 3/134).

The basic curriculum in all such schools was issued from the central Ministry of Education. If local administrators wished to add studies beyond the required list from the Ministry, they could do so by adding more class time to the instructional day.

The five principal agents participating in the development of primary- and secondary-school curricula have been: (i) the nation's parliament at the top of the decision-making ladder; (ii) the Minister of Education and his policy advisers; (iii) and (iv) two parallel curriculum-development units of the Ministry of Education; and (v) the classroom teachers who are expected to apply the recommended curricula. The following paragraphs review the roles of each of these agents.

Parliament's Role

In 1989 the Indonesian Parliament ratified a new basic education law, replacing the country's original fundamental education act of 1950. Whereas the 1950 act did not address curriculum issues, the 1989 version specified that the following subjects were to be taught in all elementary schools: moral education (derived from the nation's five basic philosophical principles of belief in God, humanitarianism, social justice, nationalism, and democratic rule), religious studies, citizenship, Indonesian language, mathematics, introduction to science and technology, geography, national and general history, handicrafts, music, drawing, health and physical education, and English language (*Undang-Undang Republik Indonesia No. 2*, 1989, chapter 9, article 39). Thus, Parliament determined the recommended primary-school curriculum at the variety-1 level of specificity.

For secondary education, the 1989 parliamentary act stated only that moral education, religious studies, and citizenship must be taught. The task of identifying the remaining subjects that would form secondary-school programs of study was left up to the Ministry of Education.

The Ministry of Education's Role

The Ministry of Education's three most important agents engaged in curriculum decisions have been the minister and his top-level advisers, the Research and Development Center's curriculum unit, and the Ministry's division of elementary and secondary education.

The Minister and his advisers

The Minister of Education is a political appointee who is not necessarily an educator by profession. (Throughout the following discussion the pronoun *he* will be used, since no woman has ever held the post.) The Minister is committed to establishing policies in concert with the political goals of the nation's President and ruling political party. In the later 1950s and early 1960s, when the Indonesian Communist Party was an increasingly influential political force, the Minister was a member of a local communist party, the Murba Party. However, since Communist parties were outlawed following an aborted *coup d'état* in late 1965, ministers of education have all been strong supporters of the current ruling party (GOLKAR) which is dominated by government employees and the anti-communist military. GOLKAR, in contrast to the outlawed Communist Party, is first *nationalistic* (in support of the government in power) and second *pro-religion* (Islam, Christianity, Hinduism, Buddhism). As a result, the Minister of Education and his top advisers, who include military officers, address their attention particulary to curriculum policies and materials that bear on matters of national socioeconomic development, citizenship, and religious education. They issue directives that affect the work of the curriculum-development agencies under their jurisdiction.

Two curriculum-development agencies

Within the Ministry, two agencies have been engaged in building curricula. They have operated in a slightly awkward competition/cooperation relationship. The two agencies are (i) the Directorate of Basic Education; and (ii) the Research and Development (R&D) Center. Their roles and status can be explained in terms of their historical origins.

From the earliest days of the Republic, the curricula for elementary and secondary schools had been created within the Directorate of Basic Education, which had separate divisions for primary schools, for general junior high schools, for general senior high schools, for various kinds of secondary vocational schools, and for special-education programs. Each division was responsible for specifying the subjects to be taught, the hours per week for each subject, and textbooks to be used in the kinds of schools under its authority. Divisions were also charged with disseminating the curricula and supervising their implementation throughout the nation's schools. Until quite recent times, each of these divisions tended to work independently of the others in the Directorate.

During the 1950s and 1960s the Directorate's divisions would occasionally issue a new curriculum plan, usually in response to significant events in the nation's general political arena. For example, the 1958 curriculum was replaced in 1964 by a new version which included provisions inserted by Ministry staff members who were associated with the Indonesian Communist Party. However, in 1966 an anti-communist army general, Suharto, became president, taking over the reins of power from the existing Sukarno government which had been blamed for the massive bloodshed following the unsuccessful leftist coup of late 1965. The Suharto government in 1968 replaced the 1964 curriculum with a new version which, among other things, included the subject of religious education as a required class for all students. Under the previous curriculum, parents had been able to excuse their children from religious education if they chose to do so. The recommended curriculum at each of these times took the form of variety 2 in our earlier list (subject titles, general objectives), plus textbooks issued by private publishers to fit the pattern of subjects and objectives in the curriculum.

The Suharto government's plan to rebuild the nation's economy and social structure included the establishment in 1969–70 of a project to assess the nation's education system (Beeby, 1979). The purpose of the project was to furnish planners with a sound base of data on which to erect educational programs that would become part of the nation's series of five-year national development plans. The resulting detailed assessment identified significant weaknesses in the country's educational system. The Minister of Education summarized the system's shortcomings in a memorandum:

> It cannot meet the challenges of this age, and in particular the challenges of a developing society.
>
> There is a barrier between the school and society, especially in (a) the content, composition, and orientation of the subject matter of the schools; (b) the methods of teaching; (c) the hierarchical structure of the school system; and (d) the evaluation techniques used.
>
> The education system is meeting more the society's subjective desires for education than its objective needs for education. (Mashuri in Soedijarto, 1976, pp. 3–4)

As a means of producing innovations to cope with the system's inadequacies, the Ministry converted the original assessment office into a full-fledged Research and Development Center which, by the mid-1970s, occupied a five-story building on the Ministry grounds in Jakarta, staffed by Indonesian educators who had been trained either within the country or overseas. The Center was assigned responsibility for devising curricula and for conducting many types of research and evaluation. By the close of the 1980s, the curriculum unit within the Center employed a large staff located in their own building, separate from the rest of the Center.

The establishment of the new Curriculum-Development Unit in the 1970s was not particularly welcomed by personnel in the Ministry's Directorate of Basic Education. The new unit meant that an important function of the Directorate would be shifted to an upstart agency. In addition, how responsibilities would be shared between the new Center and the traditional Directorate divisions was unclear. It appeared that the divisions would continue in charge of supervising the nation's elementary and secondary schools, conducting teacher-training workshops, providing advice to teachers, and supplying such instructional aids as textbooks and teachers' manuals. But debates arose about where a precise line should be drawn between curriculum development and the creation of textbooks and teachers' instructional guidebooks. A a consequence, while the Curriculum-Development Unit within the Center in the 1970s and 1980s focused attention on devising improved sets of learning goals, the divisions of elementary and secondary education continued independently to revise texts and teachers' guidebooks. As a result, in terms of our earlier list of varieties of curriculum specificity, the Center was devising variety 3 products while the Directorate's divisions were independently creating variety 4 materials.

Recognizing this problem, top-level administrators in the Ministry during the 1970s and 1980s sought to coordinate curriculum development and dissemination by encouraging more cooperation (i) among the separate divisions within the Directorate of Basic Education (elementary, secondary, vocational, special education); and (ii) between the Directorate and the R&D Center. The task of achieving a smooth-working relationship among these units was not easy, because people within the agencies sought to maintain their independence and to retain as much authority as they could manage. However, by careful political maneuvering and gradual shifts of assignments among the agencies, the Ministry was able to establish some measure of the desired cooperation by 1990.

However, problems of coordination remain. For instance, in recent years the R&D Center has specified the learning goals and subject-matter content (the course of study) that are the foundation for creating textbooks. However, the process of writing textbooks is the responsibility of an autonomous Textbook Bureau within the Ministry of Education. At the same time the Directorate of Basic Education continues to be responsible for teacher upgrading, monitoring curriculum implementation, and supervision of instruction. A team assigned to evaluate the operation of these agencies concluded in 1990 that:

> Because curriculum is designed in one office, translated into lessons in another, and implemented in still a third, the overall process often lacks integration and it suffers from bureaucratic rules and boundaries that inhibit coordination ... From the time work is begun on a text until it is published, a period of almost four years elapses. There are signs that this lengthy period is being reduced, but the fact remains that the development of 'model' curricular material lags far behind directives to implement a specific curriculum. For example, the most currently used curriculum was approved by the Minister in 1984. However, textbooks using [that curriculum's] Active Learning format have been produced only in science and mathematics. (Theisen, Hughes and Spector, 1990, pp. 15 and 18)

At the same time, private publishers outside the Department of Education who have obtained copies of the course of study have generally been quicker than the government in issuing books, which students can then obtain from commercial bookstores. Some observers have also judged the commercially prepared texts to be of better quality than the government texts.

The government's textbook publishing program during the 1980s has been massive. Between 1982 and 1989 a total of 105 million free books were distributed. However, as noted by the assessment team:

> This is a notable accomplishment until it is measured against the demand: an average of over 20 million students have been enrolled annually at the primary level. Each of them studied up to 11 subjects for a total annual demand, nearly double the total number of books produced in the last seven years. Although textbooks are theoretically free to all students, the Textbook Center is only preparing books for the approved, key fields of study: moral Pancasila, math, science, social studies, bahasa Indonesia (Indonesian language), and English (junior-high level only). (*ibid.*, p. 18)

Over the past two decades, new curriculum plans for elementary and secondary schools have been introduced on two occasions, the first in 1975 and the second in 1984. On each of these occasions, the chief formulators of the plans were staff members of the R&D Center and consultants brought in from other educational agencies, including faculty members of public teacher-training institutes and universities.

The published 1975 curriculum was comprised of (i) general aims for the education system as reflected in the nation's socioeconomic development plan and; (ii) more specific objectives derived from a logical analysis of the general aims, with the specific objectives assigned to particular subject-matter areas. Three key features of the 1975 curricula were that:

1 Specific instructional objectives were described so 'every teacher should know exactly what objectives are to be achieved by the pupils while planning the teaching-learning activities and implementing the lesson plan'. (Indonesia, 1986, p. 145)
2 Every subject taught contributes to the nation's general educational aims.
3 The nation's five basic philosophical principles, known as the *pancasila* (belief in God, humanitarianism, nationalism, social justice, democratic rule), would be taught not only in a separate class, but also integrated into the other subjects of the curriculum.

Thus, the 1975 curriculum was of variety 3 in our earlier list. Instructional objectives were provided, but the task of creating or locating instructional materials and preparing methods of teaching each lesson was left to classroom teachers. However, observations of the curriculum in practice suggested that many classroom teachers lacked the skill, resources, initiative, time, and energy to create effective learning activities for pursuing the objectives. Apparently, in most classrooms traditional lecture and question-answer methods prevailed. Teachers also continued to use traditional textbooks if, indeed, enough textbooks were available.

In order to carry the recommended curriculum toward more specific levels (varieties 4, 5, 6) several of the Center's staff members organized teacher-education workshops aimed both at (a) training classroom instructors in creating efficient teaching methods and materials; and (b) compiling a growing supply of lesson plans that might be distributed to schools. For example, in each of a series of workshops on science education, thirty or forty teachers from around the nation gathered at a central location for several weeks to view demonstrations of effective science teaching, to prepare lesson plans and reading materials for a selection of the instructional goals in the 1975 curriculum, and to try out the plans in practice. The best of the plans were then reproduced for dissemination to schools. Because teachers in one workshop created plans for a different set of objectives than did teachers in other workshops, the system proved to be a low-cost method of extending the recommended curriculum from variety 3 to variety 6 in the field of science.

During a nine-year period of evaluating the implementation of the 1975 curriculum, the Research and Development Center identified weaknesses in the relevance of curricula to the government's socioeconomic plan, in the suitability of curriculum contents to pupils' cognitive development, and in an overload of course materials in certain subject areas. A 1984 revision of the curriculum was designed to correct these shortcomings as well as to: (i) emphasize Indonesians' struggle to gain independence from colonialism; (ii) produce a more suitable combination of core subjects and elective subjects; (iii) match learning goals and activities more adequately to pupils' cognitive, emotional, and psychomotor development; and (iv) achieve a better transition from school to the world of work (Indonesia, 1986, pp. 145–6). This 1984 version continued in effect into the 1990s.

In the mid-1980s, among the problems the Center was seeking to solve was that of adjusting the national curriculum to the diverse needs of the nation's varied geographical, cultural, and occupational conditions. As a means of accomplishing this goal, the Minister of Education in 1987 called for a plan to assign to regional authorities the responsibility for planning a portion of the school program — perhaps 20 per cent — around local patterns of life. By 1990, the form this decentralization should take was still being debated (Theisen, Hughes and Spector, 1990).

Political involvement at the ministry level
Earlier it was noted that the decision about which agents in the Ministry of Education would make key curriculum decisions could vary from one subject-matter area to another. Furthermore, it was suggested that two factors influencing the decision-making assignment were the political significance of the subject-matter area and the expertise deemed necessary for making wise judgments. This interaction of politics and curriculum planning can be illustrated with the example of *Pancasila moral education*, which is a required subject of study at all grade levels in every Indonesian school.

Prior to 1975, one of the subject-matter areas in elementary and secondary schools' curricula was social studies. Then, in the 1975 curriculum this area was divided into two separate subjects: (i) social science, which was mainly history and geography; and (ii) a sort of citizenship training labeled *Pendidikan Moral Pancasila* (Pancasila Moral Education) that involved in-depth study of the five principles that have served as the philosophical foundations for the government ever since the Republic was first established following World War II. As already noted the five (*panca*) principles (*sila*) are: belief in God, nationalism, humanism, social justice, and sovereignty of the people.

To implement the Pancasila program, schools needed suitable textbooks at all grade levels. Hence, publishers began issuing new texts, with the authors drawn mainly from the staff of the Ministry of Education or from teachers' college and university faculties. A committee of military officers serving as advisers to the Minister screened the texts and all curriculum materials created in the Ministry's R&D Center to ensure that the contents were in keeping with the government's interpretation of the five principles.

Then in 1978 two interlinked events occurred that reflected increased political intervention into the realm of curriculum development.

First was the transfer of all moral-Pancasila curriculum decisions out of the R&D Center and into the hands of advisers to the Minister of Education. Second was the creation of a series of Pancasila indoctrination courses in which all government employees were required to enroll. The government's purpose was to establish tighter control over the specific elements of instruction that students and government servants would receive in the areas of citizenship and politics. The motivation behind this drive for tighter control was apparently two-fold:

(i) Government leaders feared the renewal of subversive acts by unrepentant remnants of the Indonesian Communist Party, which had been outlawed in 1966 for its ostensible role in the unsuccessful *coup d'état* of late 1965 that led to the killing of perhaps a half million Indonesians.
(ii) The government felt threatened by the growing strength of Islamic political parties, some of which were caught up in the fervor of the current worldwide Islamic revival and thus were suspected of trying to change Indonesia into a Muslim political state. (Thomas, 1981, pp. 390–2)

Stimulated by these political concerns, the Minister of Education in 1978 appointed a retired army officer and law professor, Dardji Darmodihardjo, as Director-general of Primary and Secondary Schooling. Responsibility for preparing the learning objectives and textbooks for all moral-Pancasila classes was assumed by a team working directly under Dardji's direction. The R&D Center continued to be in charge of curricula for all other subject-matter fields. In effect, the minister and his [military] advisers considered themselves more competent than the R&D professional staff to formulate politically sensitive citizenship-education materials. In contrast, the professional educators in the R&D Center were judged more competent to devise curriculum materials for such nonpolitical subjects as Indonesian language, mathematics, social science, and the natural sciences.

Individual Schools' and Teachers' Roles

The role of classroom teachers in determining the instruction students receive is a function of two principal variables. First is the level of specificity of the curriculum materials provided for teachers by the agents above them in the curriculum-development hierarchy. Second is the teachers' own abilities, time, local facilities, and dedication to the task. When the recommended curriculum that teachers receive is of variety 2 or 3, their burden of preparation is very great indeed. When it is of variety 5 or 6, their task is far easier. And because of the significant limitations among teachers in their abilities, time, facilities, and dedication, the likelihood that more effective instruction will be offered is greater when the recommended curriculum from the Ministry or from regional education officials is of variety 5 or 6 rather than variety 2 or 3.

Summary

As the foregoing overview has indicated, by 1990 the curricula for non-Islamic elementary and secondary schools was being produced by a hierarchy of agents extending from:

(i) Parliament and the nation's President at the top, where general policies bearing on instructional content were established to promote the government's socioeconomic development plan, through

(ii) the Minister of Education and his chief advisors, who cast general policies into directives and produced specific objectives and study materials for the politically sensitive moral-Pancasila citizenship classes. The general directives covering other subject-matter fields were then carried out by

(iii) the Curriculum Unit of the Research and Development Center, which prepared instructional objectives and illustrative teaching methods, materials, and evaluation techniques in cooperation with

(iv) the Textbook Bureau, which wrote the test materials, and with

(v) the Directorate of Basic Education, which supervised the dissemination of the curriculum to the schools, and finally to

(vi) the individual school and its classroom teachers, who made the ultimate determination of how the pupils would pursue the learning goals.

Islamic Elementary and Secondary Schools.

As explained earlier, an Islamic school system operates in parallel to the secular system. The Islamic schools are under the jurisdiction of the Ministry of Religion and consist of two main types known as *pesantrens* and *madrasahs*. Both types are found at elementary and secondary levels, enrolling perhaps 15 or 20 per cent as many pupils as do secular schools.

For centuries the pesantren has been a non-graded, privately-sponsored study center conducted by an imam, a Muslim scholar offering instruction to young students (santri) in the holy Quran, the Hadith (wise sayings of the Prophet Mohammed), Arabic language, Islamic law, and/or Muslim traditions. In the past, few if any secular subjects were taught. The curriculum of the pesantren has always been set entirely by the scholar in charge. Frequently the imam has specialized in a particular aspect of Islamic lore, such as religious law or the interpretation of the Quran.

The curriculum of that imam's pesantren would thus emphasize that scholar's specialty.

In the early decades of the twentieth century, when Indonesia was still a Dutch colony, progressive Muslim educators recognized that secular subjects (literacy in the indigenous and Dutch languages, mathematics, natural science, social science) were better preparation for occupational opportunity in a modernizing society than was a curriculum composed entirely of religious topics. Thus, from 1910 into the 1930s, a growing number of Islamic schools added secular subjects to the curriculum, thereby reducing the time spent on religious studies (Junus, 1960). This new type of Muslim school, combining religious and secular material, was called a madrasah, a title adopted from Muslim schools in the Middle East. Like pesantrens, madrasahs were private institutions, sometimes sponsored by religious foundations that operated a number of schools. As in the pesantrens, the curricula of madrasahs were designed by the scholars in charge.

A marked change in the administration of Muslim schools occurred after World War II when Indonesians established their independent republic. Islamic education was placed under the authority of the newly-created Ministry of Religion. As a means of directing Muslim schools into the mainstream of national development, the Ministry promoted the expansion of madrasahs by providing government funds for buildings, teachers, and textbooks. The Ministry also designed combined religious/secular curricula (variety 1 or 2) which schools were obliged to adopt in order to qualify for government monies. A recently established Research and Development Unit within the Ministry now participates in curriculum building.

Over the 1950–1990 period, pesantrens have continued to function as private schools directed by a religious scholar who independently sets the entire course of study. Pesantrens are recognized as important institutions and are afforded at least moral support by the Ministry of Religion. However, they are not obligated to abide by Ministry directives. Nevertheless, many pesantrens have introduced secular subjects into their programs of study, while others remain almost exclusively religious in their offerings. Today it is not uncommon for parents who wish to furnish their children both secular and religious training to enroll their children in the morning session of a secular public school and in the afternoon session of a pesantren.

From the late 1960s into the 1980s, top-level government officials sought to achieve greater coordination between the Ministry of Education and the Ministry of Religion in their schooling structures and curricula. These efforts were met with considerable resistance by personnel in both ministries who feared the loss of control over their own affairs. However, a major step toward coordination was taken in 1975 when a directive endorsed by the ministers of education, of religion, and of the interior stipulated that the curricula of Islamic madrasahs were to be comprised of 70 per cent secular subjects and 30 per cent religious studies (*Joint Decision*, 1975). This directive represented the triumph of secular-modernization forces in the government over traditional Islamic groups. The triumph was of particular historical interest, for it came amidst the heightened attention to the worldwide Islamic revival that accompanied the 1979 rise to power of the Ayatollah Khomeni in Iran.

The Ministry of Religion's support for increased secularization of curricula in madrasahs was further indicated in 1984 by the addition of subjects to the recommended offerings of the upper secondary school, the *madrasah aliyah* (Sjad-zali, 1984). In the Minister's directive, each student's program over the three years (six semesters) would be divided into three segments: religious education (23.3 per cent of the program), general basic secular education (43.3 per cent), and a specialization (33.3 per cent). All students took the first two segments in common. For the third segment, students could choose Program A from among four academic emphases for candidates preparing to enter a higher education institution (Islamic religion, physics/biology, economics, and culture/humanities) or Program B from among a variety of vocational emphases for students intending to join the work force directly. The vocational specializations were in religion (pastoral counseling, Islamic-court administration), industry (ceramics, leather work, sewing, automotive repair, electrical installation, electronics, carpentry, and others), business computers, agriculture and forestry, service occupations (business administration, cooperatives, bookkeeping, tourism, and others), maritime pursuits (ocean fishing, sailing), and culture and the arts. The ministerial order also advised school personnel to fit new study topics into those subject-matter areas most suitable for such topics. Examples of new topics were nutrition, school health, political education, driver/traffic education, village development, and national defense education. It seemed apparent that the Ministry was defining curriculum at the variety 1 level, leaving to the individual instructor the task of preparing specific instructional objectives, methods, and materials as well as techniques for assessing student progress.

Such a plan was a dramatic departure from the course of study of the traditional pesantren or madrasah of the 1950s and 1960s. The 1984 directive was remarkable for the unprecedented variety of opportunities it offered students in Islamic schools to prepare for diverse higher-education specializations and for a multitude of occupations. However, there is a serious question about how much of the plan could be put into practice over the latter 1980s and throughout the 1990s. Madrasahs have always faced difficulties in staffing their schools with skilled teachers in secular subjects and in supplying equipment in science and technical fields. Far greater will be the difficulties of devising educationally sound courses of study, employing skilled teachers, and providing suitable equipment for the proposed offerings in the 1984 directive. Even in such large urban centers on the island of Java as Jakarta, Bandung, Yogyakarta, and Surabaya it would be a rare secondary madrasah, indeed, that could provide even a portion of the courses suggested by the Ministry. In smaller cities, the problem of mounting such a program would be far more problematic. Consequently, much of the 1984 plan will probably remain a dream for the future rather than a program that will actually be available to students, at least in the 1990s.

Throughout the 1980s, as secular subjects made further inroads into the Islamic curriculum, the political tension between the secular/modernization forces in the Ministry of Education and the Islamic leadership of the Ministry of Religion continued to reveal itself in exchanges of correspondence between the two ministries. For instance, in 1985 the Director General of the Ministry of Religion's Islamic Section learned that the Ministry of Education planned to reduce the time for religious education in secular schools from three to two periods a week in upper elementary grades. The intention behind this reduction was to make room for subjects the Education Ministry's curriculum developers judged to be more important than religious studies. The Director General, in

217

response to this information, sent an official note reminding the Head of the Ministry of Education's R&D Center of the obligation to abide by their 1975 three-periods-a-week agreement. Also in 1985 the Head of the Ministry of Religion's R&D Unit wrote officially to his counterpart in the Ministry of Education to complain that the new kindergarten curriculum was designed to integrate subject-matter areas under topic study units rather than setting aside a specific time period for each subject. He proposed that religion be studied separately during specific periods of the week rather than merging it into other topics where it might be lost or neglected (Thomas, 1988b, p. 906).

In summary, from the mid-1970s throughout the 1980s, Islamic educators were trying to achieve two somewhat contradictory goals — make their schools more competitive with secular schools by including more secular academic subjects and vocational courses in the curriculum, while still maintaining a strong religious theme in students' lives.

Pre-school Education

Two Indonesian terms are used for identifying the nation's early childhood education — *taman kanak-kanak* (literally *kindergarten*, that is, *taman* = garden, *kanak-kanak* = children) and *prasekolah* (pre-school). Both terms refer to schools or child-care centers for children ages 3 through 6. By the mid-1980s, a total of 1,233,783 children were enrolled in kindergartens registered with the Ministry of Education, a number representing an estimated 7 per cent of the nation's children of pre-school age (*Statistik Taman Kanak-Kanak*, 1985, pp. 1–2). However, this figure can be considered an undercount, since many child-care groups throughout the country were not officially registered. Nevertheless, it is clear than only a small portion of children ages 3–6 engaged in formally organized education.

The nation's early childhood education is a cooperative venture between private women's organizations and the government, with the private groups playing the major role in extending pre-schools to all segments of the population, while the government provides support in the form of expertise in developing curricula, sponsoring teacher training, publishing teacher guidebooks, and conducting conferences (Thomas, 1988a).

Most private groups that operate pre-school facilities are members of the Indonesian Pre-school Education Association, which was organized in 1957 and since that time has held periodic national congresses at which plans are devised for the next steps in the kindergarten movement. The significance of the Association is reflected in the fact that by 1985 its members sponsored 99.8 per cent of the nation's registered 25,379 early-childhood programs, while the government (national, regional, local) sponsored the remaining 0.2 per cent (sixty schools) (*Statistik Taman Kanak-Kanak*, 1985).

Because most pre-schools are private and their sponsors are voluntarily members of the Association, neither the Association nor the government has the authority to determine the programs' curricula. Hence, the cooperative Association/government role in curriculum-building is primarily advisory and supervisory. The government publishes curriculum guidelines that have been developed with Association leaders, and these materials are distributed free to pre-schools. Furthermore, the government and Association members alike send personnel to pre-schools to offer suggestions about improving their programs.

Two of the major problems faced in upgrading preschool education in the past have been the inadequate preparation of teachers and the lack of guidance in the conduct of specific daily activities for children. Steps taken in recent times to solve these problems include increasing the number of regional workshops for teachers, providing more supervisors to guide teachers in program development, and publishing booklets clarifying the characteristics of suitable early childhood education. The greatest potential for reaching the largest number of pre-school sponsors and teachers lies in the publications issued by the curriculum-development unit of the Ministry of Education's Research and Development Center, since the printed materials can be distributed promptly to all parts of the nation at a cost far lower than that required for workshops or additional supervisors.

Indicative of the kinds of publications the government offers is the series of booklets issued in 1986. The series included: a description of curriculum goals and structure, handbooks on teaching each of the seven topic areas of the curriculum, and four guidebooks describing the recommended learning-teaching system, evaluation methods, equipment/supplies, and the professional development of preschool teachers. A brief overview of the contents of two of these publications will illustrate the kind of aid they offer to those who operate kindergartens (Thomas, 1988a).

First, the booklet on curriculum goals and structure describes three general purposes of pre-school programs:

1 Building a foundation for the development of the attitudes, knowledge, skills, and creativity that children need for succeeding in their society.
2 Preparing children to enter primary school.
3 Preparing children for self-development in keeping with educational principles, so that individuals can achieve their potential during their entire life span. (*Kurikulum*, 1986, p. 5)

In addition, the publication lists seven areas on which the learning program is to focus, along with weekly time allotments for each topic. The topics include: (i) moral education; (ii) the history of the nation's struggle for independence and unity; (iii) language skills; (iv) affective awareness of one's society and environment; (v) general knowledge; (vi) creativity; and (vii) health and physical fitness. In effect, the booklet defines the curriculum at the variety 1 level described early in this chapter. It may be apparent that teachers receiving such a list might feel lost in trying to devise meaningful ways to teach young children 'the history of the nation's struggle' or 'affective awareness of one's society' or 'creativity'. As a means of resolving such a puzzlement, the remaining booklets in the series offer specific examples of how those objectives can be pursued. The additional booklets thus qualify as examples of variety 5a in our earlier hierarchy of specificity of curriculum proposals.

For example, the second publication in the sequence, *Guide to the Learning-Teaching Process in the Kindergarten*, is a sixty-page booklet describing learning experiences for children organized around play activities that include group and individual role-playing, discussions, story telling, field trips, demonstrations, and projects using materials from children's everyday lives. Specific examples are offered to show how each of the seven aspects of the curriculum can be taught. Different ways to arrange the physical settings of pre-schools are illustrated, and evaluation techniques and forms for reporting children's progress are included (*Petunjuk Proses Belajar-Mengajar*, 1986).

An Example of Curriculum Experimentation

In their efforts to solve curriculum problems in such a large and diverse society, Indonesian educators have shown no lack of ingenuity. The sophistication and creativity that teams from the Ministry of Education have brought to the task of providing students with improved learning opportunities can be illustrated with the Development School Project, which represents an endeavor to provide recommended curricula at the variety 6 level.

As is true in most developing societies, traditional instruction in Indonesian schools has consisted mainly of teachers giving lectures, of students copying material from the blackboard, and of students reciting what they have memorized. Indonesian educational leaders in recent decades have realized that such methods often fail (i) to adjust instruction to individual students' learning rates; (ii) to engage students in an active rather than a passive learning style; and (iii) to provide learners with continual feedback, with *feedback* meaning information about how well the students were mastering the objectives. In an effort to devise a teaching-learning system that corrected these weaknesses, the Research and Development Center of the Ministry of Education introduced the Development School Project in 1971–1972, a program that continued for more than a decade (Soedijarto, 1976).

The project involved the establishment of eight experimental elementary and secondary schools, each of them located on the campus of a public teacher-education institute (IKIP or *Institut Keguruan dan Ilmu Pendidikan*). Six of the IKIPs were on the island of Java, one was on Sumatra, and one on Sulawesi.

General guidelines for devising curricula were provided by the Center in Jakarta. Within these guidelines, the participating faculty members in each IKIP were encouraged to invent effective ways to achieve the aim of active, individualized learning with continual feedback. The general system that evolved in this cooperative venture between the Center and the IKIPs was labeled 'the modular teaching-learning approach'. To begin, the specific instructional objectives for each subject-matter area at each grade level were organized into segments. Most segments usually represented from two to five days' instruction in a subject-matter area. Every segment was then organized as a teaching-learning packet called a *module*. A typical packet contained:

1   *A Teacher's Manual.*   This teacher's guidesheet described (a) the module's objectives in terms of desired student knowledge and skills; (b) instructional materials used in the module; and (c) how to apply the module successfully, such as how to furnish remediation for learners who had difficulty mastering the objectives.
2   *Preassessment.*   A means of assessing prerequisite knowledge and skills

required for succeeding with the module was provided. This was often in the form of a paper-pencil pretest. The pre-test (a) alerted the teacher to possible deficiencies in students' backgrounds that could affect their progress with the module; and (b) refreshed the students' memories regarding matters related to the module's objectives.

3 *Basic Learning Activities.* The principal learning activities in which students would engage over the two-to-five days dedicated to the module could be of various types. Three examples would be: (a) the learners' completing self-instruction workbooks that included text material interspersed with problem-solving exercises which reflected how well the students comprehended the text content; (b) the teacher demonstrating science phenomena, and students writing answers to questions about the demonstration; and (c) students orally repeating English-language phrases played on a tape-recorder.

4 *Summative Evaluation.* When a student completed the basic learning activities, his or her mastery of the module's objectives would be evaluated by means of a paper-pencil test, of a performance test, or of a work project, such as an insect collection (science), a map (geography), or a short story (language arts).

5 *Enrichment and Remediation.* The modular system provided for enrichment activities to be pursued by students who successfully completed the module early. The enrichment opportunities enabled the more adept students to use their time constructively as they waited for their less apt classmates to succeed with the basic learning goals. The system also suggested remedial measures for learners who failed to reach an 80 per cent mastery of the objectives on their first time through the basic module.

In summary, the foregoing five elements comprised the contents of the modular system. It is apparent that this system equipped teachers with a recommended curriculum at the variety 6 level.

To implement such a plan in the eight experimental schools would clearly require the expenditure of large amounts of money, the availability of experts in preparing learning materials, careful training of teachers, and constant supervision. It would also require an efficient process of assessing the effectiveness of individual modules and of feeding information about the modules' strengths and weaknesses back to project headquarters so the materials could be refined.

During the mid-1970s, high prices of Indonesia's oil exports furnished monies to support the expensive modular-instruction venture. In addition, such foreign-aid organizations as UNESCO and US-AID financed the hiring of foreign experts and sponsored overseas module-writing workshops for Indonesian educators.

From the viewpoint of the nationwide education system, the purpose of the experimental program was to provide a means of testing out and improving innovative curricula before gradually transferring the most successful modules into the country's regular schools. Over the decade of the Development School Projects' operation, continual progress was made in refining the modular approach at the eight experimental sites. However, the original ambitions of Ministry officials to make modular, individualized instruction the standard method in all the nation's schools was never realized. The project was abandoned in the mid-1980s. There are a variety of reasons that, even though the system succeeded in the eight experimental schools, it failed to be adopted nationwide.

First, the modular approach was costly. It required a constant supply of specialized reading materials, some of which were expendable. That is, worksheets and tests could be used only once and then had to be replenished. Furthermore, the results of achievement tests administered to students in the experimental schools, when compared with results from regular schools, suggested that whatever slight gains the modular-instructed students might show over the regular-school students were not worth the extra expenditure the modular approach required. In short, module instruction was judged not to be cost-effective. And concerns about cost were particularly acute in the early 1980s when oil export prices had dropped from their highs of the 1970s.

A further factor in the demise of the modular program was the appointment of a new minister of education who dismissed top-level personnel of the Research and Development Center, replacing them with appointees who were not committed to the modular experiment.

There were also serious inadequacies in the routine management of the experimental-school project which caused the educationally sound curriculum plan to fall considerably short of its potential. For example, the process of supplying module writers information about the success of their modules in classrooms started off well but broke down relatively early in the project's lifetime because suitable personnel were not permanently assigned to monitor the feedback system.

As a second example, a team of six IKIP faculty members were sent to the United States for a three-month intensive workshop in creating prototype enrichment modules. According to the plan, the six, upon their return to Indonesia, would then train additional authors of enrichment materials so that a growing supply of such modules would be fed into the schools. During their three-month study abroad, the faculty members developed an instructional handbook for writers of enrichment activities and created 210 exemplary modules covering six subject-matter areas (Thomas, 1977). However, when the professors returned to Indonesia, they went back to their separate IKIPs without the Development School Project's managers incorporating the results of the overseas experience into the system. In effect, no additional authors of enrichment activities were trained by the six faculty members, and the 210 prototype modules were not even reproduced for use in the schools.

Such management shortcomings are not uncommon in developing countries where there is a limited supply of educational experts, where the available experts take on multiple jobs, and where new opportunities for additional income attract the experts away from concentrating on the responsibilities they already bear.

The fact that the modular instructional approach was not disseminated throughout Indonesia's regular schools should not be interpreted to mean that the Development School Project failed to exert a positive influence on the nation's curriculum development. The basic personnel who were involved in the project continued to participate in the curriculum work of the Research and Development Center, applying the experience gained in the project to the revision of nationwide curricula. The modules created for the project remained available for use in whatever schools chose to adopt them. And the process of creating instructional objectives for the experimental schools contributed to the preparation of objectives for the country's 1975 and 1984 curriculum revisions.

In summary, the Development School Project was a sophisticated teaching-learning system built on a sound foundation of modern-day instructional psychology. Although it proved to be feasible and successful in the experimental-school setting, its potential level of success was limited by weaknesses in the management process. A major reason the module approach was not adopted throughout Indonesia was its high cost in relation to the benefits it would likely yield in terms of student achievement.

Concluding Comments

As the foregoing review has shown, curriculum development in Indonesia involves somewhat different actors or agents in the pre-school and primary/secondary divisions of the education system. Furthermore, these agents contribute to the recommended curricula at different levels of specificity, with the classroom teacher typically making the ultimate decision about which precise objectives are pursued and which methods of instruction are used to achieve those objectives.

Both the Ministry of Education and the Ministry of Religion maintain relatively new research and development units which currently bear much of the responsibility for preparing curriculum guidelines for secular and Islamic institutions from the preschool level through the upper secondary school. These units have brought increasingly sophisticated procedures to the process of planning and disseminating curriculum innovations.

However, a variety of problems continued in the 1990s to limit the effectiveness of curriculum planning and implementation. These included: (i) an overload of separate subjects at the elementary-school level so that students had insufficient time to master any given subject; (ii) inadequate coordination among the agencies engaged in curriculum development and utilization; (iii) too few teachers' guidebooks and textbooks to equip all schools; (iv) extensive lag time between the designing of a new curriculum and the supplying of appropriate guidebooks and texts to the schools; (v) a lack of continuous assessment of pupils' progress, (vi) indecision about how best to suit the curriculum to local conditions; and (vii) the unsatisfactory implementation of the principles of active learning and individualization of instruction (Theisen, Hughes and Spector, 1990).

Chapter 11

Curriculum Development in Malaysia

Sharifah Maimunah Syed Zin and
Keith M. Lewin

Introduction

This chapter is concerned with the process and practice of curriculum development in Malaysia. It provides a resumé of the social, political and economic context in which curriculum development has evolved since independence and outlines the basic tenets of the national education system. A discussion of the introduction of the national curriculum is followed by a review and analysis of curriculum development practices. From this, and examples drawn from the development of the new primary school curriculum (KBSR), a number of issues are identified for further consideration which are discussed in the last sections.

Social, Political and Economic Context

Malaysia was established as a political entity in 1963 through the amalgamation of three former British colonies. Geographically, it comprises Peninsular Malaysia to the south of Thailand (formerly known as the Federation of Malaya); and East Malaysia which is part of the island of Kalimantan (Sabah and Sarawak). Politically, it consists of fourteen states. It has a constitutional monarchy and an elected House of Parliament. Its 15.8 million people are drawn from three major ethnic groups. The Malays and other indigenous groups (Bumiputra) comprise 58.6 per cent of the population; the Chinese 32.1 per cent; and the Indians 8.6 per cent. Other minor ethnic groups account for about 0.7 per cent. About 82.1 per cent of Malaysia's population is in Peninsular Malaysia, 8.1 per cent in Sabah and 9.8 per cent in Sarawak. The uneven distribution of population reflects the historical, geographical and economic factors that influenced development before and during colonization. Islam is the state religion, but the worship of other religions is allowed by the Constitution. Bahasa Malaysia (The Malay language) is the national and sole official language. English is a second language.

Malaysia has an agriculturally-based economy which has been rapidly developing. The main exports are palm oil, rubber, cocoa, timber, tin, liquid natural gas and petroleum.

Industrialization has led to a substantial manufacturing sector which includes electronic and electrical products as well as automobile production. Employment is still largest in the agricultural sector (35.7 per cent of those employed) but this is a minority of the total labour force. Employment in each of the government, manufacturing, and commerce and banking sectors is between 15–17 per cent of the labour force.

Malaysia is a plural society with a diversity of cultural, social, political, religious, economic and language traditions. Hence the major task of the national development plan is to forge a nation that is united through the principles of Rukunegara (the National ideology) and through the New Economic Policy. Rukunegara was formulated as a result of the 1969 racial conflict and its principles have been the guiding force in nation building and in educational policies (see appendix 1). Its aims are to achieve a united nation with a plural society; democratic institutions through a constitutionally elected Parliament; a just society with equal opportunites for all; a liberal society of diverse cultural traditions; and a progressive society oriented towards science and technology. The New Economic Policy is aimed at the eradication of poverty and the restructuring of society to eliminate the identification of race with economic function and geographical location.

Education and National Development

The emphasis on national unity has several implications for the education system. First of all, education is seen as one of the means through which Malaysia's national objectives can be achieved. Education is considered as one of the most important social investments that will benefit the country in the long run. This important role is manifested in all the five successive national plans. An extract of the educational objectives from the Fifth Malaysia Plan (1986–1990) — representing the fourth and last segment of the twenty-year Outline Perspective Plan (1971–1990) for attaining the supreme goal of national unity — reflects the link between education and national development.

> The overall objective of education and training is to promote national unity ... the role of education and training in Malaysia is to produce knowledgeable, trained, and skilled individuals to meet the manpower requirements as well as the growing social needs. (*Government of Malaysia*, 1986, p. 483)

The importance of education can be seen in terms of government expenditure. In 1989, the total budgeted allocation education expenditure was approximately M RGT.$5203.0 million and this accounts for 18.8 per cent of the total national expenditure. (Ministry of Education, Malaysia 1990). Malaysia has consistently allocated 15–20 per cent of the national budget to education over the last two decades.

Developing a National Education System

Malaysia's formal educational programme dates from the nineteenth century. Education then was mostly conducted in the vernacular languages reflecting the country's plural society. The colonial government provided limited vernacular Malay education up to the primary level for the Malays. Chinese education was the concern of the Chinese community and Tamil education was associated with the rubber plantations where most of the Indian immigrants were employed. The English schools were provided for all races. However, since these schools were mainly established by Christian missionaries, they were mostly found in the urban centres. Due to the religious overtones and location, the schools were more accessible to the urban and immigrant population of ethnic Chinese and Indians. Only a small number of Malays attended these schools. Alongside this formal system, Koranic schools existed and predated the secular system.

Hence, during the pre-Independence years, there existed separate systems of education. The school curriculum was ad hoc, uncoordinated and generally reflected traditions from the country of origin from the different groups. It was also severely constrained by the availability of books. It was not until after the Second World War that the first steps began to be taken to reorganize and plan towards a more purposeful and nationalized system of education. Rapid political and social changes were taking place in the region and the spirit of nationalism made Malaysians realize that the country must move towards self-government and that the various ethnic communities had to be merged into one nation. The different types of schools existing relatively independently with different curricula orientations were seen as a potentially divisive factor in a multiethnic society. As stated earlier, education was seen as playing a vital role in laying the foundation for building unity and cohesion among the races. Towards this end, several committees were set up to study and make recommendations regarding a national system of education. However, it was not until 1956, on the eve of independence, that the changes under discussion began germinating into a statutory framework to provide a single national system.

The recommendations of the Education Committee of 1956 (also known as the Razak Report) formed the basis for the Education Ordinance in 1957. It is from this that the National Educational Policy was formulated. In 1960, a further review was carried out by the Education Review Committee (the Rahman Talib Report). Its recommendations, and that of the Razak Report, became the basis of the Education Act of 1961. Significant changes brought about by these Committees were the provision of universal free primary education, automatic promotion up to the third year of secondary schooling, a common content syllabus that has a Malaysian outlook, use of Bahasa Malaysia as the national language, and as main medium of instruction, common national assessment, expansion of teacher training programmes, and provision of religious and moral instruction. These recommendations were implemented over the next twenty years and a single national system of education established. The next major review of national educational policy was conducted by the Cabinet Committee from 1974 onwards and its report was published in 1979. Among its recommendations were the reform of the primary curriculum, a more broadly-based general education at the secondary level, and the introduction of vocational stream in secondary education.

Educational Philosophy, Aims and Objectives

The National Philosophy of Education has recently been defined as follows.

> Education in Malaysia is an on-going effort towards further developing the potential of individuals in a holistic and integrated manner, so as to produce individuals who are intellectually, spiritually, emotionally and physically balanced and harmonious, based on a firm belief in and devotion to God. Such an effort is designed to produce Malaysian citizens who are knowledgeable and competent, who possess high moral standards, and who are responsible and capable of achieving a high level of personal well-being as well as being able to contribute to the harmony and betterment of the society and the nation at large. (Ministry of Education, 1990)

The underlying principles and goals of the National Educational Policy and National Educational Philosophy are translated into educational programmes to achieve the objectives below:

- To provide pupils with the essential intellectual, affective and psychomotor skills in a holistic and integrated manner so as to produce individuals who are intellectually, physically, emotionally and spiritually balanced and functionally literate.
- To inculcate and nurture national consciousness through fostering common ideals, values, aspirations and loyalties in order to mould national unity and national identity in a multi-ethnic society.
- To produce manpower with the requisite skills for economic and national development.
- To inculcate in pupils desired moral values and to promote personality and aesthetic development as well as the sense of being responsible, disciplined and progressive enabling them to contribute effectively towards nation building. (Ministry of Education, 1990)

Administrative Machinery

Political, economic and social factors have resulted in the evolution of a highly centralized system of education. Within this centralized system most matters pertaining to education rest wholly with the central government. Through the enactment of the Education Act of 1961, the Ministry of Education is empowered to make decisions on all policies related to education. Its planning, development, implementation and evaluation of educational programmes are operated from four levels, i.e. federal, state, district and school levels. The Ministry at the federal level is responsible for translating educational policy into plans, programmes, projects and activities as well as coordinating their implementation. The state level is responsible for executing and supervising educational programmes, and organizing the coordination of school administration with respect to staff and personnel. With the increasing emphasis on decentralization in the execution of programmes and their administration, district education offices were established. These form the third level in the hierarchy and act as linkage between the school and the State Education Department and also assist in the supervision of programmes being implemented. The school forms the last level.

The School System

Malaysia has a 6+3+3+3 system of primary, secondary (lower and upper) and post-secondary education. Children start school at the age of 6 and until 1989, the school year began January. Parents are free to choose the type of schools for their children. In 1989, the enrolment figure for primary school was 2,390,920 and this represents 99 per cent of the population of the 6 to 12-year-old age group. (Educational Statistics of Malaysia, 1989). The dropout rate is very low. For example, of the total number enrolled in year 1 in 1980, 96.3 per cent reached year 6 in 1985. The high enrolment is due to the policy of providing free education with automatic promotion: the availability of improved facilities such as the provision of hostels in the remote areas; and increased realization amongst parents of the importance of education. Primary schools are classified as national (using Bahasa Malaysia as the medium of instruction) or national-type (using Chinese or Tamil as the medium of instruction). There is a common government examination at the end of the primary school but this does not affect promotion to the secondary schools.

Pupils from the three types of primary school merge at the lower secondary school for another three years of uninterrupted schooling. At this level, the medium of instruction in all schools is Bahasa Malaysia. Those from the national type schools spend an extra year (the first year of secondary schooling) in Remove Classes to enable them to acquire sufficient proficiency in Bahasa Malaysia before joining the main stream the following year. In 1985, the transition rate from primary to secondary level was 88.2 per cent. The reduction in enrolment ratio, considering that there is automatic promotion from the primary to secondary is partly attributable to the existence of alternative non-government educational institutions. A government examination at the end of the lower secondary level (Lower Certificate of Examination; Sijil Rendah Pelajaran) serves as a selection device in determining whether pupils continue for a further two years of upper secondary academic or vocational education or leave school and enter the labour market. This aspect is being reviewed in the light of the proposal to extend the opportunity for schooling from nine to eleven years. Figure 11.1 shows the present education system. All schools use the same syllabus, in line with the national policy of having a common Malaysian outlook. Textbooks are given to needy pupils on a free loan basis by the Ministry. One striking feature of Malaysian schools is the operation of schools in double shifts i.e. morning and afternoon. A high concentration of pupils in certain schools and the lack of space have contributed to this phenomena (both in primary and secondary schools, especially in the urban and semi-urban areas) and this feature is likely to remain in place for some time. In the more rural areas, many of the schools are small and may be single shift.

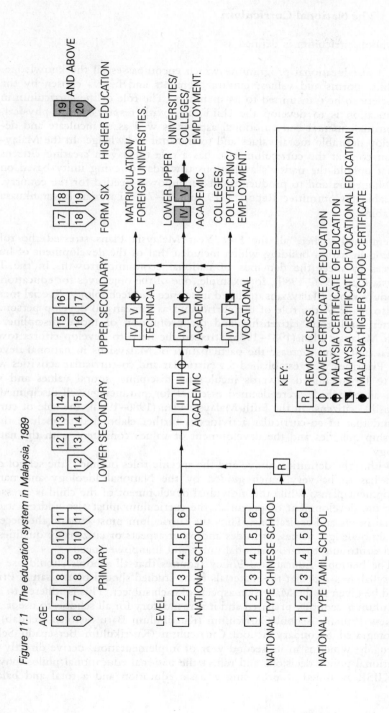

Figure 11.1 *The education system in Malaysia, 1989*

229

The National Curriculum

The school curriculum is defined as:

> ... an educational programme which encompasses all the knowledge, skills, norms and values, cultural elements and beliefs chosen by the society to be transmitted to its members. The role of the curriculum in education is to develop the child fully with respect to the physical, spiritual, mental and emotional aspects as well as to inculcate and develop desirable moral values and to transmit knowledge. In the Malaysian context the curriculum also has a role to play in creating citizens that uphold the nation's aspirations towards achieving unity based on Rukunegara and to produce trained manpower needed for the country. (Cabinet Committee Report 1979, pp. 66–7 — Laporan Jawatankuasa Kabinet)

As mentioned earlier, all the Five Year Malaysia Plans stressed the role of education in nation building which included that of the development of human resources to meet the demands of national economic growth. In the Third Malaysia Plan (1976–1980), for example, one of the objectives for education was to produce more Malaysians qualified in science and technology. Special mention was also made of the role of the curriculum as a means to develop personality, character, and good citizenship and the promotion of moral discipline. The Fourth Malaysia Plan (1981–1985) stressed the need to develop efforts towards national unity and increase the participation of Malaysians in national development. Priorities were established for curricular and co-curricular activities which were to be orientated towards inculcating discipline, moral values and work ethics, all of which were deemed essential for producing well-disciplined and responsible citizens. In the Fifth Malaysia Plan (1986–1990), the role of curriculum and that of co-curricular activities is further elaborated to include that of leadership qualities and the development of values consistent with the national ideology.

Within the definition above and the specific roles outlined, the school curriculum has to be very much guided by the National Ideology and national development plans. While the individual development of the child is stressed to enable the development of potential, the curriculum must also address itself to national needs and aspirations. Thus the curriculum must contain the necessary skills, knowledge, values, attitudes and other aspects or citizenship qualities that would contribute towards national unity and manpower needs.

The National Educational Policy requires that all schools should use common syllabuses and that the materials to be studied should be the same. Priority should be given to the Malaysian aspects of each subject. This is adhered to as the curriculum is centrally prepared and it is mandatory for all schools to use it. Both the New Primary School Curriculum (Kurrikulum Baru Sekolah Rendah), and the Integrated Secondary School Curriculum (Kurrikulum Bersepadu Sekolah Menengah) which is in its second year of implementation, derive directly from educational policy decisions and reflect the national educational philosophy.

KBSR is aimed at providing a basic education and a total and balanced

Table 11.1   *The structure of the primary school curriculum*

FIELD	COMPONENT	SUBJECTS	
		Phase I	Phase II
Communication	Basic Skills	† Medium of Instruction Bahasa Malaysia English Mathematics	Medium of Instruction Bahasa Malaysia English Mathematics
Man and His Environment	Spiritual Values and Attitudes Humanities and the Environment	†† Islamic Relig. Edu. †† Moral Education —	Islamic Relig. Edu. Moral Education Man and Environment
Individual Self Development	Arts and Recreation	Music Art Education Physical education Co-curriculum —	Music Art Education Physical Education Co-curriculum Manipulative Skills

Notes:
†   The medium of instruction in national schools is Bahasa Malaysia.
The medium of instruction in national type Chinese schools is Chinese and in national type Tamil school is Tamil.
††   When Muslim pupils and others who choose to do so study Islamic religious education, pupils of other religious denominations must study moral education.

development of the child at the primary level. Thus its emphasis is on the mastery of the skills of reading, writing and arithmetic skills. The structure of the curriculum is built around three broad areas, i.e. communication, man and the environment and individual development. The development of desirable values among children is emphasized through Islamic religious education for Muslims and moral education for the non-Muslims. An important feature in the curriculum is the introduction of Man and the Environment which integrates the elements of history, geography, science, health education and civics, thereby replacing them in the primary school curriculum. Other new elements brought in are commercial practices, manipulative skills, and co-curriculum activities. Co-curriculum is given a specific time in the formal school timetable and are provided to enrich school experience outside the constraints of the formal academic curriculum. Commercial practices is incorporated into the mathematics curriculum while manipulative skills is taught as a subject.

The planning of KBSR has been based on the principle of giving every pupil equal opportunity to obtain skills, values, attitudes and practices. It is divided into two phases. Phase I refers to the first three years of schooling and emphasizes the acquisition of the basic skills. Phase II covers the next three years and focuses on the utilizaton of the skills already acquired and the more explicit learning of knowledge. Table 11.1 shows the structure of the curriculum. The changes brought about by KBSR can be seen not only in its curricular content, but also in its teaching and learning strategy, pupils' assessment, the teachers' role, and the model of implementation and management. The following lists the major innovative intentions of the programme:

— More consideration of individual differences and the advocacy of more independent learning with the introduction of remedial and enrichment programmes and different approaches to teaching.
— An integrated approach to teaching and learning in contrast to the rigid compartmentalization of subjects in the past.
— Two separate terminal pupil assessments at the end of primary schooling, i.e. a centrally administered standardized examination (Ujian Peperiksaan Sekolah Rendah, referred to as UPSR) and school-based assessment (Penilaian Kemajuan Berasaskan Sekolah referred to as PKBS).
— The use of evaluation as an integral part of the process of teaching and learning with the following features;
  — it is decentralized to school level;
  — it aims to be diagnostic to assist in identifying learning difficulties and overcoming them;
  — it is undertaken continuously using a variety of techniques;
  — it is formulated, administered and processed by teachers.
— Monitoring of pupils' progress through teachers' observations and pupil's progress records
— Postponement of formal learning of useful knowledge to year 4 and the inculcation of study skills through the introduction of men and the environment, an integrated subject comprising the elements of history, geography, science, health education and civics.
— Teachers perceived as motivators of learning rather than givers of information. The emphasis is on teachers' creativity in integrating knowledge and giving due attention on the individual. Teachers are given more opportunity to adapt teaching materials to the local situation and be creative and resourceful.
— The role of headmasters (headteachers) places emphasis on them as professional managers of the implementation of the curriculum.
— The concept of decentralization whereby curriculum implementation is no longer the sole responsibility of the central agency, i.e. the Curriculum Development Centre, but is shared with other agencies. State Education Departments have a bigger role to play in the following areas:
  — planning for the strategy of limited and full implementation;
  — planning and organization of in-service training for teachers;
  — distribution or resources such as facilities for schools and finance;
  — curriculum maintenance (supervision, advice and other support services)

KBSR has already completed its first cycle of implementation for all grades and is now into its second year of the second cycle.

KBSM (The Integrated Secondary School Curriculum) is intended to integrate learning experiences with what is seen as the central purpose of education, i.e. producing a harmonious and balanced human being. An important feature of the curriculum is the non-selective general and comprehensive provision for all students — defined as the core curriculum, together with some guided specialization in the form of electives at the upper secondary level. Another important attribute is 'Values across the curriculum' which emphasizes the internalization and practice of spiritual, humanistic and citizenship values. The curriculum also stresses 'National language across the curriculum' in an effort to ensure consistency and correct use of the language as well as being consistent with using Bahasa Malaysia as a language of knowledge. A new subject labelled 'Living skills' has been introduced and aims to develop interactive skills and basic functional skills for daily living as well as to give students a broad exposure to technology, industry, agriculture and meaningful recreational activities. The KBSM curriculum is its second year of implementation. Table 11.2 shows the subjects in KBSM at the upper secondary level.

Curriculum Development Practices

When the national educational policy was formulated, a General Syllabus and Time-table Committee were established to ensure that aspirations for common content were met. Several sub-committees were formed to formulate the subject syllabuses. In 1965, when non-selective comprehensive education was introduced at the secondary level, subject committees were again set up to revise, amend and if necessary devise new syllabuses. The drafts prepared by these committees were circulated to schools to be tried. Amendments were made, taking into consideration views expressed during the trial. After these syllabuses were revised and approved they were made mandatory for schools to use. Once the work was over, the syllabus committees ceased to exist. Hence the committees were ad-hoc in nature. Curriculum development work then was more in terms of syllabus preparation.

During the late 1960s it was recognized that apart from the content to be learned, other aspects of the curriculum, such as teaching methods and learning materials, were also equally important if one was to improve the quality of programmes in schools. One of the early measures towards serious curriculum improvement in science education was the establishment of the Science Centre in 1969. The broader concept of curriculum and the need to systematize curriculum development work under one roof paved the way for the establishment of the Curriculum Development Centre in 1973. The original functions of the Centre are listed below:

— to identify national needs and aspirations and apply them as a basis for curricular specifications;
— to conduct research and to plan and develop curricular programmes for continuous, systematic and qualitative development in education;
— to develop and produce curriculum materials such as syllabuses, teachers' guides, pupil learning materials, evaluation instruments, audio-visual aids and prototype equipment for teaching and learning;
— to disseminate information on curricular innovations and practices to teachers in schools and others in the community;
— to organize in-service courses to communicate innovation, changes and revisions so that teachers will be able to implement them effectively in the class;
— to conduct surveys and analyses of significant trends and development in curricular specifications and teaching practices. (Curriculum Development Centre, undated)

Table 11.2 Subjects for the upper secondary level

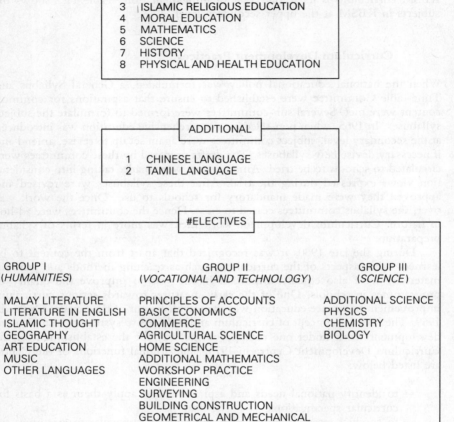

CORE

1 BAHASA MALAYSIA
2 ENGLISH LANGUAGE
3 ISLAMIC RELIGIOUS EDUCATION
4 MORAL EDUCATION
5 MATHEMATICS
6 SCIENCE
7 HISTORY
8 PHYSICAL AND HEALTH EDUCATION

ADDITIONAL

1 CHINESE LANGUAGE
2 TAMIL LANGUAGE

#ELECTIVES

GROUP I (HUMANITIES)	GROUP II (VOCATIONAL AND TECHNOLOGY)	GROUP III (SCIENCE)
MALAY LITERATURE	PRINCIPLES OF ACCOUNTS	ADDITIONAL SCIENCE
LITERATURE IN ENGLISH	BASIC ECONOMICS	PHYSICS
ISLAMIC THOUGHT	COMMERCE	CHEMISTRY
GEOGRAPHY	AGRICULTURAL SCIENCE	BIOLOGY
ART EDUCATION	HOME SCIENCE	
MUSIC	ADDITIONAL MATHEMATICS	
OTHER LANGUAGES	WORKSHOP PRACTICE	
	ENGINEERING	
	SURVEYING	
	BUILDING CONSTRUCTION	
	GEOMETRICAL AND MECHANICAL DRAWING	
	PRACTICAL IN ELECTRICAL TECHNOLOGY	
	COMPUTER SCIENCE	
	GEOMETRICAL AND BUILDING DRAWING	

Will be implemented after 1992

Currently, the Centre undertakes most of the curriculum development activities in the Ministry. Curricula for the technical and vocational area and Islamic religious education are an exception and are prepared by the respective divisions of the Ministry. Special education and music are the responsibility of the School's Division.

All decision-making related to curriculum policies and change rests with the Central Curriculum Committee. This high-powered Committee is chaired by the Director-General of Education who is an educationist and head of the professional wing of the Ministry. The Curriculum Development Centre acts as secretariat to this Committee. Curricular programmes that have financial implications or which may affect the education system are referred to the educational Planning Committee chaired by the Minister of Education.

The current process of curriculum development is still based on the statutory procedures that existed before the establishment of the Curriculum Development Centre. However, professionalization of curriculum development has meant that more steps are now included in the process. For example, between planning and implementation the drafts are subject to a series of discussion with the relevant project teams as well as core planning groups within the Curriculum Development Centre. One consequence is that a programme takes much longer to develop before it actually gets off the ground than under the previous system. The following processes have been identified by the Centre as crucial stages in curriculum development:

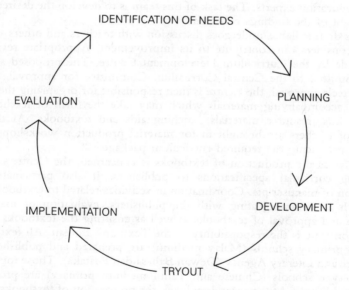

The cyclic model of curriculum development as depicted above is similar to that which has been used in some English curriculum development projects, for example by the Nuffield Foundation for the development of science materials, and has common features with Havelock's rational problem-solving model (Havelock, 1973). Since the middle of the 1970s the range of work has broadened and the patterns of curriculum development have included many different variations and it has been more difficult to identify a definitive curriculum model which has been used for all projects.

Although the diagram seems to show a smooth flow of events in the curriculum development process, in practice there is a lot of back and forth movement in between the stages. For example, at the development stage, reference may have to be made to the needs stage from time to time so that the curriculum being developed is in line with aspirations which themselves may change in the light of practical judgments about what is possible. A draft curriculum may need to be referred back to the Central Curriculum Committee a second or third time for reconsideration when problems in its specification become apparent as a result of detailed work.

A typical example where the processes are generally followed is during a syllabus revision. The Curriculum Development Centre conducts its own small-scale research projects and also collects information on the syllabus in use from other sources such as reports produced by other Divisions of the Ministry. The collective findings and proposals for change or amendments are then presented to the Central Curriculum Committee for consideration. Following the decision to revise the syllabus, a subject or project team is appointed comprising curriculum officers from the Centre, representatives of subject specialists from the School Inspectorate, Teacher Education Division, Textbook Bureau, Examination Syndicate (if the subject is an examinable one). Schools Division, Education Technology Division, practising teachers and, where necessary, subject matter or general education experts. The task of this team is to develop the desired syllabus in the light of the findings collected.

This draft syllabus undergoes discussion with teachers and others whom the Centre considers can contribute to its improvement. Appropriate revisions are then made by the Curriculum Development Centre. The proposed syllabus is then submitted to the Central Curriculum Committee for approval. After the Committee's approval, the Centre is then responsible for organizing the development of accompanying materials which may take the form of teacher guides, learning kits, resource materials, teaching aids and textbooks. At this stage, groups of teachers are brought in for material production workshops oriented towards producing the required curriculum package.

As far as the production of textbooks is concerned, the Centre's role is in providing curricular specifications to publishers. It also participates in the evaluation of manuscripts. Coordination of activities related to textbook production such as communicating with the publishers, evaluation of manuscripts, selection and approval of textbooks as well as ensuring the textbooks reach the schools on time is the responsibility of the Textbook Bureau. All textbooks for national primary schools (Malay medium) are prepared and published by the Language and Literary Agency (Dewan Bahasa dan Pustaka). Those for use in the national type schools (Chinese and Tamil medium primary) are produced by private publishers. At the secondary level, the preparation of textbooks is similar to those for the national type primary schools, i.e. undertaken by private publishers. All books used in schools as texts must have the approval of the Textbook Bureau.

The approved syllabus and accompanying curriculum materials are tried out in selected schools. Such tryouts are normally undertaken by the Curriculum Development Centre with the cooperation of State Education Departments and headteachers of schools concerned. Findings of the tryouts are then taken into consideration in the revision of the syllabus and curriculum materials.

While the draft syllabus is being tried out in schools, the design for implementation is planned. This includes the plan for dissemination. If teacher retraining is involved, the Centre then organises in-service courses at the national level for key personnel selected by the state department from amongst the teachers. These key personnel then conduct courses for the rest of the teachers in the state or districts. While all this is taking place, other divisions such as the Education Technology Division, will be involved in the development of programmes for broadcasting to schools. Often if the programme is an innovation that anticipates changes in teacher attitudes or parental support, then other means are employed. These include seminars for teachers and parents, information brochures, coverage by the media or even an announcement by the Education Minister himself.

The implementation of a programme may be phased (in stages) or simultaneous. Formative evaluation is undertaken during this time. Feedback collected through this evaluation is then fed into the revision of the programme which usually takes place after a full cycle of implementation is completed. The flowchart of the curriculum development procedure is given in appendix 2. It is this sequence of curriculum development that the New Primary School Curriculum (KBSR) was based upon. A detailed description of the process of developing the curriculum would perhaps be useful in understanding the entire process. KBSR was a review and renewal of the primary school curriculum and it was the first time a revision of the entire school curriculum was undertaken. There were several reasons for the changes.

The primary school curriculum of the seventies had been using subject syllabuses that were developed in the late sixties. As indicated earlier, although periodic reviews of these syllabuses were undertaken by the Ministry, they were done on a piecemeal basis and focused on specific aspects. For example, at one time the language curricula were changed, at another time, the science and mathematics curricula were. There was then a growing concern for the need to review the whole curriculum, especially when it was found that the syllabuses in use seemed to create educational problems. It was also felt that a review of the entire operation of the educational system was necessary, especially when it was more than twenty years since the educational policy was formulated. In 1974, the government established a special committee known as the Cabinet Committee to study and review the overall implementation of the national education policy. The Chairman was the then Minister of Education (now the Prime Minister). The terms of reference were to review the goals and effectiveness of the education system, including its curriculum, with the aim of ensuring that national manpower requirements were met and more so to ensure that the education system was able to fulfill national needs to promote unity.

The Report, made public in 1979, contained several findings and recommendations for both the secondary and primary school curricula. With regard to primary curriculum, the Report basically recommended that it should be re-examined, taking into consideration the problems that were brought to the attention of the Cabinet Committee. These concerns had been the subject of discussions in the newspapers, mass media, and among educationists. Dominant amongst these was that a sizeable number of school children were leaving primary schools and entering secondary schools without reading, writing and mathematical skills. Among the reasons cited as contributing to this state of affairs were that the curriculum in use was too academic and content-based, that it was overloaded, that it was too compartmentalized leading to learning taking place in isolation. Some of the content was thought irrelevant to the pupils' immediate environment. More emphasis on basic skills was recommended as a result.

The then Mininster of Education had taken an interest in this issue and had directed the Curriculum Development Centre to look for positive measures to ensure that each pupil would be able to read fluently after completing primary education. In 1979, the Curriculum Development Centre, catalyzed by the above-mentioned concerns, conducted a nationwide survey on the performance of pupils in reading and writing (both in Bahasa Malaysia) and in mathematical skills. A test was administered on a sample of pupils from selected schools. The criteria for selection were location (rural, semi-rural, urban), size (large, medium, small), and medium of instruction (Bahasa Malaysia, Chinese, Tamil). The tests for mathematics and Bahasa Malaysia were standardized. The result of the test, amongst other things, revealed that many of the pupils were not able to read, write and do mathematics at levels consistent with their age level norms. It also revealed that urban pupils performed far better than their rural counterparts. This confirmed the concerns mentioned earlier. This prompted the Minister of Education to instruct the Ministry to revamp the primary curriculum.

Since its inception, the Curriculum Development Centre had been conducting small scale projects such as the Integrated Curriculum Project, the Compensatory Education Project, and the Primary Science and Mathematics Project, reflecting domestic and international concerns. There was thus a dynamic base receptive to the need for an over-arching initiative to redevelop the primary curriculum as a whole. The Centre had also 'sensed' that there was a receptive climate for change in the wider community and was already having discussions with various groups on the directions change should take. With these developments, and prompted by the decision to revamp the curriculum, the planners began to develop the new curriculum, its philosophy, aims and objectives and its composition. Drafts prepared were presented to and debated by educational groups such as teachers, academicians, politicians, professionals, teachers' unions and administrators. Comments and suggestions were examined and where relevant and suitable were added to the drafts. Several subject teams were then formed to plan and develop the syllabus for each subject in the curriculum. The teams consisted of curriculum developers, and representatives of the various divisions of the Ministry as well as teachers. These drafts were discussed and debated first at the level of the Curriculum Development Centre with the various project teams. This was to ensure that the contents of the syllabuses did not contradict one another. The drafts were then discussed with groups of teachers. After final amendments were made, the drafts of the syllabus were brought to the Central Curriculum Committee for approval. Certain subject syllabuses presented were approved right away with very minor amendments, while others such as Man and the Environment were presented three times as the earlier drafts did not meet the specifications of the planners. After the approval, several workshops were organized to develop the accompanying materials. It is at this level that teachers were involved.

Since KBSR had implications for policy and finance, it was brought to the Educational Planning Committee and the Cabinet. The curriculum met the approval of the Committees and consequently all schools were given M$5000/ M$7000 launching grant for each year of the first cycle of the implementation of KBSR.

The curriculum package for KBSR comes in the form of multimedia materials such as the syllabus and handbooks (one for each subject), textbooks and workbooks, resource books and supplementary readers; learning kits (charts, pictures, reading cards, cassette tapes and other learning materials) and other aids and equipment for subjects like physical education and music. All printed materials for teacher use (except for the teaching of Chinese, Tamil and English) are in Bahasa Malaysia. Pupil materials are in the three languages. These materials are supplied to each school and each State Education Department is responsible for ensuring that the materials (except textbooks) reach the schools as scheduled. Ground work for the field trial and full implementation, such as teacher preparation, material development and supply of aids and equipment to schools, was usually completed in the preceding year. However, this was not always the case especially when other external agencies such as publishers and distributors took part.

As the main agency responsible for formulating the specifications of KBSR and for providing suggestions in the approach and methods for teaching and learning, the Curriculum Development Centre was also responsible for communicating the curriculum to the various groups concerned. The main purpose was to enable members of these groups to perform their roles. The main strategy for disseminating the KBSR to teachers was in-service courses. The aim was to orientate teachers and provide them with the necessary training for effective implementation of the curriculum in the classroom (Noor Azmi 1988).

National level courses were conducted by the developers of the curriculum themselves at the Curriculum Development Centre. Key personnel, participants in these courses, were selected by the respective state departments based on criteria such as academic and professional qualifications, competency in the subject, experience in writing materials, age (below 50 and with a minimum of five years teaching experience), ability to move around, and in-service training (courses, seminars and workshops attended). Each state was represented by two officers for each subject in the curriculum. These courses were also attended by officers from the divisions of the Minstry. These participants were to act as change agents in the implementation of the curriculum. After undergoing the centralized course, they were to conduct similar courses for other groups of key personnel. Both groups then held courses for the other teachers. They are thus agents linking the intentions of the curriculum developers with the practitioners in a cascade process of dissemination. Other methods for disseminating the curriculum used were through the curriculum materials mentioned earlier, through seminars and workshops, the mass media and a special information brochure on the curriculum.

The curriculum went for field trial in year 1 classes in 302 schools in 1982 (later 305, about 5 per cent of the total primary schools in Malaysia). Nationwide implementation of the year 1 programme began in 1983 and ran concurrent with the trial of the year 2 programme. This left very little time for significant modification as the result of formative evaluation data arising from the trial period, as noted below. By 1987, the curriculum was implemented nationwide from year 1 to year 5 and on a field trial basis at year 6.

The responsibility for implementing KBSR was shared by all concerned in the Ministry (see appendix 3). With increased decentralization, the responsibility of planning the preparation and monitoring of the implementation was left to the state and district levels. Both were encouraged to use their initiative and discretion in undertaking measures to ensure the curriculum developed as envisaged by the planners and that the momentum was maintained. To help streamline the activities, the KBSR Implementation Committee chaired by the Deputy-Director General of Education 11, was established at the federal level with the following responsibilities:

To plan strategies for the implementation with special attention to:
— suitability of teaching learning materials for all levels of primary schools;
— teacher preparation and ensuring teacher adequacy to utilize the above materials in the process of teaching and learning;
— development of additional teacher pupil materials;
— technical and professional problems which may arise; and
— monitoring the implementation of KBSR in all schools whether in trial or full national implementation (refer appendix 4)
To coordinate all implementation activities undertaken by all divisions of the Ministry.

At the national level, this Committee was assisted by the KBSR Technical Committee whose members consisted of all coordinators of the curriculum at state and divisional levels. This Committee met about once every two months to communicate feedback to the Curriculum Development Centre on the progress and problems of all aspects of KBSR.

KBSR largely followed the pattern of development laid out in appendix 2. However, there were other programmes, especially those introduced in the seventies which did not fall within this model. The Malaysian integrated science for secondary school, for example, was adapted from the Scottish integrated science curriculum (Lewin, 1981) using less comprehensive procedures. Some programmes have been referred to the Central Curriculum Comittee a second and third time, as was the case with Man and the Environment, when practical problems and detailed design work identified flaws in the original brief that needed reconsideration. There have also been cases where the processes involved in the development were short-circuited because of the inadequate time available or because of political developments external to the Ministry. The duration of tryout of programmes, for example, was either reduced or the programmes did not get tried out at all. Sometimes too, new programmes were initiated by agencies outside rather than within the Ministry, thus skipping some of the stages of consultation.

From the above description, it appears that the process of curriculum development has become more systematic than the practice before the establishment of the Curriculum Development Centre. The pattern of developing subject-based syllabuses by different committees established in the 1970s has continued. This has proved to be easier to undertake than the more recent attempts to develop curricula in an interrelated way across a number of subjects. The disadvantages of subject-based curriculum development have become clear. It has led to compartmentalization which can create contradictory approaches to similar topics occurring in different subjects; the sequencing of material which may be interdependent cannot be coordinated easily (as for example where some science teaching depends on some mathematical skills being mastered): the contents of subject-based syllabuses may overlap unpredictably; if there is unnecessary repetition problems of content overload may be exacerbated. All these disadvantages appeared in the problems diagnosed with the primary curriculum of the seventies. KBSR was conceptualized as a whole to try to overcome these. The process of discussing the drafts with project teams formed for each major area helped to avoid at least some of the problems, but at considerable cost in terms of time which had to be allocated to this.

Another characteristic of early curricular programmes was the utilization of foreign consultants to help with the conceptualization, adaptation and training of teachers. This was especially so when these programmes were supported by external agencies or adapted from programmes of another country. However, as the Curriculum Development Centre matured and more officers were trained in developing the curriculum, much of the work, including that of syllabus preparation, was undertaken by national staff. The role of foreign consultants diminished through the 1970s as this occurred and their influence ceased to be direct as it had been initially.

Curriculum Innovation

The literature on curriculum change reveals that there can be several forces that induce change. These range across educational, political, social and economic considerations. In the United Kingdom for example, the Schools Council (1973) undertook a review of why curriculum projects had been set up. The reasons given included the following: in response to technological advancement, in response to social changes outside the system, in response to special needs not previously catered for by the system, to take advantage of recent advances in educational or other research and in response to change in the education system itself. The stimulus for change can come from within or from outside the system.

In Malaysia, one of the early attempts at curricular improvement came with the country's decision to increase the school leaving age to 15 and to restructure secondary schooling along the lines of a comprehensive education system. Subjects such as industrial arts, agricultural science, home science and commerce were offered as electives so that pupils who were unable to continue their schooling would have some elements of pre-vocational training when they left school. In 1969, integrated science was introduced, also as part of the comprehensive system. The modern physics/chemistry/biology for Malaysian schools and the modern general science for Malaysian schools became new science courses for the upper secondary level in 1972 and 1974 respectively where separate subject teaching was to be retained for science students. All these courses were adapted from courses in the United Kingdom (Lewin, 1984).

Innovation in science curricula was deemed necessary as this was seen as an area that would contribute to economic growth as well as educate children to adapt themselves to the rapidly changing post-school environment. The decision to build directly on the science courses of the United Kingdom was partly because it was more economical to do so in terms of expertise and manpower, given existing familiarity with British curriculum materials. It was also to keep abreast of international developments with the assumption that courses in developed countries represented the most effective approaches to teaching and learning secondary science. With the integrated science course came tutors from the United Kingdom to provide in-service training, and donations of apparatus and books for in-service programmes. Financial assistance was also provided to enable six teachers/officers to undertake a study tour of the United Kingdom's developments in science and mathematics. Curriculum 'entrepreneurs' played their part in disseminating new programmes in science as they did in many other countries (Lewin, 1981; Chisman and Wilson, 1989).

At the Curriculum Development Centre, several other innovative projects were carried out in specific areas of the curriculum with external assistance. Many of these projects were supported by foreign agencies such as UNICEF, the Van Leer Foundation, and the Ford Foundation. Areas of concern were those that relate to specific aspects of the curriculum. The Pilot Integrated Curriculum (1974) for example, was designed to try out an integrated approach in the curriculum and to seek an alternative delivery system. The Compensatory Education Project (1974) was to develop strategies and materials for remediation for the primary schools and pre-schools and to involve the community in the early education of rural children. The Curriculum for Pahang Tenggara (1974) was a project to adapt the regular curricular programmes for use in a large land settlement scheme. Materials and teaching strategies were reviewed and adapted to suit the physical environment around the area, and to take into account differences in the groups of children whose parents had migrated to the scheme. The Multiple Class Teaching Project (1976) was aimed at the adaptation of materials, teacher roles, classroom organization and classroom facilities to cater for group differences in a multigrade class. These projects had foreign consultants attached. All these projects were experimental and although they were not subsequently implemented on a full scale basis the experience gained was incorporated into the new primary school curriculum.

Some Issues

From this analysis several issues emerge. In particular these concern the effective participation of teachers; the dissonance between intentions and outcomes; clear specification of curricula and communication difficulties during dissemination; tensions between the professional cultures of curriculum developers and teachers; and time constraints on the development process. An appropriate balance between centralized and decentralized styles of curriculum development lies behind problems in relation to most of these areas.

First we consider teacher participation in curriculum development. Many studies of curriculum change in the seventies have pointed out the need to include users in the development of the programme and this has been reinforced by case studies in the 1980s (Lewin and Stuart, 1991). Participation by the target group in all processes of change from identification of needs through to implementation is thought to speed up acceptance and help in effective implementation, especially if the innovation involves significant behavioural changes (Dalin, 1978). While this may be desirable, it has proved impractical to involve all teachers in developing programmes in the Malaysian context since the number of schools is so large. Representative participation is used in the hope that those invited to participate will represent the views and practices of the classroom teachers. Furthermore, experience has shown that sheer quantity of participation in planning can be harmful if it involves disagreement, wasted time, unclear needs assessment and frustrating meetings which often move off the task in hand (Fullan and Pomfret 1977). Also participation in development is not necessarily related to effective implementation (Gross *et al.*, 1973). It may be more realistic to think in terms of new forms of participation during implementation that allow some measure of adaptation and 'ownership' of new curricula forms within an agreed framework.

Second, one of the problems which afflicts centrally prepared curricula is the lack of congruity between intended educational objectives and those realized during implementation. Among the reasons for this identified from the experience in Malaysia are the weaknesses in the dissemination strategy (too rapid and too optimistic concerning teacher's willingness to change established practice); varied interpretations of the curriculum concept and philosophy (ambiguity, for example over the meaning of integration, at both conceptualization and materials design levels); advocacy of teaching and learning strategies that are unfamiliar and not readily grasped (for example, group work in KBSR, which is intended to be a pedagogic change, not simply a reorganization of seating plans); the difficulties of accommodating widely differing school environments within national curriculum guidelines (well resourced urban schools and remote rural schools); and support mechanisms that are not sustained over time (it has proved difficult to build on introductory in-service courses which accompany initial implementation). It has been at the implementation stage that many of the weaknesses of the curriculum development process have been revealed. Thus, to take one example, the pattern and conduct of in-service courses as a means of disseminating the curriculum and preparing teachers have been evaluated as insufficient and superficial. The cascade system of using key personnel has resulted in the dilution of the messages which the planners and developers have conceptualised. In-service courses have also exposed weaknesses in the methods used for in-service support. Studies conducted on the implementation of KBSR have consistently revealed this aspect (for example, Noor Azmi, 1988) and draw attention to emphasis on information-giving rather than competency-based training to support implementation.

Third, as mentioned above, curricula produced have sometimes lacked clear specification which would allow them to be easily understood by teachers. The case with Man and the Environment in the new primary school curriculum is an example. Man and the Environment was a new subject in KBSR. It was a curriculum innovation designed to bring about changes not only in the subject matter but also in pedagogy, teacher roles and behaviour, teacher-pupil relationship, evaluation procedures, as well as values and attitudes. The subject is organized around five general themes from three disciplines, i.e. the physical sciences, the social sciences and the humanities. Essentially it is an integrated subject replacing history, geography, science, health education and civics of the old curriculum. An inquiry-discovery approach was advocated for its teaching and learning, whereby pupils would have more control over their learning. It was envisaged that the subject would help solve the problem of overlapping content, compartmentalization of subjects and curriculum overload, as well as reorientate the curriculum away from the traditional teacher-centred approach. The Ministry initiated the innovation and the detailed conceptualization of the programme was undertaken by a group of key people specially enlisted for their expertise. The framework for implementation was also created centrally and it was then handed over to the teachers to be realized in the classroom. Man and the Environment was therefore an demanding innovation with fairly complex sets of expectations about the changes that needed to take place.

The problems and possibilities of the programme surfaced when teachers began to use it. The curriculum materials that accompanied the programme were found by many teachers to be insufficiently detailed and limited in scope compared to those they replaced. This was deliberate since the materials were designed to encourage less emphasis on content and more on thinking skills — but teachers used to teaching content did not necessarily appreciate this. The new relationship between teacher and pupils proposed was seen as problematic for the less able, the unmotivated and those who had not acquired the skills of reading and writing, who many teachers felt needed more structured learning to grasp basic skills before they were ready to take more responsibility for their own learning. This led to feelings of anxiety amongst teachers that the new integrated programme was inferior to the old subject-based curriculum. The concept of integration, a basic feature of the curriculum, was new and members of the advisory team had different interpretations of the term. Even when they agreed on the definition of the term, there were still controversies on the scope of the component subjects. Important aspects of the philosophical assumptions as articulated by the planners and developers were not included or explicitly stated in the syllabus and accompanying curriculum materials making it difficult for teachers to find out about the reasoning behind the new curriculum. In addition those teachers who previously specialized in the teaching of specific subjects, found that with integration they had to grapple with the teaching of content new to them. This posed issues of self confidence with unfamiliar content. The teaching approach added an extra burden to the teachers as they had to seek resources beyond the school textbooks which were not readily available in all the schools. Not all of these emerging difficulties were the result of unclear formulation; but most had an element of miscommunication concerning curriculum intentions.

Fourth, some of the difficulties experienced with implementation now seem to be related to the gap between the planners and developers on the one hand, and the teachers who implement change on the other. As the case with Man and the Environment, an analysis of the implementation revealed that one of the factors that led to the lack of undertanding of the philosophy and demands of the subject was that the groups involved belonged to two different cultures. The planners and developers have developed a culture of being theoretical, abstract, idealistic, forward looking, up-to-date and academic. Most of the planners were themselves above average and motivated teachers. Their reference groups are their peers and the risk exists that curricula will be designed which reflect the capabilities and motivations of such atypical staff. On the other hand the teachers exist in a school culture which does not immediately welcome change, is orientated to the practical day-to-day problems of teaching heterogenous groups of children, which values stability, and which is organized around tried and tested procedures. Teachers' own motivations vary across a spectrum from those with a high level of professional commitment beyond working hours, to those for whom teaching is a job like any other and who may not have chosen teaching as a career with any strong vocational commitment. In these circumstances it may not be surprising if the language of the developers is too technical to result in easy communication. Teachers' language is relatively free of the technical jargon which developers attached to the innovation. Teacher sub-culture tends to be relatively free of technical terms (Macdonald and Rudduck 1971). Teachers shun elaborate words and elaborate ideas. This appears true in Malaysia too (Sharifah Maimunah, 1990).

Fifth, lack of time for experimentation has been a recurring problem. In KBSR in general and Man and the Environment in particular there was a short time-lag in between experimentation and implementation. So much so that little information could be collected on the suitability of the programme and the difficulties faced by the teachers. The year for experimentation or tryout was immediately followed by nationwide implementation so that whatever feedback was obtained from the trial schools could not be effectively used for implementation in the wider scale. Indeed materials had to be finalized for large scale implementation before a whole year's tryout could be completed. And the additional burden on the staff involved of supporting in-service work further reduced the attention that could be given to formative evaluation.

In the light of these issues several steps have been taken to help overcome the problems. One is more emphasis on the professional development of head-teachers alongside that of teachers so that they can keep abreast of developments that are happening and be better managers of the curriculum at the school level. State education offices and professional bodies such as the Headmasters Council have played a part in organizing workshop sessions on specific areas of the curriculum such as the development and use of various teaching and learning materials for more effective classroom instruction. The establishment of curriculum committees at the district level has provided opportunities for the schools to share experiences and to learn from one another. The Institut Aminuddin Baki, which is a national training institute for the education services, has undertaken courses and workshops for the professional development of headteachers. The needs of schools have been given increasing attention because it is at this level that many of the problems arise. Other methods of disseminating and familiarizing teachers with curriculum changes, in addition to the face-to-face in-service courses, have also been tried, including the use of multi-media packages with some measure of success.

Concluding Comments

Many countries have established Curriculum Development Centres over the last two decades. The evolution of the Malaysian CDC shows how its role has changed as it has matured. It has retained its functions as the official channel through which government policy on the curriculum is promulgated and it continues to act as the source of professional advice in developing policy. Its initial role in focusing on projects to develop curriculum materials in particular subject areas has changed. It now takes a much more global view of the curriculum and its development across subjects as well as contributing to each separate area of the curriculum. It has also moved away from the production of materials itself towards monitoring and approving those which are produced in line with specifications that it draws up. This allows it to concentrate on the pedagogic and epistemological issues which are its strength and devolve much of the production and distribution of curriculum materials to other parts of the Ministry and the private sector. Partly as a result it has become heavily involved in in-service work. In addition, its changing role as a professional agency has allowed it to develop increased awareness of implementation problems as they emerge, since full scale implementation is the responsibility of other divisions of the Ministry.

It is clear from the account given that much has been learned about the difficulties of nationwide curriculum development and implementation from the experiences with the various projects that provides opportunities for reflection and more effective planning for the future. The cyclic model presented remains but progression through its stages is not seen as a smooth process but one which requires constant iteration to develop effectively. A balance has to be struck between the participation that is desirable and that which is practical and productive. The real limits to extending opportunities to take the initiative to the school level are being appreciated within the context of an essentially centralized system where not all teachers have the type of 'extended professionality' that allows curriculum development to become school-based. The dangers of over ambitious goals have also been brought home by experience with some new curricula.

This account demonstrates yet again how problematic implementation can be. 'Fidelity' to the original brief is only likely to be achievable within limits which recognize that 'mutual adaptation' will take place (Fullan, 1982) as curricula plans leave the minds of their originators and enter the real world of the schools for which they are intended. This is not simply a technocratic problem that can be solved by exhortation, example and accurate information on intentions. It necessarily depends on the development of a reasonable consensus concerning purposes, working practices and desirable outcomes that enter into the calculus of reward that influences teacher and student commitment to that which is new.

There is much to consider in the realization that the professional culture at the centre of curriculum development effort may not easily mesh with the professional culture of the teachers and schools expected to implement new programmes. This becomes clear when case study methods are used to probe the curriculum in action, rather than basing evaluation studies on quantitative survey techniques that can claim representativeness but lack depth and interpretive power. One of the challenges for the future is to see to what extent case study methods like those used to explore the implementation of Man and the Environment (Sharifah Maimunah, 1990) can contribute to a deeper understanding of the problems of implementation. Such qualitative work is not common in the literature on education and development and has much to offer (Vulliamy, Lewin and Stephens, 1990).

Some of the dilemmas of centralization of curriculum development are apparent from our discussion. A centrally prepared curriculum cannot meet the needs of all schools equally well since they differ in environment and locality. In principle, schools, teachers and the state education offices should be allowed to have the freedom to undertake curriculum development activities that reflect needs arising from these variations. In fact, this was the desire of the Curriculum Planning Committee. However, in practice, this is a difficult task to accomplish. Curriculum development is a specialized undertaking and few of the teachers or even those working at the state education departments have received any training in the area. Problems of content overlap and overload across the curriculum are probably best met by centrally coordinated development strategies. These are also likely to improve the sequencing or related topics in different subject areas. Centralization would seem to be much more economical both in terms of effort and resources. Malaysia's political and educational context also does not promote attempts to decentralize strongly. If we can recall, before the evolution of the national educational system, there were four systems of schooling existing side by side each with its own orientations. The system was seen to be divisive rather than to promote national unity. The common-content syllabus emphasized in the National Educational Policy was designed to ensure overcoming this problem. Given the overriding priority to support the development of a Malaysian outlook across the curriculum some amount of centralization is inevitable. This does not preclude decisions on some aspects of curricula — teaching methods used, patterns of material use — being made at decentralized levels. Nor does it lessen the need to involve teachers in the implementation process in such a way that commitment is generated.

Unlike many developing countries Malaysia has been blessed with consistently high rates of economic growth which have transformed its ability to resource high quality curriculum development. The education system has been able to develop in a way where ideas, not resource constraints, have been the central feature of curriculum development activity. And the opportunities presented by this have been well used. An active professional community has emerged whose challenge is now to remain open to new educational ideas and take advantage of the experience which has accumulated in refining the strategies employed to ensure that planned change in education is both effective and sensitive to the needs of those it serves.

Appendix 1

RUKUNEGARA

DECLARATION

OUR NATION, MALAYSIA, being dedicated

to achieving a greater unity of all her peoples;

to maintaining a democratic way of life;

to creating a just society in which the wealth of the nation shall be equitably shared;

to ensuring a liberal approach to her rich and diverse cultural traditions;

to building a progressive society which shall be oriented to modern science and technology;

WE, her peoples, pledge our united efforts to attain these ends guided by these principles:

Belief In God

Loyalty to King and Country

Upholding the Constitution

Rule of Law

Good Behaviour and Morality

Appendix 2 Flowchart of curriculum development in Malaysia

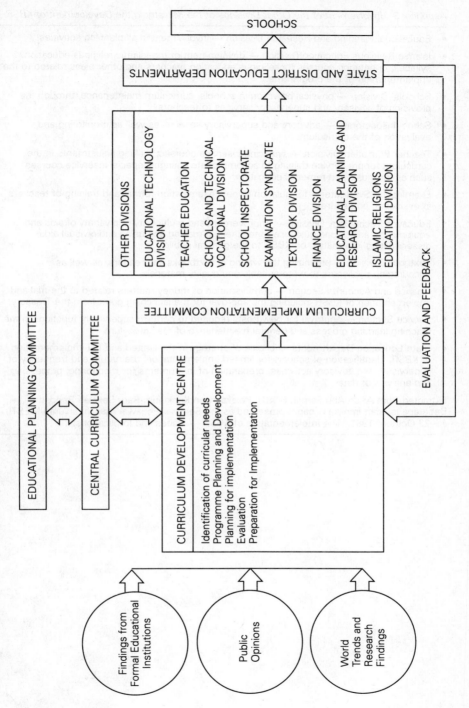

Appendix 3   Involvement of the Other Divisions of the Ministry in the Development of KBSR

- Educational Planning and Research Division — involvement in all planning activities.

- Islamic Religious Education Division — development of the Islamic religious education syllabus, orientation courses for religious education teachers and other plans related to the implementation of the programme.

- Schools' Division — physical provision in schools, curriculum maintenance, through the provision of advisory and supervisory services to teachers.

- School Inspectorate — advisory and supervisory services as well as monitoring and evaluation of the curriculum.

- Teacher Education Division — financing inservice courses, making adjustments in the curriculum for pre-service training to accommodate changes, special inservice courses such as for music and remedial education.

- Examination Syndicate — formulation of new examination format and training of teachers in evaluation procedures.

- Education Technology Division — improvement and multiplicity of a variety of aids and equipments, advice and guidance to teachers in making and using audio-visual aids, disseminating information on KBSR to the general public.

- Textbook Division — organizing the writing of textbooks and readers, as well as encouraging publishers to write suitable and quality materials.

- Finance and Accounts Section — administration of money matters related to the trial and implementation of KBSR including the approval for the launching grant from the Treasury.

- Service Section — approval for new posts required to perform supervisory functions in the teaching learning process and general maintenance of the curriculum.

- State Education Departments — choice of strategy in the limited and full implementation of KBSR, identification of schools for limited implementation, the nature and frequency of supervisory and advisory activities, preparation of instruments for monitoring, processing and analysis of data.

Extracted from Asiah Abu Samah (1981) 'Pelaksanaan Kurikulum Baru Sekolah Rendah — Beberapa Isu dan Implikasi' paper presented as the Seminar Pegawai Atasan, anjuran MESTI, 19–22 October 1981. [The Implementation of KBSR — Issues and Implications]

Appendix 4   The KBSR Committee at the Various Levels

Level of Committee	Membership	Tasks
Ministry Level: KBSR Implementation Committee	Chairman: Deputy-Director General II Members: directors of all professional Divisions, heads of three administrative Sections. Secretariat: Curriculum Development Centre	To decide policies and to oversee implementation at all levels Responsible for financial matters To ensure cooperation and coordination between all agencies
Ministry Level: KBSR Technical Committee	Chairman: Deputy-Director General II Members: KBSR coordinators from all states and professional Divisions representatives from three administrative Sections. Secretariat: Curriculum Development Centre	To deliberate and decide on details pertaining to implementation at the state level
State Level: State KBSR Implementation Committee	Chairman: State Director Members: professional officers of the state department, representatives of head teachers, School Inspectorate, and teacher education colleges. Secretariat: KBSR Unit	To plan implementation activities at the state, district and school levels To manage finances
District Level: District KBSR Implementation Committee	Chairman: Head of District Education Office Members: representatives of headteachers, teachers and Parent-Teacher Assoc.	To plan for implementation activities at the district level
School Level School KBSR Committee	Chairman: headteachers Members: all KBSR teachers and other teachers.	To provide guidance and assistance for implementation at the school and classroom levels

Source: 'Ke Arah Pelaksanaan Yang Berkesan' (Towards an Effective Implementation) in 'Berita KBSR 2' (1) 1983

Section III
Emerging Issues

Chapter 12

Patterns and Dilemmas

Paul Morris and Colin Marsh

Introduction

Section II of this book illustrates the rich diversity of approaches to curriculum development which exist in Asia. As has been pointed out the cultural context and prevailing political priorities in each country exert powerful influences on curricular issues and their resolution. But it is possible to identify common patterns within this diversity and to analyze the resulting dilemmas and problems. The concept of dilemma is employed to underline the complexity of curricular issues and to avoid any suggestion that tensions which arise in curriculum development are unidimensional in nature rather than interconnected and multifaceted. Any attempt to reach a decision about a problematic aspect of the curriculum, such as increasing the relevance of the curriculum to pupils' needs, is likely to involve a series of trade-offs with other aims such as meeting parents' expectations or maintaining academic standards.

The main issues which we address in this chapter are those which we introduced in section I, namely the slippage between policies and their implementation, the effects of low levels of teacher professionalism on curriculum development, the pursuit of élitist educational policies, the impact of a language of instruction other than the pupils' mother tongue on the curriculum and the close relationship between school curricula and broader political goals and tensions. Subsequently we discuss the implications of these for curriculum development policies.

Antecedents

Before embarking on an analysis of the current situation in the Asian countries on which this book focuses, it is important to understand their historical origins. In common with other social phenomena, patterns of curriculum development do not develop in a vacuum. Most Asian countries enjoy a rich and individual educational heritage but most have been colonized. The major exception to this is China which was never fully colonized although it experienced numerous foreign incursions since 1840 and an extended civil war. Externally determined curricula, reflecting educational traditions and conventions in the metropolitan country or in other Western societies, were introduced in most Asian countries after 1945.

As Lewin (1985) has noted, the curricula which prevailed in Asian colonies tended to reflect the more conservative and academic traditions which existed in the metropole and at the same time to support the status quo and to legitimate the socioeconomic structure of the colony. Attempts to broaden the range of educational opportunity have often been focused on school building programmes and the provision of an expanded teaching force at the expense of attention to the development of an appropriate curriculum. Hong Kong provides a good example of quantitative changes preceding qualitative changes so that a wide range of pupils has been expected to follow curricula designed for a highly selective and academic audience. In the 1960s and 1970s most countries in Asia began to develop ways to address the resulting problems, often establishing units and centres to promote curriculum reform. This has resulted in a range of different curriculum development activities, designed to create relevant and modern curricula.

This historical context has formed part of a wider political and economic context in each country in which a priority has been to develop a modern thriving economy in as short a period of time as possible. Modernization necessitated a literate, flexible and hardworking workforce who shares the goals of national development. Many of the countries analyzed in Section II have succeeded in achieving remarkable rates of economic growth. Whilst it is difficult to demonstrate that economic growth is caused by the nature and quality of educational provision it is evident that the two are mutually supportive.

In parallel with the pursuit of economic growth and modernization, schools clearly serve as the guardians of national character and are used to inculcate the prevailing moral and political sentiments. The precise form which this takes varies according to the conditions and tensions which prevail in each country. In the People's Republic of China (PRC) the pursuit of the 'four modernizations' provided the rationale and impetus for curriculum reforms, subject to the overriding goal of the Chinese Communist Party to ensure their own position and power. Consequently both major and minor changes of political orthodoxy or changes to the leadership were rapidly incorporated into the official curriculum, if not always effectively disseminated to schools. The highly centralized system of curriculum decision making and dissemination reflects that which prevails in other areas of public policy making.

In Indonesia the delicate balance which prevails in that society between the secular modernists, the demands of the Islamic nationalists and the perceived threat of Communism is reflected in the school curriculum. The mainstream curriculum reflects a secular modernist perspective while pupils are also able to receive Islamic religious instruction or to attend Islamic schools. These alternatives exist alongside a moral and civic education programme which stresses the five principles (Pancasila) which reflect the philosophical foundations of the government.

In Hong Kong the highly bureaucratic and derivative approach to curriculum development is a reflection of the pattern of decision making of a colonial government which is tolerated by the populace so long as it is able to deliver a stable and prosperous socioeconomic environment. The government is able effectively to control the content of school subjects and of textbooks but questions about which subjects are to be studied by pupils and the language of instruction are determined by parental wishes. This represents a compromise between the needs of the government to protect its own interests and the desires of parents to pursue the interests of their children. The result is, in terms of curriculum development, a compromise between a *laissez-faire* system and one which is centrally controlled. In common with the other colonial territory, Macau, there has been no attempt to use schooling to promote a sense of national identity or character.

In Macau the *laissez-faire* role of the government in all aspects of decision making has been reflected until recently in the absence of any coherent system of curriculum development. However, given the impending transfer of sovereignty to the PRC in 1999, and the government's desire to use Macau as a centre to promote Portuguese interests and culture in Asia, it has become more directly involved in policies which affect the school curriculum.

In Singapore the tension between developing a prosperous, multiethnic, modern and democratic society whilst at the same time retaining the values associated with a traditional society pervades the curriculum. Whilst most aspects of the curriculum reflect the needs of a highly competitive modern society (for example, the use of English and streaming), the recent introduction of civics and programmes designed to promote an essentially Confucian set of values, reflects the pursuit of a more traditional orthodoxy. In contrast though to the colonies of Macau and Hong Kong, the Singapore Government, as an elected and sovereign body, has the legitimacy to pursue a much wider range of policy initiatives.

Malaysia inherited one of the most ethnically diverse populations in southeast Asia from a colonial administration and set itself the task of welding these into a nation state sharing common loyalties and values. Its emphasis on centralized, common national curricula reflects this as does the commitment to promote the Rukunegara.

The pursuit of a unified national identity and the perception of an everpresent threat from North Korea is reflected in the school curriculum in South Korea. A highly uniform centralized curriculum has been devised which stresses national identity and the evils of Communism. In parallel, the returns to each level of educational achievement and the democratic political system has resulted in a highly competitive educational system which primarily functions as a selective device for access to the prestigious universities.

The Nature of the Curriculum

The dominant characteristic of the school curriculum which permeates the countries described in Section II is that it is essentially *academic* but its specific form is determined by the social, political and economic tensions which prevail in each country. It is academic in that the subjects made available for students to study are geared to the goals of tertiary education. The content is derived from the conventional academic disciplines. *Teaching methods* rely on teacher direction, with emphasis on written work and time-consuming individual study. As we saw in chapter 3, *examinations* loom large in that they provide the yardstick for entry into limited places in colleges and universities. In addition, competition for places in the more reputable schools may lead to examinations and examination pressure on students at other points in primary and secondary schooling. *Textbooks* are used extensively to focus both teachers' and students' efforts on examinable aspects of the respective syllabuses. These textbooks, along with the style of public assessment, determine, to a considerable extent, the actual teaching practices occurring in schools. The process of decision-making within this pattern is highly *centralized and bureaucratic*. It is assumed that a centralized system should be able to marshal resources most efficiently and to provide appropriate policies, guidelines and support to individual schools and their respective teachers and students. It also permits the process of schooling to be closely linked to the inculcation of national identity, the promotion of a common set of moral values and the indoctrination or socialization of pupils into the prevailing political ideology.

Content

Many of the contributing authors to Section II have emphasized the academic nature of the content of subjects taught at primary and secondary school levels in their respective countries. In many cases the content is selected by senior officials and academic professionals and often it is derived from existing overseas curriculum projects and 'indigenized' to reflect local conditions. However, the extent of dependence on overseas projects has during the 1980s declined markedly compared to the 1970s, especially in those countries which have established professional organizations to develop curricula.

In the PRC, the content taught in school subjects stresses the theoretical purity of disciplines, especially in the sciences. There has been little interest in developing subjects which integrate content over several disciplines or in selecting content on the basis of pupils' needs or interests. Whilst political considerations exert a powerful influence on the Chinese language curriculum it remains unquestionably academic and élitist in emphasis.

In Korea, since 1948, academic content has prevailed despite attempts, through national curriculum revisions, to pursue other goals such as 'relevance' and 'life centredness'. In Hong Kong examination syllabuses provide one of the driving forces for what is taught in schools and they are dominated by academic content, largely derived from Western sources. In Macau school subjects which reflect the traditional subject boundaries are derived from a variety of sources, without any attempt at indigenization.

In Singapore the school curriculum is based on the traditional academic subject boundaries and academic excellence is prized and rewarded. However a less academic curriculum is provided for a small proportion of pupils who study in Chinese.

In Malaysia the curriculum borrowing characteristic of the first wave of curriculum development has been replaced by attempts to produce Malaysian curricula tailored to Malaysian aspirations and educational circumstances. This has taken place within a centralized framework but has sought to take advantage of new pedagogy and Malaysian criteria for content selection.

An academic orientation and a reliance on conventional subject boundaries does not mean that the content of any particular syllabus is determined or that all will look alike. Content can be influenced by political considerations. Minor changes in the political leadership in the PRC have resulted in rapid changes to the content of Chinese language textbooks. In South Korea each change of government has been followed by a major revision of the national curriculum. In Singapore the academic curriculum studied by most pupils also contains a civic education programme designed to promote the four national principles. Similarly in Indonesia the five principles underlying the government's philosophy form the basis of the civics curriculum.

Teaching Methods

Some countries in East Asia have seen experiments with non-traditional teaching methods in the 1970s and 80s, but as with the experience elsewhere, there is little evidence to suggest that curriculum innovations have had a major impact on what goes on 'behind the classroom door'. The prevalent teaching method remains highly expository with pupils' 'activities' confined primarily to listening, recording and answering narrowly focused, factual questions. This experience confirms the universal nature of the problem, namely that the most difficult part of the curriculum to initiate change is the styles of teaching and learning used.

In the PRC teaching methods are very teacher-centred — 'a dogmatic Confucian pedagogical tradition which has fused effectively with the Soviet mode of instruction' as Leung describes it. The shortage of qualified teachers in the PRC has possibly exacerbated the pattern of teachers being passive adopters of the official curriculum. Teachers of Chinese language are heavily dependent on textbooks and other curriculum materials.

Korea has experienced five reform periods in which it was planned to include innovative teaching methods such as those associated with discipline-centred, humanistic-oriented and future-oriented curricula but there is little evidence that these changes have been enduring or that traditional teaching methods have been supplanted.

In Hong Kong, a local version of the Scottish Integrated Science syllabus was intended to encourage teachers to use innovative teaching methods but evaluation reveals that teachers use the content but not the guided discovery teaching approach which is required for its proper implementation. A highly didactic form of instruction is still being retained. In Singapore the teaching methods are similarly described. Teachers prepare their pupils to compete in a highly selective system of public examinations and this is seen to place a premium on covering the syllabus.

Examinations

Where an academic curriculum leads to public examinations, the teachers' selection of lesson content, the means of instruction and student activities is often driven by the style and format of the examination papers and tasks. The administration and control of examinations is generally not undertaken directly by the central government. The general pattern is that public examinations which affect access to school are administered by a regional government body or by a quasi-independent agency such as the Hong Kong Examinations Authority (HKEA). In many cases, examinations which select pupils for access to tertiary education are administered, as in South Korea, by the universities themselves or, as in the PRC, by the central government.

Examinations have been used in China from as early as the Han Dynasty (202BC–190AD). Lai uses the apt metaphor of the public examination as the 'conductor's baton' for the curriculum 'orchestra'. In the PRC, examinations are used to select students for entry to senior secondary schools and to tertiary institutions. Confidentiality of the examination papers is taken very seriously, to the extent that subject specialist examiners are required to be relocated at venues where they cannot be contacted by the public or even by their families for the period of time between the setting of questions to when the examinations have been completed by the students.

Leung refers to the 'examination hell' in the PRC. In a country where only 1 per cent of the working population obtain university degrees, it is little wonder that university entrance examinations are seen as a very important springboard. It is also important to note that the reputation and material rewards for schools in the PRC is based upon the performance of their students in the public examinations.

Territory-wide examinations are a recent phenomena in Macau. Because of inertia, the small size of the country and the informal contacts established between employers and school personnel, territory wide examinations were not found necessary. The introduction in 1990 of an entrance examination for the University of East Asia, located in Macau, may well provide an academic 'yardstick' for schools to establish their reputations with parents and students.

In Malaysia, a common government examination at the end of primary school is used for selection to residential schools but does not affect promotion of students to secondary schools. External examinations are held in years 5 and 6/7 of the secondary school for students seeking matriculation into universities. There is considerable demand for local university places, to the extent that many students (especially Chinese students) seek vacancies in overseas universities.

In South Korea the entrance examination to tertiary colleges exerts a powerful influence on the school curriculum. This is despite the fact that over 35 per cent of the relevant age group enter tertiary education and that there is a relatively high level of unemployment amongst graduates. This suggests that, as evidenced in Japan, widening access to tertiary education does not affect selection pressure and the nature of the secondary school curriculum in any simple and direct way.

Textbooks

Student textbooks are a major element of any academic curriculum as they provide the basis for the content to be taught and in many instances, the methods which will be used by teachers. In most of the countries studied, textbooks are directly produced by the government or one of its agencies. In others, such as Hong Kong and Malaysia, textbooks are produced by independent publishers but the government determines which ones are approved for use in schools. Macau has no system to produce books nor to control their content and schools use books produced for use elsewhere.

Textbooks play a major role in schools in the PRC. Not only are textbooks used extensively by teachers but teachers are encouraged to use only the officially published, unified textbooks. The government controlled People's Education Press is a very effective means of ensuring that teachers do use officially prescribed textbooks. The majority of these enormously influential textbooks are written in condensed language and literally 'crammed' with information. Textbook writers rarely make allowances for variations in resources between schools or for the needs of less academic pupils.

Textbook publication in Korea is also under strict control and teachers are required to use only government designated textbooks which are predominantly narrowly academic in style and content. Development of other forms of curriculum materials, such as videotapes, slides and tape recordings has received little attention.

In Hong Kong, textbooks are recommended for each syllabus and teachers are unlikely to go beyond these because of the influences of the external examinations. Schools are put under pressure by parents to provide subjects (and their related textbooks) which are academic in their orientation. Attempts by schools to adopt more innovative textbooks or more applied courses/units are generally not received favourably by parents.

In Macau, textbooks are very influential but in many cases they are only appropriate to the needs of the official schools which do not reflect the needs of most of the society. Commercial publishers have not been interested in publishing textbooks for the small market and as a consequence schools have had to import textbooks produced for other countries, mainly Hong Kong, Taiwan and PRC. These textbooks include few, if any, local examples about Macau and tend to focus upon geographical, historical and political aspects of their country of origin.

In Singapore, textbooks are approved by the government but produced by both private commercial sources and by the CDIS. As with other countries, the content and approach of textbooks is geared to cover the examination syllabus and to prepare pupils for the relevant examination.

Textbook provision in Malaysia is from diverse sources. Though all require approval in principle from official agencies most are produced by private publishers and substantial choice is available.

Centralized Bureaucratic Systems

Almost all the authors of the chapters in section II have commented upon the centralized and bureaucratic systems operating in their respective countries. The pattern which emerges in section II is that the extent of central control of the school curriculum broadly corresponds to the degree of centralization of the political system. Problems associated with highly centralized education systems are well documented in the literature, for example, Marsh and Huberman (1984), Morris (1984) and Lewin (1985). Yet it is important to remind ourselves of some of the advantages of centralized education systems. Centralized education systems can, and do, emphasize national goals, and provide a means for working towards uniformity of provision and for protecting schools from the demands of various pressure groups.

Governments intent on pursuing strong national goals will use centralized education systems to attain these ends. Without doubt, centralized education systems can be used very effectively to drive a curriculum which aims to promote a sense of national identity, language, culture, and political and moral values. The control of the key elements of the curriculum such as textbooks, subject content and examinations ensures that governments can exert a powerful influence on both the intended and implemented curriculum.

In the PRC, the various central agencies, such as the State Education Commission, the Department of Secondary and Primary Education and the People's Education Press, attempt to ensure that educational policies are faithfully executed in schools. These are the superordinate stake holders. By contrast, teachers have little opportunity to wield any decision-making powers.

Se-Ho and Kyung-Chui suggest that the centralized system in South Korea can lead to a considerable amount of teacher passivity and a low level of professionalism. They argue that a necessary condition for enhancing the levels of teacher involvement and professionalism is a reduction in the degree of central control of the curriculum.

In Hong Kong central education structures continue to be dominant. Ironically, whilst the government has effective control of the content of school subjects and the textbooks used, it leaves questions such as the combination of subjects which pupils study, the language of instruction and the provision of non-textbook resources to the discretion of individual schools. Recent central initiatives intended to encourage school-based curriculum development seem unlikely to succeed because of the stipulation that teachers must undertake their SBCD activities outside school hours. McClelland describes it as 'an attempt to graft increased teacher professionalism on to a bureaucratic centralised system'.

In Indonesia, there are three groups of superordinates who administer education centrally. They include the Minister and his top-level advisers, the Research and Development Centre and the Ministry's Directorate of Basic Education. The Minister and his advisers produce general policies and directives, while the R and D Centre and the Directorate of Basic Education prepare instructional objectives, teaching methods and materials in cooperation. The Directorate is also responsible for disseminating the curricula to schools. Moral education is an interesting exception, being under the control of a separate group of educators headed by a retired military officer. This reflects its important role and status in an Islamic society.

The centralized nature of the education system in Singapore has resulted in a plethora of rules and regulations for pupils and schools. This control is being relaxed in an attempt to encourage initiative and creativity but clearly this will have to occur within a framework which is supportive of the government's goals and philosophy. The official requirement that all teachers plan their lessons using specific instructional objectives demonstrates a great deal of faith in Bloom's (1956) taxonomy. However, it was perceived by teachers to actually discourage the learning of higher order cognitive skills. Thus whilst extremely attractive as an administrative tool its effects were not as intended.

In Malaysia a highly centralized form of education exists as it is argued that unity must be achieved and that it is economical in terms of effort and resources. Notwithstanding, various problems have been identified with this centralized form, including lack of congruity between intentions and implementation practices and weaknesses in dissemination activities.

Macau is the notable and instructive exception to this pattern of curriculum development. The absence of any coherent government policy on education, except for the children of Portuguese parents, creates an essentially *laissez-faire* educational environment. However, this has not resulted in a variety of school-based initiatives and teacher involvement. Instead a range of eclectic and derivative curricula has emerged, presented through the same styles of teaching and learning which are in evidence elsewhere. In itself the absence of central control is not necessarily beneficial.

Dilemmas and Problems

The concerted and enduring efforts made by a number of countries in East Asia to develop curricula has brought with them a number of attendant problems including, the *Implementation of Policies*: there is often slippage between general policies and their implementation; *Teacher Professionalism*: low levels of teacher professionalism impede the attainment of educational goals; *Elitism*: the existence of élite schools impedes development of a broad-based and equitable system; *Language*: the use of languages of instruction other than the mother tongue affects the accessibility of the curriculum.

Slippage Between General Policies and Their Implementation

Major disjunctions are evident between general curriculum policy statements and what occurs in practice. This problem appears to be accentuated within centralized education systems because the linkages or interaction between policy makers and practitioners can be minimal. Policy announcements setting out curriculum goals are made by senior officials and are often statements of ideals. Often they are motivated by political priorities and fail to take adequate account of the constraints which influence their possible implementation. It can be difficult to reconcile these general pronouncements with either the official curricula of specific subjects or the teaching styles used and learning styles encouraged in classrooms.

Several of the authors in section II noted these slippages in their respective countries. For example, Lai (chapter 5) notes the different curriculum goals promoted in the PRC by the central government and its agencies. Central government pronouncements which promote the role of language learning as a political exercise continue to be reinterpreted and adapted by the lower agencies who stress its role as a communicative tool or as a vehicle for developing an appreciation of Chinese cultural heritage.

Leung (chapter 4) uses a specific example in his chapter on the PRC to illustrate the slippage that can occur. He suggests that physics teachers in the PRC are expected to follow an inquiry-learning approach but because of a lack of resources in most schools, the subject teachers can not implement this policy.

In Hong Kong McClelland (chapter 6) describes the disjuncture which exists between the innovative and worthwhile intentions of the Junior Secondary Science Syllabus curriculum and what occurs in the classroom. He also suggests that the School Based Curriculum Project Scheme is unlikely to fulfil its purposes because it has been designed to operate within a highly centralized system of curriculum development.

In Singapore, despite a variety of reforms to the mathematics curriculum, teachers still tend to use traditional teaching styles. This encourages the mastery of skills at the expense of an understanding of concepts and the ability to solve problems. The introduction of creative thinking programmes, such as CORT are an attempt to alleviate that problem.

Se-Ho and Kyung-Chue (chapter 8) describe similar disjunctions between policy groups and specific-subject groups in Korea. One explanation they put forward for the slippage is the use of incompatible curriculum theories by the two groups as where a life-centred curriculum theory is adopted by the policy makers while a discipline-centred approach is adopted by the subject-specialists.

Sherifah Maimunah and Lewin (chapter 11) also note gaps between planners and implementers in Malaysia. They suggest that the planner's culture (theoretical, forward, academic) is very different to the teacher-implementer's culture (concrete, conservative, practical).

The innovations described in the PRC, Hong Kong and Indonesia indicate that curriculum policy makers tend to be over-enthusiastic and optimistic about what can be achieved. The first result is the promotion of selected and adapted projects which are superficially attractive but essentially impractical, given the context in which they are to be used. This may happen for a combination of reasons, such as political advantage, to obtain scarce resources and personal aggrandizement. The second result is disillusionment for other groups who are involved in implementing curriculum policies. The dilemma is complex. If educational policy makers do not promote worthwhile and radical policies then the possible costs are numerous. They include loss of political credibility, failure to obtain the necessary resources to effect developments and failure to provide the goals which might motivate teachers. On the other hand the pursuit of unrealistic goals does not improve the quality of teaching and learning while it may serve to disillusion teachers who constantly fail to achieve the goals set. This problem illustrates the extent to which the concerns and priorities of superordinate and subordinate groups can differ. Whilst policy makers are concerned with developing a worthwhile and defensible curriculum, teachers are primarily concerned with how to implement it. Thus the slippage can occur even though both groups are able to satisfy their respective concerns and priorities. An effect therefore operates in which groups can focus on the same educational policy or curriculum innovation and perceive a quite different range of issues and concerns.

Low Levels of Teacher Professionalism

An academic curriculum with a reliance on centrally provided syllabuses and textbooks emphasizing teacher-directed learning and leading to highly selective examinations, encourages and reinforces a low level of teacher professionalism. However, if the standard of teacher education and professionalism is in fact low, a highly centralized academic curriculum dependent on prescribed texts is in many ways an optimal strategy, for it mininizes dependence on the skills of individual teachers. A vicious cycle therefore operates to maintain and reinforce the role of the teacher as a technician whose only task is to transmit knowledge.

The dilemma is therefore essentially one of disentangling cause and effect. How does one develop curricula which require a high level of teacher professionalism in a society where the teacher's role has been confined to transmitting knowledge and where many components of the curriculum (for example, textbooks and examinations) and the existing levels of teacher professionalism and training reinforce that role?

Centrally controlled education systems may prefer teachers to perform as efficient technicians if this ensures that the prescribed syllabus is implemented as intended. The trade-off is that situations where teachers are not allowed opportunities to experiment with different methods and approaches provide little opportunity for raising teacher morale and professionalism.

Leung and Lai, maintain that the government of the PRC assumes that teachers will be passive adopters of the official curriculum. Instructions and information in the form of 'teacher proof' handbooks are encyclopedic and specific. Unqualified and inexperienced teachers rely particularly heavily on these handbooks. Leung concludes that there is a very low level of teacher professionalism in the PRC and that this is thwarting current efforts to bring about curriculum reform.

Se-Ho and Kyung-Chue highlight some of the problems in centralized systems where teachers' roles are heavily prescribed. They suggest that teachers will adopt very passive attitudes towards teaching if their role is seen primarily to involve the transmission to students of facts and information which have been prescribed by the central government.

McClelland, in his chapter on Hong Kong, notes that many teachers are subjected to the 'tyranny of the textbook' and have little opportunity to develop creative approaches to teaching. Examination pressures and parental demands reinforce the pressure on teachers to follow conventional teaching practices.

Sherifah Maimunah and Lewin point to some of the problems of involving teachers in curriculum development. In part these are structural, involving too many individuals can be counter-productive leading to lengthy argument, misunderstandings and frustration. They note also that a good proportion of teachers may not have the motivation or skills to become involved. Nevertheless they point out that some sense of curriculum 'ownership' is important for teacher implementors and that ways need to be found to promote this source of professional commitment.

Teacher professionalism in Macau is also noted as a problem by Bray and Hui. Many teachers in Macau schools are untrained, especially in primary schools. Over the last five years concerted efforts have been made to provide minimal training, mainly through the University of East Asia.

The Creation of Elite Schools and Problems of Equity

An academic curriculum is of greatest benefit to a small percentage of students, mainly those who have high levels of intellectual ability and who are motivated to study. The provision of school structures to enable academically talented students to maximize their educational attainments is often undertaken by governments to produce the élite citizens of the future. Differentiation through the provision of élite schools usually entails higher levels of resources for these schools with attendant reductions in provision for standard schools. There are obviously major issues of equity and justice for those students who are not recognized as intellectually talented. Their achievement and future progress may be inhibited by the diversion of resources to the schooling of the academically élite. The essential dilemma is that to provide all pupils equal opportunities, in both socially just and in utilitarian terms, will maximize the educational level of all pupils. However to provide extra resources and better schooling for the more able could act as an incentive for all pupils and could ensure the existence of a corps of well-educated future economic and political leaders.

In the PRC, keypoint schools (5 per cent of all schools) are allocated the best students and better than average teaching resources in order assist capable students to progress to higher education. This system creates inequalities between schools and intensifies pressures at the early stages of schooling as students compete to obtain access to the keypoint schools.

Different categories of schools operate in Macau. The official schools, which use Portuguese textbooks, are given much better resources than the private schools. Teachers are paid much higher salaries and class sizes are considerably smaller. By contrast, the private schools are operated by religious and social service organizations. The teachers tend to be untrained and many of the trained teachers are recruited from other countries such as Taiwan, the PRC and Hong Kong.

In South Korea, the tension between egalitarianism and élitism is very apparent. Most schools, since 1974, are assigned pupils on a random and geographic basis in an attempt to equalize schools and to break the competitive and hierarchic structure. There has, however, been an increase in the number of special schools for gifted children. More importantly the revised system of allocation brought pupils with heterogeneous backgrounds together but the curriculum and the competitive goal of schooling remained unchanged. Consequently the concern for equality has created a serious mismatch between the curriculum, which has remained academic in focus, and the needs of pupils.

In contrast to the Korean resolution of the equity-élitism dilemma, Singapore has pursued since 1980 a policy of streaming pupils by ability from primary 3. This results in 6 per cent of pupils undertaking an extended primary programme and 4 per cent following a monolingual (i.e. Chinese) course which stresses basic literacy and numeracy. Subsequent streaming takes place in schools for the majority of pupils following the normal curriculum and a comprehensive programme is provided for gifted children.

The Language of Instruction

Centralized education systems endeavour to achieve specific national goals by determining which language or languages are to be used as the medium of instruction. Sometimes the language of commerce and industry (for example, English) is preferred over indigenous languages (for example, Tamil, Hakka and Cantonese) and this is reflected in the school curriculum. Many countries in East Asia attempt to promote the language of the predominant ethnic group by requiring all students to study in this language even when it is not their mother tongue. Consequently major educational difficulties can occur for pupils when they receive instruction in a language other than their mother tongue.

In Hong Kong, the use of English as the medium of instruction in most schools means that a large number of pupils obtain little benefit from their education. However, attempts to set up a Chinese medium alternative route through school and university have not been successful, largely due to the economic benefits associated with access to English and the resulting lack of support for Chinese medium schools. The Singapore government has insisted that the majority of students study English together with any other second language, to try to ensure both a common national language and to preserve the cultural identities of their major ehtnic groups, namely the Chinese, Malaysians and Indians. The use of English has, however, been associated with the emergence of undesirable Western social tendencies such as individualism and anti-authoritarianism. Consequently pupils now study a civic/moral education programme in their mother tongue as it is hoped that this will more effectively inculcate traditional social values.

Macau illustrates some of the complex problems relating to languages of instruction. A knowledge of Portuguese is a requirement for all adults aspiring to a government post in Macau but for most citizens, proficiency in Portuguese is of little value. Schools vary in their provision with some teaching English and Chinese (Cantonese or Putonghua) or Portuguese. Recently, Chinese language has been become increasingly important for many careers in commerce but the recently opened local university (University of East Asia) uses English as its language of instruction.

Malaysian language policy allows different media of instruction in primary schools with Bahasa Malaysia in all subsequent grades. This policy promotes the national language as an integrating mechanism which can assist in the development of a Malaysian outlook.

In the PRC the pursuit of a common national identity and culture has to a large extent been achieved by requiring the use of Putonghua as the language of instruction for those pupils who aspire to tertiary education.

In South Korea, the language of instruction is not viewed as problematic with all pupils studying in their mother tongue and English being taught widely as a second language.

The central dilemmas which face countries, especially the smaller ones which rely on international trade such as Singapore, Hong Kong and Macau, arise from three distinct considerations. In educational terms pupils are clearly able to learn and interact with teachers and classmates most effectively in their mother tongue. In economic terms the returns for investment in English language proficiency are high, for it is both the language of international commerce and a major asset for persons wishing to emigrate or to study in an English-speaking country. The latter consideration is presently very influential in Hong Kong as people antici- pate the return to Chinese sovereignty in 1997. Finally, in multi–ethnic societies, such as Singapore and Malaysia, the language of instruction can be used as the vital tool for inculcating a cohesive national identity and for facilitating com- munication between ethnic groups. Thus whilst the costs of studying through a second language are high for the majority of students, the returns to the society in terms of economic prosperity and national unity can be substantial. Whilst

Singapore obtains both these benefits from the use of English as the medium of instruction, Hong Kong and Macau only serve to gain the former. This is reflected in the relative success of English language education in Singapore compared to that in Hong Kong and Macau.

Policy Implications

Three central and universal themes emerge from these chapters which have implications for policies towards curriculum development. The first relates to the nature of innovations which are selected and promoted, the second concerns the strategies used to support innovations, and the third one arises from the approaches to public assessment.

The Selection of Innovations

Innovations are often selected by superordinate decision-makers primarily with reference to their perceived worthwhileness, quality and desirability. This sometimes results in emulation of trends and fashions in the West as it allows the rapid and inexpensive adoption of 'modern' developments.

The two colonies, Macau and Hong Kong, showed a strong dependency on overseas curriculum innovations. However, Malaysia, Singapore, South Korea and Indonesia have all developed their own mechanism to develop and adapt curricula to their needs and this has meant that the dependency of the immediate post-independence period is no longer evident.

Unfortunately the experience in East Asia, as elsewhere, suggests that the intended impact on patterns of teaching and learning does not usually materialize for a range of possible reasons. In this situation it is easy for policy makers to blame teachers for their lack of commitment, professionalism or skills. The nature of the innovation itself is rarely viewed as problematic because to argue against it is to reject its self-evident worthwhileness. Thus a standard strategy of curriculum innovation follows the pattern: (a) identify the weaknesses and costs of the present styles of teaching and learning which are termed traditional, didactic, teacher centred, product oriented etc; (b) specify what benefits would arise to pupils and society if a more pupil centred, progressive, inductive, modern style were used; (c) recommend that new curricula be introduced which embody the goals identified in (b). This ensures that curriculum plans are decided primarily with regard to their intentions. Questions of relevance, feasibility and practicality are viewed as essentially technical rather than substantive issues. The very limited success of a wide range of highly desirable innovations, described in section II, arises primarily from the failure to treat implementation issues as important in policy decisions. As a result innovations are being selected without reference to information on the context in which they are to be used. Consequently teachers find themselves presented with policy initiatives which are not practical, as they do not take account of key variables such as the repertoire of teachers' skills, the resources available, the expectations of pupils and parents and the requirements of public examinations. The result is that the goals of the innovation are too distant to constitute a realistic target and the innovation is adopted at a superficial level, ignored or misused.

The situation is akin to that addressed by the theory of second best (Lipsey and Lancaster, 1957) with regard to economic policy making. This proposes that if an optimal economic policy, such as free trade, cannot for some reason be implemented (for example, because of trade barriers) then the pursuit of that goal will not be the second best policy. It is argued that the pursuit of an alternative policy with an achievable goal might in fact produce the second best results available. A corollary of the theory of second best is that the recognition of structural, or other impediments to implementation, should be followed by the identification and pursuit of a more beneficial second best alternative policy. Essentially the theory of second best merely confirms the critical need to identify policies with regard to what is both desirable and achievable. The selection of innovations needs therefore to be informed by research on what is going on in the classroom which will allow real needs and attainable targets to be identified.

Supporting Implementation

The pursuit of worthwhile goals results in a concentration upon the initiation phase of curriculum development and a relative neglect of those activities subsequently designed to support implementation. The standard pattern of centralized curriculum policy making revealed in section II primarily involves the provision of a very limited range of support activities such as information on the new policy, the provision of teacher training, classroom resource production, the revision or provision of appropriate means of assessment after the policy was adopted. Teachers are therefore often placed in a position of being expected to implement a change which they had no part in designing, of which they had a limited understanding, and with minimal or no support in terms of resources or training. Two implications arise from this.

First, there is a need to involve practitioners in the development of curriculum policy. Even within a highly centralized system, their input is more likely to lead to issues related to implementation being taken into account. However, in itself teacher involvement in not easily achieved nor is it a panacea. Logistically not all teachers can be involved in curriculum development and as has been suggested in the chapters on South Korea, Malaysia and the PRC, many teachers are unable or unwilling to become involved. Teacher participation can be also counter productive and result in a great deal of time and effort being wasted. Despite these problems a sense of ownership of an innovation does encourage implementation and teacher involvement encourages planners to address implementation problems. Those countries which have established professional organizations to support curriculum development have developed a range of methods which allow them to obtain a substantial degree of teacher input into the design of centralized curricula.

Second, the initiation of policy should not be divorced from the implementation and assessment phases of the curriculum. The provision of resources, in-service education and the identification of appropriate means of assessment should be incorporated into the process of curriculum development to ensure that the policy can be operationalized and to permit modification and adjustment of plans in the light of experience. Too frequently, piloting and trial projects which might serve this function fail to do so, for they merely serve a preliminary and self legitimating function. It is as though Tyler's classic model has been interpreted as proposing a linear sequence of stages of curriculum development with a separation of policy making (the identification of aims and objectives) from questions of implementation (pedagogy and assessment). Instead what is needed is a fluid relationship between the components of a curriculum to ensure that goals are not selected without consideration of their impact on practices, the provision of teaching resources and the choice of appropriate content. If it is evident that the goals cannot be adequately assessed or that workable resources cannot be developed, then it is the goals which need to be reconsidered.

A related point concerns the nature and purpose of supporting activities. From section II it is evident that the primary support for teachers attempting to implement curriculum policies is the provision of new textbooks, circulars, regulations or courses designed to transmit information about the policy. Whilst it is necessary to ensure that teachers are aware of a new policy, this in itself is not sufficient to ensure a change of practice. The abandonment of existing familiar practices always involves a cost and changes, especially those which affect the style of teaching and they role of the teacher, are extremely difficult to bring about.

Public Assessment

Where there is an imbalance between demand and supply (for well-paid jobs, élite schools, university places) and where there is a high rate of private return to each level of education, the educational system must incorporate some mechanism for selection and sorting. Public examinations have been widely adopted as the fairest method for determining who will obtain the scarce number of available places. Where selection pressure is high they begin to become the reason for schooling. Pupils and parents become more concerned with their certification than with their education. As we explained in chapter 3 the effect of this is that the style and format of public examinations places a very strong influence on the style of teaching used and the style of learning which is encouraged.

If a public examination, in an attempt to maximize the objectivity and efficiency of marking, consistently requires candidates to reproduce chunks of discrete and trivial information, then that is what they will be encouraged to do in class. Teachers will transmit that information and pupils will attempt to memorize it. This will exert a more powerful influence on the implemented curriculum than any other factor, especially in a society where there is a low level of teacher professionalism.

The solution does not lie in the removal of public examinations for they are merely a symptom of the essential problem which is the need to select pupils for scarce places. Nor does the solution necessarily lie with a shift from norm to criterion referenced assessments. If the latter are used to select pupils then either they lose the benefits usually associated with criterion referenced tests or selectors are required to develop other selective devices. The time and effort which is required to develop a new curriculum is likely to be wasted if the means of assessment are not able to measure those skills and understandings which are its reason for existence. The development and testing of appropriate means of assessment should therefore be considered at an early stage in the process of curriculum design. Too frequently it is undertaken by another agency long after the euphoria which accompanies the new policy has evaporated. More importantly, examiners, by virtue of the very important and practical nature of their task, are more likely to be influenced by the realities of the classroom and by the need to ensure objectivity. The result can be a massive disjuncture between plans and practices. This can be avoided only if both achievable goals and appropriate means of assessment are identified.

Notes on Contributors

Dr Mark Bray is a Reader, Department of Education, University of Hong Kong.

Dr Kyung-Chue, Huh is a Senior Researcher, Korean Educational Development Institute, Seoul.

Mr Philip Hui is a Lecturer, School of Education, University of East Asia, Macau.

Mrs Winnie Y.W. Au Yeung, Lai is a Lecturer, Department of Curriculum Studies, University of Hong Kong.

Dr Julian Leung Yat-Ming, is a Lecturer, Department of Curriculum Studies, University of Hong Kong.

Dr Keith M. Lewin is a Reader in Education and Associate of the Institute of Development Studies, University of Sussex.

Dr Colin Marsh is Director, Secondary Education Authority, Perth, Western Australia.

Dr J.A.G. McClelland is Senior Lecturer, Department of Education and Sub-Dean, Faculty of Education, University of Hong Kong.

Dr Paul Morris is Senior Lecturer, Department of Curriculum Studies and Dean, Faculty of Education, University of Hong Kong.

Dr Se-Ho Shin is President, Korean Educational Development Institute, Seoul.

Dr Sharifah Maimunah Syed Zin is a researcher in the Educational Planning and Research Division of the Ministry of Education, Malaysia.

Dr R. Murray Thomas is Professor of Education, Graduate School of Education, University of California, Santa Barbara, California.

Dr Khoon Yoong, Wong is Lecturer, Science and Mathematics Education Centre, Curtin University of Technology, Perth, Western Australia.

Bibliography

ADAMS, R.S. and CHEN, D. (1981) *The Process of Educational Innovation*, UNESCO/Kogan Page.

AFONSO, R. and PEREIRA, F.G. (1987) 'The constitution and legal system' in CREMER R.D. *Macau: City of Commerce and Culture*, UEA Press, Hong Kong.

ALTBACH, P.G. *et al.* (1956) *Excellence in Education: Perspectives on Policy and Practice*, New York, Prometheus Books.

ALTBACH, P.G. (1983) 'Key issues of textbook provision in the third world', *Prospects*, XIII 3.

ALTBACH, P.H. and KELLY, G.P. (Eds) (1978) *Education and Colonialism*, New York, Longman.

ALTBACH, P.H. *et al.* (1985) *Excellence in Education: Perspectives on Policy and Practice*, New York, Prometheus Books.

ALVES PINTO, M.C. (1987) *Ensino em Macau: Umas Abordagem S Stemica da Realidade Eductiva*, Gabinete do Secretario-Adjunto Para a Educacao e Cultura, Macau (also available in Chinese).

ANDERSON, R.M. (1983) 'Interest groups in social education', *The History and Social Science Teacher*, 18, 4, pp. 205–9.

APEID (1976) *Towards strategies of curriculum developments*, Report on An Asian Workshop, Bangkok, UNESCO.

APEID (1977) *Educational Policy, Curriculum Development and Implementation*, Report of APEID High Level Personnel Exchange Workshop on Curriculum Development, Bangkok: UNESCO.

ARCHER, M.S. (1979) *Social Origins of Education Systems*, London, Sage Publications.

AUSUBEL, D. (1963) *Psychology of Meaningful Verbal Learning*, New York, Grune and Stratton.

BAKER, E.L. (1973) 'The technology of instructional development', in TRAVERS, R.W.M. (Ed.) *Second Handbook of Research or Teaching*, Chicago, Rand McNally.

BALL, S. (1987) 'Relations, structures and conditions in curriculum change: A political history of English teaching 1970–1985' in GOODSON, I. (Ed.) *International Perspective in Curriculum History*, London, Croom Helm.

BASTID, M. (1987) 'Servitude or liberation? The introduction of foreign educational practices and systems to China from 1840 to the present' in HAYEHOE, R. and BASTID, M. (Eds) *China's Education and the Industrialized World: Studies in Cultural Transfer*, New York, M.E. Sharp Corp.

BECHER, T. and MACLURE, S. (1978) *The Politics of Curriculum Change*, London, Hutchinson.

BEEBY, C.E. (1979) *Assessment of Indonesian Education: A Guide in Planning*, Wellington, Oxford Press.

BERMAN, P. and MCLAUGHLIN, M.W. (1977) *Federal Programs Supporting Educational Change, Vol. VII: Factors Affecting Implementation and Continuation*, Santa Monica, CA, Rand Corporation.

BERNSTERIN, B. (1971) *Class, Codes and Control: Theoretical Studies Towards A Sociology of Education*, London, Routledge and Kegan Paul.

BLOOM, B.S. *et al.* (1956) *Taxonomy of Education Objectives*, Handbook 1, The Cognitive Domain, London, Longman.

BRAY, M. (1985) 'High school selection in less developed countries', *Comparative Education Review*, 29, 2, pp. 216–31.

BRAY, M. (1990) 'Provision of higher education in small states: Demands, constraints and strategies', *Higher Education Quarterly*, 44, 4.

BRAY, M. and HUI, P. (1989) 'The implications of size for educational development in small territories: The case of Macau', *International Review of Education*, 35, 2.

BRIGGS, L. (1970) *Handbook of Procedures for the Design of Instruction*, Pittsburgh, American Institute of Research.

BRUNER, J. (1963) *The Process of Educations*, New York, Vintage Books.

BRUNER, J., GOODNOW, I.I. and AUSTIN, G.A. (1967) *A Study of Thinking*, New York, Science Editions.

BURUMA, I. (1989) *God's Dust*, London, Johnathan Cape.

CALDWELL, B.J. and SPINKS, J. (1988) *The Self-Managing School*, London, Falmer Press.

CCP (1985) *Decision of the Central Committee of the Communist Party of China on the Reform of the Educational Structure*, 27 May, Beijing, Foreign Languages Press.

CENTRAL MINISTRY OF EDUCATION, PRC (1979) *A Summary of the Second National Publication and Circulation Working Conference*, CMOE, National Publication Office Beijing.

CHEN, B.X. (1987) *A History of the Development of Language Education in Modern China*, (Zhongkuo Xiandai Yuwen Jiaoyu Fazhanzhi), PRC, Yunnan Education Press.

CHEN, E.Z. (1985) 'Thirty-five years of geography teaching', *Curriculum, Teaching Materials and Teaching Methods*, (Kejing, Jiaocai and Jiaofa), 4.

CHEN, X. (1985) 'Curriculum development: Concept and principles', *Curriculum, Teaching Materials and Teaching Methods*, (Kejing, Jiaocai and Jiaofa), 13.

CHEN HSIEN, T. (1974) *The Maoist Educational Revolution*, New York, Praeger.

CHEN, X. (1988) *Curriculum* (Kecheng Lun), People's Education Press, Beijing

CHENG, K.M. (1984) 'Physics education in China: The basic facts', *Physics Education*, 19, p. 115.

CHENG, K.M. (1990) 'Financing education in Hong Kong: An international perspective' in CHUNG Y.P. and WONG, Y.C. (Eds) *The Economic Analysis of Hong Kong Education: Costs, Effects and Choices*, Hong Kong, The Chinese University Press.

CHENG, N.L. *et al.* (1973) *At What Cost? Instruction through the English Medium in Hong Kong*, Hong Kong, Shum Shing Printing Co.

CHINA EDUCATION YEARBOOK EDITORIAL BOARD (1984) *China Education Yearbook 1949–1981* (Zhangkuo JiaoYu Nanjian), China, Yearbook Publishing Press.

CHINA EDUCATION YEARBOOK EDITORIAL BOARD (1989) *China Education Yearbook 1988* (Zhongkuo Jiaoyu Nanjian), Beijing, People's Education Press, Beijing.

CHISMAN, D. and WILSON, B. (1989) *Partners in Development: A Review of Science and Mathematics Education 1965–1989*, London, British Council.

CHIU YUK SANG (1987) 'A preliminary look at education in Macau during the transitional period', unpublished paper, South China Normal University, Guangzhou (available in Chinese).

CHO, Y.T. and HUH, K.C. (1988) *A Critical Examination of the Approaches to Curriculum in Korea*, RR 88–13, Seoul, KEDI.

CHUNG, B.M. (1990) 'Education for development and beyond: A Korean perspective' in WILSON, D.C. *et al.* (Eds) *Asia and the Pacific*, Calgary, Detselig Enterprises.

CLEVERLY, J. (1985) *The Schooling of China*, London, George, Allen and Unwin.

COCKCROFT, W.H. (1982) *Mathematics Counts*, London, HMSO.

COMMENTARY (1989) Special issue on Education in Singapore, Vol. 8, Nos 1 and 2 (Journal of the National University of Singapore Society).

CONNELLY, F. and BEN-PERETZ, M. (1980) 'Teachers' roles in the using and doing of research and curriculum development', *Journal of Curriculum Studies*, 12, 2, pp. 95–107.

COOKE, B.L. *et al.* (1990) 'Research on beginning teachers in Hong Kong', *Educational Reserach Journal*, 5.

COOMBS, P. (Ed.) (1980) *Meeting the Basic Needs of Rural Poor*, New York, Pergamon Press.

CORNBLETH, C. (1979) 'Curriculum materials and pupil involvement in learning activity', paper presented at the annual conference of the American Educational Research Association, San Francisco.

COWEN, R. and McLEAN, M. (1984) 'China' in *International Handbook of Education Systems*, London, John Wiley and Sons.

CRANDALL, D. *et al.* (1983) *The Study of Dissemination Efforts Supporting School Improvement* (DESSI), Andover, MA, The Network.

CREMER, R.D. (Ed.) (1987) *Macau, City of Commerce and Culture*, Hong Kong, UEA Press.

CREMER, R.D. (1989) 'The industrialization of Macau' in JAO, Y.C., MOK, V. and HO, L.S. (Eds) *Economic Development in Chinese Societies: Models and Experiences*, Hong Kong, Hong Kong University Press.

CURRICULUM DEVELOPMENT COMMITTEE (1985) *Guidelines on Civic Education in Schools*, Hong Kong, Education Department.

CURRICULUM DEVELOPMENT COMMITTEE (1986) *Guidelines on Sex Education in Secondary Schools*, Hong Kong, Education Department.

CURRICULUM DEVELOPMENT COMMITTEE (1987a) *Paper 9/87: Proposals for Curriculum Development and the Reorganization of the Curriculum Development Committee*, Hong Kong, Education Department.

CURRICULUM DEVELOPMENT COMMITTEE (1987b) *Paper 11/87: The School-based Curriculum Project Scheme*, Hong Kong, Education Department.

CURRICULUM DEVELOPMENT COMMITTEE (1987c) *Paper 15/87: The General Principles Governing the Award and Administration of the Curriculum Project Grant*, Hong Kong, Education Department.

CURRICULUM DEVELOPMENT COUNCIL (1988) *Paper 5/88: Review of the Senior Secondary Curriculum*, Hong Kong, Education Department.

CURRICULUM DEVELOPMENT COUNCIL (1990) *Paper 6/90: Procedure for the Development of Syllabuses for New Examination Subjects to Be Followed by the HKEA and CDC*, Hong Kong, Education Department.

CURRIN, C. (1987) *Curriculum Development for Basic Education in China*, Textbook Development Project, China Department, Washington DC, World Bank.

DA, Z.L. (1988) 'Multiformity, the inevitable tendency of the curriculum in senior middle schools', paper presented at the symposium on Curriculum Development and Continuing Teacher Education, University of Hong Kong, December.

DALIN, P. (1978) *Limits to Educational Change*, London, MacMillan.

DALIN, P. and McLAUGHLIN, M.W. (1975) *Strategies for Innovation in Higher Education*, Educational Research Symposium on Strategies for Research and Development in Higher Education, Stockholm, Sweden.

DENG, X.P. (1977) *Respect Knowledge, Respect Trained Personnel*, speech on 24, *May Selected Works of Deng Xiaoping*, Beijing, Foreign Languages Press.

DEPARTMENT OF EDUCATION AND SCIENCE (1985) *The Curriculum from 5 to 16*. London, HMSO.

DORAISAMY, T.R. (Ed.) (1969) *150 years of Education in Singapore*, Teachers' Training College (later became the Institute of Education), Singapore.

DORE, R. (1976) *The Diploma Disease: Education, Qualification and Development*, London, George Allen and Unwin.

Bibliography

DOVE, L.A. (1980) *Curriculum Reforms in Secondary Schools; A Commonwealth Survey*, London, Commonwealth Secretariat.

EBEL, R.L. (1979) *Essentials of Educational Measurement*, (3rd ed.), New York, Prentice Hall.

EDMONDS, R.L. (1989) *Macau*, World Bibliographical Series Vol. 105, Oxford, Clio Press.

EDUCATION DEPARTMENT (1974) *Report on First Year Trial of Integrated Science Project*, Hong Kong, Education Department.

EDUCATION DEPARTMENT (1975) *Evaluation of Second Year Trial of Integrated Science Project*, Hong Kong, Education Department.

EDUCATION DEPARTMENT (1990) *Directory of School-based Curriculum Projects 1988–89*, Hong Kong, Education Department.

EGAN K. (1986) *Teaching as Storytelling*, London, Ont., Althouse Press.

EGGLESTON, J.F. *et al.* (1975) *Processes and Products of Science Teaching*, London, Macmillan Education.

EISNER, E. (1969) Instructional and Expressive Objectives, Monograph No. 3. Washington, DC, AERA.

EISNER, E. (1974) 'Instructional and expensive objectives', in GOLBY, M. (Ed.) *Curriculum Design*, London, Open University Press.

EISNER, E. and VALLANCE, E. (Eds) (1974) *Conflicting Conceptions of Curriculum*, Berkeley, McCutchan.

ENG, S.P. (1981) *State of Moral Education in Singapore Schools*, Occasional Paper No.17, Singapore, Institute of Education.

FEITOR, R. (1987) 'Macau's modern economy' in CREMER, R.D. (Ed.), *Macau: City of Commerce and Culture*, Hong Kong, UEA Press.

FONG, W.C. (1988) *The Use of Specific Instructional Objectives for Effective Teaching and Testing*, Singapore, Ministry of Education.

FRASER, S.E. and HAWKINS, J.N. (1973) *Educational Reform and Revolution in the People's Republic of China*, Phi Delta Kappan.

FULLAN, M. (1982) *The Meaning of Educational Change*, New York, Teachers' College Press.

FULLAN, M. and POMFRET, A. (1977) 'Research on curriculum and instruction implementation', *Review of Educational Research*, 47, 1, pp. 335–97.

FUNG, Y.W. (1986) 'Education' in CHENG, J.Y.S. (Ed.) *Hong Kong in Transition*, Hong Kong, Oxford University Press.

GAGNE, R.M. (1962) *Psychological Principles in System Development*, New York, Holt, Rinehart and Winston.

GAGNE, R.M. (1968) 'Educational technology as technique', *Educational Technology*, VIII.

GAMBERG, R. (1977) *Red and Expert: Education in the Peoples' Republic of China*, New York, Schockem Borks.

GIFFORD, P. *et al.* (1971) 'African education in a colonial context: French and British styles' in PROSSER G. and LOUIS, W.R. (Eds), *France and Britain in Africa*, New Haven, CT, Yale University Press.

GLASER, R. (1963) 'Instructional technology and the measurement of learning outcomes: Some questions', *American Psychologist*, 18, pp. 519–21.

GLASER, R. (1981) 'The future of testing: A research agenda for cognitive psychology and psychometries', *American Psychologist*, 36, pp. 923–36.

GOH, K.S. *et al.* (1980) *Report on the Ministry of Education 1979*, Singapore, Ministry of Education.

GOODSON, I.F. (1983) *School Subjects and Curriculum Change*, London, Croom Helm.

GOVERNMENT OF MALAYSIA EDUCATION ACT (1961) Kuala Lumpur, Government Printers.

GOVERNMENT OF MALAYSIA (1979) *Cabinet Committee Report on the Review of the Implementation of the National Education Policy*, Kuala Lumpur, Dewan Banasa dan Pustaka.

GOVERNMENT OF MALAYSIA (1976) *Third Malaysia Plan 1978–1980*, Kuala Lumpur, Government Printers.

GOVERNMENT OF MALAYSIA (1981) *Fourth Malaysia Plan 1981–85*, Kuala Lumpur, Government Printers.

GOVERNMENT OF MALAYSIA (1986) *Fifth Malaysia Plan 1986–90*, Kuala Lumpur, Government Printers.

GOVERNMENT OF MALAYSIA EDUCATION COMMITTEE REPORT (1956) Kuala Lumpur, Government Printers.

GRIFFIN, P. and NIX, P. (1990) *Educational Assessment* Sydney, Harcourt, Brace Jovanovich.

GROSS, N., GIACQUINTA, J. and BERNSTEIN, M. (1973) *Implementing Organizational Innovations: A Sociological Analysis of Planned Educational Change*, New York, Basic Books.

GUANGZHOU EDUCATION OFFICE (1986) *Examination Syllabus Guide for Junior Graduate Examination 1987* (available in Chinese).

GUTHRIE, G. (1986) 'Current research in developing countries: The impact of curriculum reform on teaching', *Teaching and Teacher Education*, 2, 1.

HALL, G.E., GEORGE, A.A. and RUTHERFORD, W.L. (1979) *Measuring Stages of Concern About the Innovation: A Manual for Use of the SoC Questionnaire* (2nd ed.) Austin, TX, University of Texas, Research and Development Center for Teacher Education.

HALL, G.E. and LOUCKS, S.F. (1977) 'A developmental model for determining whether the treatment is actually implemented,' *American Education Research Journal*, 14, 3.

HALL, G.E. and LOUCKS, S.F. (1979) 'Teacher concerns as a basis for facilitation and personalising staff development' in LIEBERMAN, A. and MILLER, L. (Eds) *Staff Development: New Demands, New Realities*, New York, Teachers College Press.

HALL, G.E., WALLIS, R.C. and DOSSETT, W.F. (1973) *A Development Conceptualization of the Adoption Process within Educational Institutions*, Austin, TX, University of Texas.

HARGREAVES, A. (1988) 'Teaching Quality: A sociological analysis', *Journal of Curriculum Studies*, 20, 3.

HAVELOCK, R.G. (1973) *The Change Agents Guide to Innovation in Education*, Englewood Cliffs NJ, Educational Technology Publications.

HAVELOCK, R.G. and HUBERMAN, A.M. (1977) *Solving Educational Problems: The Planning and Reality of Innovation in Developing Counties*, Paris, UNESCO.

HAWES, H.W. (1985) *Curriculum History: Third World Countries*, International Encylopaedia of Education, London, Pergamon.

HAWKINS, J. (1983) *Education and Social Change in the People's Republic of China*, New York, Praeger.

HAYHOE, R. (1984) *Contemporary Chinese Education*, London, Croom Helm.

HAYHOE, R. and BASTID, M. (1987) (Ed.) *China's Education and the Industrialized World: Studies in Cultural Transfer*, New York, ME Sharpe Corp.

HE, B.C. (1986) 'Hidden crisis in Chinese education', *Future and Development*, Vol. 4.

HE, D.C. (1988) 'Rural education should serve local construction', *Chinese Education News* (Zhongguo Jiaoyu Boa), 1 March.

HE, M.H. (1985) 'On reforming curriculum for rural schools,' *Curriculum, Teaching Materials and Teaching Methods*, (Kejing, Jiaocai and Jiaofa), 6, pp. 61–5.

HE, X.W. (1980) 'The practice of classical language teaching of the consolidation of the teaching reform at East China Normal University No. 2 secondary school,' *Language Learning* (Yuwen Xuexi), 9.

HENRY PARK PRIMARY SCHOOL (1988) *A Project on Thinking Skills*, Singapore, Curriculum Development Institute of Singapore.

HEYNEMAN, S.P. (1987) 'Uses of examinations in developing countries: Selection, research and education sector management', *International Journal of Educational Development*, 7, 4, pp. 251–63.

HEYNEMAN, S.P. *et al.* (1984) 'Textbooks in the Philippines: Evaluation of the pedagogical impact of a national investment', *Educational Evaluation and Policy Analysis*, 6, 2.

HOLLOWAY, S.D. (1988) 'Concepts of ability and effort in Japan and the United States', *Review of Educational Resarch*, 58, 3.

HOLMES, B. and McLEAN, M. (1989) *The Curriculum: A Comparative Perspective*, London, Unwin Hyman.

HONG KONG GOVERNMENT (1982) *A Perspective on Education: Report of a Visiting Panel* (The Llewellyn Report) Hong Kong, Government Printer.

HONG KONG GOVERNMENT (1989) *Measures to Improve Language Teaching in Schools: Report of a Government Education Department Working Party*, Hong Kong, Government Printer.

HOUSE, E. (1979) 'Technology versus craft: A 10-year perspective on innovation', *Journal of Curriculum Studies*, 11, 1.

HUA, M. (1980) A discussion on the 1963 secondary school language syllabus and textbooks (Tantan 1963 Nian de Zhongxue Yuwen Jiaoxue Dagang He Kebun) *Secondary School Language Teaching* (Zhongxue Yuwen Jiaoxue), 5.

HUANG, G.S. (1980) 'About the revision of the secondary school language syllabus' (Tantan Zhongxue Yuwen Jiaoxue Dagang De Xiuding) *Secondary School Language Teaching* (Xhongxue Yuwen Jiaoxue), 8.

HUBERMAN, A.M. and CRANDALL, D. (1982) *A Study of Dissemination Efforts Supporting School Improvement (DESSI). Vol. IX, People, Policies and Practices, Examining the Chain of School Improvement*, Andover, MA, The Network.

HUNG, C.L. (1988) 'A study of the teaching methods used by integrated science teachers in Hong Kong secondary schools', unpublished MEd dissertation, University of Hong Kong, Hong Kong.

HUO, F.Y. (1988) 'The necessity of integrated science and integrated biology in junior middle school', paper presented at the Symposium on Curriculum Development and Continuing Teacher Education, University of Hong Kong, December.

HURST, P. (1983) *Implementing Educational Change — A Critical Review of Literature*, Occasional Paper, No. 5, Department of Education in Developing countries, University of London.

INDONESIA (1986) *In Elementary Primary School Curriculum in Asia and the Pacific — National Reports: Volume 1*, Tokyo, National Institute for Educational Research.

JENNINGS-WRAY, S. (1984) 'Teacher involvement in curriculum change in Jamaica: Advocacy and reality', *Compare*, 14, 1, pp. 41–58.

JIANG, S.Y. (1988) 'A basic problem in the overall structure of the secondary school curriculum', paper presented at the Symposium on Curriculum Development and Continuing Teacher Education, University of Hong Kong, December.

JOHNSON, K. (1983) 'Language Policy in education in Hong Kong', *Asian Journal of Public Administration*, 5, 2.

JONES, R.C. and BRAY, E. (1986) *Assessment: From Principles to Action*, London, Macmillan.

JOYCE, B. and WEIL, M. (1980) *Models of Teaching*, Englewood Cliffs, Prentice-Hall.

JUNUS, M. (1960) Sedjarah Islam di Indonesia, Jakarta, Pustaka Mahmudiah.

KEDI (1988) *Educational indicators in Korea*, IM 88–1, Seoul, KEDI.

KIM, J.S., LEE, Y.D., HWANG, J.K. and LEE, H.W. (1987) *Curriculum and Educational Evaluation*, Seoul, Educational Science Publishing Co.

KIRST, M.W. and WALKER, D.F. (1971) 'An analysis of curriculum decision making', *Review of Educational Research*, 41, 5, pp. 479–509.

KO, P.S. (1987) 'The cognitive and social development of pre-school children in Singapore', *News and Views*, Singapore, Institute of Education.

KOHLBERG, L. (1966) 'Moral education in our schools' *School Review*, 74.

KWAK, B.S. and HUH, K.C. (1988) 'A Study on the 5th revision of the general guidelines of the Korean school curriculum', Regular Report 86–2, Seoul, KEDI.

KWO, O. (1987) 'Language policies in Hong Kong secondary education', *The Chinese University Education Journal*, 15, 1.

KWONG, J. (1979) *Chinese Education in Transition: Prelude to the Cultural Revolution*, Montreal, McGill Queen University Press.

LAUGLO, J. (1986) *The Control of Education*, London, Heinemann.

LAW, S.S. (1989) 'Vocational training in Singapore', *Commentary*, 8 (1 and 2), pp. 108–18.

LAWTON, D. (1980) *The Politics of the School Curriculum*, London, Routledge and Kegan Paul.

LAWTON, D. (1986) *Curriculum Studies and Educational Planning*, London, Hodder and Staughton.

LEE, M.F. *et al.* (in press) *Growing up in Singapore: The Pre-school Years*, Singapore, Longman.

LEE, P. and LAW, M.T. (1988) *An Introduction to Educational Assessment for Teachers in Hong Kong*, Education Department, Hong Kong, Frith Word.

LEITHWOOD, K.A. (1981) 'The dimensions of curriculum innovation', *Journal of Curriculum Studies*, 13, pp. 25–36.

LEITHWOOD, K.A., ROSS, J. and MONTGOMERY, D. (1982) 'An Investigation of Teachers' Curriculum Decision-making', in LEITHWOOD, K.A. (Ed.) *Studies in Curriculum Decision-making*, Toronto, OISE Press.

LEMLECH, J.K. (1984) *Curriculum and Instructional Methods for the Elementary School*, New York, Macmillan.

LEUNG, Y.M. (1989) 'A Study of curriculum innovation in post-1976 China: With special reference to the design and implementation of the senior middle school geography curriculum', PhD thesis, University of Sussex.

LEVIS, D.S. (1985) 'Teaching strategies in school' in BAUMGART, N.L. (Ed.) *Education: A Map for Introductory Courses*, Sydney, Ian Novak.

LEWIN, K. (1981a) 'Science Education in Malaysia and Sri Lanka: A Curriculum Development and Course Evaluation 1970–78', unpublished DPhil thesis, University of Sussex.

LEWIN, K. (1981b) 'Curriculum research and examination reform: A case study from Malaysia', *Bulletin*, 11, 2, Institute of Development Studies, University of Sussex.

LEWIN, K. (1984) 'Selection and curriculum reform' in OXENHAM, J. (Ed.) *Education versus Qualifications*, London, Unwin Education.

LEWIN, K. (1985) 'Quality in question a new agenda for curriculum reform in developing countries', *Comparative Education*, V, 21, 2.

LEWIN, K. (1988) 'Curriculum reform in Asia: What's right in the past and what's left for the future', paper presented at the Symposium on Curriculum Development and continuing Teacher Education, University of Hong Kong, December.

LEWIN, K. and STUART, J.S. (1991) *Educational Innovation in Developing Countries: Case Studies of Change Makers*, London, Macmillan.

LIANG K.H. (1983) *A Brief Introduction to the Language Teaching Material Selected Independently by Yucai Middle School*, in Language Teaching Correspondence (Yuwen Jiaoxue Tongxun) 8.

LILLIS, K.M. (1984) 'Africanising the school literature curriculum in Kenya: A case study in curriculum independency' in TREFFGARNE, B.W. (Ed.) *Reproduction and Dependency in Education*, Part 2, Occasional Papers No. 7, University of London Institute of Education.

LIPSEY, R. and LANCASTER, K. (1957) 'The general theory of second best', *Review of Economic Studies*, 24, 63.

LITTLE, A. (1984) 'Combating the diploma disease' in OXENHAM, J. (Ed.) *Education versus Qualifications*, London, Unwin Education.

LIU, K.Z. (1981) 'About a few issues concerning secondary school language teaching reform' (Tantan Zhongxue Yuwen Jiaoxue Gaige), *The State of Art and Assumptions of Secondary School Language Teaching*, (Zhongxue Yuwen Jiaoxue Xianxang He Shexiang) PEP.

LO, C.Y. (1990) 'A review of the characteristics of school-based curriculum projects', unpublished seminar paper, University of Hong Kong, Hong Kong.

Lo, S. (1989) 'Bilingualism in Macau: English as the Lingua Franca', unpublished paper, School of Education, University of East Asia, Macau.

Lofstedt, J. (1979) *Chinese Educational Policy: Changes and contradictions 1949–79*, Stockholm, Amqvist and Wikshell International.

Lofstedt, J. (1980) *Chinese Education Policy: Changes and Contradictions*, Stockholm, Amqvist and Wikshell.

Lofstedt, J. (1984) 'Educational planning and administration in China', *Comparative Education*, 20, 1.

Lord, R. and Cheng, H.N.L. (Eds) (1987) *Language Education in Hong Kong*, Hong Kong, Chinese University Press.

Loucks, S.F. (1976) 'An exploration of levels of use of an innovation and the relationship to student achievement', paper presented at the annual meeting of the American Educational Research Association, San Francisco.

Loucks, S.F., Newlove, D.W. and Hall, G.E. (1975) *Measuring Levels of Use of the Innovation: A Manual for Trainers, Interviewers and Raters*, Austin, TX, University of Texas.

Lu, A.Q. (1986) 'Analysis of the reasons for my school being our province's champion of performance in the 1985 geography higher school examination', *Geography Teaching*, (Dili Jiaoxue), 1, pp. 26–9.

Lungu, G.F. (1985) 'Elites, incrementalism and educational policy-making in post-independence Zambia', *Comparative Education*, 21, 3.

Ma, L. (1985) 'Modification of the teaching requirement of subjects is a positive measure to raise the quality of junior middle schools', *People's Education* (Renmin Jiaoyu), 9.

Macau, Governo de (1984) *Linhas de Accao Governativa: Plano de Investimentos*, Macau, Imprensa Nacional.

Macau, Governo de (1987) *Macau em Numeros*, Macau, Direccao dos Servicos de Estatistica e Censos.

Macau, Governo de (1989a) *Inquérito ao Ensino 1987/1988*, Macau, Direcção dos Servicos de Estatístics e Censos.

Macau, Governo de (1989b) *Macau: A Educação em Números*, Gabinete de Estudos e Planeamento da Acção Educative, Macau, Direccça dos Serviços de Educação.

Macau, Governo de (1990) *Proposta de Lei-Quadro do Sistema Educativo de Macau: Ante-projecto*, Macau, Gabinete do Secretário-Adjunto para a Educação e Administração Pública.

Macdonald, B. and Ruddock, J. (1971) 'Curriculum research and development projects — Barriers to success', *British Journal of Educational Psychology*, XLI.

Macdonald, B. and Walker, R. (1976) *Changing the Curriculum*, London, Open Books.

Macdonald, J.B. and Leeper, R.R. (Eds) (1965) *Theories of Instruction*, Alexandria VA, ASCD.

Madaus, G. *et al.* (1983) *Evaluation Models*, Amsterdam, Kluwer.

Magendzo, A. (1988) 'The application of a cultural analysis model to the process of curriculum planning in Latin America', *Journal of Curriculum Studies*, 20, 1, pp. 23–33.

Mager, R.F. (1962) *Preparing Instructional Objectives*, Palo Alto, CA, Fearon.

Mann, F. (1976) 'Making change happen', *Teachers College Record*, 77, 3, pp. 313–22.

Marimuthee, T. (1990) 'Schooling and Citizenship in Malaysia' in Wilson, D.C. *et al.* (Eds) *Asia and the Pacific*, Calgary, Detselig Enterprises.

Marsh, C. and Huberman, M. (1984) 'Disseminating curricula: A look from the top down', *Journal of Curriculum Studies*, 16, 1, and 16, 3.

Marsh, C.J. and Stafford, K. (1988) *Curriculum: Practices and Issues*, (2nd ed.) Sydney, McGraw-Hill.

Maslow, A. (1962) *Toward a Psychology of Being*, Princeton, Van Nostrand.

Matthews, J. (1989) *Curriculum Exposed*, London, Fulton.

MATTHEWS, J.C. (1985) *Examinations: A Commentary*, London, George Allen and Unwin.

NCNEIL, J.D. (1977) *Curriculum: A Comprehensive Introduction*, Boston, Little Brown.

MCNEIL, J.D. (1985) *Curriculum: A Comprehensive Introduction*, (3rd ed.) Boston, MA, Little, Brown and Co.

MELLOR, B. (1988) *The University of East Asia: Origin and Outlook*, Hong Kong, UEA Press.

MINISTRY OF EDUCATION, KOREA (1990) *Education in Korea: 1989–1990*, Seoul, MOE.

MINISTRY OF EDUCATION, MALAYSIA (1985) *Education in Malaysia*, Educational Planning and Research Division, Government of Malaysia.

MINISTRY OF EDUCATION, MALAYSIA (1989) *Education in Malaysia 1988*, KL, Government of Malaysia.

MINISTRY OF EDUCATION, MALAYSIA (1990) *Education in Malaysia 1989* KL, Government of Malaysia.

MINISTRY OF EDUCATION, PRC (1982) *On Offering Senior Middle School Geography*, internal circular to schools.

MINISTRY OF EDUCATION, SINGAPORE (1986) *Learning Skills in Content Areas: A Resource Book*, Singapore, MOE.

MINISTRY OF EDUCATION, SINGAPORE (1989) *Education Statistics Digest 1989*, Singapore.

MORRIS, P. (1982) 'A study of economics teaching in Hong Kong: Curriculum rhetoric and Reality,' PhD thesis, University of Sussex.

MORRIS, P. (1983) 'Teachers' perceptions of their pupils: Hong Kong case study', *Research in Education*, 28, pp. 3–18.

MORRIS, P. (1984) 'Curriculum innovation and implementation: A South East Asian perspective', *Curriculum Perspectives*, 4, 1, pp. 3–18.

MORRIS, P. (1985) 'Teachers' perceptions of the barriers to the implementation of a pedagogic innovation: A South East Asian case study', *International Review of Education*, 31, 3.

MORRIS, P. (1986) 'Identifying the strategy of curriculum development within a highly centralised educational system', *International Journal of Educational Development*, 6, 3, pp. 171–82.

MORRIS, P. (1990) 'Bureaucracy, professionalization and school-centred innovation strategies', *International Review of Education*, 36, 1, pp. 21–41.

MORRISON, K. and RIDLEY, K. (1988) *Curriculum Planning and the Primary School*, London, Paul Chapman.

NAKAYAMA, S. (1984) *Science in Japan, China and the West*, Tokyo, Tokyo University Press.

NATIONAL PRODUCTIVITY COUNCIL TASK FORCE (1985) *Career Guidance in Schools*, Singapore, National Productivity Board.

NEUMANN, P.H. (1980) *Publishing for Schools — Textbooks and Less Developed Counters*, Washington, D.C., World Bank.

NEUMANN, P.H. (1986) *Publishing for Schools — Textbooks and the Less Developed Countries*, Washington DC, World Bank Staff Working Paper No. 398.

NG, S.M. (1987) *Research into Children's Language and Reading Development*, Singapore, Institute of Education — Educational Research Unit.

NOAH, H.J. and ECKSTEIN, M.A. (1989) 'Tradeoffs in examination policies: An international comparative perspective', *Oxford Review of Education*, 15, 1, pp. 17–27.

NOOR AZMI BIN IBRANIM (1988) 'In-service courses and teacher professionality; the implementation of the KBSR in Malaysia', Unpublished DPhil, University of Sussex.

NUTTALL, G.O. and SNOOK, I. (1973) 'Contemporary modes of teaching', in TRAVERS, R.M.W. (Ed.) *Second Handbook of Research on Teaching*, New York, Rand McNally.

OGUNDERE, S.F. (1988) 'Curriculum Development: A Description of the National Curriculum for Primary Social Studies in Nigeria', *Educational Studies*, 14, 1.

OLIVA, P.F. (1988) *Developing the Curriculum* (2nd ed.) Glenview, IL, Scott Foresman and Co.

Bibliography

OLIVER, D.W. and SHAVER, J.P. (1966) *Teaching Public Issues in the High School*, Boston, Houghton Mifflin.
ONG, T.C. *et al.* (1979) *Report on Moral Education*, Singapore, Ministry of Education.
OXENHAM, J. (Ed.) (1984) *Education versus Qualifications*, London, Unwin Education.
PAN, M.Y. (1986) *Traditional Teaching Methods and Reforms*, Shanghai, East China Normal University Press.
PANG, K.C. *et al.* (1985) *School-Based Inset: Hong Kong and Beyond*, Hong Kong, Hong Kong Association for Science and Mathematics Education.
PEARCE, D. (1982) *Textbook Production in Developing Countries: Some Problems of Preparation, Production and Distribution*, Paris, UNESCO Studies on Books and Reading, No. 7.
PEOPLE'S EDUCATION PRESS (1982) *Education Year Book*, PRC, PEP.
PEOPLE'S EDUCATION PRESS and BEIJING TEACHER'S COLLEGE (1981) *Secondary School Language Teaching* (Zhongxue Yuwen Jiaoxue), Beijing People's Education Press.
PEOPLE'S EDUCATION PRESS SECONDARY SCHOOL CHINESE LANGUAGE EDITORIAL OFFICE (1981a) *The Rationale for the 3:3 System Secondary School Language Textbook* (Bienxie 3:3 Zhi Zhongxue Yuwen Kebun De Shexiang) Secondary School Language Teaching, 3.
PEOPLE'S EDUCATION PRESS SECONDARY SCHOOL CHINESE LANGUAGE EDITORIAL OFFICE (1981b) 'Thinking and exercise,' *The Newly Selected Teaching Material in Junior Secondary School* (Chuzhong 6 Ca Xin Xuan Jiaocai Cikao He Lianxi) Secondary School Language Teaching (Zhongxue Yuwen Jiaoue), 7.
PEOPLE'S REPUBLIC OF CHINA, CENTRAL MINISTRY OF EDUCATION (1978) *Full Time 10 Year Programme Teaching Outline — Language*, PRC, People's Education Press.
PIAGET, J. (1952) *The Origins of Intelligence in Children*, New York, International Universities Press.
PIRES, B.V. (1987) 'Origins and early history of Macau, in CREMER, R.D. (Ed.) *Macau: City of Commerce and Culture*, Hong Kong, UEA Press.
POLLARD, A. and TANN, S. (1987) *Reflective Teaching in the Primary School*, London, Cassell Educational.
PRICE, R.F. (1970) *Education in Communist China*, New York, Praeger.
PRICE, R.F. (1976) 'Community and school and education in the People's Republic of China', *Comparative Education*, 12, 2.
PRICE, R.F. (1977) *Marx and Education in Russia and China*, London, Croom Helm.
PRICE, R.F. (1981) 'China: A problem of information', *Comparative Education Review*, 25, 21.
PU, T.S. (1985) *The People's Education Press and I*, Prospect of the People's Education Press, PEP.
QIN, XIN (1987) 'Examine curricular structure and reform of teaching materials in middle schools', *Curriculum, Teaching Materials and Teaching Methods*, (Keching, Jiaocai and Jiaofa), Vol. 8.
REID, W. (1988) 'The technological society and the concept of general education' in WESTBURY, I and PURVES, A.C. (Eds) *Cultural Literacy and the Idea of General Education*, Chicago, IL, University of Chicago Press.
ROBINSON, F. (1982) 'Superordinate curriculum guidelines: Their role in classroom decision-making' in LEITHWOOD, K.A. (Ed.) *Studies in Curriculum Decision-making*, Toronto, OISE, pp. 132–54.
ROGERS, W.C.R. (1969) *Freedom to Learn*, Columbus, Charles Merrill.
ROGERS, E.M. and SHOEMAKER, F.F. (1971) *Communication of Innovations*, New York, Free Press.
ROSA, A. (1989) 'Education in Macau's transitional period: Present situation and perspectives', paper presented at the Symposium on Reform of Education in Macau, Macau.
ROSA, A. (1990) 'Macau education in the period of transition: An overview and prospects', paper presented at the UNESCO International Congress on Planning and Management of Educational Development, Mexico City.

ROWNTREE, D. (1977) *Assessing Students: How Shall We Know Them?*, London, Harper and Row.

RUDDUCK, J. (1980) 'Curriculum dissemination as planned cultural diffusion', paper presented at the annual meeting of the American Educational Research Association, Boston.

RUDDUCK, J. and KELLY, P. (1976) *The Dissemination of Curriculum Development*, Slough, NFER.

SAUNDERS, M. and VULLIAMY, G. (1983) 'The implementation of curricular reform: Tanzania and Papua New Guinea', *Comparative Educational Review*, 10, pp. 351–73.

SCHOOLS COUNCIL (1973) *Pattern and Variation in Curriculum Development Projects*, London, Macmillan.

SEDC ELEMENTARY and SECONDARY SCHOOL TEACHING MATERIAL OFFICES (1986) *A Collection of the Language Teaching Outlines for Secondary and Elementary Schools since the Founding of the Country*, Curriculum, Teaching Material Research Institute, PRC, Beijing.

SEDC OFFICE (1986) Minutes of the Second Meeting on the Publication and Distribution of Teaching materials, Held on April 5, 1979 in Selected Education Working Document — 1979 (Internal Publication), PRC, Beijing, PEP.

SHANGHAI EDUCATION PRESS (1983–85) *Language Learning* (Yuwen Xuexi), PRC, Shanghai, SEP.

SHARIFAH MAIMUNAH, S.Z. (1990) 'Curriculum innovation — Case studies of man and the environment in the Malaysian primary school curriculum', unpublished DPhil thesis, University of East Anglia.

SCHOOLS COUNCIL (1973) *Evaluation in Curriculum Development: Twelve Case Studies*, Schools Council Research Series, London, Macmillan.

SHI LIYING (1988) 'The development strategy and objectives of Chinese Educators', paper presented of Faculty of Education Symposium, University of Hong Kong.

SHIN, S.H. (1990) 'The evolution and direction of South Korean social studies curriculum since 1945' in WILSON, D.C. *et al.* (Eds) *Asia and the Pacific*, Calgary, Detselig Enterprises.

SHIPMAN, M.D. (1971) *Inside A Curriculum Project*, London, Methuen.

SHUFELT, G. and SMART, J.R. (1983) *The Agenda in Action. 1983 Yearbook*, Washington DC, National Council of Teachers of Mathematics.

SINGAPORE TEACHERS' UNION (1987) *Survey on the Writing and Use of Specific Instructional Objectives*, Singapore, STU.

SJADZALI, H.M. (1984) *Keputusan Menteri Agama Republik Indonesia Nomor 101, Tahun 1984, Tentang Kurikulum Madrasah Aliyah* [The Decision of the Minister of Religion of the Republic of Indonesia No. 101 Regarding the Curriculum of the Senior-Secondary Madrasah]. Jakarta, Departemen Agama.

SKILBECK, M. (1984) *School-Based Curriculum Development*, London, Harper and Row.

SKINNER, B.F. (1953) *Science and Human Behaviour*, New York, Macmillan.

SKINNER, B.F. (1968) *The Technology of Teaching*, New York, Appleton-Century-Crofts.

SOARES, M. (1989) Address, delivered to the assembly at the University of East Asia on the occasion of the visit of His Exellency.

SOEDIJARTO (1976) *The Modular Instructional System as the Teaching-Learning Strategy in the Indonesian Development School.* Paris, International Institute for Educational Planning.

SOMERSET, H.C.A. (1982) 'Examination reform: The Kenyan experience', *World Bank Report*, Brighton, IDS.

SOMERSET, H.C.A. (1984) *The Development of Public Examinations in Nepal*, Nepal, Ministry of Education and Culture.

SOMERSET, H.C.A. (1985) 'Examinations as an instrument to improve pedagogy', paper submitted to the Workshop on Standardised Tests and Selection Examinations, Beijing.

SOON, T.W. (1988) *Singapore's New Education System: Education Reform for National Development*, Singapore, Institute of Southeast Asian Studies.

SPEAK, C. (1988) 'Aspects of cross-cultural curriculum development: A case study of the problems of education and geography in Hong Kong, unpublished MPhil thesis, University of Bath.

TABA, H. *et al.* (1967) *Handbook for Teaching Elementary Social Studies*, Reading, Addison-Wesley.

TAN, B.G. (1989) 'The gifted education programme', *Commentary*, 8, 1 and 2, pp. 102–7.

TAN, E. (1988) 'Job preferences of secondary school pupils in Singapore', *Teaching and Learning*, 9, 1, pp. 86–99.

TAN, H.H. (Ed.) (1989) *Singapore 1989*, Singapore, Ministry of Communications and Information.

TANG, S.C. (1985) *Continue the Tradition of Serving Text Construction*, Retrospect and Prospect of the People's Education Press, Beijing, PRC, PEP.

TANG, T. and MORRIS, P. (1989) 'The abuse of educational evaluation: A study of the evaluation of the implementation of the Civic Education "Guidelines"', *Educational Research Journal* (HK), 4, pp. 41–49.

TEIXEIRA, M. (1982) *A Educação em Macau*, Macau, Direcção dos Serviços de Educação e Cultura.

THE PEOPLE'S PROGRESSIVE PARTY LIBRARY (1983) *Index to Secondary School Language Teaching Reference Materials*, autumn, PRC, Beijing.

THEISEN, G., HUGHES, J. and SPECTOR, P. (1990) *An Analysis of the Status of Curriculum Reform and Textbook Production in Indonesia*. Washington, DC, USAID.

TIEN, X.L. (1983) *The Revision of the Short Essays on Language Knowledge in the Secondary school Language textbooks* Language Learning, 7.

THOMAS, R.M. (1973) *A Chronicle of Indonesian Higher Education*. Singapore, Chopmen.

THOMAS, R.M. (1977) *A Handbook for Authors of Enrichment Modules*, Santa Barbara, Graduate School of Education.

THOMAS, R.M. (1980) 'An instructional model for studying cognitive development and readability of instructional materials', *Aids to Programming Unicef Assistance to Education*, No. 40. Paris: Unesco.

THOMAS, R.M. (1981) 'Indonesian education: Communist strategies (1950–1965) and governmental counter strategies (1966–1980)', *Asian Survey*, 21, 3, pp. 369–92.

THOMAS, R.M. (1988a) Dividing the labor: Indonesia's government/private early childhood education system, *Early Child Development and Care*, 39, pp. 33–43.

THOMAS, R.M. (1988b) 'The Islamic revival and Indonesian education', *Asian Survey*, 28, 9, pp. 897–915.

TORRANCE, P. (1962) *Guiding Creative Talent*, Englewood Cliffs, Prentice Hall.

TOWARDS EXCELLENCE IN SCHOOLS (1987) *A Report to the Minister for Education*, Singapore, Singapore National Printers.

TSENG, D. (1986) *The Relationship between Education System, Technological Revolution and Economic Development, World Economics*, (Shijie Jingqi) 4, pp. 28–32.

TSUI, H.K. (1988) 'Restructuring the junior secondary English language curriculum' in McCLELLAND, J.A.G. (Ed.) *School-based Curriculum Development*, Education Paper No. 3, Faculty of Education, University of Hong Kong.

TYLER, R.W. (1949 and 1950) *Basic Principles of Curriculum and Instruction*, Chicago, IL, University of Chicago Press.

UNGER, J. (1982) *Education under Mao*, New York, Columbia University Press.

VULLIAMY, G., LEWIN, K.M. and STEPHENS, D. (1990) *Doing Educational Research in Developing Countries: Qualitative Strategies*, London, Falmer Press.

WAN LI (1985) 'Speech at the Work Conference on Education', *People's Daily*, May 17, 1985.

WANG, F.L. (1988) *Several Problems of the Construction of a Teaching Force for Compulsory Education*, Education Forum, (Jiaoyu Luncong), 2, pp. 16–19.

WANG, W.Z. (1986) *Labour Technology is A Compulsory Middle Curriculum*, People's Education, (Renmin Jiaoyu), 6.

WANG, X.C. and BAI, N.F. (1986) *An Economic Field Study of China's Backward Regions*, Chengdu, Szechuan People's Press.

WARMING (1982) 'Textbooks', *Encyclopaedia of Educational Research*, New York, Free Press and MacMillan, pp. 1934–36.

WATSON, J.K.P. (1979) 'Curriculum development: Some comparative perspectives', *Compare*, 9, 1.

WATSON, K. (1982) 'Colonialism and educational development' in WATSON, K. (Ed.) *Education in the Third World*, London, Croom Helm.

WATTS, A.G. (1988) 'Changing conceptions of careers guidance and a proposed model for Singapore schools', *Singapore Journal of Education*, 9, 1, pp. 28–36.

WEINSTEIN and FANTINI (1970)

WEB, PO (1990) 'Attention should be paid to ideological education in secondary schools English teaching', *Curriculum, Teaching Material and Method*, People's Education Press.

WEN P. (1990) 'Attention Should Be Paid to Ideological Education in Secondary School English Teaching', *Curriculum, Teaching Material and Method*, 9, 19–20, Beijing, People's Education Press.

WHITE, R.T. (1973) 'Research in learning hierarchies', *Review of Educational Research*, XL III, 3.

WHITE, G. (1981) *Party and Professionals: The Political Role of Teachers in Contemporary China*, Armork, M.E. Sharp.

WONG, K.Y., LIM, Y.S. and LOW, K.G. (1989) *SEAMEO-RECSAM Computers in Education Project, Country Reports Singapore*, Penang, Malaysia, RECSAM.

WONG, P.M. (1985) 'An analysis of the planned and implemented strategies of curriculum development in Hong Kong since 1972', unpublished MEd dissertation, University of Hong Kong.

WOODHOUSE, H.R. (1984) 'Beyond the hidden curriculum in Nigeria' in TREFFGARNE, C.B.W. (Ed.) *Reproduction and Dependency in Education*, EDC Occasional Papers, No. 7.

WORLD BANK (1980) *Education Sector Policy Paper*, Washington, DC, World Bank.

WORLD BANK (1984) *Report on Chinese Education*, Washington, DC, World Bank.

WU, J. (1986) *On Teaching and Learning — A Historical Development of the Theories of Teaching and Learning*, Jilin Education Press.

YAN, Z.H. (1986) 'Summary of the symposium on primary and middle school teaching plans jointly held by the State Education Communision and the Central Institute of Educational Research', *Curriculum, Teaching Materials and Teaching Methods* (Kejing, Jiaocai and Jiaofa) 3.

YE, L.Q. (1985) *Inheritance, Development and Progress*, Retrospect and Prospect of the PEP 1950–1985, PRC, People's Education Press.

YE, L.Q. (1987) 'Discussions on the curriculum reform of primary and middle school curriculum', in SHAO, J. and WU, Y. (Ed.) *Reform of General Education*, Beijing, People's Education Press.

YOUNG, J. (1979) 'The Curriculum Decision-making Preferences of School Personnel', *Alberta Journal of Educational Research*, 25, pp. 20–29.

YOUNG, J. (1985) 'Participation in Curriculum Development: An Inquiry into the Responses of Teachers', *Curriculum Inquiry*, 15, 4, pp. 387–414.

YOUNG, M.F.D. (Ed.) (1971) *Knowledge and Control: New Directions for the Sociology of Education*, London, Macmillan.

YU, Y. (1984) *Selected Lesson Plans by Yu Yi — Selected Lesson Plans by Special Grade Teachers*, 1, Shanghai, Shanghai Education Press.

Bibliography

Zepp, R.A. (1987) 'Interface of Chinese and Portuguese cultures' in Cremer R.D. (Ed.) *Macau: City of Commerce and Culture*, Hong Kong, UEA Press.

Zhang, D.Y. and Lu, S.H. (1983) 'Understand the syllabus guide thoroughly and manage the teaching of reading well', *Secondary School Language Teacher*, 1, p. 22.

Zhang Z.G. (1984) and (1985) Some tentative idea about reforming the language lessons, language teaching materials and language teaching, Curriculum, Teaching (Material and Teaching Method.) (Part 1 — 1984.6) (Part 2 — 1985.1) (Part 3a — 1985.3) (Part 3b 1985.5) Material and Teaching Method.

Zhang Lianfeng (1985) 'Inherit and foster the good traditions of the People's Education Press', *Retrospect and Prospect of the People's Education Press 1950–1985*, Beijing: People's Education Press.

Zhong, Q.C. (1989) *Modern Theory of Curriculum* (Xiandai Kechenglun) Shanghai, Shanghai Education Press.

Index